83-84 app

Y0-ALJ-104

IREX
655 THIRD AVENUE
NEW YORK, NEW YORK 10017

THE GROWTH OF
THE LAW IN
MEDIEVAL RUSSIA

The Growth of the Law in Medieval Russia

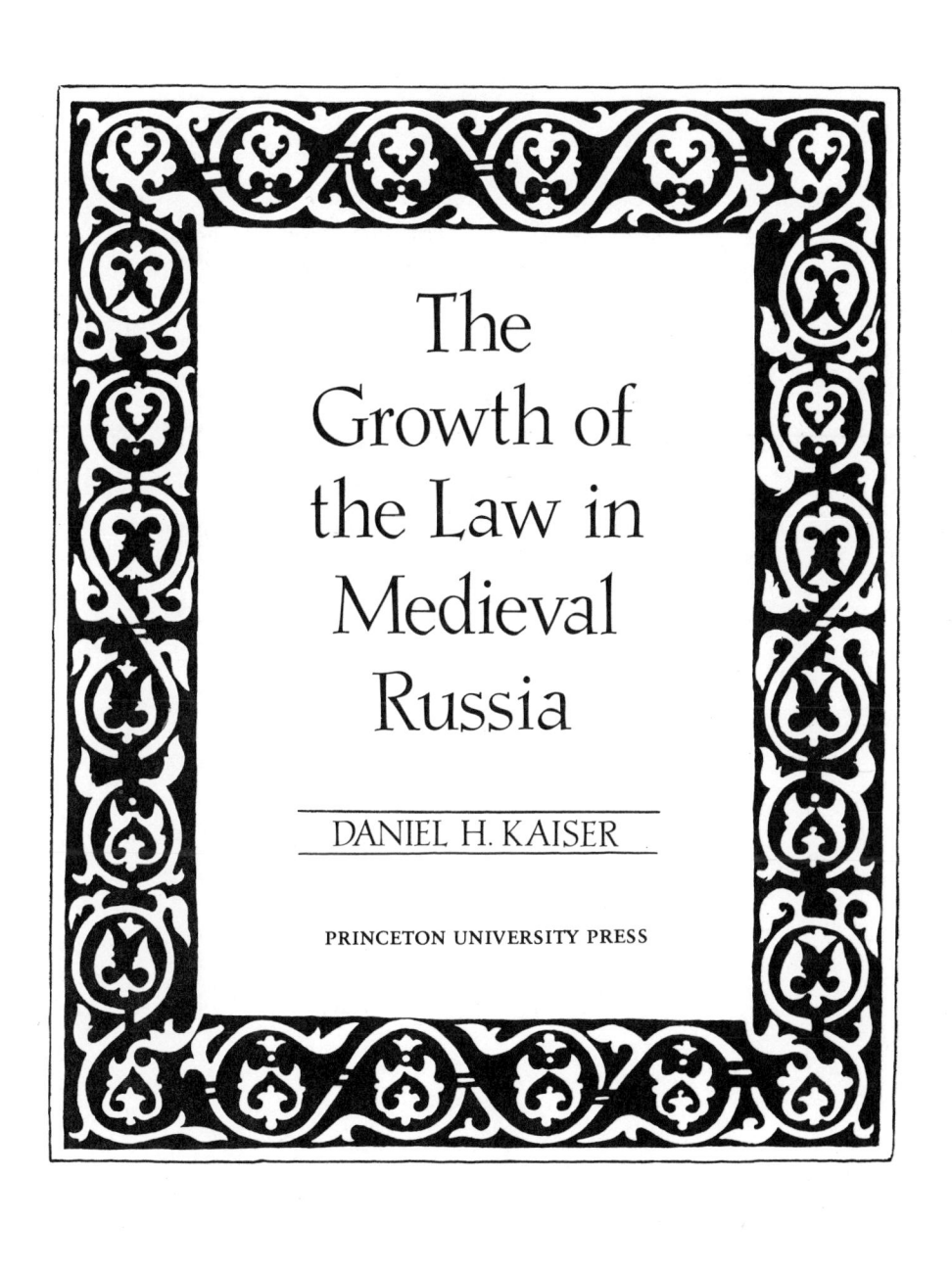

DANIEL H. KAISER

PRINCETON UNIVERSITY PRESS

Copyright ©1980 by Princeton University Press
Published by Princeton University Press, Princeton, New Jersey
In the United Kingdom: Princeton University Press,
Guildford, Surrey

All Rights Reserved

Library of Congress Cataloging in Publication Data will be
found on the last printed page of this book

This book has been composed in VIP Sabon

Clothbound editions of Princeton University Press books
are printed on acid-free paper, and binding materials are
chosen for strength and durability.

Printed in the United States of America by
Princeton University Press, Princeton, New Jersey

To Jill

CONTENTS

PREFACE	ix
CHAPTER 1	
Notions of Law and Legal Development	3
CHAPTER 2	
Sources of the Law	18
KORMCHAIA KNIGA	19
MERILO PRAVEDNOE	23
MISCELLANIES	25
THE RUSSKAIA PRAVDA AND ITS HISTORIOGRAPHY	29
REGIONAL LEGAL TEXTS	37
MUSCOVITE LAW	39
THE RUSSKAIA PRAVDA AND THE LAW IN MEDIEVAL RUSSIA	41
ZAKON SUDNYI LIUDEM	46
PRINCELY STATUTES	50
SOURCES OF MEDIEVAL RUSSIAN LAW	60
CHAPTER 3	
Sanctions and the Law	62
HOMICIDE	63
ASSAULT	80
THEFT AND ROBBERY	82
CONCLUSIONS	90
CHAPTER 4	
Development of Judicial Personnel	94
THE ORIGINS OF JUDICIAL PERSONNEL IN RUSSIA	96
JUDICIAL PERSONNEL IN NOVGOROD AND PSKOV	101
MUSCOVITE JUDICIAL PERSONNEL	114
JUDICIAL PERSONNEL AND THE NEW LEGAL ORDER	125
CHAPTER 5	
Patterns of Evidence	127
TESTIMONY	128
ORDEALS	148
PHYSICAL EVIDENCE	152
WRITTEN EVIDENCE	153
EVIDENCE AND THE LAW	163
CHAPTER 6	
Medieval Russian Society and Legal Change	164
THE ROLE OF THE CHURCH IN RUSSIAN LEGAL CHANGE	165
SOCIETY AND LEGAL CHANGE	174
LEGAL CHANGE AND MEDIEVAL RUSSIA	186

ABBREVIATIONS	189
NOTES	190
GLOSSARY	269
SOURCES CITED	275
INDEX	305

PREFACE

Several observations are in order before introducing the reader to this book's argument. We may begin with definitions. This study is titled *The Growth of the Law in Medieval Russia*, and that alone may be enough to distress some of my colleagues. Please note that I have not labeled it *The Evolution of the Law*. I have no confidence that the law, or any other facet of culture, must move inevitably along some progressive continuum. On the contrary, anyone who has read the literature on sanctions must at least doubt the wisdom of contemporary notions of deterrence and criminal law. On the other hand, it seems to me that the law does grow as the informal constraints of traditional society recede, for whatever reason those constraints recede. The law's growth is not uniformly beneficial—in fact it need not be uniform at all. But, in general, larger societies with a more heterogeneous makeup demand a larger body of enunciated law for effective regulation of behavior.

Scholars interested in modernization theory will have noticed that I introduced into the preceding paragraph a term now slightly out of vogue. In recent years the whole idea of traditionalism has been much discussed, and I confess to having stumbled upon the debate unwittingly. Furthermore, I would very much like to stay out of it altogether. Nevertheless, I have employed the word and idea of traditionalism in these pages, and I offer here a few words in its defense. What I intend by tradition is that tendency "to accept the givenness of some past event, order or figure . . . as the major focus" of a society's collective identity, as S. N. Eisenstadt puts it. I realize that the simplicity of my construct hides the rich diversity of cultures. Indeed, what strikes my eye is precisely the fact that some societies feel no need to elaborate in detail their norms or the means for ensuring socially acceptable behavior. Consequently, I find very palatable Edward Shils's suggestion that we conceive of tradition as "society's reservoir of behavior and symbols." In medieval Russia it was that reservoir of symbols which resisted the introduction of new legal norms, not necessarily because the old were superior to the new, but simply because the old norms were old norms.

Again I hasten to assure the reader that I do not intend to denote or connote by "tradition" some lesser state of civilization. Inasmuch as I subscribe to a pessimistic view of man, it is difficult for me to suppose that man is necessarily building over the course of time a qualitatively better society. As in most things, notions of quality vary with time and place, and I do not here propose a unilinear, infinite progression. That having been said, I find no persuasive reason to abandon the idea of traditionalism.

Still another aspect of this book's title deserves a few words of explanation. Western historians are well accustomed to the term medieval, by which they mean that period which separated Europe's rediscovery of classical culture from classical culture itself. Recent scholarship continues to expand our comprehension of exactly how much of the classical heritage was known and valued in medieval Europe, but the basic utility of the term medieval remains manifest. Russia represents a different situation. At no time before the modern age did Russia receive any significant portion of the classical heritage, so it is inaccurate to perceive there a renaissance of classical learning, just as it is inaccurate to imagine that the classics penetrated Russia before the Slavs settled on the East European plain. For Russia there never was a "Middle Age" which separated two worlds inundated in classical learning.

Nevertheless, I have labeled as medieval the thirteenth, fourteenth, and fifteenth centuries, in part simply because the word itself has wide currency among historians who are not alerted to the peculiarities of Russia's situation. It is my hope that this book will be of interest to historians of medieval Europe, and I did not wish to exclude them from the list of potential readers by offering them some scholastically accurate, but foreign title. Likewise I have hopes that scholars of other disciplines might find here something instructive, and I am anxious to hear their comments.

My colleagues might have preferred that I title my book *The Growth of the Law in Rus'*, and I myself should have found nothing objectionable in this. Rus' is the term by which medieval Russian society knew itself, even if in a slightly confused way. At a very early point Rus' signified especially the southern territories surrounding the ancient capital city of Kiev. Later the term was grafted onto the northeastern territories as Old Rus'; the latter term, however, causes some difficulty. In Russian the same word denotes Old Rus' and Old Russian. Most folk will not be aware of any cause for concern, but my colleagues in Russian studies are sensitive to the history of Great Russian domination over other ethnic groupings on the East European plain. The translation Old Russian connotes that the culture of Old Rus' was necessarily Russian, when in fact it had several components of different ethnic origins, as I point out in chapter 6.

I am aware of the scholarly issue at stake here, but have decided

PREFACE   xi

for simplicity's sake to continue the usage "Russian" rather than some artificial substitute term. Furthermore, this study is concerned primarily with northeast Rus', the homeland of the Great Russians, so I feel somewhat less constrained in my terminology than I might have were I discussing developments over a broader geographical perspective.

There remains the pleasant duty of acknowledging my debts. This book originated as a dissertation at the University of Chicago. I owe the University a great deal, and it is my hope that this book will reflect well on that institution's distinctive commitment to multidisciplinary history. Much of the original spadework was done under several fellowships which the University provided: the Lamson Scholarship, the Ford Fellowship for Dissertation Research, and the William Rainey Harper Fellowship. The manuscript was written and prepared for publication while I was Visiting Assistant Professor of Russian History at the University in 1977-78. I am grateful for the confidence in me which the University of Chicago has demonstrated.

I owe a special debt to Richard Hellie. It was in his seminar on the 1649 Ulozhenie that I first learned of the possibilities of comparative legal history, and my subsequent work benefited greatly from his steadfast interest. He has been generous with his time and scholarship during the book's several redactions, and much of what is good in this book belongs to him. I also had the benefit of counsel and criticism from Stanley Katz and Richard Wortman, both of Princeton University; Harold Berman and Edward L. Keenan, both of Harvard University; James Capua of the University of Rochester; Zack Deal of Boston College; Horace W. Dewey of the University of Michigan; Charles J. Halperin of Indiana University; Ann M. Kleimola of the University of Nebraska-Lincoln; and Marc Zlotnik of the Federal Broadcast Information Service.

Both the International Research and Exchanges Board and the Fulbright-Hays Program provided me with the funds for travel and study in Moscow and Leningrad. I am grateful to A. K. Leont'ev, my advisor at Moscow State University, for his help. Likewise, Ia. N. Shchapov of the Institute of History AN SSSR was generous in sharing with me his vast knowledge of the manuscripts of the Kormchaia Kniga and related materials. I am also indebted to the staffs of several Soviet libraries and manuscript repositories: the Manuscript Section of the Lenin Library, Moscow; the Manuscript Section of the State Historical Museum, Moscow; the Central State

Archive of Ancient Acts, Moscow; the Archive of the Academy of Sciences of the U.S.S.R. in Leningrad; the Manuscript Section of the Saltykov-Shchedrin Public Library, Leningrad. Likewise I enjoyed the assistance and resources of the Regenstein Library of the University of Chicago and Widener Library and the Law School Library of Harvard University.

Early drafts of this book were written at Harvard University's Russian Research Center where I was settled as a Visitor in 1975-76 and as a Research Fellow in 1976-77. Everyone there received me well, and I am indebted to the Center for its support and a stimulating environment in which to work.

Preparing a manuscript is dependent upon the people who transcribe the author's scratchings into readable typescript. I am grateful to Elizabeth Bitoy and Marnie Veghte of the University of Chicago for typing much of this work. My editors at Princeton, Gail Filion and Judith May, have been efficient and enthusiastic, characteristics bound to endear them to any author. Finally, I am delighted to acknowledge my gratitude to my wife, Jill, who has willingly taken on herself much of the work of preparing the book for publication. No one has contributed more to its success. All errors which remain are my responsibility.

Oak Park, Illinois
20 July 1979

THE GROWTH OF
THE LAW IN
MEDIEVAL RUSSIA

CHAPTER I

Notions of Law and Legal Development

Despite the political and social turmoil which accompanied the decline of Kiev and the appearance of the Mongol overlords, the period which separated the thirteenth-century Russian code, the Expanded Russkaia Pravda, from the late fifteenth-century Muscovite code, the Sudebnik, was juridically stagnant, if one may judge from the surviving legal sources. While chronicle compilation continued with vigor in these centuries, few legal texts appeared to supplement our understanding of what must have been a period of significant social change. In addition to the dramatic political changes wrought by the growth of Moscow, there is evidence that the law itself underwent significant alteration. Whereas the Russkaia Pravda paid little attention to state functionaries and outlined a judicial procedure which was essentially self-help, the 1497 Sudebnik was devoted almost exclusively to the role of state officials and detailed a judicial apparatus over which the Moscow grand prince reigned. Clearly things had changed a great deal.

The sources, however, do not make this change apparent. The Russkaia Pravda was copied continuously throughout the thirteenth, fourteenth, and fifteenth centuries with only minimal changes. The statutory law of Novgorod and Pskov survives only from the moment of Moscow's collision with these city-republics in the late fifteenth century. Although traces of earlier codification are discernible in the Novgorod and Pskov codes, in their fifteenth-century guise the progression of legal change is difficult to separate from the random compilations. Finally, only beginning with the late fourteenth century does the documentary base of private law help clarify the blurry image of these centuries conveyed by statutory law.

Consequently, historians of medieval Russian law have treated the growth of the law somewhat cavalierly, generalizing backward from the Sudebnik or forward from the Russkaia Pravda as it suited them. It is cause for little wonder, then, that the historical narratives of late medieval Russia often strongly resemble either an earlier or later era. But the illusion of stagnation is belied by careful examination of the legal sources, which give evidence of significant change. Medieval Russian law developed notions of sanction, evidence, and a judiciary, none of which had been prominent in the eleventh and twelfth centuries. How these changes arose, and from what sources, remain unanswered questions, although some tentative explanations are offered in the final chapter of this study. But the growth of the law is clearly demonstrable, and itself is symptomatic of the changing social structure of late medieval Russia.[1]

If the extant sources themselves are not sufficient to illustrate all the details of legal change, there is help available in the enormous literature on comparative law which has grown up in the last century. Particularly within the last several decades, jurisprudential theory has been enriched by the considerable fund of ethnographic reports which treat legal institutions as one of the basic facets of society. The acute observations of trained scholars who have examined the passage of societies from traditional to modern are especially illuminating for the historian of medieval Russia whose institutions experienced similar alteration. By the beginning of the sixteenth century Russian law had taken on many of the characteristics of the law of modern states, but in its infancy Russian law came much closer to the system of consensual norms which governs those societies without a developed state structure, without a high degree of social differentiation, and without large doses of foreign state law. It is precisely societies of the latter type that have drawn the sustained attention of ethnographers and social anthropologists, and their records will prove illuminating for discussion of some concepts and institutions of Russian law which have mystified researchers.

The nature of law itself in traditional societies has been the subject of much learned debate among jurisprudents. Since the extraordinary growth of national states in nineteenth-century Europe, statist conceptions of law have dominated jurisprudential theory. The law has come to be identified with notions of authoritative state structures and coercive penalties inflicted by agents of those structures upon social deviants. Long after John Austin's formulation of this "key to the science of jurisprudence,"[2] respected jurisprudents continued to call for an understanding of the law exclusively in terms of coercive sanctions and hierarchical state structures. But coercive-law theory, born in an imperialistic era, not only undervalued traditional society as encountered in the colonies of the European powers. It also obstructed examination of legal development. For the coercive-law theorists, there was only one law, and Europe was its prophet.

The emergence of twentieth-century sociology did not temper this bent in the literature. Max Weber, for example, while on the one hand denying that law "exists only where legal coercion is guaranteed by the political authority," on the other hand, specifically allowed that only those orders enforceable by a "staff of people holding themselves specially ready for that purpose" qualified as law. It is true that Weber admitted some legal role for blood venegeance and feud, coercive results of social deviance not tied directly to state institutions. But Weber himself was not happy with this situation, and was obliged to reiterate that behavior supported by convention or the expectation of disapproval and reprisals did not constitute law. Weber's perception of legal development from categories of irrationally formal legal thought to logically formal rational legal thought remains a useful guide, at least for certain aspects of European legal development. But his insistence on examining the growth of rational categories in connection with the growth of the *imperium* and its officials obscures the earlier phases of legal change.[3] Rationality is demanded in the law when traditional authority breaks down, but that represents only a switch in sources of legitimacy, not the difference between law and something non-legal.[4]

The introduction of concepts of social relations into notions of the law helped stimulate a more comprehensive approach to legal institutions. Roscoe Pound, for example, attempted to integrate the law into the fabric of society, and even went so far as to estimate the parallel utility of ethics and morals, kinship and religion in restraining social deviance. For all that, he had difficulty in abandoning the idea of state institutions. In the final analysis, law was reduced to an instrument for reconciling human wants and needs "by an ordering of human conduct through politically organized society." In one case, Pound admitted the priesthood to such an understanding, but only in the context that it declared precepts "enforced by penances and exclusion from the society of the pious."[5]

Recent jurisprudential theory has sought still more independence of law from consequences attendant upon social deviance. Hermann Kantorowicz, among others, proposed an understanding of law as "a body of rules aiming at the prevention or the orderly settlement of conflicts," or, more particularly, "a body of rules prescribing external conduct and considered justiciable." Kantorowicz correctly understood that narrowly prescriptive definitions of law impose hindrances to understanding judicial process and the social functions of law, and proposed that the haggling over definitions in the abstract should yield to a more practical evaluation of the utility of a definition for the particular science in which it is used.[6]

Several creative attempts to rethink our understanding of law have resulted from the effort to escape Austinian models. Some, like Hans Kelsen's "Pure Theory of Law," are less successful than others. Kelsen, in trying to free jurisprudence from all alien elements, cannot escape the dominance of sanctions, even though sanctions themselves are liberally interpreted. In reducing law to Kelsen's positivist approach, one may construe the norms of social behavior as law only with the imprimatur of legal institutions—courts and other agencies of sanction. Consequently, prescribed norms of behavior become law only with the attachment of the condition of effectiveness, that is, on the condition of legal sanction.[7] But systems of social control may and do operate effectively without institutionalized sanction.

That sanction is not vital to the law is demonstrated quite well in another attempt at revising Austinian jurisprudence. H.L.A. Hart successfully formulated a view of the law which makes sanctions no more than an appurtenance of some kinds of law. Hart's construction envisions two types of rules: primary rules which prescribe norms of behavior or confer powers, and secondary rules which govern the implementation of primary rules. Included among the latter are the rules of recognition, change, and adjudication, the last of which includes the establishment of sanctions. Hart's efforts in the main effectively escape the restrictions of command-law theory. In particular, the system of rules allows for situations certainly deemed legal though no sanctions may conceivably be attached to the rule—for example, rules which confer powers. More than that, Hart's system allows for a more productive use of law in analyzing social structures. Societies dominated by primary rules of behavior are conceivable in conditions where uninstitutionalized social pressure is still operative. Secondary rules accompany the further centralization of social pressure, an event which is likely to occur in concert with the development of legal sanctions. In short, Hart, while not specifically intending to do so, has succeeded in laying out a broad spectrum of combinations where we may understand law to be functioning.[8]

Assistance in the struggle to find a satisfactory conception of law which embraces divergent social structures has come from various quarters. In particular, the field work of anthropologists has stimulated promising comparative investigations in international law. Like the stateless societies of the so-called primitive world, contemporary international relations are governed by notions of law which preclude the imposition of sanctions, strictly conceived. Relations between formally equal power centers are governed by characteristics such as restraint, reciprocity, and mutual agreement. Recognition of law without sanctions has prompted some scholars to propose a theoretical spectrum of legal relations which emcompasses both the hierarchical power structures of the modern nation-state and the nonhierarchical orders present in relations between states.

It is a small but significant step to transfer this model to the much wider conception of legal development, including structures dominated by self-help and self-restraints as well as those controlled by Austinian sovereigns. Vertical legal systems in which orders and threats of sanctions prevail are paralleled by a hierarchy of institutions which may compel obedience to their commands. Horizontal systems, on the other hand, rely upon less formal means to regulate behavior. Where vertical systems utilize particular personnel to mediate and adjudicate, as well as to enforce dispute resolutions, horizontal systems depend upon conventionalized dispute regulation in which the two primary actors themselves resolve the conflict.

Horizontal systems reveal little evidence of the visible apparatus of law and politics. Official institutionalized intermediaries are absent, a situation which has given rise to labeling such systems dyadic, dominated by the actions of the offender and the victim. Triadic systems earn that designation by virtue of the fact that the disputants are joined by official agents of reconciliation. Whereas in horizontal systems the victim must undertake his own investigation and receive satisfaction in accordance with procedures accepted within the jural community, officials in vertical systems, specifically designated for conducting investigations and adjudication, take steps decreed by existing state order, and ultimately fix the state's penalties upon those judged to have violated behavioral norms.[9]

Horizontal systems therefore depend on other kinds of strictures in order to maintain harmony within the community. Societies where this kind of justice prevails are usually homogeneous, small, and bound by kinship relations. Resolution of conflict depends upon what one scholar calls "invisible mediators," those conventions hallowed by consensus within the jural community.[10] With growing social differentiation the task of mediation also becomes differentiated, falling increasingly within the exclusive jurisdiction of a particular person or caste.[11] Typically, such mediators fulfill their arbitration duties in addition to other tasks, which they execute by virtue of their standing in the community. Their role may be a result of wealth, expertise, or some other trait highly valued in the society. But in those systems where homogeneity breaks down, where internal bonds such as kinship are weak, deviant behavior is less susceptible to correction through informal resolution. Counsel, official mediators, and police are all associated with societies characterized by division of labor, some use of writing, and money.[12]

With the exception of the evolutionary values which sometimes freight these models, the attempt to relate law to social structure has found an enthusiastic welcome in several different quarters.[13] Particularly apt has been the application to the sociology of law. The Scandinavian sociologist, Vilhelm Aubert, has successfully charted the extremes of conflict resolution on the basis of the structure formed by the participants. Where law is least developed, the third party, where present, is vaguely defined and possesses little authority. By contrast, what Aubert calls triadic relations function most strongly in an atmosphere of centralized authority where potential rewards and sanctions serve to stimulate conflict resolution.[14]

Sometimes the sociological contrast is framed in different terms. William Evan, for example, in an article which examines the relationship of subsystems within the state organization, suggests a distinction equally useful in casting law on a developmental spectrum. Public legal systems, characterized by all the formal institutions of adjudication, are based upon territorial conceptions of the state, whereas private legal systems, relatively deprived of formal intermediaries, acquire jurisdictional rights on the basis of the subsystem's own characteristics. It is true that Evan does not associate the distinction between private and public legal systems with the difference between so-called primitive societies and modern state structures. In one place, he specifically suggests that public legal systems exist even among preliterate societies. However, in analyzing the modes of change in private and public legal systems, Evan actually proposes a theory of legal modernization quite in keeping with the transformation currently under way in formerly traditional societies of Africa and Asia.[15]

Anthropology has added even more to our understanding of the dynamics of legal change. Sir Henry Maine was perhaps the first to state in a thorough and well-documented way a theory of legal development. Surveying ethnographic reports and the history of the ancient world, Maine proposed a steady sophistication of legal norms from those governed by social station and kinship to those warranted by the binding convention of individual contract.[16] His proposals, however, like those of his immediate successors, for all their ingenuity, suffered from the relatively small fund of ethnographic reports then available, and therefore dealt with fairly simplistic models of social structure. In the meantime, a wealth of ethnographic data on judicial and protojudicial institutions and their relation to social structure has come to the fore.[17]

A question more serious than the small factual base for such generalization is the appropriateness of projecting western jurisprudence upon the legal systems of traditional society. Maine, like many of his contemporaries, assumed that the law evolved from traditional to modern. That assumption has come under increasing criticism. Maine's view has found the most vigorous support in the person of Max Gluckman. Trained as an anthropologist, Gluckman did field work with the Barotse in present-day Zambia, where he was first induced to observe the vitality of traditional forms of adjudication. Subsequent study of ethnographic reports convinced him of the correctness of Maine's basic postulates. Gluckman went so far as to posit that the reasoning of judges in traditional societies was based upon categories similar to those used by Western jurists, a position which antagonized a sizable portion of the community of lawyer-anthropologists.[18]

Much of the opposition resists any neat systematization of legal development. For example, Sally Falk Moore objected to the value judgments attached to evolutionary perspectives—the law does not always change for the better. On another level, Moore's protests are less persuasive. In particular, she objects to depictions of institutional progression where individual responsibility grows at the expense of collective responsibility, where self-help yields to state action, and where relations described above as horizontal yield their places to institutions of centralized authority. At bottom, Moore's point is simply that these seemingly distinct forms of legal relations in fact overlap in societies of differing composition.[19] Other data which illustrate the relationship between particular legal institutions and social orders show Moore to be correct.[20] But one may wonder whether the attempt to chart a model of legal change implies that the model must have uniform application to all societies. To suggest, as Moore does, that characteristics which prevail in most traditional societies persist in subdued form in centralized societies in no way dismisses the general observation that traditional societies evidence certain traits which distinguish their legal systems from those of hierarchical societies.

In fact most studies which integrate notions of contemporary jurisprudence with a comprehensive examination of a society show the utility of the developmental model. E. Adamson Hoebel's characterization of primitive law, despite the sustained insistence upon the role of sanction in forming the law, demonstrates that various societies with widely differing geographic bases share certain fundamental approaches to the law. Likewise, Max Gluckman's attempt at synthesis, although restricted to societies where courts and justiciaries are clearly pronounced, offers similar help.[21] Less comprehensive but equally useful studies complement these works.[22] If used with care, the correlation of legal institutions and social development provides hope for charting a model of social history which need not dictate universal applicability nor connote evolutionary perspectives.

Among contemporary historians of comparative law, A. S. Diamond stands out by virtue of his attempt to include all aspects of society in a single evolutionary pattern of growth. Breaking down human civilization into three basic stages, Diamond attempts to correlate modes of income production, social ordering, and forms of conflict resolution along the entire scheme of human history throughout the world. In its bare skeleton, Diamond's hypothesis proves appealing, suggesting a prevalence of private wrongs in the least centralized societies and the emergence of clear criminal law in the most hierarchical societies. But in its particulars, Diamond's theorizing is less useful. In his eagerness to increase the acceptability of his findings, he is reduced to quantifying the frequency with which one encounters various factors in the ethnographic literature.[23] Statistical confirmation assumes uniform observation by the ethnographers and random sampling of the societies observed. Neither assumption seems warranted.

Although a science of legal development must remain for the present an unachievable ideal, the basic idea of correlating social structure with the law continues to stimulate serious analysis. Indeed, the persistence which marks these analytical forays is itself indicative of the common sense upon which the correlation of law and society rests. The terminology often varies, but the literature on legal and social change continues to expand, even in the face of sophisticated critiques like those of Bohannan and Moore.[24] To be sure, the case may easily be overstated, but it is counterproductive to assert the uniqueness of Western institutions which regulate social behavior, and thereby pronounce traditional societies bereft of institutions with similar functions. Certainly no two societies are exactly alike, and no society exactly replicates the social or legal institutions of another. But to assert distinctiveness does not release us from the task of classification. The fact is that some societies are more clearly related than others, and recognizing their similarities does not necessarily exclude their differences.[25]

Until such time as more comprehensive analyses of ethnographic data are performed, it is useful to understand the distinctions between legal structures in terms of the participants in conflict resolution. Horizontal societies, as they will be understood in this study, represent those societies where conflict resolution is essentially a matter for the parties directly involved—offender and victim. Each party is on an equal footing, restrained only by the norms which the jural community, loosely understood, will permit. At the most violent level, these bilateral relations will function under the norms of retaliation or revenge, but the alternatives still utilize horizontal forms of reconciliation, relying upon compensation and composition. Nevertheless, whether the dispute is resolved through retaliation or compensation, the scales of reciprocity are established in the consensus of the jural community. Even without codification, the range of satisfactions becomes part of the community's consciousness.[26] When the schedules of compensation are reduced to writing, the legal system reveals symptoms of change, although formally relations between the offender and the offended continue to operate on a dyadic basis.

Upon discovering some injury, whether to person or property, the victim himself must seek restitution through the channels established to bring the perpetrator to account. In traditional societies members of a kinship group often bear responsibility collectively, so that revenge and composition alike fall on the heads of the relatives of the offender. Nevertheless, the reconciliation takes place exclusively between the two affected parties, whether the principals themselves or their sponsoring kinship group. Only gradually does any form of mediation intrude on this essentially horizontal relationship. Where intermediaries exist in societies already observed by anthropologists, the middlemen tend to be the wealthy, respected members of the community who have earned their station by virtue of their association with religion or a past record of wisdom.[27] Typically, these mediators exert no force in bringing about a resolution, but merely serve to connect the two disputants.[28] Consequently, procedure remains essentially horizontal and informal, supported only by consensus.

Disruption in this pattern occurs with the development of a strong third party. In the history of colonial law, the intrusion of

Western legal notions and judiciaries upon the existent native structures interrupts horizontal systems.[29] But it is clear from some of the samples of ethnographic reports that the same trend may be observed in traditional societies whose own structures changed before their exposure to the centralized systems of the European colonialists.[30] In either case, the emergence of a power hierarchy is associated with those polities where cultural and ethnic homogeneity and consensus no longer work. In order to unify the culturally diverse elements, a vertical political institution must enforce its will upon the disparate elements of the society.[31] Therefore, hierarchies are institutionalized at the expense of the previously equal centers of power. Mediators acquire the ability to impose solutions, a factor that has its impact upon the conduct of procedure. The exclusive claims to authority that the vertical power structure makes imply the impermissibility of independent conflict reconciliation, so that increasingly all conflicts must be channeled through the official intermediary.

The most elemental form of mediation is a system of courts. Only those individuals invested with authority to hear and settle disputes may serve to bring justice to the disputants. At the same time, this authority compels those adjudged to be in the wrong to pay whatever price the justices set. From the point of view of the power structure, litigation may prove profitable if the proceeds are monopolized effectively. Consequently, matters once settled by restitution between the disputants by becoming the affair of a professional third party, become liable to his exactions. In this simple step there occurs the transition from private to public, from civil to criminal law.[32]

The appearance of criminal law represents an important stage in the development of legal relations. Criminal offenses constitute harms inflicted on the entire community, as interpreted by the power structure. As a result, what an exchange of blows or goods once rectified now finds remedy in the imposition of third-party exactions, either financial or physical. Again, there can be no question that the imposition of financial sanctions which do not directly profit the victim cannot exist without the state hierarchy and its subservient institutions. Corporal sanctions come into being under the same conditions, often to the total confusion of peoples accustomed to a different way of doing things.[33] Infliction of physical pain upon someone in and of itself offers the victim little satisfaction, unless it is the victim who inflicts the punishment. The psychological satisfaction presumed to accompany this process will be considerably less than that derived through a restoration of the relations which previously existed between the two parties.[34]

Sanctions have special allure for functionaries of the state apparatus. In addition to providing the community with a sense that in fact there are limits to acceptable social behavior, sanctions also serve to buttress legislation, legal norms which may have no root in the customary norms of the jural community.[35] In this context, sanctions stand as presumed deterrents to deviancy, warning the citizenry to abide by those regulations which the central power regards as inviolable. As the recent literature on deterrence suggests, physical sanctions may not achieve their desired ends.[36] Perhaps the stubborn commitment to the role of sanctions in deterring deviancy may put to rest the suggestion that vertical structures represent some higher phase of legal evolution. Sanctions oblige compliance with norms undigested by the community only with a great investment in enforcement. Again, the experience of the colonial powers will be instructive in understanding the futility of imposing prohibitions upon the behavior of a citizenry which adjusts its relations by other norms.[37]

Legal procedure also distinguishes horizontal from vertical systems. Societies without clearly defined hierarchies demand proofs of guilt or innocence by appeal to some supernatural power.[38] Inasmuch as neither the litigants, if that they are, nor any other member of a horizontal society may impose his judgment upon an equal, the decision rests with various forms of ordeal designed to release from responsibility each member of the society. Trial by water, fire, and oath are widely known in traditional societies, and their results find acceptance in the jural community.[39]

Vertical systems, for their part, engage in more direct forms of investigation and prosecution. Far from ceding their powers to unknown divinities, these power systems attempt to obtain as much control as possible over the process of finding, judging, and punishing deviants. Rules of procedure, what Hart calls secondary rules, are designed by the power hierarchy in much the same way as the primary rules, the norms of behavior. Within the context of a complex social fabric possessing numerous subcultures, the state mechanism undertakes to reduce the role of the unknown, and to submit as many elements as possible to verification by its own agents. Therefore witnesses are obliged to relate only that information which is verifiable with the senses; legal decisions of whatever type are increasingly consigned to paper, a medium which has no prejudice for either side; finally, even the issuance of paper guarantees is monopolized by the state institutions which alone may invest them with legal standing.[40]

Indeed, legal standing comes to depend exclusively upon the will of the power hierarchy. Whereas the memory of the community was once sufficient to guarantee the validity of behavioral norms and their restitutive value, the social differentiation evident in vertical societies produces a demand for a medium of stating norms enforceable by state institutions. The result is a legal code.[41] Weber correctly noted that in its earliest stages the process of codification represents little more than an attempt to generalize the prevailing norms to all the citizenry. Ultimately, however, the code serves as a means of including within the rubric of law behavioral prescriptions which were not generated from the community itself.[42]

To suggest these trends in the law is not to underestimate the particular solution which each society applies to regulating social behavior. Societies represent various points along a broad continuum of legal systems. The prevalence of blood revenge and feud are well documented; composition as an alternative is even better known.[43] Mediation in its various guises has been detected among the North American Plains Indians, the Ifugao of the Philippines and numerous African societies.[44] The switch to formalized adjudication was noted in several colonial societies, and the concomitant growth of judicial agencies also has been observed.[45] Colonial societies demonstrate equally well the movement toward sanctions, both physical and pecuniary.[46] Consequently, there is a large base of residual data to tack on to the model explicated above.

Even in the face of so much ethnographic support, the image of the law's relationship to social structure remains blurry. In the best-documented societies from which a relatively reliable sample was taken, much is still unknown. In comparison with the extended period during which these societies have operated, we have peeked into their internal structure only for a moment. Furthermore, despite the general apparent conformity of the known data to the scheme laid out above, exceptions have already been noted, and doubtless more will be uncovered.[47]

Nevertheless, the model of legal change described above has considerable importance for historians of societies at the dawn of significant change. Their own records of themselves often appear only at that moment when the change is already well under way, a fact which the appearance of writing itself seems to support.[48] For those societies already changed, there is no chance of retreating into their consciousness, no chance for firsthand observation of the type that contemporary ethnographers have done for the traditional societies still active in our era.[49] The records bequeathed by the participants of long-gone societies have themselves weathered the intervening centuries only at the cost of considerable loss. Terms once understood within the context of the society in which they were written have either totally lost their original meaning or have acquired an altogether new meaning which obscures our vision of the past.[50]

The model of legal change described above is especially useful for enlarging upon the laconic description of medieval Russia contained in the extant historical sources. At the beginning of the thirteenth century, Russian society was essentially horizontal. Surviving documentation attests to the fact that blood revenge had only recently been supplanted by composition. Procedure, such as there was, dictated that the victim initiate his claims against the alleged offender, who in turn was obliged to fend off the accusation as best he could. Various forms of ritual expurgation acted as ultimate spokesmen in cases where more mundane evidence was not available. Sanctions remained rare, in the main still subsidiary to composition, itself institutionalized in code form. Some cases of financial sanction do appear, probably in the late twelfth or early thirteenth century, but physical sanctions remained unknown. Thirteenth-century Russian society demonstrates all the traits of horizontal legal relations: procedure was dyadic and no sanctions were attached to the commission of private wrongs.

In contrast to the system of self-help outlined in the first codes, later legal texts give evidence of the rapid and steady undermining of the bilateral process. Instead, triadic forms of conflict resolution appeared with specialized mediation personnel. Courts, unknown by any direct reference in the first codes, gradually assumed definite composition and functions, and were staffed with their own hierarchies of supplementary personnel. One of the duties which devolved upon these intermediaries was the infliction of coercive and pecuniary sanctions, to the virtual exclusion of restitutive penalties. Private wrongs became more difficult to conceptualize, inasmuch as private settlement with various offenders became an offense specifically prohibited by princely legislation. Monopolization of the power to inflict sanctions grew in tandem with a monopolization of the authority to judge, record, and certify the results of litigation. In sum, late fifteenth-century Russian law may aptly be described as vertical, characterized by formally unequal centers of power.

To associate the change in legal relations with changes in social structure is more hazardous. Diamond, Gluckman, and others have already suggested that certain traits often, although not always, accompany legal change. One may expect, for example, that fifteenth-century Russian society grew absolutely, that its occupations became more clearly differentiated, and that a money economy became more usual than was apparent three centuries earlier. Likewise traditional forms of social organization may be expected to have receded in the face of the growing presumptions of state organs. Kinship ties may have lost their former strength, and larger associations of kin may have followed the trend toward individualization and differentiation. Religion, too, deprived of its former strength as an arbiter, likely diminished in importance, increasingly replaced by the rational formal modes examined so brilliantly by Weber.

Even alerted to the precariousness of inferring social change too rigidly from the model of legal change, one is still forced to acknowledge some obvious parallels in late medieval Russian society. The role of kinship as understood in pre-Christian Russia did undergo significant changes in the face of the church's own understanding of the appropriate relationship of blood relatives and affines. The prolonged howl of churchmen against the incestuous morality of the day suggests that the old conceptions had not yet died out, and that communal kinship organizations may still have exercised some of their social functions. Although the nuclear family became ever more usual in these centuries, the data introduced below demonstrate that extended kin ties, far from dying out, retained some measure of vitality even in early Muscovy.

The import of all this is considerable for our depiction of the demise of Kievan Russia and the rise of Muscovy. The persistence of community kinship ties helps explain Muscovy's reliance upon local institutions, even after the annexation of Novgorod and Pskov. The gradual sophistication of legal arrangements, expressed in rules of procedure, the application of sanctions, and the growth of a judiciary, become more comprehensible in the context of the church's preoccupation with the law. While on the one hand churchmen supplied models of procedural and criminal law, on the other hand these same churchmen were engaged in a struggle against traditional institutions rooted in the deep past when kinship and pagan religion played much greater roles. The net effect of this two-sided contribution was the growth of secular state institutions at the expense of traditional social structures.

In any case, the basic alteration in medieval Russian law is inescapable. Although its course was halting and uneven, Russian society of the thirteenth, fourteenth, and fifteenth centuries moved from a legal system dominated by horizontal, dyadic relations to one characterized by vertical, triadic relations. This pattern is evident in the development of sanctions, the appearance of judicial personnel, and the changing norms of procedure and evidence.

CHAPTER 2

Sources of the Law

Many of the difficulties which attend the study of medieval Russian law are the result of ambiguities inherent in the texts which survive. Not only are the sources characterized by antique terms, but the regulations themselves are often couched in the most laconic grammatical structures which breed endless debates over origins and meanings. Historians who have successfully piloted a course through these difficulties are often trapped in quagmires of nationalism. The result is an historiography filled with exceptions and qualifications, a patchwork of guesses, surmises, and deductions which obscure the larger issues concerning the nature of juridicial institutions and conceptions.

The passing of time has not removed all the impediments to a coherent study of medieval Russian legal relations, but it has provided a considerably enriched body of knowledge on which to base an analysis of the process of legal development. In addition to the publication of several critical editions which rely on a very broad source base, studies of recent years have also unearthed several supplementary monuments of law that help to fit together the complex puzzle.

Nevertheless, the extant sources pose serious problems for a legal historian. Most obvious is the chronological discrepancy between the surviving copies and their originals. The overwhelming majority of the surviving texts are copies made several centuries after the presumed time of initial compilation. The Expanded Russkaia Pravda, for example, though linked by internal evidence to the eleventh and twelfth centuries, survives in one thirteenth-century, two fourteenth-century, twenty-eight fifteenth-century, forty-eight sixteenth-century, and sixteen seventeenth-century manuscripts.[1] Not only does this differential complicate analyses of the original structure of the text, but it also raises questions about the Pravda's role in defining the law in centuries subsequent to its origin. Furthermore, although internal evidence indicates that the Expanded Pravda represents a revision of legal norms as elaborated in the Short Pravda, the manuscript tradition does nothing to support that conclusion. While the Short Pravda is extant in two fifteenth-century copies and some eighteenth-century copies, the Expanded Pravda survives in numerous transcriptions which antedate the

SOURCES OF THE LAW

oldest copy of the Short Pravda. It is not at all clear what such information means for the relative times of origin of these texts, significantly different in their understanding of legal relations. The problem is further compounded by the fact that similar complications attend most of the legal texts which have retained a large manuscript base.

A complex and chronologically idiosyncratic manuscript tradition leads to another serious problem. The vast majority of the legal texts are part of manuscript collections which themselves have a complex history of compilation. The bulk of the collections are clearly church documents where the canons of the ecumenical councils, local councils, and church fathers were joined to texts such as the Russkaia Pravda and the Statutes of the early Russian princes. This coincidence served not only to support views of legal development that relied on church law to explain legal sophistication in medieval Russia, but also has contributed to the difficulties in resurrecting the text history of each of the so-called secular monuments.[2]

Those who hope to find here a final resolution of each of these problems will be disappointed. Much remains to be done, work that is not the primary aim of the present study. However, recent reexamination of these difficulties permits a thorough, if conservative, estimate of the time and place of origin of the documents in question. This information is sufficient to provide an historical framework for an analysis of legal institutions and their transformation in medieval Russia.

Kormchaia Kniga

The place to begin such a study is with the legal collections whose copying was sponsored by church institutions. The most widely known collection and the most complex in composition is the Kormchaia Kniga, roughly translated as Pilot's Book.[3] This name came to be applied to collections of church canons, epistles, sermons, Byzantine secular legislation, and such Russian monuments as the Russkaia Pravda and the princes' Statutes. In other words, the Kormchaia Kniga is the medieval Russian equivalent of the nomocanons long known in Byzantium.[4]

The Kormchaia includes three basic redactions in manuscript form: the Efrem, Serbian, and so-called "Russian" redactions. The Efrem Kormchaia—so named because the oldest extant manuscript of this redaction is accompanied by several notes from its copyist,

Efrem—represents a Slavonic version of the Byzantine Syntagma of Fourteen Titles, and is provided with none of the glosses characteristic of later Kormchie.[5] Though undated, the oldest copy (Synod no. 227) is generally regarded as belonging to the twelfth century, but some linguistic data suggest that it may have originated as early as the eleventh century.[6] Since no part of the text's contents may be dated later than 912, and since only one article of native Russian origin is present, it seems likely that the Efrem Kormchaia's protograph was compiled outside the Russian lands, perhaps for the South Slavs early in the tenth century.[7] Within a century copies of this redaction were in use in the Kievan lands.[8]

Relatively few copies of the Efrem redaction survive, but they are spread out over several centuries.[9] In the course of time copyists regularly revised the Kormchaia's contents, presumably with an eye to adjusting the text to changing conditions. Revision reached extreme proportions in the so-called Ustiug Miscellany, the manuscript of which once belonged to the Ustiug Archangel Monastery.[10] Based upon a different canonical collection, the Scholasticus Nomocanon, the Ustiug Miscellany was supplemented with materials taken from the Efrem version. Although Pavlov strenuously argued that this was indeed Russia's first Slavonic nomocanon, the apparent borrowings from the Efrem Kormchaia have induced later scholars to reject Pavlov's view in particular, and to doubt the official status of the Ustiug Miscellany in general.[11]

Despite the relative antiquity of the Efrem Kormchaia, it is clear that the canonical books in use for the first three centuries of official Christianity in Russia proved unsatisfactory. The remarks of Metropolitan Kirill addressed to the Vladimir Council of 1273 suggest that there was considerable confusion over the content of church law.[12] It was this imbroglio that had induced the Metropolitan to request a new nomocanon from Bulgaria sometime in the 1260s.[13] Based upon a revision of the canons performed somewhere in the Balkans early in the thirteenth century, the new Kormchaia, like the Efrem, was centered upon the Nomocanon of Fourteen Titles. But it differed from the Efrem Kormchaia in that the compilers had utilized the abbreviated canons and accompanied them with the detailed glosses of Aristinus and Zonaras.[14] Imported to help reform the Russian clergy, this so-called Serbian Kormchaia has a relatively weak manuscript tradition in Russia.[15] Although it served as the basis for the 1280 Riazan' copy, the Serbian Kormchaia soon fell into disuse as a result of further revisions in the canon law of northeast Russia. The Serbian text remained in use in much of the

Ukraine and Belorussia, but reemerged in northeast Russia only in the seventeenth century in connection with the preparation of the new printed Kormchaia of 1649-1653.[16]

Perhaps more important is the fact that the imported Serbian Kormchaia served as the stimulus for an entirely new edition of the church texts in the thirteenth century. This redaction, probably compiled in connection with the 1273 Vladimir Council called by Metropolitan Kirill, combined the canonical texts in their complete form as presented in the Efrem Kormchaia with the glosses included in the Serbian canonical texts.[17] The original product of this combination did not survive, but nevertheless did serve as the basis for two subsequent reworkings—a protograph of the southern redactions of the Kormchaia (the Vladimir-Volynia and the Ukrainian Lukashevich Kormchie) and a protograph of the northern redactions, compiled perhaps in Pereiaslavl'-Zalesskii in 1280.[18] The northern protograph in turn had two recensions active in the northeast—the Varsonof'ev-Barsov and the Synod-Tikhomirov groups, the oldest of whose manuscripts belong to the fourteenth and thirteenth centuries respectively.[19] Only the last, the Synod Kormchaia, includes the Russkaia Pravda or similar secular legal monuments of medieval Russia, a deficiency in some cases corrected by later copyists.[20] The Vladimir-Volynia Kormchaia and the Ukrainian Kormchaia evidently were in wide use in the southern principalities, which explains their omission of two articles of northern origin—the Questionary of Kirik and the Canons of Il'ia—included in the thirteenth-century northern Kormchie.[21]

Consequently the Kormchaia, especially in its northern copies, is an ideal source from which to extract information about the legal norms of medieval Russia.[22] It has a large manuscript tradition both in the number of surviving copies and the contents of those copies. Particularly useful to the historian of law are the Synod Kormchaia and the Kormchie Knigi which developed from it. The Synod Kormchaia itself represents in a very early copy the revision of church law undertaken in the thirteenth century, and contains the oldest extant copy of the Expanded Russkaia Pravda.[23] A fourteenth-century addition also preserved the oldest copy of Vladimir's Statute, another document important for defining Russian legal institutions in medieval times.[24]

The impact of the Synod Kormchaia was magnified as it became a source for other legal texts. The Sophia Kormchaia, created in the late fourteenth century,[25] the Miasnikov Kormchaia, also devised in the fourteenth century, possibly for the Dvina lands,[26] the so-

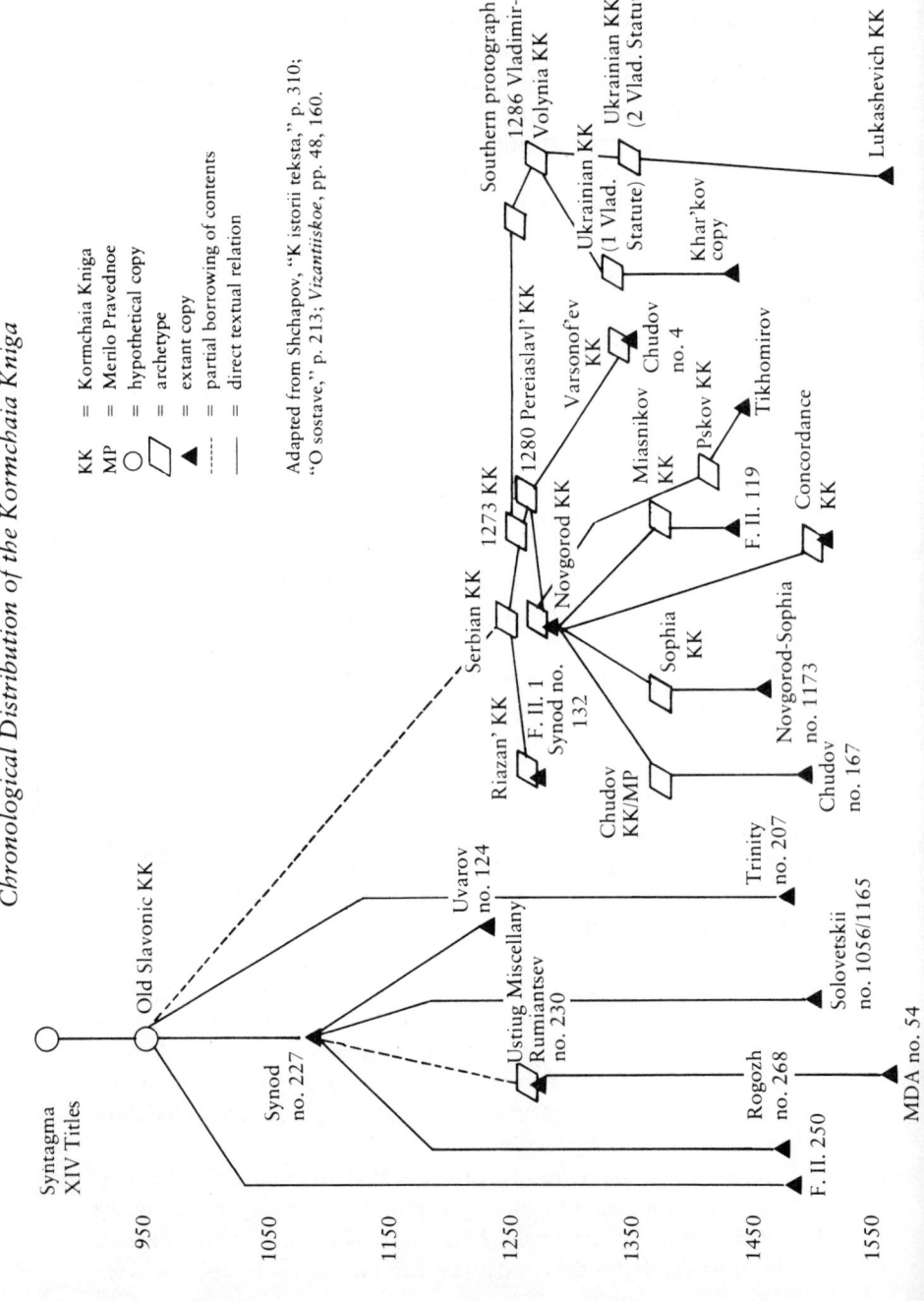

called Concordance Kormchaia, a generalizing collection whose history is tied to the debate over church lands in the sixteenth century,[27] and the Chudov Kormchaia, probably of fourteenth-century origin[28]—all sprang from the Synod Kormchaia. Not only do these descendants constitute a rich and continuous source for legal texts of the fourteenth and fifteenth centuries, but they also attest to the prolonged vitality of particular texts and the changes introduced in them in the late medieval period.

Merilo Pravednoe

Further testimony to legal developments in this period is contained in another collection of legal texts whose creation evidently depended upon the church. The Merilo Pravednoe, or the Just Measure, like the Kormchaia Kniga, is characterized by a complex composition. Although only five copies survive, the structure is identical in all but one.[29] The manuscript consists of two parts. The first is devoted largely to presenting various episcopal lessons, sermons, and pithy observations of churchmen on the general theme of justice. The second section includes various kinds of legal texts—for example, Selections from the Mosaic Law (*Izbranie ot zakona bogom dannogo*), a series of Byzantine regulations concerning marriage, the complete texts of the Procheiros Nomos and Ecloga, and a number of articles which originated in Russia. Included among the last is the Russkaia Pravda in its Expanded redaction, as well as a provision related to clerical jurisdiction, On Church People (*O tserkovnykh liudekh*).[30]

The oldest surviving copy of the Merilo Pravednoe is reliably dated to the fourteenth century, and its predecessor may well have arisen late in the thirteenth century when the Kormchaia Kniga itself was undergoing its distinctive reworking.[31] Two fifteenth-century copies and one sixteenth-century copy duplicate the composition. Only one early sixteenth-century text offers any significant variants.[32]

Like the Kormchaia Kniga, the Merilo had its origins in church circles in medieval Russia. Ownership of three of the four later manuscript copies has successfully been tied to Russian Metropolitans, a factor which suggests that the Merilo Pravednoe was composed especially for the Metropolitan.[33] The oldest extant copy is a particularly fine example of elaborate manuscript ornamentation of the type likely to be used for an important official such as the Metropolitan.[34]

Merilo Pravednoe and Iushkov's Reconstruction of Its Origins

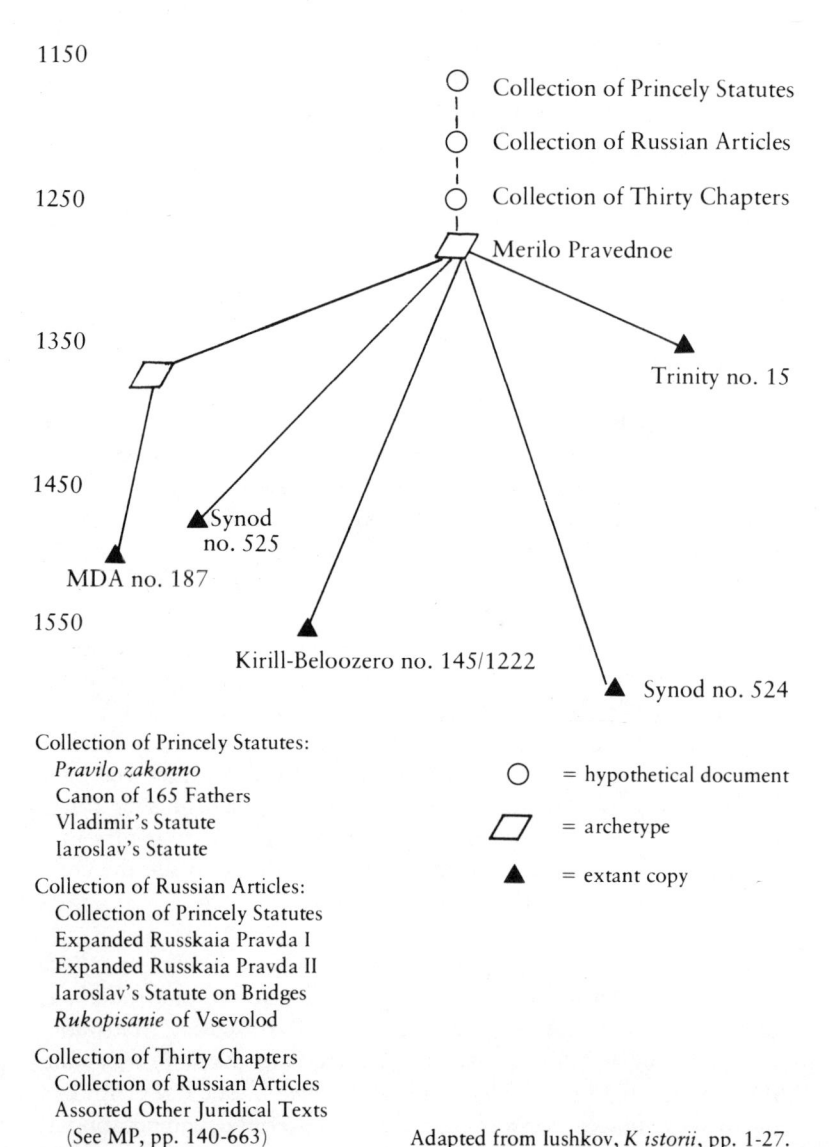

1150 ○ Collection of Princely Statutes

○ Collection of Russian Articles

1250 ○ Collection of Thirty Chapters

▱ Merilo Pravednoe

1350

▱

▲ Trinity no. 15

1450

▲ Synod no. 525

▲ MDA no. 187

1550

▲ Kirill-Beloozero no. 145/1222

▲ Synod no. 524

Collection of Princely Statutes:
  Pravilo zakonno
  Canon of 165 Fathers
  Vladimir's Statute
  Iaroslav's Statute

Collection of Russian Articles:
  Collection of Princely Statutes
  Expanded *Russkaia Pravda* I
  Expanded *Russkaia Pravda* II
  Iaroslav's Statute on Bridges
  Rukopisanie of Vsevolod

Collection of Thirty Chapters
  Collection of Russian Articles
  Assorted Other Juridical Texts
  (See MP, pp. 140-663)

○ = hypothetical document

▱ = archetype

▲ = extant copy

Adapted from Iushkov, *K istorii*, pp. 1-27.

The Chudov recension of the Kormchaia represents a unique combination of the Kormchaia of the Novgorod type with the Merilo Pravednoe. It seems likely, as Tikhomirov has suggested, that the Chudov Kormchaia arose in the fourteenth century, probably in northeast Russia.[35] The logic of combining the Merilo with the Kormchaia is not apparent, although it may point to particular juridical needs of churchmen in the northeast principalities. In any event, the Chudov combination demonstrates again that legal norms were a subject of interest in the fourteenth century and makes more substantive the church connections of the Merilo Pravednoe.

Miscellanies

Several manuscripts of complex composition which exhibit no clear signs of official origin or acceptance also survive. The oldest is the so-called Musin-Pushkin Miscellany, named for its early nineteenth-century owner. The Expanded Russkaia Pravda, the Zakon Sudnyi liudem (Court Law for the People), Selections from Mosaic Law, the 1229 Smolensk Treaty, Iaroslav's Statute on Bridges, and an introduction on judges make up the contents. The collection probably was compiled in Novgorod in the fourteenth or late thirteenth century.[36]

A similar collection is included in the Archeographic copy of the Novgorod First Chronicle, a fifteenth-century text. Like the Musin-Pushkin Miscellany, the Novgorod Chronicle text contains the Russkaia Pravda, the Zakon Sudnyi liudem and Iaroslav's Statute on Bridges, but also includes several additional articles—the Statutes of Vladimir, Iaroslav, and Vsevolod.[37]

The proximity of several articles of Russian origin in monuments of complex composition has provoked a good deal of speculation about the role and significance of these collections in medieval Russia. Some attempt to elucidate the relationship of the particular documents to the larger convoy was made in the nineteenth century, but the source base was insufficient to permit a very complete picture to emerge.[38] Only with the early years of the twentieth century did this methodology begin to yield any substantive results. After V. N. Beneshevich had prepared a critical edition of two of the Russian princes' church statutes,[39] one of his students, S. V. Iushkov, published an original study of the basic juridical miscellanies which included the princes' statutes as part of the fundamental convoy. Summarized in a 27-page booklet with a very small printing, the basic propositions of Iushkov's work were slow in finding an audience.[40] He therefore repeated his findings in each of his subsequent monographs, but despite the hammering produced by this repetition, his general approach did not win many converts among Soviet students of old Russian law.[41]

Iushkov's work centered on the Statutes of Princes Vladimir and Iaroslav, texts associated with other Russian legal documents in complex collections. Painstaking examination of the manuscript collections yielded seven basic combinations of legal and semi-legal texts. Although the earliest manuscripts for any of these combinations belonged to the fifteenth century, Iushkov theorized that the components had come together much earlier to form an integral juridical handbook. As evidence for his judgment, he pointed to the history of the inclusion of the legal texts in monuments of complex composition such as the Kormchie Knigi and the various legal miscellanies.[42]

Several stages attended this process. The basic components, those comprising what Iushkov called the Collection of Princely Statutes, were the *Pravilo zakonno* (a document similar to Vladimir's Statute, perhaps an introduction to the Statute), the Canon of the 165 Holy Fathers, which defended church property interests, and the Statutes of Vladimir and Iaroslav.[43] As the list clearly shows, the ground common to all the components is a concern for church jurisdiction, which suggests that such a collection may have been designed for church courts.

Iushkov suggested that the core of legal documents was later supplemented by other articles of similar thrust—the Statute of Prince Vsevolod, the Tale on Marriage (*Skaz' o zhenitve*), and two confirmation charters of Grand Prince Vasilii Dmitrievich, the first concluded with Metropolitan Kiprian (1402) and the second with Metropolitan Fotii (1419), by which the preceding princely Statutes were officially confirmed. These last provisions, each added at different times for different redactions of the Collection of Princely Statutes, were useful therefore in tracing the later history of the Collection itself.[44]

The Collection of Princely Statutes, according to Iushkov, was then absorbed into a compilation of still more complex composition. The Collection of Russian Articles, as he named it, included versions of the basic articles enumerated above. In addition, however, the Russkaia Pravda in the form of two separate Statutes—

of Princes Iaroslav and Vladimir Vseslavich—was joined to the Collection, along with Iaroslav's Statute on Bridges and the *Rukopisanie* of Vsevolod. The importance of this collection, as Iushkov reconstructed it, lies in its combination of church law with texts of secular law. Consequently, Iushkov visualized the existence of two distinct judicial powers—church and state—as early as the beginning of the thirteenth century.[45]

In its turn the Collection of Russian Articles was joined to several other texts in an anthology called the Collection of Thirty Chapters, the existence of which is easy to establish, given its place in the Merilo Pravednoe. Chapters 1-26 consisted of various texts of foreign law, and Chapters 28 and 29 were formed from the two parts of the Expanded Russkaia Pravda. The final chapter included several small, independent texts.[46] Chapter 27, however, far from including all the contents of the hypothesized Collection of Princely Statutes, contained only the *Pravilo zakonno*. Consequently, while the preceding and succeeding chapters consist of lengthy entries, the *Pravilo zakonno* occupies only one side of one folio.[47] Comparison of the relative size of all the other chapters led Iushkov to theorize that Chapter 27 was somehow corrupt, deprived of its usual convoy.[48]

While the more tenuous of Iushkov's arguments may require further substantiation, there is reason to believe that legal codification of the sort that he described was under way as early as the thirteenth century. At a minimum, the Collection of Thirty Chapters clearly had a separate identity before its inclusion in the Merilo Pravednoe, since in the latter it bore a separate numeration setting it apart from the more prosaic eulogies to justice in the Merilo's first section.[49]

Least successful among Iushkov's arguments is his understanding of the last stage of the process of combination and codification. From the Merilo Pravednoe, according to Iushkov, these legal texts fell into the Kormchaia.[50] On a scale much less grand than he intended, his observation is indisputable. The Chudov recension of the Kormchaia, that branch which combines the usual composition of the Synod Kormchaia with the Merilo Pravednoe, clearly marks the assimilation of the Merilo, evidently sometime in the fourteenth or early fifteenth century. It is more difficult to accept such a progression for other families of the Kormchaia, where many of the same texts—the princes' statutes, Russkaia Pravda, and others—appear, but not in the company of the complete convoy displayed in the Merilo Pravednoe. Only if the Merilo Pravednoe preceded the Kormchaia as a judicial handbook for clerics may we see any rationale for Iushkov's sequence.

Nevertheless, the evidence is sufficient to justify Iushkov's assertion that some such collation did take place in the fourteenth and fifteenth centuries. This conclusion recently has gained more respectability with the work of another Soviet scholar, Ia. N. Shchapov. Like Iushkov, Shchapov was attracted to legal texts by an interest in the Statutes of Vladimir and Iaroslav.[51] Examining chronicle texts in fifteenth-century copies, Shchapov found collections similar to those uncovered earlier by Iushkov. The Karamzin copy of the Sophia First Chronicle, for example, included the Russkaia Pravda, Iaroslav's Statute on Bridges, the Zakon Sudnyi liudem, and a provision on torture. This seemingly secular compendium was enlarged in the Bal'zerov family of the same chronicle which added to the above the Statute of Vladimir, the Canon of the 165 Holy Fathers, the Canon on Church People, the Statute of Iaroslav, and the 1402 confirmation charter of Grand Prince Vasilii to Metropolitan Kiprian.[52]

The first of these collections, which Shchapov visualizes as a secular collation, was made part of the Chudov Kormchaia, a Moscow-based revision of the Kormchaia and Merilo Pravdenoe carried out in the fourteenth or fifteenth century. The second, enlarged collection, composed of secular and church texts, was inserted into the chronicle text (*svod*) of the 1430s and may well have entered its source, the *Polikhron*. Inclusion of the 1402 Charter of the Moscow Prince serves to convince Shchapov that this basic chronicle compilation belonged to Moscow rather than to Novgorod.[53]

Shchapov traces another juridical complex in the Novgorod First Chronicle. The Archeographic copy (Arch. no. 240) contains a collection prefaced by an extract from a Canon of St. Basil on the courts, and includes the Russkaia Pravda, a provision devoted to dishonor payments (*bezchest'e*), the Zakon Sudnyi liudem in its expanded redaction, and Iaroslav's Statute on Bridges. Immediately preceding the complex is the miscellany which Iushkov tied to the entire development of legal texts in the early period—the Collection of Princely Articles. The presence of Vsevolod's Statute in the latter collection and Iaroslav's Statute on Bridges in the former serves to underline the Novgorodian origin of both parts of the compilation, created perhaps contemporaneously with the copying of the surviving texts in the heat of Novgorod-Moscow rivalry.[54]

Though Iushkov's claims for the existence of specialized legal collections may remain unproven, the sum of work done by Iushkov and Shchapov demonstrates clearly that during the fourteenth and fifteenth centuries, if not the thirteenth, there was an intense and clearly defined interest in the compilation of legal texts. This manifested itself not only in church circles, where the Kormchaia Kniga and Merilo Pravednoe took shape, but also among those concerned to extend the range of law governing purely secular concerns.

The Russkaia Pravda and Its Historiography

Nevertheless, the great majority of the surviving legal texts do not confront us with manifest convoy implications. This reality has helped to bury the conclusions of Iushkov, and simultaneously has spurred the examination of each separate text within the larger complexes. Internal criticism was urged upon scholars in no small part by the nature of the texts themselves. The Russkaia Pravda, the greatest beneficiary of the impulse to textual criticism, has been described alternately as a concordance of Russian princely law or a collection of native customary law. Its local origin places the Pravda in stark contrast to other collections such as the Kormchaia Kniga where the diligent reader must plow through the canons of the seven ecumenical councils, canons of the Orthodox saints, and folios of Byzantine secular legislation before he reaches "native" Russian law.

It is no surprise, then, to discover that the Russkaia Pravda was the first to be subjected to detailed textual criticism. Already V. N. Tatishchev had discovered the Short Pravda in the 1730s, but his history of Russia bears only slight traces of the discovery. Evidently Tatishchev intended to publish an edition of the Pravda with other "ancient laws" he had uncovered, but he never succeeded in this aim.[55] Only in 1767 did A. L. Schlözer fulfill the task, publishing the Short Pravda according to the Academy copy discovered by Tatishchev. That same copy was the basis for the edition in the first volume of the *Prodolzhenie drevnei rossiiskoi vivliofiki* under the direction of S. Ia. Rumovskii.[56] The third volume of that series contained a significant addition to the knowledge of the Russkaia Pravda. In 1788 V. V. Krestinin published a copy of the Expanded Russkaia Pravda, the original of which was, until recently, thought subsequently to have been lost. But, like the preceding editions, Krestinin's was devoid of any critical approach, based as it was on a single copy.[57]

The first step in the direction of a more sophisticated understanding of the Pravda's textual history was taken by I. N. Boltin in his 1792 edition. Using seven copies of the Expanded Pravda plus the Academy copy of the Short Pravda, Boltin concluded that the Expanded Pravda represented a simple combination of laws of Iaroslav and Iziaslav.[58] The task of gathering additional copies of the Pravda received a substantial boost with N. M. Karamzin's appointment as the Empire's official historian by Alexander I. By imperial order, Karamzin was permitted into numerous achives, where he discovered several copies of the Expanded Pravda, including those now known as the Synod, Pushkin, and Karamzin copies.[59] It fell to Konstantin Kalaidovich to publish the Synod text in 1815, and shortly thereafter Pavel Stroev published the Voskresensk copy.[60]

The task of collecting and codifying Russian imperial law, begun anew by M. M. Speranskii under the patronage of Alexander I, proved to be a stimulating atmosphere for the study of the Pravda as well. G. F. Ewers, for example, was invited to Moscow to work on the codification, and soon fell in with Karamzin, who alerted the German scholar to the existence of the Russkaia Pravda's Synod copy. Although his 1816 German translation of the Pravda did not utilize the Synod text, Ewers was already aware of the distinction and relative age of the two redactions of the Pravda, a fact underlined in his study of medieval Russian legal development published a decade later.[61]

None of the early studies had paid any attention to the manuscript convoy in which the Pravda was found. G. A. Rosenkampf's work was a useful corrective, since Rosenkampf identified the Pravda and several other texts as a composite part of one of the Kormchaia's basic redactions. It proved more difficult to account for copies not found in the Kormchaia, but Rosenkampf had demonstrated effectively that attempts to date and explain the Russkaia Pravda without reference to its manuscript convoy were bound to fail.[62] Initially this contribution was lost in the charged debate between Westernizers and Slavophiles, an exchange which had a continuing impact on the monographs devoted to the Pravda published in the 1830s and 1840s, during which time not one study contributed in any meaningful way to advancing the Pravda's textual history.[63]

Only with the publication in 1843 of the entire Musin-Pushkin Miscellany did the issue of convoy again come to the fore. The new edition finally made available the Pushkin copy of the Expanded Pravda discovered several decades earlier by Karamzin,[64] and as a result, comparison of the Pravda's redactions was made substantially easier. Although subsequent histories continued to be preoccupied with the question of the national origin of the legal norms contained in the Pravda, studies such as those of E. S. Tobien already demonstrated a basic understanding of the Pravda's two essential manuscript families and their chronological relationship.[65] But Rosenkampf's work had contributed more than that to the subsequent literature. Nikolai Kalachov, poring over the copies of the Kormchie Knigi known to him, had managed to amass fifty copies of the Pravda.[66] Utilizing a method essentially similar to that espoused by Iushkov seventy years later, Kalachov divided the families of the Russkaia Pravda according to their convoy. He was thus able to isolate copies in (1) the Novgorod First Chronicle, (2) the Kormchie Knigi and Merila Pravednye, (3) Stroev's *Sofiiskii vremiannik*, and (4) juridical collections which possessed no definitive structure. Within the second group, clearly the largest in terms of surviving manuscripts, Kalachov isolated the Synod text, which he regarded as the most important copy of the Expanded Pravda, the Obolenskii and Tolstoi IV copies, now usually identified as the Abbreviated Pravda, and a third category to which he consigned all the rest.[67] In actual publication of the texts of the four basic families of the Pravda, Kalachov printed the Academy, Trinity (in place of the Synod copy already published in 1815 by Kalaidovich), Karamzin, and Obolenskii copies, each representing a different redaction. Successive reprintings of this edition are witness to its prolonged dominance in the subsequent historiography.[68]

Only in the 1890s did the profession catch up with Kalachov's enormous contribution. The first systematic attempt to rethink the entire classification of copies on the basis of a broad source base was undertaken by V. I. Sergeevich. Using more than fifty copies, Sergeevich deduced that the Pravda consisted of three families, different in size, content, and time of compilation. Although skeptical about the actual application of the Pravda's regulations, Sergeevich saw some chronological trend in the creation of the Short, Expanded, and what he called a Middle redaction. His conclusions appeared originally in a brief article which was published without any accompanying texts.[69] By the time Sergeevich published his edition of the Pravda's texts, he had significantly altered his views. In the 1904 edition he posited not three but four redactions, a conclusion based upon his willingness to subdivide the Short Pravda into two component parts: the first section, now usually described as the Drevneishaia (Oldest) Pravda, representing legal norms of the early eleventh century; and the second part, often called the Pravda Iaroslavichei (of Iaroslav's sons), norms of the late eleventh century. In other respects Sergeevich stuck to his original conclusions, stipulating a separate redaction for the Expanded Pravda and his Middle Pravda.[70]

Sergeevich's work had considerable impact on monographs devoted to Russian law. Especially provocative was his suggestion to divide the Short Pravda into two basic redactions, an idea that led some historians of law to seek a much earlier date for the Short Pravda's roots than the eleventh century. Sergeevich's attempts to debunk the official origin of the Pravda helped to antiquate its legal norms. By denying the authenticity of the Pravda's ascription to Iaroslav, Sergeevich freed himself and other scholars from the chronological restraints previously imposed by the Short Pravda's supposed age. Although the Russkaia Pravda was preserved in a fifteenth-century copy, it now became possible to suggest that at least the Pravda's first provisions belonged to the pre-Christian epoch of the eighth and ninth centuries. Critics of this view did not conceal their dislike for its arbitrariness, but nevertheless, the basic work of collecting and examining the documents carried out by Sergeevich was the most complete such study since Kalachov.[71]

Despite Sergeevich's attempt at reclassification, Kalachov's 1846 edition continued to prevail in early twentieth-century studies. In 1914, A. I. Iakovlev, frankly admitting his dependence on Kalachov's work, published a new textbook edition of the Pravda in which he included the Academic, Trinity, Karamzin, Synod, and Obolenskii copies.[72] Meanwhile furious debate continued over such questions as Byzantine and Roman influences on medieval Russian law,[73] the Kievan roots of the Pravda,[74] and the whole issue of the Short Pravda's origin, a problem which had festered since Sergeevich's bold hypothesis that the Short Pravda itself constituted two separate redactions.[75]

When a new textbook edition of the Russkaia Pravda appeared in 1928, Kalachov's classification, published three-quarters of a century earlier, still had not been displaced.[76] But the groundwork for a completely new edition of the Pravda was laid in the early 1920s, and by 1928 work was officially under way for the publication of the Russkaia Pravda in an edition prepared by the Academy of Sciences. The timing, however, did not prove propitious for commencing such long-term projects, and the task was interrupted in 1929.[77] Nevertheless, the first fruits of this work began to appear soon thereafter.

In a 1930 publication E. F. Karskii produced a complete edition of the Synod text. Together with a photographic reproduction of the Synod copy, Karskii presented a critical edition of the text adorned with variants from no less than nineteen other copies. This factor alone was enough to constitute a considerable advance over previous editions.[78] Still, a comprehensive edition of all the redactions, based upon all the copies, remained an unfulfilled goal.

While the anticipated Academy edition awaited publication in the capital, S. V. Iushkov managed to get a fairly sophisticated edition of the Pravda published in Kiev in 1935 under the auspices of the Ukrainian Academy of Sciences. In the most comprehensive collection of manuscripts to that date, the Ukrainian edition relied upon a total of ninety-four copies, the chief variants of which were introduced in the notes. The Pravda was divided into five redactions, a system favored by Iushkov, where the Short Pravda was represented by the Academy copy and the Expanded Pravda, subdivided into three recensions, represented by the Synod, Pushkin, and Trinity copies. The final three redactions were based exclusively upon the convoy, and were represented by the Archeographic no. 23, Archeographic no. 240, and the Tolstoi II copies.[79]

As with Iushkov's earlier work, an apathetic response greeted the new edition, despite the heroic accomplishment of collecting nearly twice as many copies as Kalachov, an authority still in vogue as late as 1928, had used in 1846. But work on the central Academy of Sciences' edition of the Pravda resumed in earnest in the mid-1930s with the publication of a proposal for a four-volume edition composed of texts, manuscript descriptions, literature on the Pravda, and a separate volume of indices. No less than fifteen complete texts were to be printed in their entirety in parallel columns. Photoreproduction of the texts also was proposed.[80]

Textbook editions of the Pravda continued to appear in the 1930s, capped finally by Grekov's textbook edition, published in anticipation of the nearly completed Academy edition. Based upon the largest number of copies ever used, Grekov's text followed the same division later introduced in the more prestigious publication of the Academy. Only two redactions of the Pravda, Short and Expanded, were included. Adopting the same preference for copies that the Academy edition was later to show, Grekov published the Academy copy of the Short Pravda and the Trinity copy of the Expanded Pravda.[81]

The concentrated attention devoted to the Pravda in the 1930s and 1940s produced new findings on a wide variety of topics related to the development of legal norms in medieval Russia. Most notable among the scholars involved in this work was M. N. Tikhomirov who, though a member of the editorial board of the Academy edition, dissented from the basic classification system adopted for that publication. Just preceding the release of the Academy's first volume, Tikhomirov published his findings in a short article. Paying some attention to the convoy approach pioneered by Iushkov, Tikhomirov distinguished between the Short and Expanded Pravda, the former compiled in the early twelfth century and the latter in the late twelfth or early thirteenth. Most controversial was his contention that the Abbreviated Pravda, consigned to a recension of the Expanded Pravda in the Academy edition, constituted a separate redaction whose rise was connected to events in Perm' in the fifteenth century.[82]

Tikhomirov reproduced these views in much more detail in a 1941 monograph. Here he carefully analyzed the connections between individual texts, their larger manuscript convoy, and the political and cultural developments of medieval Russian society. Although Tikhomirov altered somewhat his calculations for dating the rise of the Short Pravda, his conclusions on the other two redactions remained unchanged.[83] In scope and attention to detail this work remains unsurpassed, but Tikhomirov did supplement it with the 1953 publication of a textbook edition of the Pravda. Well prior to the appearance of the Academy's volume of photoreproductions of the basic texts, Tikhomirov included photographic prints of the Academy and Trinity copies. In addition to that, as one of the consequences of his own monograph of a decade earlier, he devoted space to other legal texts of the period, most notably the Zakon Sudnyi liudem and the Pravosudie Mitropolich'e.[84]

Tikhomirov was not alone in conceptualizing the Abbreviated Pravda as a separate redaction. Another study devoted to this question appeared in 1940. N. A. Maksimeiko, also taking issue with the planned absorption of the Abbreviated Pravda, examined both the lexicon and the structural changes evident in the abbreviated copies and thereby convincingly demonstrated that they represented a later, conscious reworking of the Expanded Pravda. The terminology especially suggested an origin in Moscow, perhaps as late as the seventeenth century, since some of the legal norms coincided with seventeenth-century Muscovite legislation.[85]

Meanwhile, work continued on the Academy edition. Another preliminary article by Liubimov laid to rest the false start initiated by Sergeevich on the division of the Short Pravda into two redactions.[86] Finally, the first volume of the long-awaited Academy edition of the Russkaia Pravda appeared in 1940. Much as Liubimov had suggested in his 1936 article, the initial volume contained texts of the fifteen basic copies with variants from all the surviving manuscripts. Using 87 of the 102 copies known to them (not counting the three Tatishchev copies), the editors of the Academy edition divided the Pravda into two redactions, Short and Expanded, the latter subdivided into three groups and thirteen types. As Liubimov had proposed earlier, the Abbreviated Pravda was absorbed into the Expanded Pravda, as it represented only a simple selection of regulations from the latter. A second volume, devoted to surveying the extensive literature on the Pravda, emerged in 1947, and the final volume, photoreproductions of the basic fifteen copies, did not appear until 1963.[87]

Despite the prestige which the new edition carried, its conclusions were not uniformly accepted by all members of the academic community. For one thing, Iushkov did not abandon his own orientation toward the convoy of the Pravda. In a 1939 article and in his much more detailed 1950 monograph, he continued to hammer away at the convoy theme.[88] The publication of various texts of Russian law, a series commenced in 1952 under Iushkov's direction, also rejected parts of the system proposed by Liubimov. In the first volume of that series, largely devoted to texts of the Russkaia Pravda, the Abbreviated Pravda earned a separate place as a redaction of the late sixteenth or early seventeenth century.[89]

Despite the disagreements which the classification system produced, the Academy edition filled a need that had been felt since the early years of the nineteenth century. While Kalachov had attempted a systematic survey of all copies of the Pravda, and while he was concerned with the surrounding convoy, the intervening hundred years had produced no publication where the basic texts of the Pravda itself were made widely available in the company of the critical variants of so broad a manuscript base. Although the Academy edition to some extent overlooked the role of convoy, scholars like Tikhomirov and Iushkov could make use of the published texts to advance their work on the more complex collections in which the Pravda was found.

The Academy edition marked a significant advance in another way. Studies of the Russkaia Pravda published subsequently have concentrated on approaches dominated by internal criticism. A very productive aspect of this labor has been the effort devoted to examining eighteenth-century copies of the Pravda in search of evidence for the existence of other copies lost through fire or the simple passage of time.[90] The most creative work has been produced by the linguists, and the least productive and most popular work involves attempts to subdivide the Pravda's contents on the basis of vague ideological premises.[91]

There has also been some interest in social history as refracted through the lens of the law. N. L. Rubinshtein, although best known for his study of Russian historiography, contributed a very insightful piece relating the content of the Short Pravda to the social structure of medieval Russia. In another case, Mark Kosven, an ethnographer trained in the 1920s, concentrated attention on the relation between social units depicted by the Pravda and the principle of resolving conflicts. More recently, A. A. Zimin has produced some innovative examinations of the Pravda. But, except for the occasional republication of the basic two or three copies of the Pravda, this is the sum of Russian work drawing on the most comprehensive edition of an historical text in the history of Russian scholarship.[92]

The Academy edition sparked the interest of Western historians as well. In 1947 the Russian emigre scholar George Vernadsky published an English translation of the Academy text of the Short Pravda and the Trinity copy of the Expanded Pravda. Although Vernadsky performed a useful service in first making the Pravda available to English-speaking persons, his translation is marred by serious errors and reveals none of the texts' intricacies.[93] These inadequacies become more readily apparent in the few studies devoted to the Pravda which appeared in English in the subsequent two decades.[94] Meanwhile Marc Szeftel produced a series of studies of early Russian legal norms which culminated in the publication of a French translation of several texts. Szeftel's commentary often resembles a summary of the historiography, but unlike other Western students, he attempted to trace legal development in the pre-Muscovite period.[95] Recently another French translation of the Pravda has appeared, but it makes no attempt to examine the pace of legal change in medieval Russia.[96]

Particularly grievous among the omissions in the literature is the failure to monitor adequately the changes introduced in the legal

SOURCES OF THE LAW 37

norms of the Pravda as they passed into subsequent texts. Novgorod documents of the late thirteenth century reflect very clearly the basic postulates of the Pravda. Inasmuch as many scholars are willing to admit the connection of the Russkaia Pravda with the city-republic of Novgorod, there is less reluctance to examine the interrelationship of the legal norms presented in parallel texts. But a similar affinity with the legal notions of the Pravda may be discovered in Pskov and even Smolensk, though the subsequent influence of Western law diluted the Pravda's impact there.[97] Nevertheless, as later Lithuanian law demonstrates, the Russkaia Pravda continued to have legal force in the thirteenth and fourteenth centuries in the western territories which came under Lithuanian control.[98]

REGIONAL LEGAL TEXTS

It is important to confirm the role of the Pravda in the law of the western Russian lands in order to establish the general validity of the Pravda, a document whose actual application was doubted by scholars as important as Sergeevich.[99] But beyond that, the widespread application of the norms of the Pravda in twelfth- and thirteenth-century documents gives some chronological basis to the Russkaia Pravda, and in that way helps sort out some of the ambiguities introduced by the complex textual history of its manuscripts. Finally, the application of the Pravda in other monuments of law serves to underline the essential integrity of the tradition of legal institutions examined in this study.

The Novgorod Treaty with Gotland and the German towns represents the oldest extant treaty negotiated between the Russians and the northern and western Europeans. It is dated to 1189-1199, although the copy in which it survives belongs to the second half of the thirteenth century. Reprinted several times in the twentieth century, the treaty offers a concise explanation of some norms for trade relations and criminal law in Novgorod.[100] The Smolensk Treaty of 1229, which calls itself a Pravda, is known through a much more complex manuscript tradition. Surviving in six or seven copies, depending upon the criteria applied, the Treaty is divided into two redactions—Gotland and Riga—which reflect the international character of the document's compilation.[101] It is sufficient to note here that the text survives in a copy very close to the 1229 original, three other thirteenth-century copies, and two fourteenth-century copies.[102] In short, the Smolensk treaty texts clearly relate the legal norms of the Expanded Russkaia Pravda to the thirteenth century. The connection is only strengthened by the existence of a project for still another treaty of Smolensk with the Germans, a document which probably belongs to the last half of the thirteenth century.[103]

Similar links with the legal norms of the Pravda may be isolated in the legislative codes of the two main northern city-republics of this era. The Novgorod Judicial Charter survives in a single copy, itself incomplete, so that we do not possess the whole code.[104] The contents are further compromised by the fact that the collection in which the code survives is a compendium of documents pertaining to Moscow's absorption of Novgorod in 1471.[105] The literature analyzing the Novgorod Charter, consequently, is strewn with theories of the code's construction, most recently based on a combination of internal criticism and Marxist logic.[106] By the most modest standard, then, one can relate the charter only to the second half of the fifteenth century, although it seems likely that various provisions originated much earlier.

The Pskov Judicial Charter survives in more complete form, containing fully 120 articles, but it too is characterized by a weak manuscript tradition. The complete text is extant in a single copy, supplemented only by a fragment containing the last eleven articles.[107] Originally the Pskov code was known only in the form of this fragment, published in Karamzin's history of Russia. This final portion of the Judicial Charter was republished several times early in the nineteenth century before the complete text was discovered in a private manuscript collection.[108] A transcription of the code was published in 1847, furnished with an explanatory glossary and a one-page reproduction to demonstrate the handwriting.[109]

Discovery of the complete Pskov Charter greatly increased the material available for the study of Pskov legal and social history and provoked a surge in the literature on these subjects. Within twenty years several detailed studies of Pskov's legal institutions appeared, works which still bear considerable value.[110] A second printing of the Charter appeared in 1868, and most documentary collections for the next forty years relied upon this text.[111] The prolonged dependence upon the printed text of the Pskov Charter helped stimulate a new edition based solely upon the document itself, a publication which appeared in 1914. The editors included a detailed description of the manuscript, and published the text of the entire code as well as the separate fragment known already to Karamzin. A photocopy of the original was appended to allow for a comparison with the printed text.[112]

SOURCES OF THE LAW 39

Perhaps as a result of the timing of the new edition, there was no large stir from the academic community. P. E. Mikhailov published two specialized studies on aspects of legal relations defined by the Charter, but the more substantive work took a new course.[113] Most Soviet studies devoted to the Pskov Charter concentrated on the question of textual history. The first of them, by M. K. Rozhkova, suggested a complex history for the different sections of the code whereby the last section actually constituted the oldest part of the Charter. Among the other subdivisions she saw, none was arranged strictly chronologically, but instead reflected the long history of editorial changes inflicted on the text.[114] Subsequent studies have adopted most of Rozhkova's conclusions, although the subdivisions within the text sometimes vary.[115] Soviet publications have also made available the text and its translation several times, though no significant changes have been introduced since the 1914 edition.[116] The major innovation, if it may be called that, introduced by Soviet historians is the attention paid to the development of seigniorial relations as outlined in the Charter.[117]

Pskov law, even more clearly than the surviving regulations from the Novgorod Charter, demonstrates the changes taking place in legal norms in the fourteenth and fifteenth centuries. Nevertheless, a significant portion of the Russkaia Pravda still shows through. The city of Pskov, long influenced by its larger sister city, Novgorod, could hardly have escaped the legal foundations upon which Novgorod law had been built.[118] And while the commercial activity which flourished in both Novgorod and Pskov undoubtedly contributed to the extinction of the old legal formulas, the traditional patterns of conflict resolution enunciated in the Pravda still were not erased in the fifteenth century.[119]

Muscovite Law

Muscovite law likewise fell under the considerable influence of norms customary in Russia since the twelfth century. The earliest of the Muscovite texts, the Dvina Administrative Charter, although brief and slanted toward the more centralized administration favored by the Moscow princes, still relied upon the basic institutions created for the resolution of conflict in the era of the Russkaia Pravda. The Dvina Charter, issued in 1397 in connection with Moscow's temporary control of the Dvina lands, formerly Novgorodian territory, also survives in a single copy within the same collection of documents that contains the Novgorod Judicial Charter.[120] Although in this form it represents a relatively late copy, late fifteenth- or early sixteenth-century, the institutions developed in it can leave no doubt regarding the document's fourteenth-century origin. Many of the institutions prescribed by the Charter bear close resemblance to institutions of the Russkaia Pravda.

Despite the fact that the text of the Charter has been published many times since Karamzin first introduced it,[121] the exact significance of its juridical norms is not clear. The brevity of the document's actual application in the Dvina lands, soon restored to Novgorodian control, may account for a certain amount of caution in evaluating the Dvina Charter.[122] But the institutions included in its text did not collapse with the expiration of the Charter's application in the Dvina lands. Subsequent administrative charters issued by the Moscow princes, first in 1488 in Beloozero, and then repeatedly in the early sixteenth century for a wide variety of places, demonstrate the continuing life of legal institutions defined in the Dvina Charter.[123] Of course, the vertical structure implicit in the government of the Moscow grand princes continued to develop under these same documents, but resolution of such serious offenses as murder and theft remained within the traditional modes of satisfaction.

The 1497 promulgation of a new code of laws by the Moscow Grand Prince Ivan III interrupted this trend. Though known to us through a single copy, the 1497 Sudebnik has a long history in the literature on Muscovite law.[124] The sixteenth-century German visitor to Muscovy, Baron Sigismund von Herberstein, on returning home published in Latin his observations on life in that foreign land, and included among his reflections an abstract from the 1497 code.[125] Until the nineteenth century Herberstein's Latin text remained the historian's only information regarding the Sudebnik, even though a parallel code from 1550 had been published in Russian in the eighteenth century.[126]

The single extant manuscript of the entire 1497 Sudebnik was discovered only in 1817 and published two years later by Kalaidovich and Stroev. The same edition was later reprinted, although other editions appeared in the interim.[127] Growing interest among historians in early Russian sources led to the publication of several editions of the same copy of the 1497 Sudebnik. But the 1550 Sudebnik, a text which survives in a much stronger manuscript tradition, exerted more influence on the literature.[128]

Studies which preceded the 1917 Revolutions attempted to tie the 1497 Sudebnik to the entire history of legal relations in Muscovy, and, though useful, were not substantial contributions.[129] The first of the Soviet editions of the Sudebniki was not especially distinguished, but the 1952 edition of the 1497, 1550, and 1589 Sudebniki included the code's text, translation, commentary, and a poor photographic reproduction. At roughly the same time, a fairly good textbook edition of the Sudebnik appeared.[130] These publications made it possible for Western scholars to perform a thorough analysis of the 1497 Sudebnik and its legal norms. The 1955 doctoral dissertation of Horace W. Dewey was the first work in a long series of articles devoted to that task.[131] The edition also served to permit Western scholars, isolated from the original document, to comment upon the paleographic aspects of the lone manuscript, and thereby judge the Sudebnik's worth as an historical source.[132]

Application of textual criticism, heavily tainted with Marxist conceptions of the world order, to the 1497 Sudebnik had results identical to those born of a similar approach to the Pskov Charter and the Russkaia Pravda. Although Iushkov in the 1920s had already attempted to treat the subject in more than a perfunctory manner, the dominant approach to the study of the Sudebnik continued to rely upon formal textual analyses.[133] However, although the Sudebnik's single copy may now be safely dated to a time very close to 1497, which in turn provides a fairly reliable index of its actual promulgation, the contents of the code betray a heavy orientation toward procedural questions to the virtual exclusion of criminal and civil law.[134]

The Russkaia Pravda and Law in Late Medieval Russia

The Sudebnik's attention to procedural law contrasts sharply with the content of the Russkaia Pravda where criminal and civil matters occupy the great bulk of the text. The importance of this comparison is underlined by the textual history of the Russkaia Pravda itself. While the Sudebnik, the Novgorod and Pskov Charters, and the bulk of Muscovite legislation survive in single copies, the Russkaia Pravda is represented by more than seventy-five copies made throughout the thirteenth, fourteenth, fifteenth, and sixteenth centuries.[135] The coincidence of the interrelationship of contents between the Sudebnik and the Pravda, on the one hand, and the Pravda's rich manuscript base on the other, suggests a continued role for the Pravda's legal norms, even in the heyday of Muscovite power.

The Short Pravda, reflecting fewer legal norms than its larger

Extant Copies of the Russkaia Pravda

--- Short Redaction
—— Expanded Redaction

Sources: Kolycheva, *Kholopstvo*, p. 203; Shchapov, "Russkaia Pravda," pp. 70-72.

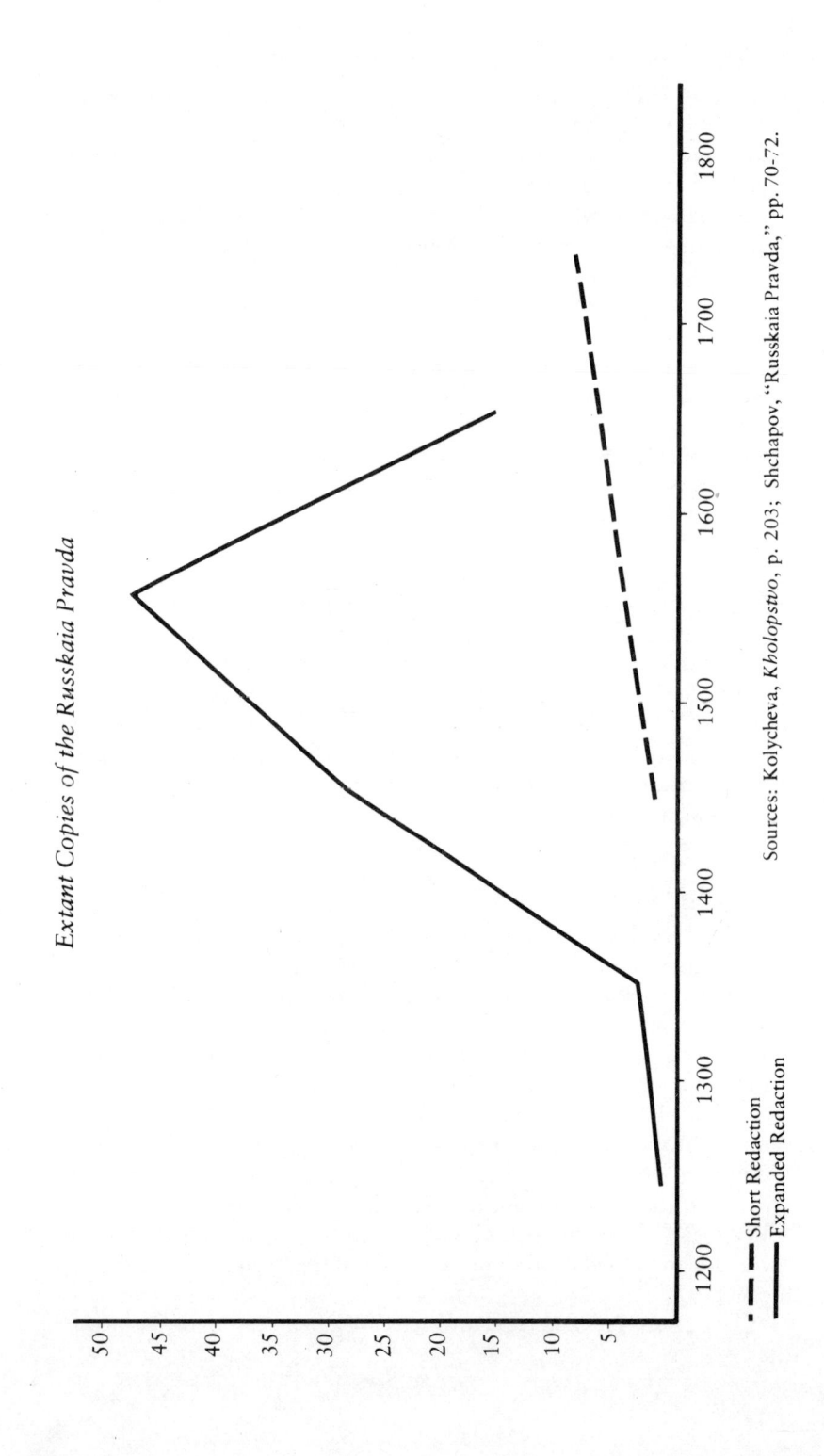

parallel, clearly was of limited use to Muscovite society. Essentially a list of appropriate compensations for various torts, the Short Pravda had little to offer the complex society centered around Moscow in the fifteenth century. This fact is reflected in the manuscript tradition of the Short Pravda, which survives in two fifteenth-century copies, and a number of eighteenth-century copies which certainly had no legal status. Both language and content of the extant texts suggest that the Short Pravda must have preceded its Expanded counterpart, itself known in the thirteenth century.[136] The more hypothetical analyses which project the Short Pravda's norms into deep antiquity may be discarded, if for no reason other than the weakness of the bases upon which such arguments stand.[137] The attribution to Iaroslav contained in the document's heading need not be abandoned simply because the extant copies are of late origin. Even if the regulations contained in the first part of the Pravda were shaped in some pre-Christian era, that circumstance would not invalidate their attribution to the codifying pen of Iaroslav's court.[138]

The second portion of the Short Pravda bears an attribution to Iaroslav's sons. Again, no substantive reason has yet been found to oblige us to abandon that simple indication of source.[139] Certainly the content of the regulations allows for the eleventh-century origin which the document claims for itself. The growth of princely administration and the transition to more formal means of conflict resolution are suggestive of the emerging power structure controlled by the princes as well as the more complex social system which attended the breakdown of small groupings highly dependent upon kinship ties. In short, these two parts of the Short Pravda, along with the clearly defined appendices setting fees for particular services, give every evidence of belonging to the eleventh century. The dissecting influence of internal criticism cannot undo the fact that at some point in the eleventh century all the norms contained in the Short Pravda were accepted into a single codification.[140]

The enormous number of surviving manuscripts alone makes more difficult the task of unraveling the textual history of the Expanded Pravda. Though it is certain that the compilers of the Expanded Pravda utilized and developed the norms expressed in the Short redaction, it is equally certain that the Expanded version reflects considerable innovation. Long complexes of articles devoted to matters of commercial law, inheritance, and slavery, all absent in the Short Pravda, demonstrate the changing economic and social circumstances in which the Expanded Pravda appeared. Like the

Short Pravda, the Expanded redaction was probably compiled in a series of layers, a conclusion that the texts themselves support.[141] But the complete text as it appeared in the thirteenth-century Synod Kormchaia, and as it was copied persistently in the succeeding three centuries, attests to the fact that the Expanded Pravda as a whole already constituted a single monument in the thirteenth century, if not earlier. That such a significant development should take place in this century should provoke no surprise. The thirteenth century also witnessed a vigorous reexamination of legal sources conducted within the church in connection with the compilation of the new Kormchie Knigi. Furthermore, as the history of subsequent copying of the Pravda shows, churchmen continued to display interest in the law.[142]

The Pravda's textual history mirrors the church's association with princely law. The three manuscript groups of the Expanded Pravda—the Synod-Trinity, Pushkin, and Karamzin—represent significantly different origins. The Karamzin group stems from a relatively late reworking of the first two groups. Although this synthesizing work may have begun in the fourteenth century, the three basic recensions of the Karamzin group are all represented in fifteenth-century copies.[143] Inasmuch as other documents, such as the Pravosudie Mitropolich'e, examined in more detail below, demonstrate that jurists continued to revive norms of the Russkaia Pravda in the fourteenth or fifteenth century, the revisions in the Karamzin group in no way vitiate the Pravda's legal force.

The Pushkin group probably constitutes a new phase of editorial work on the Pravda carried out in Novgorod in the late thirteenth or early fourteenth century. The oldest copy of the group, the text of which is included in the Musin-Pushkin Miscellany, belongs to the mid-fourteenth century, while a copy of its cousin recension, the Archeographic, stems from the mid-fifteenth century in a copy of the Novgorod First Chronicle. These copies, while among the oldest of the surviving set, include various corruptions.[144]

Consequently, the Synod-Trinity group is the most useful for understanding the Pravda's legal norms in the period closest to its compilation. The Synod recension, as noted above, is represented by a copy in the Novgorod Kormchaia of 1282, and as such constitutes the oldest surviving copy of any redaction of the Russkaia Pravda.[145] The Trinity recension, on the other hand, is represented in the oldest of the surviving manuscripts of the Merilo Pravednoe, reliably dated to the middle fourteenth century. Probably compiled at the Metropolitan's court, this copy suggests that the Pravda was

SOURCES OF THE LAW   45

known in the northeastern principalities well before the push toward a new codification in Muscovy in the fifteenth century.[146]

Other recensions in this group may also be tied to the activity surrounding the collection of church law in the Kormchaia Kniga or the Merilo Pravednoe. The Miasnikov recension, surviving in a manuscript belonging to the early fifteenth century, probably developed in the fourteenth century, perhaps in Novgorod in connection with the Moscow occupation of the Dvina lands.[147] The Sophia recension, also connected with the composition of a new Kormchaia, likewise originated in Novgorod late in the fourteenth or early in the fifteenth century. The recension's oldest extant copy, however, may be dated only to the late fifteenth century.[148]

The Russkaia Pravda:
Recensions of the Expanded Redaction

GROUP	CENTURY OF ORIGIN	RECENSION	OLDEST COPY	CENTURY OF COPY
Synod-Trinity	XIII-XIV			
		Trinity	Trinity no. 15	XIV
		Synod	Synod no. 132	XIII
		Novgorod-Sophia	Novgorod-Sophia no. 1173	XV
		Rogozh	Rogozh no. 256	XVI
		Miasnikov	F. II. 119	XV
		Rosenkampf	Uvarov no. 556/791	XV
		Ferapontov	Egorov no. 248	XVI
Pushkin	XIII-XIV			
		Pushkin	TsGADA, f. 135, no. 383	XIV
		Archeographic	Archeographic no. 240	XV
Karamzin	XIV-XV			
		Trinity	Trinity no. 765	XV
		Obolensk-Karamzin	TsGADA, f. 135, no. 382	XV
		Museum	Museum no. 1009	XV

Adapted from PR 1:55-59.

The largely independent construction of the Kormchie Knigi and of the Merilo Pravednoe dominated the first century or so after the importation of the so-called Serbian Kormchaia. These two strains of legal compilation did combine, however, in a separate recension, the Rosenkampf, the earliest copies of which belong to the late fifteenth century. Probably the original editorial work took place earlier in the same century.[149]

The last of the major recensions of the Synod-Trinity group, the Ferapontov, belongs to the mid-sixteenth century, and was developed in the context of the legal reform associated with the compilation of the 1550 Sudebnik. Well represented in sixteenth-century copies, the Ferapontov recension probably served as the basis for the compilation of the Abbreviated Pravda.[150] Both texts cover legal developments well beyond the chronological boundaries of this study, but it is useful to note the long-lived interest in the legal norms of the Pravda and the association of the reworkings of the Russkaia Pravda with the compilation of church law.

Zakon Sudnyi liudem

The development of church law involves far more than simply the history of the Kormchie Knigi. Evidently, from the early years of Christianization, the church played a sizable role in the administration of justice, a role considerably enlarged with the broadened efforts to convert native pagans in the thirteenth, fourteenth, and fifteenth centuries.[151] Their traditional morality, especially as reflected in marriage and death ceremonies, challenged some of the doctrines most crucial to the Christian faith, and served as the pretext for extending clerical jurisdiction.

This pattern was already apparent in the early activities of Byzantine missionaries in the lands of the South and West Slavs. The combination of emerging statehood, Christianization, and the intoxicant of the civilization represented by the literate Mediterranean states contributed to the rapid absorption by the Slavs of legal norms from the Judeo-Christian tradition. The resulting cultural transfer is reproduced most luminously in the Zakon Sudnyi liudem (Court Law for the People).

Like the Russkaia Pravda and certain other legal texts examined here, the Zakon Sudnyi liudem is tied to the textual history of larger collections of legal materials such as the Kormchaia Kniga. Although this condition makes study difficult enough, lucid treatment of the Zakon is hampered further by the chauvinistic views which dominate the literature. The majority of studies concentrate upon establishing the country in which the document originated, rather than upon the legal norms which the code propounds.[152]

The Zakon Sudnyi liudem survives in three basic redactions—Short, Expanded, and Concordance. The greatest number of copies and the least useful discussion belong to the Short redaction, known mainly through the Kormchaia Kniga. The text appears in the thirteenth-century Synod Kormchaia, the fourteenth-century Varsonof'ev Kormchaia, and the Ustiug Miscellany of roughly the same date.[153] The Short redaction is also part of the fourteenth-century Trinity and later copies of the Merilo Pravednoe.[154] Most of the extant copies appear in the Chudov recension of the Kormchaia in which the Merilo Pravednoe was joined to the Russian Kormchaia late in the fourteenth century or early in the fifteenth. At approximately the same time another recension developed in Novgorod and entered the Novgorod-Sophia Kormchaia.[155]

By contrast, the Expanded and Concordance redactions make up part of several chronicle texts. The Expanded redaction, interesting for the large number of articles it includes as well as the kind of legal norms it establishes, is known through the Novgorod chronicle of the fifteenth century.[156] But this redaction is surely much older than that, since a copy also survives in the fourteenth-century Musin-Pushkin Miscellany described above.[157] Both texts link the Expanded redaction to Novgorod, and suggest a time of origin roughly contemporary with the burst in codification which took place in the late thirteenth and early fourteenth centuries. Other, later copies of the Expanded redaction took their places in collections of more complex composition, including some Kormchie and chronicle texts.[158]

The Concordance redaction of the Zakon Sudnyi liudem, an obvious attempt at reconciling the divergent contents of the Short and Expanded redactions, belongs to the early fifteenth century. And while it, too, serves as proof of the vitality of legal reform, its meager innovations make it less useful for tracing the course of medieval Russian legal change. The Concordance redaction appears to be no more than a mechanical coalescence of the two basic redactions.[159]

The Short Zakon consists of a series of provisions, a third of which are lifted from the Byzantine Ecloga, which examine offenses against morality, property loss, judicial procedure, and the protection of church property.[160] Offenses under these headings were made punishable under a dual system of sanction, secular and clerical. Reliance on the Ecloga, an eighth-century Byzantine code, rather than on the ninth-century Procheiros Nomos, suggests an early date for the original compilation of the Short Zakon Sudnyi. Linguistic observations also indicate a West Slavic origin at some time soon after the ninth-century expedition of SS. Cyril and Methodius to the Slavs.[161]

Long before any critical edition of the Zakon Sudnyi liudem had appeared, a large literature had already developed over the question of the document's origin. The primary argument has pitted Bulgarians against the Czechs, with subsidiary battles fought over the identity of the composer of the Short redaction. The Czech case rests largely on linguistic similarities with the literary works associated with the school developed around Methodius and Constantine-Cyril. The penances that form part of the Zakon's penalties have induced some to see the influence of the Western Church on the Zakon, either through Frankish missionary activity in Pannonia or as the result of the visit to Rome by the two missionaries, Cyril and Methodius.[162] Still another viewpoint, while admitting Methodius to authorship of the Zakon, propounds a much earlier origin in Macedonia.[163]

The Bulgarians rely upon evidence of a more circumstantial nature. The coincidence of Bulgaria's Christianization and the statehood developed at Byzantium's expense in the ninth century indicated to some scholars a vacuum in legal norms which the Zakon Sudnyi fills admirably. Indeed the correspondence which took place between the Bulgarian Prince Boris (852-89) and the Roman Pope Nicholas is most interesting. Although only the contribution of the Pope survives, the contents indicate that Boris had posed some questions relative to particular aspects of the law which the Zakon Sudnyi liudem seems to answer.[164]

The essential arguments in the debate were expounded long prior to the publication of any comprehensive edition of the texts. During the nineteenth century, Russian scholars had published a copy of the Concordance Zakon, the fourteenth-century Pushkin and fifteenth-century Archeographic copies of the Expanded Zakon, and the Varsonof'ev Short redaction copy.[165] Shortly thereafter a series of Bulgarian studies emerged with texts included.[166] The Archeographic copy was reprinted in 1935 in Iushkov's edition of the Russkaia Pravda, and printed again in conjunction with the edition of the complete Novgorod First Chronicle in 1950.[167] Only in 1959 did the Bulgarians produce a detailed critical edition of the Zakon Sudnyi, though its small printing made it an instant rarity. A few years later a Soviet edition of all three redactions appeared, complete with photographic reproductions of the basic copies in each redaction.[168]

The significance of the modern editions is to point out that all copies of the Zakon Sudnyi upon which any textual history must be based are preserved in medieval Russian manuscripts. Regardless of what that may mean for the debate over the country of origin, it is clear that the preservation of the Zakon Sudnyi was in the interests of the Russian clergy; and furthermore, the reworking of the legal norms within the Zakon, as expressed in the Expanded redaction, took place only within Russia. Consequently, an understanding of the juridical significance of the Expanded Zakon Sudnyi is crucial for a study of early Russian legal institutions.

Part of the importance of the Zakon Sudnyi liudem lies in its relation to the general process of codification which took place in the thirteenth, fourteenth, and fifteenth centuries. It was this aspect of the problem that first drew the attention of Russian scholars. Rosenkampf's study of the Kormchaia Kniga, Kalachov's attempt to classify the copies of the Russkaia Pravda, and Pavlov's interest in the process of Russian absorption of foreign legal norms—all these nineteenth-century investigations contained lengthy considerations of the Zakon Sudnyi liudem.[169] The heated debate over Byzantine influence in the earliest Russian laws also involved detailed examination of the role of the Zakon Sudnyi as a medium of transfer.[170]

Nevertheless, a comprehensive examination of the legal norms contained in the Zakon and their relation to the broader issue of legal change is only beginning to appear in the literature. Iushkov understood the significance of the association of the Russkaia Pravda and the Zakon Sudnyi, but he never undertook to treat the Zakon's importance as a monument of law in Russia.[171] Tikhomirov first examined that matter in his 1941 monograph on the Russkaia Pravda, although the conclusions reached there constitute only an initial step in the task. By including in his textbook edition of the Pravda selected articles by which the Zakon Sudnyi and the Russkaia Pravda were joined in some manuscripts, Tikhomirov later reasserted his conviction of the interrelationship of these two texts.[172] Little more could be expected before a satisfactory critical edition appeared.

The 1959 Bulgarian edition and the 1961 Soviet editions stimulated further work on the juridical significance of the Zakon Sudnyi within the legal milieu of medieval Russia. Especially notable is the work of L. V. Milov and Ia. N. Shchapov, both of whom draw upon the Zakon Sudnyi in the course of treating early Russian legal development.[173] But there is still much more to be extracted from this code.

The Princely Statutes

The Statutes of Princes Vladimir (980-1015) and Iaroslav (1019-1054) represent the most promising source base for a comprehensive analysis of legal change. Like the Zakon Sudnyi liudem and the Russkaia Pravda, the statutes are associated with the complex manuscript history of the Kormchaia Kniga and similar legal compilations. Copies of both statutes survive in relatively late manuscripts, despite the internal attributions to the tenth-century Prince Vladimir and his son Iaroslav. Vladimir's Statute contains a general prescription of church income, as well as some vague descriptions of judicial competency for clerical courts. Iaroslav's Statute demonstrates more variety and specificity in content, but at bottom consists of particular formulations for crimes against morality and family life.

The oldest surviving copy of Vladimir's Statute is contained in an appendix to the thirteenth-century Synod Kormchaia. The appendix is reliably dated to the fourteenth century.[174] Still, the document purports to be the Statute formulated to support the young Russian Church sometime before Vladimir's death in 1015. The chronicle accounts mention that Vladimir issued some sort of income-providing charter in 996, but it is not clear that the surviving Statute in any way reflects the original provision.[175] This uncertainty, taken together with the late date of the manuscript sample, induces some caution in evaluating the document's own statements of its origin. Besides, it is worth noting that the Synod Kormchaia, in which the Statute currently survives as an appendix, did not originally contain the Statute, although its importance to the church would seem to have been considerable.

These factors notwithstanding, it is clear that very soon after the Synod Kormchaia was compiled, if not before, Vladimir's Statute became very important to the church, as the bounteous supply of extant copies demonstrates.[176] Unfortunately, textual inconsistencies within the Statute are nearly as numerous. One of the most striking incongruities is the frequently repeated assertion that Prince Vladimir's conversion originated with the Byzantine Patriarch Photius (ca. 820-97), a man who died almost a full century

Vladimir's Statute

REDACTION	RECENSION	CENTURY OF OLDEST EXTANT COPY
Oleninsk		
	Archangel	XV
	Pushkin	XV-XVI
	Archeographic	XV
	Markelov	XVII
	Archive	XV
Synod		
	Synod	XIV
	Krestinin	XV
	Rumiantsev	XV
	Volokolamsk	XVI
	Stoglav	XVI
	L'vov	XVIII
Varsonof'ev		XIV
Volynian		XV
Pechersk		XVII
Trinity		XVI
Stepennaia Kniga		XVI

Adapted from Shchapov, *Drevnerusskie*, pp. 12-84; *Vizantiiskoe*, pp. 270-71.

Kormchaia at different times, in the fourteenth or early fifteenth century, inasmuch as one copy of the Volynian Kormchaia contains the Statute only once. Marginal notations indicate that copies of the Volynian Kormchaia originated in the Belorussian and Ukrainian lands late in the thirteenth or fourteenth century.[192]

Two more redactions seem to have originated in the southern principalities. The oldest surviving text of the Pechersk redaction belongs to a seventeenth-century copy of the Kievan Paterikon. Although mention of certain terms suggests an origin earlier than the seventeenth century, it is difficult to ascribe to this variation a more concrete date of creation.[193] The Oleninsk redaction is represented by a wide sample of copies, mostly from the fifteenth century. The text's lexicon suggests some ties with the Ukraine or Belorussia, and probably it originated somewhat earlier than the surviving copies would indicate. It is more difficult to prove the contention of both Shchapov and Iushkov that the Oleninsk redaction originated early in the thirteenth century.[194]

While none of the reconstructed datings may be taken as definitive, even the most conservative dating reveals that Vladimir's Statute exercised broad influence on legal codification in Russia in the fourteenth and fifteenth centuries, and at that period was clearly recognized as an authentic guarantee of the church's right to income and the immunity of clerical jurisdiction. More specific statement of the church's legal rights surfaced only with the completion of a companion regulation.

Iaroslav's Statute addresses several particular areas in which the church had special jurisdictional interest, but its utility to scholars is lessened by the fact that extant copies include none older than the fifteenth century. Consequently, prolonged scholarly debate has focused upon the document's authenticity, especially since it purports to stem from the eleventh-century Prince Iaroslav Vladimirovich.[195] Some misgivings about the Statute's reliability are related to the norms of family and marriage law propounded within it, norms that show a striking similarity to Byzantine legislation and cast doubt on the native origin of the code. Furthermore, both content and terminology vary considerably among the Statute's basic redactions.

Absence of a thorough critical edition long hampered proper investigation of these questions. The occasional publication in the nineteenth century of isolated copies served only to further the prejudices of the debate's participants. Beneshevich, instrumental in presenting a critical edition of Vladimir's Statute, had intended to perform the same task for Iaroslav's Statute. But, although his work was nearly ready for printing as part of *Russkaia istoricheskaia biblioteka*, Beneshevich died before the material was published.[196] Subsequently, Iaroslav's Statute has drawn only incidental scholarly attention.

The lone exception to the tradition of inattention is the Soviet scholar, Ia. N. Shchapov. More than a decade ago, Shchapov published a detailed examination of the manuscript history of Iaroslav's Statute, but only recently has the critical edition appeared.[197] The enormous base of manuscripts from which he works serves to strengthen his rehabilitation of the Statute, although no copies older than the fifteenth century have yet been discovered.

Like Vladimir's Statute, Iaroslav's Statute is associated with the history of the Kormchaia and similar collections of complex composition. The Short redaction is tied to the so-called Chudov Kormchaia, in which the Merilo Pravednoe and the Kormchaia were combined. This collation certainly took place somewhere in northeast Russia, perhaps in Moscow, either late in the fourteenth or early in the fifteenth century.[198] All recensions of the Short redaction supply clues which support this geography and chronology. The Academy recension, for example, is replete with references to princely authority, suggesting that the prince did the punishing (*kniaz' kaznit'*) where other texts assign the right to impose a monetary fine to the bishop. In addition, copyists also found it necessary to particularize the grivna by which the fines were described, mentioning grivny of silver or gold. All these data suggest a relatively late origin, probably fifteenth-century.[199]

The Frolov recension offers more tangible reasons to relate it to the fifteenth century. Each of its two types is linked to charters concluded by the Moscow Grand Prince Vasilii Dmitrievich (1380-1425) early in the fifteenth century with two successive Metropolitans—one to the 1402 charter with Metropolitan Kiprian and the other to the 1419 charter with Metropolitan Fotii. Linking Iaroslav's Statute with these charters is crucial not only for dating the Statute's appearance, but also because the charters themselves guaranteed the church all previously granted judicial rights enjoyed by the clergy, rights spelled out in the princely statutes joined to the confirmation charters.[200] This association reconfirms that the princely statutes were part of medieval Russian law at least early in the fifteenth century, if not before.

Another recension, which Shchapov calls the Bal'zerov recension, is part of the first Sophia Chronicle.[201] It too is joined with the 1402 concordat between the Grand Prince and Metropolitan, but includes a number of variants that separate it from other texts tied to the charter. Most significant, for purposes of dating, is the reference to metropolitans in the plural, a situation possible only briefly in the fourteenth or beginning in the mid-fifteenth century when two metropolitans were seated in Russia.[202] Tied as the Statute is to the 1402 charter with the Moscow prince, it seems likely that the Bal'zerov recension too arose in the Moscow principality. The last recension of the Short redaction also belongs to the north, most likely to the Beloozero region. The oldest extant copy is associated with the Kirill-Beloozero Monastery in a collection of materials defending monasterial landholding rights, and there are hints within the Statute itself of a similar anxiety over clerical jurisdiction. The oldest copy is from the fifteenth century, and lexical evidence supports the notion that the Beloozero recension belongs to the same time.[203]

For the purposes of examining juridical norms, the Expanded

redaction of Iaroslav's Statute offers more of interest. Besides the inclusion of nearly twenty additional articles devoted to special problems of family law, the Expanded redaction also includes a long article examining the conditions under which divorce was acceptable. Displaying the usual complex interrelation of legal texts of the period, the Expanded redaction survives in texts whose history is even more involved than that of its briefer counterpart. The Archeographic recension, represented by a fifteenth-century copy in the Novgorod First Chronicle, suggests an origin in Novgorod, not only because it survives in a Novgorod text, but also by its provision for monetary equivalencies between the ruble and grivna ("2 rubles or 12 grivny"). Mention of the *tamga*, a customs duty known in immunity documents only from the late fourteenth century, indicates that the Archeographic recension could not have appeared long before the fifteenth century.[204]

Other recensions of the Expanded redaction seem to have originated in the western Russian lands at about the same period. The Archive recension, for example, survives in the text of the Chronicler of Pereiaslavl'-Suzdal', a fifteenth-century compilation which relies in part on an earlier annalistic text from Belorussia. The monetary provisions in the Statute are expressed in *groshi*, typical for the western lands under Lithuanian influence. Other provisions indicate that the Orthodox may have been in conflict with the Catholic Christians, a tableau which also points to the lands under Lithuanian hegemony in the late fourteenth or early fifteenth century.[205] Hints of a similar origin also appear in the so-called Basic recension, surviving in a copy from the late fifteenth or early sixteenth century. Although fines are described in rubles, the Statute characterizes the Metropolitan as Metropolitan of Kiev and All Rus', a title given the Metropolitan in Russian materials only late in the fourteenth century.[206]

The oldest extant text of the Statute in any redaction is preserved in a manuscript belonging to the early fifteenth century. The text of the Expanded redaction is abbreviated somewhat here, although the articles touching matters of church property remain at the expense of those devoted to adultery and immorality. This feature persuaded Shchapov to connect the Hypatian recension to the Orthodox struggle within the Catholic Lithuanian Principality, though one may wish for more believable support. Of more importance, perhaps, is the demonstration in this copy that the Expanded redaction was already known early in the fifteenth century.[207]

The last recension of the Expanded redaction, the Markelov, and

SOURCES OF THE LAW

Iaroslav's Statute

REDACTION	RECENSION	CENTURY OF OLDEST EXTANT COPY
Expanded		
	Basic	XV-XVI
	Hypatian	XV
	Archeographic	XV
	Markelov	XVII
	Archive	XV
Short		
	Kormchaia Kniga	XV
	Frolov	XV
	Academy	XVI
	Bal'zerov	XV
	Beloozero	XV
	L'vov	XVIII
Rumiantsev		XV
Tarnov		XV
Svitok Iaroslavlia		XVI
Ustiug		XVI

Adapted from Shchapov, *Drevnerusskie*, pp. 85-139.

the two concordance redactions, the Rumiantsev and Tarnov, offer fewer clues regarding the development of legal norms in medieval Russia. The Markelov recension is represented by a seventeenth-century copy related to the fifteenth century only with considerable strain.[208] The concordance redactions, though surviving in fifteenth-century manuscripts, evidently belong to the last stages of the development of Iaroslav's Statute, taking extracts from both the Short and Expanded redactions. Likewise, both show traces of origin in the Ukraine in the fifteenth century, a circumstance which reduces somewhat their utility for the present study.[209]

Cursory examination of their manuscript histories demonstrates the value of the princely statutes for a study of legal norms in Russia in the thirteenth, fourteenth, and fifteenth centuries. While it will require more data to connect the Kievan Princes Vladimir and Iaroslav with the documents bearing their names, it is beyond any question that the Statutes as they survive constitute church juridical rights as they existed in the fourteenth and fifteenth centuries, if not earlier, throughout the Russian principalities.[210] The compilers' attempts to link these Statutes to the revered names of Vladimir and Iaroslav, no matter how small a part of the documents' contents originated with these princes, reveal the emerging recognition of the evolving role of the prince in legislation, a pattern already established in Muscovite administration in the fifteenth century.

Finally, one may observe the correlation of the Statutes' texts with the growing interest in law, as manifested in the multiplication of legal collections such as the Kormchaia Kniga and Merilo Pravednoe. In conjunction with the growth of a chronicle tradition which united the Kievan past with the Muscovite state, the evolving legal collections reflected a historical preoccupation with the past and a sense of a new order.

The legal historian will find supplements to the church-state nexus in several regional statutes. The Statutory Charter of the Smolensk Prince Rostislav Mstislavich survives in a single sixteenth-century copy, although it is dated to the years 1137-1150.[211] Like Vladimir's Statute, the Smolensk Statute provided for income to the local episcopal see and guaranteed judicial immunity for certain types of cases.[212] The occasion for granting the Charter was the founding of the Smolensk bishopric in the second third of the twelfth century.[213] The jurisdiction here assigned to clerical courts—namely, cases involving family and marriage law and some forms of criminal offenses connected with the church—fits the pattern outlined in the Statutes of Vladimir and Iaroslav. In Smolensk, too, clerical courts were primarily interested in issues of moral law.

The Statute of the Novgorod Prince Vsevolod closely resembles Vladimir's Statute. The text itself has no date, but this Statute is generally attributed to the thirteenth century, and its sources perhaps to the reign of Prince Vsevolod Mstislavich (1135-1137).[214] The surviving copies do not approach this time limit, the oldest being part of the mid-fifteenth-century copy of the Novgorod First Chronicle.[215] To speculate upon the earlier history of the text is tempting, but it will suffice for the present to observe its confirmation of the principles of jurisdiction which Vladimir's Statute traces, and of the geographical distribution of the principles which Vsevolod's Statute helps to establish. In Novgorod, as elsewhere in the medieval Russian principalities, churchmen claimed exclusive jurisdiction over their own personnel and over subjects connected with the spiritual welfare of their flocks. Likewise, the tithe was promised to help sustain the clerics' earthly duties.

The last of the princely statutes belongs to the reign of Novgorod Prince Sviatoslav Ol'govich (1136-1138, 1139). It survives in two copies, the oldest in the same fourteenth-century appendix to the Synod Kormchaia that contains the oldest copy of Vladimir's Statute.[216] Despite its weak manuscript tradition, Sviatoslav's Statute is important for understanding the emergence of the church as a social institution, and the extent to which the princes financed this development. The Statute includes specific incomes which Sviatoslav guaranteed the church in consonance with the tithe policy operative before the new agreement. The figures themselves supply a rough estimate, therefore, not only of church income, but also of the prince's expectations from traditional fees extracted for criminal offenses.

The picture of sources of the law in early Russia will not be complete until two other collections are examined. The Pravosudie Mitropolich'e represents a rough reworking and abstract from both the Russkaia Pravda and Iaroslav's Statute, a collation that results in a haphazard content. Known only through a single copy from the sixteenth-century, the Pravosudie Mitropolich'e became a subject of discussion only after its publication in 1928.[217] Iushkov speculated that the Pravosudie was compiled for use in church courts and originated sometime in the late thirteenth or fourteenth century, a deduction based largely on the document's lexicon. L. V. Cherepnin indicated that the Pravosudie, although composed in Moscow in the 1380s to 1390s, was designed for the Metropolitan's Court in Novgorod. In 1953 M. N. Tikhomirov suggested a fourteenth-century connection with Novgorod, but Zimin shortly thereafter proposed a much later date of origin, sometime after the publication of the 1497 Sudebnik. According to Zimin, the Pravosudie grew out of an attempt to reintroduce into practice old Novgorod norms of law, already long forgotten by the late fifteenth century. Once more before his death, Tikhomirov returned to study the manuscript in detail, suggesting this time that the Pravosudie originated in Perm' in the fifteenth century.[218] Although it is impossible to sort out the divergent views with any sense of finality, it is clear that the norms reflected in the Pravosudie, norms consonant with the Russkaia Pravda and Iaroslav's Statute, still had an audience in the Russian lands in the fifteenth century. This fact serves to underline the importance of the Russkaia Pravda in the same period, and emphasizes the prolonged significance of the norms contained there.

Large collections of foreign law in early Russia were not unique to the Kormchaia Kniga. There also survive some independent collections of law, primarily Byzantine, whose existence was not connected with the Kormchaia. Most famous of these are the Knigi zakonnye, an accumulation of Byzantine statutes in the areas of marriage law, criminal law, and procedural aspects of testimony, together with a reworked version of the Byzantine Farmers' Law.[219] The Knigi zakonnye drew scholarly attention only after Pavlov published the entire text along with a Greek counterpart in 1886, although several attempts to publish portions of the Knigi, especially the Farmers' Law, had preceded Pavlov's edition. The publication created a stir in the late nineteenth century, but, except for a few references in later literature, the Knigi zakonnye have slipped into relative obscurity.[220]

Part of the neglect stems from the nature of the document's contents. The relatively sophisticated notions of criminal law and punishment, safeguards of testimony, and the complex computation of relations within which marriage was precluded seemed inapplicable to twelfth- and thirteenth-century Russia, which was the time and place Pavlov suggested for the origin of the Knigi. Furthermore, the manuscript in which the Knigi zakonnye survive is relatively late, and has no parallel manuscripts.[221]

Recent discoveries of abstracts of Byzantine law in independent collections help support Pavlov's notion of the applicability of the Knigi, especially in light of the fact that the same subjects treated in the Knigi gained the attention of other medieval copyists. Both marriage law regulations and stipulations of evidentiary acceptability are now known in other manuscripts, and in translations not identical to those of the Knigi zakonnye.[222] Byzantine criminal law remains so far unattested in medieval texts, but its significance for seventeenth-century Muscovy is by now well documented.[223] This corroboration, however slight, serves to suggest, at the very least, that Byzantine notions of crime and punishment, testimony, and marriage were known in early Russia, a situation that could not help but exert an influence on the compilation of native law.

Sources of Medieval Russian Law

The surviving corpus of law is sufficient to establish a basic chronology from the Russkaia Pravda, whose Short redaction was completed either late in the eleventh or early in the twelfth century, and the Expanded redaction, completed in the thirteenth century, to the 1497 codification expressed in Muscovy's Sudebnik. The thirteenth-century source base is supplemented by collections based upon the Pravda, monuments such as the Smolensk and Novgorod treaties, while the intervening period is supplemented by the codes of the city-republics of Pskov and Novgorod and the early Muscovite administrative statutes. Church law, for its part, is represented by the princely statutes, the Zakon Sudnyi liudem, the Kormchie Knigi, Merilo Pravednoe, and independent collections such as the Pravosudie Mitropolich'e.

While these texts represent the full chronological range of the period here under review, they also constitute a fair indication of the geographical distribution of the same legal norms. Although the majority of the texts were associated with the northeast and the north, the manuscript tradition of some, like the Statute of Iaroslav, and to a lesser extent, the Russkaia Pravda itself, continued to display vitality in the Ukraine and western Russian lands. The political destiny of these areas, altered significantly in the centuries under examination here, precludes their inclusion in this study; but in the thirteenth century, at least, the norms of the Russkaia Pravda and clerical participation in adjudication were certainly phenomena known throughout the Russian territories.

In sum, the sources reveal an active legal tradition which underwent considerable reworking in the thirteenth, fourteenth, and fifteenth centuries. This activity took place in concert with the growing influence of the church and parallel to the extension of the Moscow grand princes' authority. Ultimately, the prince and his officials came to dominate a new power structure that doomed the lateral relations predominant in Russian law at the beginning of the thirteenth century. It was Muscovite princely law that supplanted the customary institutions of justice of early medieval Russia.

CHAPTER 3

Sanctions and the Law

As recent studies have shown, the appearance of formal sanctions is closely connected with the maturation of legal structures. Horizontal systems, not disadvantaged by the limits imposed upon large heterogeneous societies, may rely upon informal sanctions to regulate behavior. The relatively small size of the social grouping permits effective advertisement of behavioral norms, and at the same time, emphasizes the effect of deviance.[1] In this context the force of personalized public opinion monitors social norms, and a wide variety of informal actions censures unacceptable behavior.

Blood revenge, carried out by kin of the aggrieved party, is representative of the earliest stage of lateral legal relations. Here the community's estimate of deviant behavior is so uniform that the offender's own kin accept the vengeance act without retaliation.[2] But horizontal relations take on a different character in those societies where property interests facilitate the transition to composition. Revenge yields to restitution payments, still carried out by the interested parties, and the same social pressure which legitimized satisfactions through revenge supports norms by which values for various torts are established. Kinship and face-to-face acquaintance help reinforce the approved means of conflict resolution.[3]

By contrast, a high level of centralized authority characterizes vertical systems, which therefore are well suited to the administration of formal sanctions upon deviants. The reduction in personal acquaintance within the community and the lessened role of kinship relations in regulating behavior vitiate the informal sanctions operative in horizontal societies. At the same time, social differentiation and its accompanying labor specialization make possible the creation of a staff of persons specially commissioned to administer sanctions in place of the informal censure operative in horizontal systems.[4]

All this suggests a developmental pattern for sanctions, from revenge or informal restitution, present in most traditional societies, to the institution of formal sanctions and the appearance of the concept of felony. It is important to establish that it is not the severity of the sanction that identifies the different systems, but rather the nature of its imposition. It may be argued, for example, that revenge is a severe form of punishment, but the importance for our study is that revenge, like restitution, involves only the affected parties, while formalized sanctions rely upon a specialized staff of enforcers. Broadly conceived, the enforcement staff includes the judiciary as well as its police accompaniment. Both elements belong to the third party which is responsible for legal satisfaction. Consequently, while restitution and revenge both rely upon the consensual support of the community, an enforcement staff operates on the basis of authority vested in it by the vertical structure.[5]

The evolutionary pattern in the development of sanctions is fully apparent in the law of medieval Russia, especially in the period from the thirteenth to fifteenth centuries. Still an essentially agrarian society, still influenced by kinship organizations and under the influence of a foreign conqueror, Russian society of the thirteenth century had not yet developed a vertical state structure or the organs of enforcement inherent in this concept.[6] Three centuries saw all that change.

Homicide

Lateral legal relations in matters of homicide were expressed in early Russia in several institutions, chief among which was revenge. Both the Short Pravda and its more modern parallel, the Expanded Pravda, begin with a provision permitting revenge within a circumscribed kinship unit. The texts authorize retaliation among brothers, fathers, and sons, and nephews and their uncles.[7] The usual scholarly treatment of these provisions is confined to observing the attempt of the Iaroslavichi to abolish revenge. Brief forays into the kinship affiliations of the proposed avengers likewise are not uncommon. But the general result of these analyses is totally unsatisfactory inasmuch as most studies deny the existence of revenge, and avoid the obvious relation of kinship to the practice of revenge.[8]

Revenge may have persisted quite late in Russia, even under the guise of Christian morality. The Expanded Zakon Sudnyi liudem, for example, in a passage absent in its parallel redaction, affirms the basic wisdom of the Mosaic Law's preference for talion: a hand for a hand, eye for eye, head for head, and even a leg for a leg.[9] The spirit of tailoring the punishment to fit the crime is precisely the perspective which Muscovy eventually adopted in its criminal code, but the morality of talion found other outlets as well.[10] Early in the eleventh century, Prince Iaroslav, having arrived at the spot where his sainted brothers Boris and Gleb had been martyred, is alleged to have used the Biblical story of Cain and Abel to ask revenge for his brothers' deaths.[11]

It is usual to argue that Iaroslav's sons expunged vengeance justice in homicide cases by a provision included in the Expanded Pravda. The thrust of the regulation was to replace blood revenge with composition.[12] But despite the appearance of the new rule, the successful abolition of revenge by the Iaroslavichi seems unlikely. Inclusion of the old revenge statute in the article immediately preceding the new regulation raises some questions about the reformers' intent. Were revenge totally eliminated, article two would have sufficed, and could have displaced the older provisions of article one. Failure to excise the revenge stipulations indicates some continued recognition of their utility. Consequently, revenge probably still was practiced at the beginning of the thirteenth century, the time of the Expanded Pravda's compilation.[13]

The hesitancy with which the Iaroslavichi seem to have rejected revenge may be traced to still another factor—their real inability to eliminate the practice by decree. Replacing revenge with composition would certainly provoke dissatisfaction among elements of society imbued with traditional values. Consequently, a logical first step in altering this form of censure was to offer the potential combatants a choice—revenge or composition. Article one provides that option: "if someone will not avenge him, then provide [*polozhiti*] 40 grivny for his head [*za golovu*]." In this way, article one stipulates the open conclusion of revenge and simultaneously dignifies the alternative. Under conditions of settled habitation and the growth of a money economy, the economic interests expressed by composition supplanted the psychological basis of revenge.[14] The emergence of the financial alternative to vengeance is poorly documented in medieval Europe, so that even Maitland could not ascertain firmly the sequence by which composition displaced vengeance. Written English law begins with composition, and provides for revenge only after all monetary avenues have been exhausted. But the fleeting hints of the persistence of vengeance in European texts allude to the possibility that Europe, too, experienced the same sequence.[15] But where European comparative materials will not suffice, the Russian texts themselves propose exactly that pattern of legal development—revenge first, and then composition.

Not all homicides were susceptible to composition. Murderers who fled or who could not be identified made difficult the process of restitution. The Expanded Pravda provided that the homicide of a princely servitor accomplished by some unidentified criminal

SANCTIONS AND THE LAW

obligated the community where the body was found to make an eighty-grivna payment. The death of an ordinary man required only a forty-grivna fee.[16]

The major thrust of the article seems to be an attempt to protect princely personnel and to distinguish them from their less notable compatriots. In that sense the regulation serves as a reinforcement of article one. Whereas the Short Pravda protected all freemen by the same forty-grivna fee, the Expanded Pravda doubled the price for the homicide of one of the prince's officials.[17] But the fee stipulated here, and developed in several subsequent articles, is not described as composition. Instead, a new term (*verv'naia* or *virevnaia*) was introduced. This payment is clearly an innovation, inasmuch as similar regulations in the contemporary Smolensk documents continued the principle of simple composition (*za golovu*). In other respects the Smolensk texts reinforce their similarity to the Russkaia Pravda in their treatment of the absent offender (*razboinik*), but there is no sign of the new payment.[18]

The Expanded Pravda confuses the matter somewhat by introducing still more new terminology. By the provisions of article four, the community (*verv'*) was required to make a special payment (*dikaia vira*) as long as a killer was not handed over.[19] The subsequent article specified the dimensions of the payment by examining the case of the murderer's return. By coming back, the killer brought on himself the obligation to pay his share of the *vira* (which totaled forty grivny), and to pay alone the head fee (*golovnich'stvo*, another forty grivny). Individuals who did not belong to the communal payment system were obliged to pay everything without any aid. Finally, murder committed without cause (*bez vsiakoia svady*) need not force the community to pay the *dikaia vira*, as long as the offender was surrendered to the prince. The criminal (*razboinik*) and his family were subject to special punishment.[20]

Three items in this corpus merit special attention. Perhaps most important is the implication that physical punishment is decreed for criminals for whom the community felt no responsibility. The texts assign the perpetrator and his family to *potok i razgrablenie*. The first term is usually understood as imprisonment or exile, based on an etymology using the Slavonic *potochiti*. More radical and less likely interpretations deduce from this term execution or enforced slavery.[21] *Razgrablenie* indicates some form of property confiscation, an explanation based on the verb *razgrabiti*, to despoil.[22] *Razgrablenie* is found only this one time in the Pravda, but *potok* appears in two other cases. According to the first, a horse thief was to be given to the prince for punishment (*vydati kniaziu na potok*).²³ The second case connects *potok* with property raids in cases of arson committed in threshing courts or residences. Here, however, the prince did not perform the primary role in rectifying the wrong. Instead, the victims first were satisfied from the arsonist's property, and only then did the prince act.²⁴

Some clarification of the expression appears in the 1229 Smolensk Treaty. Article six established that a Smolensk merchant indebted to a Westerner was to pay his debt first, and only after that was the prince entitled to extract what remained to assuage his own complaint. In one phrase the Smolensk text even uses *rozgrabiti* to indicate the prince's method of expressing his dissatisfaction.²⁵ The parallel article included in the 1230-1270 project for another treaty specifies quite directly the implications of sanction. As before, merchant indebtedness was to be settled first, but the offended official (archbishop, master, or judge) had to defer his intentions to punish the culprit (*a v"skhocheti i kazniti* [emphasis added]) until all claims of indebtedness were settled.²⁶ If it is the prince's prerogative which here was replaced, then *rozgrabiti* must have indicated some form of sanction.

The Smolensk treaties confirm the principle worked out in the Russkaia Pravda for cases of arson—the victims were satisfied first, and the prince took what remained. Were the same order observed in homicide suits for which the community chose not to pay, handing over the criminal (*razboinik*) for *potok* and *razgrablenie* would constitute a transitional stage. The victim's kin surely did not forfeit their compensation as decreed by articles one and two of the Pravda. No doubt they took the amount to which they were entitled, and what happened subsequently depended upon the prince. It is not known whether the prince exercised his option through physical or pecuniary sanctions. In either case, *razgrablenie* represents a variation of the old composition system, brought closer to the precedent of pure sanction by the prince's participation.

Potok is another matter. Imprisonment as a judicial sanction was not practiced widely in Russia before the sixteenth century. Even the existence of jails before this time is debatable. The few surviving references to incarceration as a judicial penalty are drawn mainly from the thirteenth-century Smolensk treaties, and both instances provide for imprisonment only if no bond were raised.²⁷ Although these provisions occur in close proximity to the *razgrablenie* regulations of the Smolensk treaties, it seems unlikely that they represent any allusion to *potok*.

Those who suggest that *potok* signifies expulsion or exile usually rely upon chronicle passages that rarely are as lucid as their explicators pretend.[28] The word's more widely utilized meaning refers to a stream or brook, a definition without much utility for explaining the punishment in the Pravda.[29] Consequently, some apologists have resorted to combing the texts for places where *razgrablenie* is paired with a prescription for exile. For example, the Hypatian Chronicle mentions *razgrablenie* in one case where Prince Vladislav blinded one of his servitors, cut out his tongue, ravaged his property, and expelled him with his wife and children. The coincidence by which the poor man's family was exiled with him and the presence of *razgrablenie* proved too strong a lure for some, but coincidence cannot serve as a convincing argument to identify *potok* as exile.[30]

One copy of the Expanded Pravda's Novgorod-Sophia recension does substitute expulsion (*pognanie*) for *potok* in article seven, but retains the older word in two other articles.[31] In other respects, however, the great majority of copies of the Novgorod-Sophia version display total confusion in their renditions of *potok*—four copies contain only the first two letters of the word, eleven copies replace *potok* with *boi* (fight, assault), and still another omits the parallel word *razgrablenie*, and replaces *potok* with *pognanie*.[32] The Abbreviated Pravda omits *potok* altogether in article seven.[33] Nevertheless, even in the face of this obviously poor comprehension, virtually all other versions in all their copies retain *potok*.[34] One sixteenth-century text even attempts a translation of the term, substituting imprisonment (*zatochen'e*).[35]

Clearly the term was not familiar even to all the medieval scribes; any further modern clarification of its meaning is not to be expected. Its ancient origins and pairing with *razgrablenie* make tempting the suggestion of the two terms' identity.[36] At any rate, *potok* certainly was associated with some form of sanction, as article thirty-five indicates: "If [the man apprehended by confrontation] is a horse thief, hand him over to the prince *na potok*."[37] It is true that other provisions of both redactions of the Pravda assign simple composition for horse theft, but the special designation of a horse thief (*konevyi tat'*) in article thirty-five points to a particularly serious kind of recidivist theft directed against the horse supply deemed vital for military operations on the steppe.[38]

All the texts which deal with recidivist crime show some overlapping of popular law, still essentially horizontal, with princely law, implicitly vertical. Whereas the Russkaia Pravda prescribed no punishment for thieves convicted through the confrontment process, the horse thief and threshing-floor arsonist were identified as especially undesirable and undefended by the community. The recidivist (*razboinik*), too, found no communal protection and was handed over to the prince for appropriate sanction (*potok i razgrablenie*). These cases, essentially unsuited to the satisfaction process of composition, fell most easily to the prince's judicial pretensions. In a situation identical to that which confronted authorities dealing with unknown offenders, there was no way to make recidivists abide by the rules of restitution and support the community's norms. Afflictive punishment carried out by the prince's personnel offered an easy remedy and constituted a first step away from horizontal legal relations.[39]

Recidivism is associated with a second item of importance in this complex of articles. The *dikaia vira* was clearly a payment separate from the restitution expected in cases of homicide (*za golovu, golovnich'stvo*). The new payment indicates that the prince became involved in punishing homicide through financial sanctions at a time when composition still operated. There is nothing extraordinary about this, inasmuch as the European monarchs of the early Middle Ages attempted to extract a similar share (*fredus*) from restitution fees.[40]

The situation in Russia, however, was not quite so simple. Although the bloodwite continued to be collected by Russian princes even into the sixteenth century, the payment was expected exclusively in those cases where the community either failed to identify the murderer or refused to yield him once discovered.[41] In situations in which the murderer was unknown, restitution was impossible, and the prince's intervention was easy to achieve. This sort of offense represented a tort unresolvable by the methods of lateral legal relations. Likewise, unidentified corpses discovered within a community's territory also fell afoul of the compositional system.[42] Where in the one case the offender was unknown, in the other the victim was unknown. In both cases dyadic negotiation was out of the question. Like the offense of the recidivist criminal, these cases presented opportunities for the intrusion of princely jurisdiction.

Still a third aspect of the regulations on communal bloodwites deserves examination. The wergeld prescribed by article one of the Short Pravda is limited to a single sum—forty grivny. By contrast, in the so-called Pravda of Iaroslav's Sons which makes up the second part of the Short Pravda, the prince's steward (*ognishchanin*) and other estate chiefs were protected by a fee twice the size of that extracted for ordinary mortals. Virtually identical regulations were included in the Expanded Pravda, and were generalized there by article one—all the prince's men were protected by an eighty-grivna fee.[43]

The debate over these provisions concerns the extent of the prince's interference in the horizontal system of composition. In the first case, that is, the composition for the homicide of princely officials who operated the stable, farm, and palace, the text offers no indication that the fees received went to the prince. One may speculate, as have others previously, that restitution makes sense here since the prince, having lost the valued services of his lieutenant, was, after all, the victim.[44]

But the legal texts themselves suggest that the head payment (*za golovu*) could have gone just as easily to the victim's kin as to the prince. While the prince may have lost valued services, the victim's kin lost a source of income and a position in society. Even the indication of the enormous size of the composition for princely personnel, double that for a commoner, may indicate merely the increased prestige and income-drawing power of princely men.[45] In fact, the 1230 Smolensk project for a treaty with the German merchant towns specifically provided that the homicide of an emissary or priest (!) required double payment of the head fee (*za golovu*). The last expression, "for the head," is identical to that used to describe the Pravda's new composition system which replaced revenge, and indicates that the payment was made not to the prince but to the victim's kin.[46]

The clue to the size of this fee is found in the Expanded Pravda's discussion of the *dikaia vira*. Although the community was obliged to pay for murderers undiscovered or not surrendered, the killer who returned to face the consequences had to pay both the *dikaia vira* of forty grivny and the head fee (*golovnich'stvo*) of an equal amount. This provision is but one of a series which begins with article three, where princely men were protected by an eighty-grivna fee and others by a forty-grivna payment. In this context, it is clear that the eighty-grivna sum was meant to consist of two parts—the usual head fee and the extraordinary payment made to the prince.[47] Consequently, princely interest in homicide satisfaction had its beginning in an overlay of the already-defined lateral system.

The entire order of composition schedules demonstrates some further movement away from the pattern of simple equivalencies evident in primary legal systems. Not only does the Russkaia Pravda distinguish between princely personnel and ordinary freemen (*liudi*), but it separates various social inferiors as well. Domestics, slaves, contract laborers (*riadovniki*), and peasant agriculturalists (*smerdy*) each had a wergeld considerably lower than that of either princely personnel or normal free men.[48] In fact, composition for domestics and their ilk was even less than that assigned for a free woman, who was valued at twenty grivny.[49] Consequently, the process of social stratification suggested by these values implies the development of primitive hierarchies and indicates the introduction of some other forms of change in the legal conceptualizations of Russia. It is not surprising therefore to discover some variations on the theme of homicide restitution.

On the surface, payment did not depend upon the circumstances of the homicide, still less on motive. None of the basic articles that prescribe either revenge or restitution mention the conditions of the offense. The only relevant consideration was the presence of a corpse.[50] But the conditions of the crime enter into consideration elsewhere. Two articles of the Short Pravda describe instances where the steward (*ognishchanin*) was killed. According to the first, a steward killed *v obidu*, in Vernadsky's translation "deliberately," was avenged by payment of eighty grivny by the murderer himself instead of by the community.[51] Of course, such a regulation had the effect of concentrating responsibility directly upon the culprit, and undermined the collective protection which the community supplied.

The phrasing of the text, however, is not so clear. *Obida* carries the general meaning of offense or slander, and is known in documents from the Zakon Sudnyi liudem to the Beloozero Administrative Charter.[52] Olga's revenge for the murder of her husband, Prince Igor, was based upon her right to avenge the offense (*obida*).[53] Consequently, at its root the term denoted an unfriendly act, an action subject to tort. With the change in the forms of legal satisfaction, *obida* gradually took on aspects of material loss, constituting, in effect, economic revenge.[54] But in the fifteenth century *obida* could still be conceptualized to include such offenses as theft and slander. Therefore the steward's death described in the Pravda may well have occurred during a theft or robbery.[55]

Article twenty-one of the Short Pravda gives some support to such an explanation. It provided that the steward killed near a barn (*klet'*), near the horses or cows, was to be avenged instantly. The murderer was to be "killed like a dog."[56] That such an article makes no concession to the principle of composition is clear, but why these particular circumstances provoked such a deviation is not so manifest. It may be that the association of murder with theft was in itself sufficient provocation for the princely authority to be brought to bear on the thief-murderer.[57] The intervening article, devoted to the payment of the *dikaia vira* by the commune, does describe an offense roughly parallel to that of article twenty-one. Here the steward killed during an attempted robbery (*v razboi*) is protected by the community's obligation to find (actually, to seek, *iskati*) the offender or to pay the bloodwite. A parallel passage in the Expanded Pravda used the same expression.[58]

The term *razboi* was used widely in documents of medieval Russia. It served as the root for the contemporary word for robber (*razboinik*), and from an early time must have been connected with property seizure committed under conditions of assault.[59] However, *razboiniki* are also known as murderers.[60] The nineteenth-century historian of law, Nikolai Kalachov, suggested that the term originally bore a dual meaning—robber-murderer—and only later became separated from homicidal acts. The multiple uses to which the term is put seem to support Kalachov's hypothesis.[61]

These articles point to a change in the legal relations between the victim's kin and the perpetrator. The new norms make the penalty conditional upon some particular set of events, perhaps defined by property concerns, where the volition of the actor becomes crucial to determining the kind of penalty. Volition is expressed through the habitual nature of the delict (hence *razboi*) or by the peculiar circumstances (hence robbery at the barn). In either event, one observes here a society's first hesitant steps toward acceptance of notions of guilt, and a peculiar reaction to the problem of recidivism.[62]

The definition of circumstance finds one further refinement in the Russkaia Pravda. Both the Short and Expanded redactions include articles devoted to the capture of a thief caught stealing at a barn or stable. Such a thief killed on the spot evidently was not to be avenged nor were his kin to receive restitution. But should the thief be bound and held, and then subsequently killed, the killers were liable for a twelve-grivna payment. The captured thief held until daylight was to be brought to the prince's court (*dvor*), though for what purpose the articles do not say. Like the previous regulations, these two touch on the circumstances of the delict, and perhaps even point more definitely to the element of motive. To kill a thief was permissible, if done in the heat of the moment or the darkness of night. But to kill a thief in daylight after he had been bound was an offense for which the perpetrator had to pay. One may observe only that he had to pay much less.[63]

This particular tableau was already part of Byzantine law, a factor that has prompted considerable speculation about Byzantine influence upon the Russkaia Pravda.[64] But the Zakon Sudnyi liudem also provided for dealing with *razboiniki*. In prescribing summary justice, the Expanded Zakon condemned the robber to execution by the sword, a penalty unknown to the Russkaia Pravda and essentially foreign to Muscovite law as well.[65] It is not likely that decapitation could have been practiced in Russia at the time of the compilation of the Expanded Zakon Sudnyi.

Another article of the same text, however, harks back to Old Testament principles. In a provision borrowed from Exodus, the Zakon Sudnyi examined the case of a thief discovered at his occupation (*v" pod"kopanii*). If he were killed on the spot, no charges ensued, but were he held until the sun rose, the thief's blood lay on the killer's head.[66] Clearly this text is the basis for the Byzantine as well as the later Russian passages molded on the same lines. Like the situation described by the Russkaia Pravda, homicide committed in the heat of the moment was tolerated, but delay bred suspicions about the motives of the killer.

With respect to the development of sanctions, the interesting feature in this article of the Pravda is the role that the prince played. It is conventional to count the twelve-grivna fee as a fine payable to the prince, since a parallel provision stipulated that the thief bound till daylight was to be brought to the prince's court.[67] But several difficulties plague this interpretation. One may observe in the first place that the payment is not specifically awarded the prince, nor is the term appropriate to the prince's exactions (*vira* or *prodazha*). That alone does not rule out use of the twelve-grivna fee as a sanction. However, the size of the fee itself approaches neither the wergeld of freeman or servitor, nor the prince's bloodwite for homicides committed by unidentified persons.[68] In sum, it is like no other homicide sanction known in the Pravda.[69]

It is true, of course, that the princes did attempt to control the punishment of homicides. As noted above, murder of princely personnel offered the first opportunity for interference in the horizontal settlement pattern operative in early Russia. But even in those cases, motive played no special role. However, other cases demonstrate the emergence of a particular kind of homicidal crime whose effect was aggravated by the conditions of the crime. Although the

Pravda does not specifically identify the crime as murder, it is that idea which undergirds the law's intent.

In fact, the crime of murder did come under the princes' exclusive control no later than early in the fifteenth century. Immunity charters of that time specifically excluded jurisdiction over murder from the list of privileges offered the immunity recipient.[70] What this reservation meant is more difficult to determine. None of the surviving charters indicate what the prince or his henchmen did to murderers. Furthermore, it was a church text, the Pravosudie Mitropolich'e, which first prescribed afflictive sanctions for murderers. The offender was to be decapitated and his property confiscated, penalties directly attributed to Byzantine law.[71] Among the secular codes, the Pskov Judicial Charter and Muscovy's 1497 Sudebnik ordered the execution of certain criminals, but both omit directives on the actual execution.[72] The 1488 Beloozero Administrative Charter was more explicit in some respects, appointing the prince's lieutenants to extract the costs of the complaint from thief, robber, or murderer. However, the provision also stipulates that robbers and murderers were to be handed over to the *namestnik* for fines and punishment (*v prodazhe i v kazne*), an ambiguous expression which might or might not indicate that capital punishment was involved.[73]

Although sixteenth-century materials continued these vague prescriptions for physical sanctions, far more persistent and specific are the formulas for monetary sanctions.[74] The *dikaia vira* prescribed by the Expanded Pravda obligated the community to pay for homicides in those cases where the killer remained undetected. The same regulation was repeated in the 1397 Dvina Administrative Charter, but the fee was changed to ten rubles.[75] Although not mentioned in the Sudebnik, the *vira* was prescribed in the 1488 Beloozero Administrative Charter, two 1506 Administrative Charters for Pereiaslavl' peasants, a 1509 Administrative Charter for Dmitrov beavermen, and numerous other sixteenth-century documents connected with administrative reforms.[76] The same prescription appeared in immunity charters. Several fifteenth-century charters ordered a two-ruble *vira*, while the usual sixteenth-century formula provided for a four-ruble payment.[77] Most of the texts specify that the fee was collected by the prince himself or by his officials serving in the hinterland.

The basic feature of the bloodwite system was the opportunity it presented the nascent enforcement structure to capitalize upon consensual backing for behavioral norms. The implicit community support of dyadic satisfaction through revenge or composition constituted a convenient tool for isolating malefactors. Although the community's refusal to yield murderers was admitted by the *dikaia vira* regulations, the usefulness of local investigation was not abandoned. The texts repeatedly urge the community to seek out wrongdoers, an operation that made considerably easier the prince's attempts to root out offenders. Community investigation had a long life in Muscovy, flowering in the investigative procedures of the sixteenth and seventeenth centuries.[78]

Perhaps even more important is the fact that the princes found in the bloodwite a promising source of income. The pledges of church tithes incorporated in the statutes of the Kievan princes included the *vira* as one of the income bases, but its precise value is difficult to determine.[79] If one may judge by the figure that Sviatoslav promised to supply in place of the usual tithe of bloodwites and fines, the expected income from this source was already sizable even in the twelfth century.[80]

The Russkaia Pravda provides little specific information on the size of judicial income. The Short Pravda offers a brief and confusing statement on the collection of the bloodwite. In addition to support payments enumerated in kind, a handsome sum of more than sixty grivny—larger than the wergeld of any freeman—was awarded to the official who presumably collected the *vira*, the *virnik*. It may be, as Tikhomirov has suggested, that this extraordinary sum represents some particular collection whose amount inadvertently was left in the text, but the theory has little to recommend it.[81] The Expanded Pravda fixed the *virnik*'s portion at twenty percent of an eighty-grivny payment (sixteen grivny) and also included the support levies outlined in the Short Pravda. In the text which parallels the Short Pravda's sixty-plus grivny, the Expanded redaction envisions another twenty percent fee (eight grivny), presumably extracted from a forty-grivna bloodwite.[82] The same document cites still another judicial fee collected in connection with a homicide case.[83] Consequently, the figure included in the Short Pravda must represent an error of some kind.

A convincing explanation of the meaning of the Pravda's judicial fees is yet to be found.[84] The twenty percent norm for the *virnik*'s portion is easy to accept. However, such a judgment implies that the Short Pravda's compilers did not understand very well the *virnik*'s role in homicide satisfaction—they grossly exaggerated the size of his fees. In itself misapprehension of the fees connected with homicide cases suggests that bloodwites may not yet have become part of standard practice by the time that the Short Pravda was compiled. But the bloodwite is conspicuous in the early sources. One chronicle entry dated to 854 characterizes the early Russian princes as reasonable fellows who oppressed the people neither with the bloodwite nor with fines (*prodazhi*). Although this wishful thinking is present in the Novgorod First Chronicle and several later chronicle texts, the story is absent in the Primary Chronicle.[85] Instead, the latter contains only one reference to the bloodwite, a tale present in many other chronicle redactions.[86] There the story is couched in a long narrative which depicts Prince Vladimir in an exceptionally pious light. The year of the entry, 996, was auspicious for the church, as Vladimir that year celebrated the building of the Church of the Mother of God in Kiev, fulfilling the promise of his conversion pledge. The event was of special importance to the clergy since Vladimir also donated a tenth of his income to the support of the new church. So eager was the pious chronicler to praise the generous Christian prince that Vladimir's hasty flight from the Pechenegs, recorded in the same entry, drew no reproach. On the contrary, when Vladimir vowed to found still another church because of his successful flight, the chronicler indulged in a long eulogy to the prince.[87] Only then does the chronicle entry treat the problem of justice.

The Kievan bishops are said to have approached Vladimir to advise him of the multiplication of crimes (*razboi*), and to ask why he did not punish the offenders. Vladimir's self-professed righteousness ("I am afraid of sinning") was not sufficient for the bishops, who countered by arguing that God had put the prince in power to punish the evil and to be merciful to the just.[88] Graciously Vladimir assented and began to punish (*kazniti*) the *razboiniki*. The shortsighted bishops promptly saw the financial error of the new program, and returned to urge the prince to resume the traditional collection of the bloodwite, so as to enable him to arm his retinue. Once more the agreeable prince gave in to the behests of the clerics, and returned to the "customs of his father and grandfather."[89]

The story is present in both the Hypatian and Laurentian redactions of the Primary Chronicle, and therefore must belong to one of the twelfth-century revisions of the chronicle which preceded the separation of the text's branches.[90] Nevertheless, several items in this narrative raise suspicions about the authenticity of the events described here. On the face of it, Vladimir would seem to have been utterly without opinion on a subject vital to his realm; even the bishops perceived that without the income presumably derived from the bloodwite the prince would have been deprived of the means of supporting his military servitors. Passively acceding to the bishops' various and contradictory suggestions, Vladimir as pictured here contrasts vividly with the more decisive Vladimir depicted elsewhere in the Primary Chronicle.[91]

Despite the tale's incongruities, no serious doubts about its early origins have yet been raised.[92] On the contrary, the legend has stimulated arguments that depict tenth-century Russian law as already embarked upon a course of monetary and afflictive sanctions.[93] But evidence to support the early administration of homicide sanctions, as noted above, is not strong. The Short Pravda mentions the bloodwite only once, prescribing provisions for the collector of this fee, the *virnik*. But it gives few specific details—no dimensions of the fee or conditions of its application, for example.[94] The Expanded Pravda, in addition to repeating the *virnik*'s provisioning requirements, adds several particular instances of the bloodwite's application.[95] Consequently, while it is possible that the bloodwite flourished during the twelfth century as the Expanded Pravda suggests, there are no sources, with the exception of the tale related above, to indicate that it already was entrenched as a homicide sanction in the tenth century.[96] This difficulty, however, has not deterred numerous scholars who have assumed that the regulations described in the Russkaia Pravda actually reflect judicial custom prevalent in Russia from very ancient times.

The Primary Chronicle itself assumed the bloodwite's antiquity. After Vladimir had supposedly experimented with afflictive sanctions, he returned to the practice of collecting the *vira*, referred to in the chronicle as the "custom of his father and grandfather." But there is direct evidence that Vladimir's grandfather, if not father, practiced revenge rather than the bloodwite. The 944 Treaty negotiated by the Byzantines with Prince Igor, Vladimir's grandfather, contains a regulation that specifically admitted the legality of vengeance justice. In phrasing similar to the revenge statutes of the Russkaia Pravda, the treaty permitted relatives to exercise their vengeance if they could. Failing that, composition was acceptable.[97] Comparison of this regulation with the 911 Treaty demonstrates that the regulation was not an innovation.[98]

Certainly these treaties are not without their own source problems, but any discussion of homicides in medieval Russia must at least take them into account.[99] In this case, there are no grounds for assuming that the revenge statutes reflected Byzantine law, in which homicides had fallen under the authority of the state long before the

SANCTIONS AND THE LAW 77

tenth century. Indeed, it was precisely the Byzantine preference for afflictive sanctions that gave rise to the account in the chronicle of the bishop's interference with Vladimir's judiciary.[100] After all, it was a clerical text, the Pravosudie Mitropolich'e, that first directly alluded to Byzantine law in prescribing punishment for homicides.[101]

Nevertheless, it seems likely that the church's increased sway in legal affairs, especially in the compilation of suitable codes, was felt only gradually in relation to homicide, where traditional formulations of reconciliation must have continued to have force. The prolonged existence of the bloodwite suggests that lateral forms of satisfaction remained in operation. But the apocryphal story of Vladimir and the bishops was not lost on later Moscow sovereigns. The prescriptions for execution found in the 1497 Sudebnik and the various sixteenth-century documents of local administration existed side by side with the continued expectation of bloodwite payments.[102] Consequently, physical sanctions, part of the new vertical order of Muscovite politics, and financial payments, transitional consequences of homicide that relied upon principles of restitution, struggled for predominance. The ultimate victory of afflictive sanctions was signaled in the Nikon Chronicle's account of Vladimir's encounter with the bishops. Here the prince specifically acknowledged punishment by divine law, and the chronicler omitted altogether the conclusion of the story as given in the Primary Chronicle. No longer did the chronicler feel obliged to relate that Vladimir returned to the collection of the bloodwite. Instead, the powerful prince who executed evildoers was characterized by a cunning understanding (*smyslen v razume*).[103] The old order was doomed.

What the old order was is still not clear. Contrary to the usual depictions of medieval Russian justice, the bloodwite cannot have been extracted for each homicide. Not only is the term itself virtually unknown in sources that antedate the Short Pravda, but even the Pravda itself offers a most confused explanation of its exaction. Certainly the Expanded Pravda reveals a more systematic understanding of the bloodwite, but the allusions to forty- and eighty-grivna *viry* in themselves do not indicate that the prince had jurisdiction over all murder cases. What these figures do indicate is that the prince attempted to control the consequences of homicides directed against his own staff. The persistence of revenge and the late eleventh-century attempt to introduce composition suggest that the state authority could hardly have accomplished still another major change by the early thirteenth century.[104] On the contrary, the persistence of the *dikaia vira* into the sixteenth century serves to underline the slow pace of the change in jurisdiction over homicide.

On the other hand, there is no need to deny the *virnik*'s activity or his right to percentages of both forty- and eighty-grivna bloodwites. While the highest echelon of court servitors was protected by the eighty-grivna payment, the Expanded Pravda prescribed forty-grivna fees for lesser servants of the prince.[105] Doubtless the *virnik*, like his medieval European counterparts, took his fees from homicides of both categories.[106]

Besides that, the prince also had access to the *dikaia vira*, a kind of substitute for afflictive sanctions. This, too, had its parallel in medieval European law. Early English practice obligated the local residents to bear responsibility for persons killed within their district. Their first duty was to demonstrate to the satisfaction of the Normans that the dead man was not French. Otherwise a heavy fine fell on the community where the corpse was discovered. But although the English rule clearly had as its aim the protection of the newly arrived Normans, very soon the *murdrum* came to signify a secret homicide, since ultimately the fine was exacted at each homicide unless the dead man's English ancestry could be proved.[107] In other words, medieval Russia had all the elements for just such a transition.

The elaborate description of the *dikaia vira* in the Expanded Pravda evidently appeared simultaneously with the new legislation which protected princely personnel. The antagonism to secret homicide expressed in the regulations punishing recidivist criminals (*razboiniki*) facilitated a second avenue of princely interference in normally horizontal legal relations. Finally, the immense sums which the bloodwite came to represent for the prince's treasury may be explained only by resorting to the general extension of the prince's jurisdiction over all such secret homicides.

Sviatoslav's Statute for the Novgorod region, for example, allowed that the sum of bloodwites and fines (*prodazhi*) exacted from one village must have approached 400 grivny in terms of money of the Russkaia Pravda.[108] The most recent studies indicate that this sum must represent the amount collected from an entire region, but even this perspective does not significantly reduce the dimensions of the judicial success of the prince.[109] It may be that medieval Russia, like medieval England, witnessed a great many homicides, and that, as in England, the culprits themselves were but

SANCTIONS AND THE LAW 79

rarely brought to justice. Instead, communities continued to bear the burden of paying the many pecuniary exactions.[110]

The enormity of the sum which Sviatoslav exacted may have another explanation, however. Although the *prodazha* ultimately came to represent a judicial sanction, the first uses of the term in the Expanded Pravda imply that initially its meaning was not so distinct.[111] For example, there are numerous instances in the chronicles where *prodazha* appears in a different light, far removed from judicial proceedings. In 1093 Prince Sviatopolk anticipated raising an army, but his advisors counseled him against such an operation because "the land is impoverished from war and tax payments (*prodazhi*)."[112] In another case *prodazha* is paired with the tribute (*dan'*) in describing the oppressive reign of the Rostislavichi in the Rostov and Suzdal' lands.[113]

All the citations leave the impression that the princes were able to increase the yield of *prodazhi* in a manner not unlike that used to collect the tribute. Even fourteenth-century chronicle entries reveal similar traces. One tale complains of the great suffering (*tomlenie velie*) which fell on the boyars and servitors of Prince Vsevolod Aleksandrovich. The onerous punishment is then delineated— pillaging (*grablenie*) and *prodazha*. The taxpayers suffered under a large *prodazha* tribute payment (*danaa* [sic] *prodazha velia*).[114] Other texts of the same period make similar comparisons. Several texts, although linking the *prodazha* to judicial proceedings, assign its collection by districts as for any revenue operation.[115]

None of this negates the fact that *prodazha* as a judicial sanction was already known in the fourteenth century.[116] But these citations do suggest an evolutionary history for the term, and indicate that even while fiscal sanctions may not yet have developed early in the thirteenth century, princes could still have extracted considerable income from the populace under the general rubric of *prodazha*. Consequently, while the *prodazha* as a judicial sanction may not be dismissed, it is considerably easier to understand the heroic proportions of its collection in twelfth-century Novgorod if its extrajudicial functions are admitted.

In summary, then, medieval Russian law on satisfaction of homicides bears several traces of the transition from dyadic to triadic forms of resolution. Revenge persisted, although no doubt increasingly elbowed aside by composition. The prince, like his counterparts in early medieval Europe, gained the right to penalize those cases not resolvable by the old system—propertyless recidivists and unknown murderers. In addition, the prince extracted pecuniary sanctions for homicides committed against his own servitors. This state of affairs, outlined in the Expanded Russkaia Pravda, is the context into which the new legal collections of the thirteenth century fell. Their advent gave still more dramatic impetus to the movement toward vertical legal relations and to the accompanying notions of sanction.[117]

Assault

A similar pattern is detectable in cases of assault. In a series of parallel articles, both versions of the Russkaia Pravda enumerate the compositions for such offenses.[118] To be hit with club, rod, bowl, unsheathed sword, or sword hilt called for a financial restitution. Should the blow be serious enough to result in the loss of an arm, leg, or tooth, again composition was in order. But even in these provisions there lies latent the old principle of revenge. One article of the Short Pravda provided for composition only in the event that the offender did not suffer immediate recompense in kind from his victim. Still another article of that same redaction called upon the sons of the man lamed by a blow to punish the offender. The Expanded Pravda, too, allowed the enraged victim to retaliate without penalty when struck by a sword.[119]

The provisions of the Pravda which stipulate restitution are sometimes understood as statements of monetary sanction imposed by the prince.[120] It is true that all the articles do not specify to whom the payments should go, but the usage points very clearly to the victim receiving restitution. Like composition for homicide (*za golovu*), restitution also was paid for assault (*za obidu*). Article two of the Short Pravda connects revenge with the principle of compensation. If a man was assaulted by another, and could not avenge himself, he was to take three grivny for the offense (*za obidu*).[121] Corroboration of this usage is found in thirteenth-century Smolensk law. A regulation parallel to that of the Pravda established payment "for the eye . . . , for the arm . . . , for the leg" (*za oko . . . , za ruku . . . , za nogu*).[122] A later reworking specifically provided that a man wounded by the sword or knife and thereby lamed was to be given three grivny of silver (*dati emu 3 griv[ny] serebra*).[123] All this conforms to the program of restitution discernible in regard to homicide cases.

However, the principle of monetary sanctions also makes an appearance in company with the composition schedules. The article just cited from the Short Pravda, providing a payment when an assault victim could not avenge himself, was mirrored in the Expanded Pravda. This time the assailant was required to "pay him [whom?] a *prodazha* of three grivny" (*no platiti emu prodazhiu 3 grivny*).[124] Certainly the *prodazha* came to constitute a fine, a monetary sanction, but its placement in this particular article implies that it may originally have stood for composition payments.[125] The article bears the same structure as its counterpart in the Short Pravda, maintaining even the designation of the recipient (*emu*). The prince is not referred to either in this article or in its immediate predecessor, so that it is hardly evident that the vague reference in the text alludes to him.

On the other hand, the provision for the victim avenging himself is gone. In its place the Expanded Pravda introduces certain evidentiary requirements that indicate some significant changes in the juridical concept of assault.[126] Furthermore, the immediately preceding and succeeding articles clearly distinguish a fine (*prodazha*) from composition.[127] This information, together with the numerous other references to *prodazhi* in the Expanded Pravda, would seem to indicate that the payments in fact were fines destined for the prince's treasury.[128]

This view is not without difficulties. For one thing, the article devoted to assault assigns responsibility according to one's guilt. For example, the man who complained of his wounds and subsequently was proven to be the instigator of the fight, received no sanction whatever—"then that [his wounds] will suffice for payment [*za platezh'*], that they beat him."[129] Presumably the other combatant experienced similar results, even though he did not initiate the pugilistics. One may hardly describe this kind of happenstance as sanction. Furthermore, another article in the same section of the Expanded Pravda prescribed a *prodazha* of twelve grivny *za obidu*, an expression met earlier in situations of pure composition. Other articles in the complex contain similar ambiguities.[130]

The interchangeability of meaning suggests that articles twenty-seven to thirty-one of the Expanded Pravda reflect the early stages of a transition in policy. The regulations attempt to play both sides, at least initially, prescribing the prince's fine as well as a fee for the victim. The same evenhandedness appears in other provisions as well. One article of the Short Pravda, in particular, often the object of dispute for other reasons, provided that a peasant agriculturalist (*smerd*) tortured without the prince's word was to receive three grivny for the offense (*za obidu*), whereas the same regulation in the

Expanded version provided for a three-grivna fine (*prodazha*) and one grivna for the torture (*za muku*). Both articles continue by making similar provision for princely servitors.[131] Clearly this is part of the trend toward subordinating the interests of the victim to the profit of the increasingly long arm of the prince. What previously was a simple tort was converted into a felony, sanctioned by a fine, though some form of restitution persisted.

Ambivalence in the compensation for crimes of assault even penetrated the Pskov Judicial Charter, a text that in other respects represents a fairly clear delineation of vertical interests and the accompanying notions of sanction. For example, a blow levied against one's opponent in court was rewarded not only with the anticipated restitution—a ruble to the victim—but also was penalized by a fine paid to the prince. Another article, envisioning a fight among five or ten men, provided that both compensation and fines were collectable.[132]

Nevertheless, the Pskov code did take a significant step toward vertical legal relations. Although often relying upon provisions of the Russkaia Pravda, the Pskov code made explicit a notion only implied in the Pravda—felony.[133] At one point the Pskov Judicial Charter inveighs against those litigants who, upon receiving a court summons, used that device to strike fear in the hearts of their opponents by beating or torturing them. The aggressive litigant risked prosecution as a murderer should his contestant die. The same attention to the circumstances of assault, an attitude only weakly developed in the Pravda, appears elsewhere in the Pskov code.[134]

Theft and Robbery

The movement toward actual sanctions rather than compositions is illustrated best in crimes of theft and robbery. Whereas one must struggle with terminology and the tantalizing laconisms in cases of homicide and assault, both redactions of the Russkaia Pravda outline in detail the mechanisms for resolving theft and robbery claims and make the transition from composition to sanctions comparatively clear.

In the Short Pravda, the procedure for regaining stolen property is manifestly horizontal. The confrontation (*svod*) was prescribed as a means for securing one's own property from someone else's possession. The owner was specifically enjoined from seizing it outright, and was to prevail upon his opposite to help him to establish the actual thief through a series of regressing interrogations of the individuals through whose hands the object in question had passed. In sum, the owner of the misappropriated property took upon himself its recovery and, perhaps more amazing to those accustomed to modern legal relations, the person in whose possession the property was now found was presumed to comply.[135] There is no trace here of the intrusion of the prince's agents, nor any final threat to guarantee the peaceable outcome of the proceedings. No sanction was invoked against the thief ultimately discovered in this way. The obvious, though undeclared, interest of the provision is the simple return of the property to its rightful owner.[136]

It is doubly interesting, therefore, to see in the Expanded version that confrontment was not only retained, but considerably amplified. An entire series of articles was devoted to the explanation of the method whereby the aggrieved party could legitimately reacquire his lost property.[137] One article describes an aspect of the process which no doubt was functioning even under the Short Pravda, but was not specifically mentioned there. The slaveowner whose subject had disappeared was obliged to make an announcement to this effect in the central market (*na torgu*). Anyone who concealed the slave for more than three days after the announcement was made was adjudged guilty, and the owner was authorized to take back his property.[138] Again the presumption is compliance, although the reasons for a three-day period of deliberation will probably remain unknown.[139] It is clear that the slaveowner knew where his slave was concealed (how else could he take him at the expiration of the three-day limit?), and that his claim to the property was not contested (again, how else could he seize the slave?).

The remaining provisions of confrontment reinforce some of the conjectures offered above. The individual ultimately determined to be the thief was responsible for seeing that the owner received his property in good condition. In addition, the Expanded Pravda prescribed an undetermined fine, a feature absent in the Short Pravda.[140] The Expanded redaction also enlarged the slave's role in the inquisitorial process. As before, the culprit, once found, was to return the stolen property, but now, in addition to paying costs (*protor*"), the thief also had to contend with the prince. Slave theft earned the prince a twelve-grivna fine.[141]

The Expanded Pravda's new provisions illustrate an instance of princely authority intruding on the seemingly satisfactory dyadic relations embodied in the provisions of the Short Pravda. The encroachment is all the more remarkable in light of the absence in the process of any role whatever for the prince or his lieutenants. Procedure, as before, was confined to the confrontation of owner and the accused, and only at the conclusion of the business did the state authority make its presence felt in collection of a fine. As comparison of the slave-theft provisions makes clear, monetary sanctions were added on to the forms of reconciliation already operative under customary law. The absence of any princely official at the conduct of these operations makes doubtful any effective collection of fines, but the attempt to lay claim to them is indicative of the changed order of things.

That no third-party officials took part seems clear from the other articles devoted to the confrontment process. When confrontment led beyond the boundaries of the commune (*verv'*), the process came to a halt, and the last one known to be in possession of the stolen property had to pay up, even though someone else was implicated. Should the plaintiff not succeed in recovering the entirety of his lost property, he, like the innocent participant, could do nothing but regret the loss. In the last of the regulations, the text relieved the original plaintiff of the need to participate in the entire process. Having completed the third confrontment, the plaintiff need go no further if the investigation led to another town. At this point the burden shifted to the opponent, who was to endure to the end. Only then could the original plaintiff expect to receive his composition. The thief thus apprehended was liable for damages and a fine.[142]

The system of confrontment, born in a society where consensus was strong enough to advertise and support behavioral norms, was still the order of the day in the thirteenth century. No role for the prince or his subordinates may be observed in the method prescribed for recovery of stolen property and discovery of the thief. Therefore, it is difficult to believe that the call for a fine was heeded. To be sure, even the presence of the idea of sanction is indicative of the increasing potential of the prince's authority in legal affairs, and may have signaled the end of horizontal relations. But, just as surely, the additional space given to confrontment in the explication of procedures and restitutions in the Expanded Pravda is testimony to the continued vitality of horizontal legal relations.

Further proof of the longevity of dyadic process can be found in the authorization for the confrontment procedure in the Dvina Administrative Charter. The innovation here is precisely the factor omitted in the provisions of the Russkaia Pravda: the prince's lieutenant (*namestnik*) and bailiff (*dvorianin*) evidently took part, supervising the investigation by confrontment. Furthermore, actual sanctions are delineated. The first-time offender had his property sold to compensate for what was stolen, or, failing that, was himself sold into slavery. The thief also was branded, thereby allowing the authorities to recognize recidivists. Captured in theft a third time, irredeemable criminals were hanged.[143]

At this point it can no longer be argued that sanction was not an actual and integral part of the law. But it is instructive to observe that even in this late fourteenth-century document, even in the context of such severe sanctions, the essentially dyadic nature of the investigation was not altered. The litigants themselves still bore the responsibility for carrying out the investigation. Even the Pskov Judicial Charter, a code where both physical and financial sanctions were commonplace, found room to summarize the confrontment procedure still another time. As in the other codes under discussion, the victim was expected to make a public declaration, and the possessor of lost property could escape conviction only by oath or the testimony of respected citizens.[144]

Among the developments in the Pskov Charter is the pronounced presence of third-party enforcement personnel. Not only was the investigation to take place under the direct auspices of the constables (*pozovniki*), but the resolution evidently took place before a court, an eventuality never mentioned in the Russkaia Pravda.[145] In addition to the inevitable composition still characteristic of theft cases, the court found it within its right to apply sanctions against the thief.[146] The overlapping of fines and compensation in the various theft provisions demonstrates the increasing conflict of princely and private interests.

A series of articles in both versions of the Russkaia Pravda deal with horse theft, an especially serious offense. The unauthorized rider of someone else's horse was liable to a three-grivna payment, clearly simple composition as the succeeding articles show.[147] Even the theft of a horse required of the culprit only that he pay three grivny for the offense (*za obidu*).[148] The chief distinction developed in these articles is the different estimates placed on the prince's horse and that of an ordinary mortal. But despite this difference, reminiscent of the protection of princely personnel in article one of the Expanded Pravda, there can be no doubt that these fees, too, simply constituted a definition of appropriate restitution. The other items of property lumped with the horses—mare, ox, cow, calf, ewe, and ram—all received a value estimate.[149]

Traces of sanction do appear, however, in other regulations addressed to the same subject. The Expanded Pravda ordered the deviant who maimed or killed either horse or cattle to make amends, as before, and to pay a twelve-grivna fine.[150] But the seriousness of the offense provoked an even more drastic response. The horse thief was joined with the recidivist criminal (*razboinik*) of article seven—both earned special sanction (*potok*) from the prince.[151] This association feeds the speculation that the horse thief of article thirty-five was a professional, a recidivist easily remanded to the prince's punishment. But even omitting that consideration, the twelve-grivna fine constituted an indisputable monetary sanction, and allowed the prince to interfere in a matter which at one time was conceptualized as strictly private. Consequently, it is odd that the Pskov code, so inclined to vertical authority and its accompanying sanctions, should allow horse theft to be regarded so lightly. The Pskov Judicial Charter, in one of the last references in a secular code to this particular type of criminal activity, allowed the accused to swear that the animal in question was his own, and the matter seemingly ended there.[152]

The reasons for the twelve-grivna fine imposed by the Expanded Pravda only may be conjectured. It is likely that the princes regarded horses as a kind of state resource mobilized for military campaigns, a conclusion that finds some support in other texts. Both redactions of the Zakon Sudnyi liudem linked the theft of horse and weapon in regulations that provided for the thief's beating and sale into slavery. Another article introduced a variation of the situation envisaged by the Russkaia Pravda: one who rode the horse of another without first acquiring the owner's permission was consigned to a beating for three days and then sold into slavery as a thief. Finally, the Zakon Sudnyi provided limits of responsibility for the horse borrowed and used in accordance with the rules outlined by its owner.[153]

The interest of the provisions from the Zakon Sudnyi liudem is not confined to their regard for the horse. For the purposes of legal development, we may note in passing that these regulations, present in early Russia and widely distributed from the thirteenth century onward, introduced the notion of sanction for an offense generally conceptualized in the Pravda as meriting simple composition. Even if it be granted that the Russkaia Pravda does reveal the prince attempting to impose some kind of financial sanction, the Zakon's regulations go one step further and introduce physical punishment and isolate the offender from society, the effective result of sale into slavery.

These particular sanctions are of considerable interest because of their subsequent history. Flogging became a principal sanction imposed by Muscovite officials even as early as the 1497 Sudebnik. By the same token, the offender was also sold in order to allow the victim to recoup his losses.[154] The Sudebnik's bias toward executions sometimes foreclosed this possibility, but much later forced sale was still practiced.[155] Although similarities represent no proof of the Zakon's influence, they do fit a pattern of interdependence noticeable elsewhere in medieval Russian law.

A simpler and probably older form of sanction appeared in another church text. The fourteenth-century Trinity copy of the Merilo Pravednoe contains an unusual insert concerned with theft cases. "On the Procedure for Theft" (*O ustavlen'i tatby*), together with an article on marriage procedure, is placed on a blank folio which interrupts the text of the eighth-century Byzantine code, the Ecloga. Both the content and lexicon of the theft provision point to a clerical provenance roughly contemporary with the Expanded Russkaia Pravda. But despite the similarities of language, the import of the theft statute is quite distinct from the Pravda. The essential aim of the provision was to establish procedures for the proper transfer of fines and stolen goods from the jurisdiction in which the thief was captured to that in which the offense had occurred. The official in the first district was given his choice in dealing with the crime—he could extract his fine or resort to physical sanction.[156]

The chronology of theft penalties fits well with the pattern of sanctions observed in homicide and assault cases. The Russkaia Pravda treated theft in a manner primarily oriented toward the restitution of stolen property. Only gradually did the principle of monetary sanction appear, at first in an overlay of terminology,[157] and then in combination with composition.[158] Finally, monetary sanctions yielded their place to physical sanctions, a process not fully complete at the time of publication of the 1497 Sudebnik.[159]

The law's ambivalent view of sanctions is discernible in a wide range of legal texts from these three centuries. The Pskov code, for example, assigned cases of livestock theft to the jurisdiction of the prince's court.[160] At the same time, another provision listed restitutions for some of the same animals mentioned in the Russkaia Pravda. Again, the formula not only conforms to the structural peculiarities observed in similar situations elsewhere (*za golovu, za obidu, za ovtsy*), but the owner is mentioned directly as deserving the restitution fees.[161] Even as late a document as the Pravosudie Mitropolich'e followed the same practice.[162] To find such admitted composition in these late texts amply warrants the suspicion that the parallel allowances in the Russkaia Pravda were fashioned on that same principle.

The Russkaia Pravda, therefore, provides still further mystery when it utilizes the traditional formula for composition in connection with cases pertaining to stolen livestock, but appends a clause by which peasants (*smerdy*) were permitted to receive these fees if they made a payment to the prince. Conventional wisdom has been satisfied with an exceptionally tortuous explanation of this regulation. Modern partisans of princely power find no difficulty in saying that the peasants were eligible to receive composition only if they paid the prince a fine (*prodazha*), although the text itself identified the payments as fees (*urotsi*). The usual explanation seeks to distinguish freemen, who paid the prince fines, from the slaves mentioned in the succeeding article who were not the prince's subjects, and therefore not liable to such sanctions.[163]

Another explanation may be proffered. The basic construction of the article undoubtedly was designed to regularize compositions, and the peculiar nature of the final attachment suggests that this provision may be one more expression of that ambivalence toward composition and princely sanctions which reigned in the time of the Expanded Pravda.[164] The payment of fines was instituted over those peasants who worked the prince's land as a preliminary to general application of fiscal sanctions. As with the protection first extended to the prince's personnel, the judicial power of the prince was asserted most easily where the prince's authority was least challenged. Even the Pravosudie Mitropolich'e did not escape this approach. In one provision it called for a one-grivna fine (*vina*) for anyone who killed a dog or cat, and went on to prescribe restitution ("a dog in place of a dog, a cat in place of a cat").[165]

Similar alternation is characteristic of the majority of the remaining provisions of the Expanded Pravda which deal with theft. The theft of hay and wood was assigned a nine-kuna payment in both Short and Expanded versions. Though not mentioned specifically in either redaction, a fine is implicit in the Expanded version, inasmuch as it specifically added to the nine-kuna fee a novel provision by which the owner was recompensed at a rate dependent upon how much was stolen. In view of the fact that even the most diehard advocate of the early role of the prince and his fines will admit that the predominant mode in the Short Pravda is compensation, the particular mention of composition in the second part of the article implies a different function for the first payments.[166]

In the context of safeguarding the property of agriculturalists, both editions of the Pravda undertook to settle conflicts which arose out of theft from barns, threshing pits, and households. The Short Pravda used a formula by which each thief was responsible for payment for his own offense. The same principle was endorsed in the Expanded Pravda. The seriousness of the offense may be measured by the fact that arson affecting these facilities could lead to penalizing the offender, once the costs were deducted from his property.[167] The Pskov Judicial Charter makes the serious nature of the offense even more clear by assigning these cases to the prince's court.[168] Though perhaps less direct, the provisions of the Russkaia Pravda, by allotting responsibility to each participant, indicate that the intent of the law was to affix individual responsibility and thereby introduce a measure of sanction.

It is worth noting that Iaroslav's Statute defended barn and threshing floor by similar provisions. Although the texts made no concession to the principle of composition, they did make provision for twofold sanction—fines were levied by the church and at the same time the guilty party was assigned to the prince for punishment. At first glance, the presence of these formulations in church codes may seem contradictory and point to a conflict of jurisdiction. But from another perspective, one may observe that the farmstead regulations had their roots in Byzantine legislation, a source hardly utilized by the compilers of the Russkaia Pravda's customary law. Therefore, one may surmise that the codifiers of church law, simultaneously accommodating the financial needs of the church (hence the church fine) and instituting Byzantine prescriptive sanctions, attempted to appropriate this subject for their own jurisdiction.[169] Precedents for the church's preoccupation with this theme may be found in the Zakon Sudnyi liudem, whose statutes defend not only agricultural inventory, but link it to church losses through fire.[170]

Other forms of property connected with agriculture also received protection in the Russkaia Pravda. The Short Pravda threatened the man who made mischief for the prince's beehives with the obligation to make composition. A series of articles in the Expanded redaction prescribed the payment of fines, although it is not clear that the prince was the owner of the hives.[171] Boats too had their price and fine.[172] Other regulations express the same vacillation between clearly expressed sanctions and a willingness to retain the principles of composition. Hunting property, almost certainly the reserve of the prince and his comrades, was protected by both sanction and forced restitution.[173] But here, too, a certain archaism creeps into the stolid theories of sanction. The commune (*verv'*) was to find the poacher if there were evidence of some violation of the hunting preserves.[174] With the princely apparatus either unable or unwilling even to seek the perpetrator of such crimes as these, it is difficult to visualize the systematic investigation of the same crime by the commune. The successful capture of the poacher, perhaps a member of the commune, would seem to be no more palatable to the community than the capture of one of its members as a murderer.[175]

In consonance with the bucolic tone of the Pravda, both versions devote particular attention to questions of land boundaries and their violation. While the Short Pravda awarded the landholder twelve grivny if someone plowed beyond his border, the Expanded Pravda fined the man who felled a landmark tree.[176] The first regulation alone found echo in the Expanded Zakon Sudnyi. The farmer who plowed beyond his border was censured by deprivation of his own plowland (*oranie*).[177] Nearly identical passages in the Dvina and the Beloozero Charters provided for fines for such border violations. The difference between the texts, however, is instructive. While the Dvina regulations prescribed fines in kind and established no role for the princely agents, the Beloozero Charter converted the payment into money and assigned it to the prince's lieutenants (*namestnik* and *tiun*).[178] Finally, the 1497 Sudebnik, in a much-enlarged draft of these regulations, punished the one who plowed over or cut down border markings of the power elite (grand prince, boyars, or monasteries). The sanction included both the extraction of a fine and a sound beating. Violation of peasant village boundaries led to the exaction of a fine, as before.[179]

Conclusions

The pattern of the evolution of sanction is illustrative of the general history of medieval Russian law. The basically dyadic stance of the Short Pravda was influenced by the growing role of the prince in medieval Russian society.[180] The old formulas of the violations of individual rights were generally couched in terms of simple torts, even when there is evidence of the prince's authority intruding into the strictly bilateral relations. The principle of revenge, ameliorated into composition, dominated even violation of that most valuable of human rights, the right to life. Originally, Russian law codified the gradual violation of dyadic legal satisfaction only in cases of property loss. At first confused with composition, then separated to protect princely interests, monetary sanctions came to play an important role. These, in turn, were displaced by physical sanctions only in Muscovy, with the consolidation of power in the hands of the Moscow grand princes.

The law of the city-republics of Novgorod and Pskov helps us to unravel the intermediate stages of this process, a clarification especially useful in light of the ambiguity often demonstrated in the Russkaia Pravda. Generally inclined to monetary fines, the Novgorod code also included provision for restoration of losses incurred by the victim.[181] But, like its Muscovite successor, Novgorod took care to compensate the emerging bureaucracy for the myriad tasks associated with litigation in Novgorod.[182] By contrast, Pskov, though just as concerned for the financial position of its officialdom, combined a policy of pecuniary and afflictive sanctions.[183] A first or second theft was punished by a fine; three-time offenders lost their lives. Recidivism was not tolerated for arsonists, traitors, horse thieves, and those who stole from the city citadel. Such serious breaches of the community norms earned their perpetrators immediate execution.[184]

Muscovite policy followed these precedents. The Dvina Charter gave the thief three chances: a first offense was punished by a fine, a second by property confiscation, and a third offense resulted in hanging.[185] The Beloozero Charter was not so precise, calling upon the officials to administer punishment against those condemned for serious crimes.[186] A twin passage in the 1497 Sudebnik made it clear that that punishment was execution, and the costs of the suit were extracted from the criminal's possessions.[187] The Sudebnik shows the same impatience with recidivism that appears in the Pskov and Dvina codes: first-time thieves with a clean reputation were flogged and assigned to make up the losses inflicted on the plaintiff; repetition brought inevitable execution, even if the plaintiff's losses remained uncompensated.[188] In this way lateral legal relations and their primary regard for the litigants were essentially doomed. The plaintiff's concerns had become assuredly secondary to those of the society at large, whose interests were assumed by the state. This stance enlarged the role and conception of sanction, and at the same time diminished the rights of the victim to his compensation.

So drastic a change obviously cannot have been accomplished immediately and effectively everywhere. There is no reason to believe that the apparatus at the disposal of the Moscow grand prince reached each corner of the principality.[189] Even the Sudebnik provides some evidence that the administration of these far-reaching solutions depended rather significantly upon roles performed by citizens-at-large. Representatives of the communal structure were coopted into participation at the courts of the prince's lieutenants, and much of the prosecution rested upon accusations lodged by citizens in good standing.[190] Even the imposition of physical sanctions depended to a large degree on the local reputations earned by the criminal offenders.[191]

It was exactly this group of deviants, whom the Muscovites called "known evil men" (*vedomye likhie liudi*), against whom the law was mustered in its full force. Attempts were made to identify such repeaters, but given the state of the bureaucratic apparatus, the burden of proof lay on the so-called "good men" (*dobrye liudi*). Their accusation was sufficient to bring about the execution of someone once apprehended in connection with a serious crime.[192] But reliance on unofficial enforcement procedures serves to underscore the very weakness of the system—in the absence of consistent, predictable penalties, even the severest of punishments has little deterrent effect.[193] One may speak of the ultimate deterrence imposed by capital punishment, inasmuch as the offenders are thereby rendered incapable of repeating their crimes.[194] Although not very sophisticated, the level of criminology in Muscovy clearly went no further than this. Recidivism was ruled intolerable, and culprits convicted of such deviance were guaranteed speedy relief from the troubles of this world.

In other respects, Muscovy's dealings with hardened criminals anticipated much of the consensus now developing in the study of deviant behavior. Current research has shown that the appeal and role of sanctions in deterring deviant behavior is dependent, among other things, on the person's perception of the sanction's consequence. In particular, it is evident that certain groups are highly resistant to the deterrent effects of sanctions, even those sanctions which carry a high physical cost.[195] Muscovy's recidivists evidently demonstrated resistance even to the severest of sanctions. Consequently, offenders characterized as socially reprobate (*likhie liudi*) were dispatched forthwith.[196]

Some of the recent literature examining capital punishment suggests that this penalty, whatever its effect on recidivists, has a salubrious effect on the society at large whose behavioral norms are thereby reinforced.[197] The Sudenik's pronouncement and occasional fulfillment of such formal sanctions may have had the same effect. No doubt Muscovite society could have profited from such support in the tumult of the fifteenth century. But the role of sanctions in Muscovy seems to be merely symptomatic of the changed legal position of the political authority, rather than an actual achievement of judicial science. As before, the Russian lands were largely governed by the customary norms elaborated in the Russkaia Pravda.[198] Only where the Moscow grand prince or his various agents could effectively wield their power was there any sustained application of physical sanctions.

CHAPTER 4

Development of Judicial Personnel

Vertical legal systems are impossible without the appearance of the third party: the judiciary and its pertinent assistants. Studies based on ethnographic data suggest that the development of a police presence is dependent upon a substantial division of labor and the growth of a money economy. A less clearly defined form of third-party presence, mediation, appears more frequently, and seems to evolve before police institutions, though not necessarily in conjunction with the latter. For example, the use of money shows a much more consistent correlation with societies that have official police enforcement than with societies where mediation remains the strongest form of third-party presence.[1]

Nevertheless, the usual explanations of the rise of the police rely heavily upon contemporary conceptions of statehood. Max Weber, for example, attempted to isolate his notions about police agency from the notion of a state, but in constructing a definition of "legal order" made central the presence of a clearly defined enforcement staff.[2] Although Weber was disposed to admit as sanctions even seemingly informal punishments administered under the rubric of revenge, he was obliged to recognize such a prescription as "the very limit of what can still be regarded as 'legal coercion.' " In fact, Weber went on to add that "mere social disapproval and reprisals on the part of those who are harmed ... merely by convention and self-interest rather than by a staff of persons whose conduct is *specially* oriented toward the observation of the regulatory order" does not fall within the scope of law. As a result, rule by a "legal order" was reserved exclusively for those state systems which sought enforcement through formal sanctions.[3]

While more material is still desirable, the available fund of ethnographic data indicates quite clearly that the appearance of a third-party mechanism for resolving disputes is connected with the level of social organization. Gluckman's typology of development, for example, shows the transition from self-help to some form of mediator when the social grouping exceeds a few hundred members. Though Gluckman found cases of self-help societies even in the presence of nascent vertical systems, the appearance of police as such is strongly associated with that vertical political system he identified as "authoritative chieftainship."[4] An institution such as the police, the prototypical embodiment of Weber's staff of enforcers, often emerges then from a series of more informal intermediaries.

The range of mediators known from ethnographic reports points to an equally broad range of relationships between litigating parties. The simplest societies—least fractured by societal complexity and social differentiation, least affected by the intrusion of foreign members and values, and smallest in terms of absolute numbers—exercise a form of conflict mediation that has been labeled in the literature "invisible."[5] This mediation is the simple operation of normal social constraints where retaliation, for example, is admitted by the community for the aggrieved party. More distinct forms of mediation follow with differentiation. Various experts serve as consultants and impose their authoritative judgments upon the litigants. Such an intermediary stance may at first rely upon supernatural bases, and examples of sorcerers or religious intermediaries are widely attested.[6] Weber took cognizance of this reality, and appropriated religion as one of the early forms of enforcement of social norms, which thereby converted norms into law. In this context, priests as well as police assume a stance between litigants.[7] Only with increasing societal complexity may one observe the separation of religion and other conceptual frameworks from law.[8]

Further changes in the kinds of mediation keep pace with society's own alterations. In general, various forms of explicit mediation become more visible under the conditions of absolute growth of a society and development of a money economy.[9] Even such enforcement-conscious analysts as Hoebel must admit that the trend in law is the shift in responsibility for norm maintenance from the individual and his kinship group "to agents of the body politic as a social entity."[10] Gradually mediators assume a more visible, aggressive, and formal role in ordering social relations, and become involved in enforcing compliance with the norms of societies themselves increasingly heterogeneous.[11]

The changes in the movement toward third-party mediation outlined above are descriptive of the process that took place in Russia in the centuries between the appearance of the Russkaia Pravda and the 1497 Sudebnik. Although Weber claimed to see in the Russkaia Pravda itself the beginnings of this process, his position has not been popular with most historians of Russian law.[12] Considerations of a nationalistic and political character have imposed on the Pravda a particular role, making it a product of princely legislation, the fruit of a fully developed "feudal" system furnished with a host of judicial functionaries.[13] These ideas, as noted in the preceding chapter, rely upon certain views of sanction and its application in medieval Russia. But careful examination of the development of specialized judicial personnel shows that only slowly and gradually did such enforcement functionaries appear in early Muscovy. Their antecedents performed a variety of implicit tasks that ultimately came to construct the legal triad typical of vertical systems.

The bulk of the historical literature, however, does not share this modest assessment of the early princely officials. Among pre-revolutionary scholars, the devotion to the idea of early state development has guaranteed its corollary of a host of specialized judicial officials. The most famous monograph devoted to this problem is A. E. Presniakov's *Kniazhoe pravo* (Princely Law), a survey of the prince's position in Old Russian society in the tenth, eleventh, and twelfth centuries. The essential point of Presniakov's work is to establish the predominance of the prince in early state development in general, and in the Russkaia Pravda in particular. Presniakov attributes the existence of nearly every component of specialized personnel to its association with the prince.[14]

Soviet typology of history has somewhat different motives for visualizing an essentially identical construct. The "feudal fragmentation" traditionally assigned to the centuries with which this study is concerned was preceded by the development of a state apparatus manned by the Riurikid princes. In order to justify the appropriate levels of exploitation, it is convenient for Soviet scholars to credit the princely administration with a fairly sophisticated level of labor differentiation. Such wishful thinking often penetrates discussion of the princely juridical structure.[15] Of course medieval Russia did develop a princely administration, and these princes were surrounded by their own servitors, who are known in the texts as the retinue (*druzhina*). But given the private nature of princely income in the period before the thirteenth century, the private nature of the retinue seems undoubted as well.[16] Although it falls outside the bounds of this study to examine the origins of each of the princely servitors, a careful inspection of the judicial staff supports the notion of a private princely apparatus, distinct from the institutions of customary law in medieval Russia.[17]

The Origins of Judicial Personnel in Russia

The Short redaction of the Russkaia Pravda mentions few officials, and reveals little about their functions. One officer who was featured here is the *ognishchanin*. In provisions announced by Iaroslav's sons sometime late in the eleventh century, the Pravda protected his life with the normal bloodwite (*vira*) when he was killed in an assault (*v razboi*) and the murderer remained undiscovered. Killing an *ognishchanin* in an quarrel (*v obidu*) caused the exaction of eighty grivny from the killer. Another article associates his demise with overt theft in an agricultural setting ("at a barn, or near a horse, or with a bull or a cow"), and thereby implies that he may have carried out his duties regularly on the prince's estates. Similar regulations applied to the *tiun*, who was an estate steward, so that it is likely that the *ognishchanin* also fulfilled private economic functions for the prince.[18]

Despite the parallelism, many scholars have found difficulty explaining the meaning of the term. Since the suggested roots of the word all derive from notions of the hearth or household, it seems incontestable that the *ognishchanin* originally was a household servitor of the prince.[19] But the subsequent nature of his functions remains unclear. Although he is mentioned in Novgorod texts of the twelfth and thirteenth centuries, there are few clues to his duties.[20] The thirteenth-century Expanded Pravda penalized his torture in a provision paralleling a similar regulation in the Short Pravda. After this, he appears no more in the sources. All this suggests that the *ognishchanin* still had a place in the prince's estate in the thirteenth century, even if only in Novgorod.[21] But none of the available information points to any formal role for him in judicial matters.

Only the association of the *ognishchanin* with the *tiun* raises the possibility of judicial functions. Several sources indicate that the *tiun* acted as a judge, a role that lasted at least until the sixteenth century.[22] The Smolensk Treaty of 1229 specifically identified the *tiun* as a judge who served in place of the prince.[23] Similarly, Vsevolod's Statute protected church courts from the incursions of *tiuny* and other judges.[24] Later Muscovite and Novgorod courts surely were operated by *tiuny*, while chronicle notices also indicate that the *tiun*, at least on occasion, fulfilled administrative functions in the towns in close conjunction with the policies of the princes.[25] Evidently the *tiun* also sometimes served as a kind of special ambassador for the princes, a factor underlined in the Smolensk treaties where the *tiun*'s life was protected in the same way as that of an emissary.[26]

The elevated nature of the *tiun*'s position at court must be contrasted with several other circumstances relating to his social station. For one thing, the *tiuny* seem to have been slaves. The Expanded Pravda notes that the *tiun* who accepted the position without first concluding an exemption agreement (*riad*) was thereby automatically enslaved.[27] Later wills and testaments of the princes enforce this assessment by manumitting *tiuny* in the princes' personal service.[28] Finally, the 1497 Sudebnik repeated the Pravda's formula, excluding only the old proviso of escape by previous contractual agreement. Thereafter all *tiuny* surely were slaves. Consequently, at least in early Muscovy, a significant layer of the judicial stratum was occupied by slaves, personally dependent upon prince or princely officials.[29]

The association of the *tiun* with the *ognishchanin* seems to cast him in an agricultural setting, as a kind of estate manager.[30] But the Expanded Pravda provides even more direct pointers to the *tiun*'s early involvement with agriculture. Discussing fees payable for the homicide of princely men, the Expanded Pravda groups together household (*ognishchnyi*), stable (*koniushii*), farm (*sel'skii*) and field (*ratainyi*) *tiuny*.[31] These then are all members of the personal, household staff of the prince, a factor that explains the prince's desire to protect their lives by special fees, and also makes more comprehensible their slave status.

Consequently, although the *tiuny* appear as judges in some texts, the entire collection of testimony about them indicates that they fulfilled a wide variety of roles entrusted to them by their lords and owners, the princes. Like the *ognishchanin* with whom they are so closely identified, they must have originally occupied a position in the prince's court, and from that position undertaken the various responsibilities assigned them by the texts: emissaries, judges, and temporary administrators, as well as estate stewards. It should be noted that the early sources which identify them as judges primarily supply that information in a negative construction, urging the *tiuny* not to interfere in church courts.[32]

Other officials of the Russkaia Pravda occupy a less ambiguously judicial post. Foremost among them is the *virnik*, the bloodwite collector. Even the Short Pravda includes a provision according to which the *virnik* was to be supplied with goods in kind during his travels through the territory. The parallel passage in the Expanded Pravda mentions an assistant (*otrok*) who seems to have accompanied the *virnik* on his rounds.[33]

Actual data on the duties of the *virnik* are scant, and aside from the texts of the Pravda itself, nothing is known of this functionary.[34] The only other provisions of the Pravda that deal with the bloodwite collector concern themselves with assigning him his portion of the fees collected for princely personnel.[35] The text hints that the collection drive took place periodically, recalling both the system of tribute collection (*poliud'e*) practiced by the Kievan princes, and the references to subsequent traveling courts (*sudy proezdnye*).[36] This impression is sustained by the inclusion of horse provender among the provisions in kind which the populace was obliged to produce on the occasion of the appearance of the bloodwite collector.[37]

More light may be shed on the *virnik*'s duties from the more clearly documented record of his assistant, the *otrok*. On the basis of presumed knowledge about the former, it has become customary to describe the latter as a "lesser judicial agent,"[38] but the bulk of the references to him offer a much more generalized impression. At its root the word *otrok* denotes a youth, though chronicle references primarily mention him simply as a member of the prince's retinue.[39] In one provision of the Expanded Pravda the *otrok* is grouped with the princely cook (*povar*) and groom (*koniukh*). Other groupings indicate a generalized military function, but the *otrok*'s association with personal service to the prince may not be doubted. In fact, the single reference which may be used to argue police functions for the *otrok* is the Pravda's reference cited above. That the Pravda also established for him fees and feeding requirements demonstrates only that both the bloodwite collector and his assistant were fed by the local populace while in pursuit of princely income, some of which evidently was derived from bloodwites for princely personnel.[40]

The *otrok* was paralleled by a number of other officials who performed similar functions under different names. The Expanded Pravda also includes a *metel'nik* in the division of the bloodwite collector's fees. Here he is grouped with the *otrok*, but in the summary of fees enumerated in article 107, the *metel'nik* replaces the *otrok*, suggesting their identification. The same article expands the notion of judicial participation by the prince's men by broadening their judicial responsibility beyond simply collecting the bloodwite ("And regarding all other suits, four grivny apiece to whoever helps, and six *vekshi* to the *metel'nik*").[41] Nevertheless, so little is known about the *metel'nik* that serious scholars are reduced to speculating that his name was derived from his particular apparel rather than from any duties he performed.[42]

The *otrok* was accompanied as well by a scribe (*pisets*).[43] The position and function of the scribe are not clear, inasmuch as he received no part of the fees enumerated elsewhere for the bloodwite collector and his assistants, but found consideration only in the section dealing with the provisioning requirements (*korm*) and the *perekladnoe*, evidently a special fee paid to the bloodwite collector.[44] If the forays into the countryside by the prince's officials were chiefly for the purpose of collecting revenues, as suggested above, the scribes could have fulfilled the prince's interest by inventorying his accessions on these trips. But the presence of the scribe is also a persuasive piece of evidence to indicate an interest in the writing of judicial decisions, or, at the least, the listing of the judicial fees so collected.[45]

The officer later developed in Muscovy to fulfill scribal functions in the grand prince's own domain and in the Muscovite state bore a different name, *d'iak*, connected in origin with its Greek counterpart. The *pistsy*, like those named in the Pravda, are mentioned both before and after the appearance of *d'iaki* in matters of revenue collection and inventorying undertaken with revenue in mind.[46] In a more general sense, the same word was used to apply to all who could write. For example, it was the term *pisets* which the chronicler used to describe the great translation and copying work performed in the eleventh century at the request of Iaroslav the Wise.[47] But even from an early time, *pisets* also bore a more specific meaning connected with judicial functions. The compilation of the 971 Greko-Rus' Treaty was carried out by a *pisets*, and the later Pskov Judicial Charter charged the *pisets* with writing up the results of land litigation and compiling court summonses and default charters.[48]

Despite all this, the Expanded Russkaia Pravda carries no job description of the *pisets*. Like the bloodwite collector and his assistant, whose duties are equally ill-defined, the *pisets* occupies no definite place in the administration of justice. The ambiguity of his function is only multiplied by the fact that Muscovy's scribes (*d'iaki*) were not the direct heirs of the *pistsy*, whose fifteenth-century namesakes were charged with inventorying property for tax purposes. While none of the citations are decisive as to whether the *pisets* of the Pravda executed judicial tasks, they do underline the tenuousness of those arguments which read considerable sophistication into the judicial process of medieval Russia.

The ambiguity surrounding officials mentioned in the Russkaia Pravda is alleviated only slightly by considering the remaining personnel. The Short Pravda, in addition to the *ognishchanin* and *tiun*, also protects the *mechnik*, someone who evidently bore a sword.[49] Protected in both redactions of the Pravda by a forty-grivna fee, he is not associated with the prince's men elevated to special protection in the Expanded Pravda.[50] His torture was specifically punishable under the Short Pravda, but this injunction disappeared in the corresponding passage of the Expanded text.[51] Nevertheless, the *mechnik* seems to have continued to fulfill actual functions even in the thirteenth century, as he was assigned a special fee for his role in administering the iron ordeal. It seems likely that he was more than an ordinary member of the prince's military contingent.[52]

The *mechnik* was assisted in the iron ordeal by a *detskii*, a term destined to have a long life in Muscovite administration. In meaning its root is similar to that of the *otrok*, and indeed the evidence suggests that they may have been one and the same.[53] Like *otrok*, the term *detskii* seems to have had a generalized meaning which characterized its bearers as princely men.[54] The familiarity of Prince Andrei Bogoliubskii with his *detskii* is demonstrated in the assassination scene recorded in the chronicle. The conspirators undertook to kill the prince, and sought entrance to his chambers with disguised voices. But Bogoliubskii recognized the voice of his *detskii*, and although this knowledge was not sufficient to foil the murderers, it does indicate the regular presence of the *detskii* at the prince's court.[55] Most other references suggest only that the *detskii* performed military service.[56]

The Pravda, however, reveals that the *detskii* did in fact fulfill some mediating functions. In disputes about inheritance brought by brothers before the prince for arbitration, the *detskii* was assigned a fee for his work in separating the disputing parties.[57] This type of police function is underscored in the Smolensk treaties of the thirteenth century. In one text the *detskii* is adjured to "guard" or "carry out" (*pristaviti*), a term that is associated with fifteenth-century police officials in Muscovy. Likewise, unsuccessful litigants who proved slow in settling their debts could be stimulated by the *detskii*'s intervention. Later amplification of this text explicitly provided that the *detskii* was to take the litigants to the judge.[58]

Judicial Personnel in Novgorod and Pskov

Intimations about the *detskii*'s judicial functions are reinforced by comparison with his contemporary, the *birich*, an official known from numerous Novgorod and later Muscovite documents.[59] The provision of the Expanded Pravda which assigned the *detskii* a role in maintaining the peace in inheritance cases has a parallel in an early fourteenth-century charter, except that the *detskii* there is replaced by the *birich*.⁶⁰ It may be that the *birich* represents a common Slavic official who was originally associated with the collection of a special tax, the *bir*.⁶¹ But the ancient origins are hardly clear. What is certain is that in later times the *birich* was common in Novgorod whose cadasters and chronicles frequently name him.⁶² Furthermore, Vsevolod's Statute, an addendum to the Novgorod chronicle, also depicts the *birich* as a judicial officer.⁶³ Even in Muscovite redactions of the chronicles, the *birich* is connected with Novgorod and with other personnel attached to the courts there.⁶⁴

The parallel with the *detskii* is even more direct in the extant judicial documents. In one redaction of the Smolensk-Riga Treaty of 1229, in the same article where the *detskii* was assigned the task of presenting the litigants before the elder (*starosta*), the obverse of the provision, making the regulation applicable to the Livonians, forsook the term *detskii* and used *birich* instead.⁶⁵ The Novgorod Judicial Charter outlined the functions of the *birich* in a pair of articles. According to the first, the *birich* and his equivalents were compensated according to a specified schedule for their trouble in fetching witnesses, a regulation reminiscent of the fee schedule for bailiffs in the 1497 Sudebnik. The second article, also strongly reminiscent of later Muscovite norms, provided that a default judgment could be issued if the litigant did not appear at court at the specified time, even after the *birichi* had shouted out the appointment.⁶⁶

The Novgorod Judicial Charter, however, does not consistently identify and distinguish these functions by name. In Novgorod texts the *birich* was paired with the *izvetnik, podvoiskii, sof'ianin* and others, none of whom was consistently distinguished from the others. The *izvetnik* received but one identification in the Novgorod Charter alongside the *birich*.⁶⁷ By the terms of the 1470-1471 Treaty of Novgorod with Lithuania, the *izvetnik* was to carry out court summonses. But only once does the *izvetnik* appear in Novgorod chronicles, and only several times in later Muscovite redactions.⁶⁸ In short, there is not sufficient information to determine if the *izvetnik* actually represented a formal, specialized intermediary. The fact that the *birich* is sometimes paired with the *iabetnik* has prompted some speculation that the *izvetnik* and *iabetnik* shared a common origin, but there seems to be little basis for such a conclusion.⁶⁹

The *iabetnik* is mentioned in the list of protected officials in article one of the Short Pravda.⁷⁰ The link with the *birich* suggests that he fulfilled some sort of judicial function, but the later history of this term is associated with an entirely separate strain of interpretation to do with slander and false accusations.[71] It may be that the very exercise of a bailiff's functions brought the *iabetniki* into the regular practice of calumny as a means of enrichment, since criminal conviction brought judicial officials various fees and led to the confiscation of the criminal's property.[72] The same argument is used to deduce somewhat tenuously the exercise of judicial functions by *iabetniki* in Novgorod from allusions in a twelfth-century birch bark document.[73] In fact, however, there are no solid explanations for the origin of the term or the functions its bearer executed.[74]

Still more ambiguous is the term *sof'iane*, evidently derived from the attachment of these servitors to the court of the Novgorod Archbishop at the Cathedral of St. Sophia. Mentioned only once in the Novgorod Judicial Charter in the same collective with the *birich* and *izvetnik*, the *sof'iane* may have acted as special bailiffs or police agents for the Archbishop's court, though there is no direct confirmation of that.[75] As before, such an understanding is dependent upon the simple association of the *sof'iane* with the *birichi*, also presumed to be some sort of court agents.

The key figure in such an argument by association is the *podvoiskii*, a term which, like *detskii*, made the transition from the northwestern city-republics to Muscovy's judicial chancelleries. The *podvoiskii* may well have originated as a military rank in much the same fashion as the *mechnik* or others in the prince's retinue. The etymology of the name, based on the word for army (*voi*), seems to support that origin.[76] In at least one reference, the *podvoiskii* is grouped with the notables who fell in battle, and even is identified with boyars.[77] As a judicial officer, the *podvoiskii* seems to have appeared first in Novgorod, and is recalled in its chronicle in that function under the years 1200, 1231, and 1269.[78] By the time of the promulgation of the Novgorod Judicial Charter, the *podvoiskii* was an established, though perhaps not a standing judicial officer, since confusion persisted among several apparently equivalent titles.[79] Together with the *birich*, *sof'ianin* and *izvetnik*, he is mentioned in a single article of the Novgorod Judicial Charter according to which travel fees were paid for bringing witnesses to court.[80] His bailiff functions are identified absolutely in the 1471 Karostyn Treaty with Moscow. The summonses that applied to residents of Novgorod districts were to be carried out by *podvoiskie* both of the Muscovite grand prince and Novgorod.[81] A fourteenth-century Novgorod contract features the *podvoiskii* in clear exercise of a bailiff's duties—presenting the contracting parties before the court.[82] An earlier reference to the *podvoiskii* permits a less juridical implication, and suggests that the *podvoiskie*, like some other officials of princely estate, had their origin in the personal domain of the prince.[83]

Pskov law contains even more frequent and detailed references to the *podvoiskie*. The *podvoiskii* was an agent of the city assembly (*veche*), as indicated by the fact that Pskov law contrasted him with the prince's men sent on missions of summons. His travel fees were listed by distance, as in Novgorod.[84] In each case the activity of the *podvoiskii* and the prince's men is associated with a term (*pristavnoe*) whose root denoted a fifteenth-century Muscovite bailiff (*pristav*). Nevertheless, Muscovy, too, adopted the *podvoiskii*. The 1397 Dvina Administrative Charter clearly identified the *podvoiskii* as the official responsible for summoning litigants to court, and provided for his sustenance from trade fees.[85] Since the Dvina land was previously under Novgorod's control, Muscovy may well have simply adopted local terminology. But the *podvoiskii* makes an occasional appearance in later Muscovite documents as well, including the 1497 Sudebnik.[86]

Careful scrutiny of each of the early police or bailiff functionaries reveals certain common features. It must first be noted, however, that the information on the earliest such officials suspected of fulfilling the most elementary forms of mediation is not very clear, and deductions based on these skimpy citations must be viewed with caution. The common thread by which the various proto-bailiffs are linked is their participation in the prince's personal retinue. This duty, in turn, brought each of the servitors the responsibility for military service. Such circumstances suggest that when completing their appointed proto-judicial functions, they were only fulfilling tasks assigned on an informal and temporary basis, as opposed to the specialization observable in the later bailiff's activities. From the earliest citations it is certain only that the *detskii* and *mechnik* had some role in the administration of the iron ordeal. In Smolensk the *detskii* evidently fulfilled the basic obligations of presenting litigants to the court. On one occasion the *detskii* was confused with the *birich*, an official with similar duties in Novgorod. The *birich*, in turn, is linked to several functionaries each of whom fulfilled the minimal tasks of presenting litigants and witnesses before the court. Only one official, the *podvoiskii*, has a sufficiently well-documented history to allow us to see in him a genuine predecessor of the Muscovite bailiffs. But even this development is far removed from the information supplied by the Russkaia Pravda, and is documented in judicial codes of a relatively late period from the northwestern city-republics.

To be sure, judicial tasks increasingly became the preserve of a specialized staff of enforcers, especially under the aegis of the city-republics of Pskov and Novgorod. Here officials once sponsored by the princely court came under the protection of the municipal structure, and in later documents were distinguished from the princely bailiffs. In the same cities general social differentiation made the most significant advances, a situation that must be expected to have had its consequences in the general administration of the city as well. But even in the Novgorod and Pskov codes the specialization in administration was evidently not secure. Both the Pskov and Novgorod Charters include a number of different terms to describe what seems to have been the same job.[87] In these cities, where the role of written evidence and the assignment of court appearance through documents had made such headway, there existed a natural base for the increased specialization of court personnel, both in the composition of court documents and in their execution by the bailiffs. It was this tradition which found such a warm reception in Muscovite law.

Still, all the court's petty officials and their tasks, to the extent that anything is known about them, are connected only with one aspect of the intermediary process. The *detskii* was to separate litigants in inheritance suits; in Smolensk he was to present the disputants at court, essentially the same task elaborated upon in Pskov and Novgorod somewhat later. In none of this was any bailiff charged with executing sanctions upon the guilty. In fact, it was only in Pskov that the administration of physical sanctions was assigned to the bailiffs, thereby converting their functions into something closer to those of police.[88] Nevertheless, even by Weber's most guarded definition it is difficult to see in the various bailiffs of medieval Russia, at least in the thirteenth century, a staff of persons specially oriented toward the observation of the regulatory order. These elementary mediators constituted a weakly developed form of third-party presence, something more forceful than the "invisible mediator" of Barkun, and something more than the mediator-experts that seem to serve as a transition to more formal modes of arbitration. But in light of the evidence available, they fall far short of the demands that command-theory would make of them, and illustrate further the essentially dyadic nature of conflict resolution in Russia in the thirteenth century.[89]

The development of a formal system of mediation in early Russia occurred first in Pskov and Novgorod. The administrative and power hierarchy which characterized Muscovy late in the fifteenth century was not fully achieved, however, even in Novgorod and Pskov, possibly because of the mixture of claims there among church, prince, and what might be called democratic elements. Intermediary institutions fell under disparate influences, a consideration which was reflected in the uncertain identification of the police apparatus.[90]

Novgorod had removed itself from the dominance of the Kievan princes and made the transition to a republican form of government in the twelfth century.[91] The main administrative figure that emerged from the events of the third and fourth decades of that century was the mayor (*posadnik*). This office had originated with princely administration of an early date. Vladimir had placed such representatives in numerous towns as early as 988, but in Novgorod the mayor was known even earlier.[92] The *posadnik*'s name seems to have been derived from the very process of representing the prince, whereby the prince placed (*posadi*) his men in the towns, including Novgorod.[93] Such an explanation is supported in the scholarly literature by those who see the *posadnik* as an antecedent to the prince's representative in later Muscovy, the *namestnik*.[94] As the evidence from Novgorod and Smolensk indicates, only in the twelfth century did the mayor fall from under the aegis of the princes and become an instrument of municipal administration.[95] The Novgorod Charter, copied after the Moscow takeover, reinforces the distinction and often specifically contrasts the mayor with the prince's men.[96]

In Novgorod the mayor was empowered to hear suits in conjunction with the prince's representative, the *namestnik*. But review of court proceedings was reserved strictly for the prince and the *tiun*, his assistant in these matters.[97] Consequently, despite the power rivalries built into Novgorod judicial proceedings, the court system implies the vertical drift of litigation that became so pronounced in later Muscovy. In fact, the referral (*doklad*) outlined later in the Charter strongly resembles the process adopted in the 1497 Sudebnik.[98]

A far larger role in the secular courts of Novgorod was played by the *tysiatskii*, still another member of the judiciary of medieval Russia who had his origins in the exercise of military functions.[99] The Russkaia Pravda underlines the military role of the *tysiatskie*, who are identified as members of the princely retinue.[100] But in Novgorod the *tysiatskii* served as a judge in certain trade cases, and in others acted as an assistant to the mayor.[101] At least one text suggests that the *tysiatskii*, like the archepiscopal representative (*namestnik*) and the municipal mayor, supervised a staff of judges.[102] The Novgorod *tysiatskii* dates back to the twelfth century in Novgorod's treaty with Gotland. There he was contrasted with the prince and joined already with the mayors and the other Novgorodians.[103] The succeeding thirteenth-century treaties between Novgorod and its princes reveal the same association of mayors and *tysiatskie*, both contrasted with the prince's position.[104] Even late in the fifteenth century the court of the *tysiatskii* maintained a lively and strictly defended existence.[105]

The *namestnik*, the name given to the prince's representative in Novgorod, also exercised judicial functions, and was aided in this task by a deputy (*tiun*).[106] As always, the Novgorodians were anxious to protect their court rights against infringement by the prince's officials. The fifteenth-century treaty with Lithuania shows their apprehensions about incursions into Novgorodian courts by the prince's deputies.[107] The *tiun*'s court was to be conducted in the presence of a bailiff (*pristav*) from outside, presumably another attempt at limiting the scope of the prince's judicial apparatus.[108] The same general line of defense is repeated many times in Novgorod's thirteenth-century agreements with its princes.[109] Subsequently the deputy's court found a secure place in the prince-centered judicial hierarchy of Muscovy.[110]

Pskov's judicial system closely resembled that of Novgorod. There, too, the mayor headed the city's court administration. The Pskov Judicial Charter emphasized the mayor's importance by requiring that all cases pending before his court had to be completed before the end of any mayor's term of office.[111] As in Novgorod, Pskov adjudication was sought jealously by a number of aspirants to power. The church had its court, headed by the archbishop's *namestnik*.[112] The prince, too, was involved in matters of justice. Although the text mentions the prince himself as a judge together with the mayor, doubtless much of his court function was delegated to assistants whose judicial role is attested elsewhere in the charter.[113]

In both cities, then, one may see a certain confused movement toward vertical structures, obscured somewhat both by the relative power of the church and the limitations on princely authority. The judicial authorities of Pskov and Novgorod show a certain affinity with the shadowy characters of earlier princely administration, and only with the twelfth century seem to have shed their linkage with the personal suite of the princes. The mayor, the direct heir of the prince's system of apportioning the spoil and reins of government throughout early Russia, and once the temporary, unspecialized representative of the prince's personal authority, became in Novgorod a nominee of the city assembly. From this position, he conducted trials in conjunction with the prince's appointee and thereby effectively institutionalized his role as mediator, and simultaneously established the lines of authority. The *tysiatskii*, too, moved from princely to popular patronage. As was the case with many of the agents of judicial administration already examined, his military origins facilitated the transfer to judicial functions, and, once severed from the princely connection, the *tysiatskii* developed into a specialized judicial officer.

The trend toward judicial specialization among the officials of the popular courts had its parallel among the officers of the prince's court. The prince's adjutant (*namestnik*), after 1471 the heir to the role once played by the *posadnik*, found a specialized judicial function even under the limiting circumstances of litigation in Novgorod and Pskov. One may doubt whether he performed these duties to the exclusion of the myriad other matters in which the prince was interested, but even on the basis of the surviving documentation it is clear that the prince's adjutant already performed a significant role in the conduct of trials in early Novgorod.[114] The archbishop's court likewise was represented by a *namestnik*.[115] A portion of these judicial functions came to be appropriated by the adjutant's deputy (*tiun*), who also had emerged from earlier service in the personal retinue of the prince to develop considerable leverage in adjudication both in Pskov and Novgorod. His judicial power is attested by the frequent expression of concern for the maintenance of proper balance in the deputy's court.[116] Although the local judicial organs did not survive either as an incorporated part of the Muscovite system or on an independent basis after Muscovite annexation, both the prince's adjutant and his deputy survived in the judicial administration created in the fifteenth century by the Muscovite princes.

In its most visible form, mediation is carried out not only by judges, but also by the police, who assist the courts in bringing conflicts to a resolution. The *detskii, mechnik,* and *podvoiskii* fulfilled some police functions in the thirteenth and fourteenth centuries, especially in Smolensk. In both Pskov and Novgorod, police duties took on a more permanent aspect, and at the same time, by absorbing some of the tasks of enforcement, moved closer to being a kind of formal enforcement staff.

The differentiation of police duties took some time. The list of Novgorod officials charged with such tasks demonstrates some overlapping among *podvoiskii, sof'ianin, birich, izvetnik, pristav, dvorianin,* and *pozovnik*.[117] Most of these officials disappeared with the rise of Muscovy. Of the first four, only the *podvoiskii* continued to be mentioned in later Muscovite judicial texts. The last three functionaries had a longer history. The *pozovnik* clearly derived his name from the particular duty to which he was assigned—the calling of litigants or witnesses to trial.[118] It is certain from fifteenth-century sources that this task was subsequently appropriated by various bailiffs, but the *pozovnik* indicates the early specialization under way in Novgorod's judiciary.[119]

The term *dvorianin* embodied a more generalized meaning, derived evidently from someone present at the prince's court (*dvor*).[120] The basic root (*dvor*) is shared with a host of other terms applied to various princely functionaries—*dvorskii, dvoretskii, dvornik*. Though each term seems to have followed an independent course, they are all linked by the proximity of their bearers to the prince.[121] The *dvor* is identified in the Russkaia Pravda as the princely estate, and its early administrators, the *ognishchanin* and *tiun*, probably represent the antecedents to the later *dvoriane*.[122] Muscovite documents use the term *dvoriane* in the sense of the prince's assistants, thereby continuing the original meaning.[123] Novgorod texts connect the *dvoriane* with the prince's revenue-gathering, and serve to underline the still indistinct job differentiation.[124]

The *pristav* also originated in the exercise of indeterminate functions. The root of the word by which he is described denotes the issuance of an order (*pristaviti*) which the *pristav* carried out.[125] Again, his specific functions are not identified, and like the *dvorianin* the *pristav* must have had his beginnings in the exercise of general service to the prince. Two of the earliest references connect him with the Tatars, though an immunity charter of the early fourteenth century uses a specifically Tatar term (*begul*) to signify a *pristav*.[126] One of Novgorod's thirteenth-century treaties identifies the *pristav* with the prince's administration, though it is not clear that he exercised judicial tasks.[127] But the term begins to appear regularly in princely treaties and wills in the second half of the fourteenth century, and in the surviving documents of private law only in the fifteenth century.[128] In the Novgorod chronicle, he is mentioned only in two fifteenth-century entries, while the single birch bark charter which includes the *pristav* seems to belong likewise to the fifteenth century.[129] The relatively late appearance of this term in the thirteenth century suggests that the office which it described was perhaps a refinement of earlier, undefined activities carried out by the *detskii, otrok, mechnik*, and others.[130] The apparent confusion in terms used to describe the activities of bailiffs in the Novgorod and Pskov Charters seems to confirm such a view. But in both codes, at least in the redactions in which they survive, the *pristav* stands out as having already attained a predominant position in the execution of tasks associated as well with the *birich, izvetnik, podvoiskii*, and *dvorianin*.[131] While these last officials virtually disappeared as judicial intermediaries in Muscovy, the *pristav* occupied a prominent place in the major Muscovite legal texts of the fifteenth century.[132]

According to the Novgorod Judicial Charter, the *pristav* was to be present at the *tiun*'s court, one *pristav* for each litigant. Likewise at the review hearings conducted at the Archbishop's court, each side was fortified by the presence of its own *pristav*.[133] The partisan nature of these officials is indicated specifically still a third time in the Novgorod Charter. In cases of land litigation where the judge delayed the proceedings unreasonably, the plaintiff could select *pristava* to attend the proceedings, thereby presumably prodding the tardy adjudicator into completing the case. In this setting the *pristava* were taken from the city administration.[134]

The final mention of the *pristav* in the remaining portion of the Novgorod Charter confirms his association with the administration. The issuance of a judgment charter was the signal for the loser to comply with the court's requirements including the payment of the appropriate fees. Failure to comply within a month led to the plaintiff's petition for satisfaction, an action insured by the release of *pristava* from the city assembly (*s vecha*). Intentional shirking of obligations outlined in the court decision led to the malingerer's punishment on behalf of the city itself ("then let all Novgorod the Great punish him").[135]

The introduction of the *pristav* into the business of sanctions and the enforcement of judicial decisions represents a crucial step toward the establishment of police officials in a vertical system. Though the *pristav* may have continued the less formal tasks associated with summoning defendants and witnesses, and the informal mediation like that described for the *detskii* in the Russkaia Pravda, the Novgorod Charter makes clear that the right to dispense the services of the *pristav* was the prerogative of the political authority, in this case, the assembly.[136] To be sure, the specialization of tasks still was not firmly established, given the propensity of the Charter's compilers to utilize other similar officials for similar tasks.[137] But the predominance of the *pristav*, coupled with his association with the Novgorod city assembly, suggests the emergence of a public police apparatus, even in the confused political circumstances of Novgorod.

The police functions of the *pristav* are displayed more clearly in Pskov law. A long provision of the Pskov Charter outlined in detail the obligation incumbent upon the *pristav* to investigate criminal offenses. As in Novgorod, the authority to permit investigative activity was reserved to the political structure, in this case, the prince and mayor.[138] The *pristav* was not alone responsible for carrying out the investigation, since the plaintiff was expected to accompany him on the search. The instigator of such actions also was held responsible for the *pristav*'s fees in the event that the investigation did not reveal evidence of the offense for which the bailiff had been summoned.[139] Consequently, while the *pristav* represented a specialized assistant to the litigant, his presence did not affect the essentially dyadic nature of litigation.

As in Novgorod, the Pskov *pristav* functioned as a kind of community representative. In this capacity he was required to be present at the conclusion of agreements. The sale of a tenant's goods, conducted in his lord's interest in recouping his original investment in the tenant's agricultural inventory, also was to be completed in the *pristav*'s presence. The process was initiated in the same way as were criminal suits, the plaintiff petitioning for a *pristav* from the prince or mayor. In this way the *pristav* affirmed the validity of the transaction on behalf of the political structure.[140] Likewise the *pristava* were expected to be present, one to a side, at the conduct of judicial duels.[141]

The *pristav*, however, was not the sole executor of constabulary functions in Pskov. As before, the *podvoiskii, dvorianin,* and *pozovnik* are recalled in this sense, though the text makes clear that they are but particular names for the general activity of the *pristav*.[142] A new term, *podvernik*, derived presumably from this official's position at the door (*dver'*), also is associated with *pristav* activity. The *podverniki* were adjured not to ruin the innocent, a situation reminiscent of another provision designed to aid in eliminating the corrupt bailiffs from the Pskov court system.[143]

Increasingly the *pristav* was associated with the prince's administration, sometimes replaced in the text of the Pskov code by the more generalized expression, the prince's man (*kniazhei chelovek*). At the same time the *podvoiskii* was appropriated by the Pskov city assembly structure.[144] This represents the same process of institutionalization which took place in Novgorod, but one may find in Pskov law a more direct application of the *pristava* to the work of sanctions. In one article, the previously developed features of bailiff work, namely the delivery and presentation of litigants and witnesses, were grouped with the task of securing the defendant in chains.[145] By the terms of another provision the *pristav* was recognized as possessing the right to arrest a thief or debtor. The context of the article, indicating that the defendant's wife suffered a miscarriage, implies that the transaction took place under conditions of coercion.[146]

It is important to recall that the *pristav* did not execute all these functions at his own instigation, nor even at that of the prince's or city's courts. The plaintiff himself was obliged to seek redress by addressing himself to the prince and mayor. He accompanied the *pristav*, as is obvious not only from the direct notices of the Charter, but by the Charter's concern for plaintiffs who conducted their own justice, once confronted by the accused. The instigator of a suit which proved unsuccessful had to bear the costs of dispatching the *pristav*. Therefore, when disputes were settled amicably without recourse to the police apparatus, no fees were collectable. Furthermore, the *pristava* evidently could legitimately refuse to fulfill a commission entrusted to them.[147] In Novgorod the plaintiff himself could summon the defendant to court, even without the aid of the *pristav*.[148] All this emphasizes the persistence of horizontal legal relations and their retardant effect on the development of a third-party enforcement staff.

The nascent administrative specialization in Novgorod and Pskov was not limited to enforcement personnel. In particular, a staff of intermediaries, connected with litigation only by virtue of their relation to the compilation and issuance of various written materials, makes a conspicuous appearance. The Russkaia Pravda made only slight reference to the composition of documents connected with judicial proceedings, and but one reference to a secretary (*pisets*).[149] But in Novgorod and Pskov litigation involved several elements of document preparation and authentication.

Novgorod's legal texts introduce a new term for a judicial secretary (*d'iak*). As noted above, the word bears a Greek root, and implies that the literate and juridically well-staffed church may have exerted some influence on the development of this position.[150] In any case, the Novgorod Judicial Charter required the participation of the secretary in various phases of litigation. He was expected to record judicial proceedings, and draw up judgment charters which solemnified the decision.[151] Presumably the secretary was also responsible for preparing documents which assigned dates of court appearances, and default charters which penalized those who missed their court date.[152] It is likely that court summonses, similar to the later bailiff documents of Muscovy, were executed by these same secretaries.[153] Exactly when the *d'iak* began to perform these duties is not known, but the practice of issuing documents in connection with litigation dates from at least the thirteenth century in Novgorod.[154]

Information about Pskov's scribal practices is more complete. Pskov did in fact use a written summons, the *pozyvnitsa*, read by the bailiff (*pozovnik*) before the church, either with or without the object of the summons present at the reading. The summons was followed by a bailiff document (*pristavnaia*), and either a default charter (*bezsudnaia*) or record of the litigation result (*sudnitsa*). Each was to be authenticated by the attachment of a seal, affixed either by the prince's representative or by an agent of the Holy Trinity Cathedral, the repository of official documents in Pskov.[155] The scribes identified in the Pskov Charter are not *d'iaki* but *pistsy*, a distinction that harks back to the scribal practices of the Russkaia Pravda. Only one article of the Pskov code mentions *d'iaki* in connection with the town administration and that of the prince.[156] The difference in terminology from both Novgorod and Muscovy indicates that Pskov's path to document compilation differed from that of its sister city, Novgorod, and from Moscow, its successor.

The judicial systems established by Pskov and Novgorod law reveal characteristics of both lateral and vertical legal relations. The development of effective intermediary personnel clearly did not reach such levels that the investigation and prosecution of criminal activity were appropriated exclusively by state organs. At most, the Pskov and Novgorod police agents assisted the complainants in the resolution of their disputes, and in restricted cases seem to have been responsible for carrying out the verdict of the court. The duties of applying sanctions are less clearly spelled out, though there is reason to think that the various bailiffs did on occasion undertake these functions too.[157] But even here, the police officials were not distinguished by job specialization.

Muscovite Judicial Personnel

The maturation of the trend toward vertical legal relations took place only in Muscovy, both the conqueror of the political structures of the city-republics and heir to the legal institutions developed there. The victory of Moscow, and the implicit victory of the church whose head was allied with the Moscow princes, also signaled the victory of the prince's men and institutions in matters of administration and justice.

The early history of Muscovite administration is shrouded in that mystery born of insufficient documentation. The earliest form of local administration to emerge from the Moscow principality was the *put'*. The meaning of this term, a path or route, suggests that at its root it may have resembled the old form of revenue collection practiced by the Kievan princes (*poliu'de*), whereby the prince and his retinue traveled through the lands subject to princely authority and collected tribute (*dan'*).[158] In fact, some of the earliest references to the *put'* connect it with the collection of tribute and the provisioning (*kormlenie*) requirements of its collectors. A Novgorod document of the late thirteenth or early fourteenth century, for example, prescribes income collection "along the tribute route" (*po dannichu puti*). The text adds the prince's concern for the provisioning requirements.[159] One fourteenth-century treaty, in discussing the tribute collections by the princes' boyars, prescribed that these agents were to give the prince what was collected "in the course of provisioning and along the [tribute] route" (*po kormlen'iu i po putem*).[160] Other inter-princely agreements also tie the *put'* to general revenue collection. One document, for example, calls for the distribution of half the taxes (*poshliny*) of Nizhnii Novgorod— "and Kurmysh with all the villages and with the beehives and with the *puti* and with [those] fees and from everything which is subject to taxation in [those villages]."[161]

To be sure, a few references are not conclusive evidence that the prince's officials made infrequent forays into the countryside for revenue collection and that subsequently the tribute routes were converted into judicial circuits. But the early history of European justice developed precisely according to this pattern. The English sheriff, perhaps the best documented medieval officer who had any judicial obligations, was responsible nevertheless for the king's revenue above all else. Naturally the sheriffs fell victim to accusations of financial oppression, a not unlikely consequence of the relatively loose controls which the king exercised over the sheriffs who "farmed" their local districts for all they were worth.[162] From an early time the sheriff made periodic visits throughout the countryside in search of revenue, and the local populace had to bear the costs of feeding and provisioning him and his assistants.[163] Among the assistants may be counted some form of under-bailiff and a clerk or scribe. They, too, were unsalaried and fed off the general revenue which their rural excursions produced.[164] Certainly the exercise of justice played a part in revenue production, but justice was not the sole, or even the most important, source of revenue for the medieval English officials. At various times they collected the royal revenues, supervised royal estates, and in general performed any request made of them by the king.[165] The mixture of judicial, administrative, and financial functions was not unique to the English sheriffs, but colored the activity of medieval royal servants in much of Europe.[166]

It is not outrageous, then, to suspect that the medieval servants of the Russian princes may have performed similarly diverse duties. Clearly the *put'* remained a vital income source for the early Muscovite princes, who sometimes assigned their sons such *puti* as a suitable means of maintaining the young princes.[167] There are traces surviving from the mid-fourteenth century that others of the prince's own household staff held sway over particular *puti*: the falconer, gardener, stable-master, and huntsman.[168] From the fifteenth century we have relatively few references to the *puti*, but these too suggest that the *put'* still existed as a simple means of enriching the administrators associated with these districts.[169]

At some point the term *put'* was applied to the administrative unit itself, a factor which has introduced considerable confusion into the discussion. It may be that the process of income production became identified with the territory where it was carried out, and in that sense survived in later documents.[170] The first instances where judicial fines (*prodazhi*) are mentioned also convey the impression that the initial attempts of the medieval Russian princes to control justice were little more than a variation on taxation.[171] Furthermore, while the English monarchs, for example, attempted to control the rapacity of their underlings from a very early time, limitations on bribe-taking and justice for profit made little progress in Russia before 1497.[172]

The irregular sources of revenue and justice could not last long in view of the new demands made upon Muscovite administration, especially with the annexation of new territories late in the fifteenth century. The new administrative forms that developed in Muscovite territory suffered none of the encumbrances of overlapping authority that were so evident in Pskov and Novgorod. The Muscovite princes were not obliged to share power with a popular assembly like those which emerged in the city-republics. The church officials who resettled in Moscow in the fourteenth century cast their lot with the princes, and subsequently never effectively challenged the growth of the vertical structure developed by them.[173]

The temporary advantage of Moscow in the Dvina lands gave the Moscow Prince Vasilii Dmitrievich the chance to demonstrate the best of administrative innovations. The Dvina Administrative Charter presents the *namestnik*, also encountered in Novgorod's princely administration, who was to act as the prince's personal deputy in the hinterland. In some respects the *namestnik* institutionalized the formal intermediary, especially in light of the prohibition of private justice.[174] In other respects the lateral legal relations of the Russkaia Pravda continued with some vitality. The confrontment procedure (*svod*), for example, was recognized in the code, and the prince's officials were specifically excluded from collecting fees in this process. Similarly, the identification and pursuit of murderers was left to popular initiative, and the bloodwite remained payable to the prince's deputy when the offender was not produced. Reconciliation among disputants at banquets (*piry*) also brought no interference from the prince's adjutants, as long as the dispute did not linger beyond the banquet itself.[175]

Despite this bow to custom and the dominance of lateral relations, the new apparatus made a sizable showing. Most impressive is the presumption of hierarchy expressed by the Moscow Grand Prince, Vasilii Dmitrievich. He, Grand Prince of all Russia, granted his Dvina boyars the Dvina lands, and pledged that his *namestnik* would operate according to the provisions of the document he had issued. Violators were threatened with punishment. Thefts committed against the Dvina people in the towns of Ustiug, Vologda, or Kostroma could cause the convocation of court before the grand prince himself. In short, the Dvina Administrative Charter promulgates in outline a judicial hierarchy centered in Moscow.[176]

The *namestnik*, however, was not a Muscovite innovation.[177] As noted above, the early princes of Kievan Russia used the term to identify their officials; and Novgorod and Pskov law, too, accorded the *namestnik* a place in administration. One redaction of Vladimir's Statute also mentions the *namestnik*, along with the *tiun* or judge, as one who might impinge upon the immunity that the Statute granted to church courts.[178] This reading is included in the Synod Kormchaia addenda copied sometime in the fourteenth century, which seems a likely time of origin for the term, at least in the sense in which it was used in later medieval administration.[179] Variations in later copies of the Russkaia Pravda support this chronology. Two Muscovite copies (Karamzin group) provided for the *namestnik*'s participation in apprehending fugitive slaves. A slaveowner who discovered his slave missing was to communicate this finding to the *namestnik*, and take from him an *otrok*, presumably to assist in the capture.[180] Since the copies themselves date from the late fifteenth or early sixteenth century, and since fourteenth- and early fifteenth-century copies do not reflect the new term, it seems likely that the two Karamzin copies simply accommodated themselves to the prevailing forms of administration of that period.[181]

At any rate, only in the fourteenth century does the *namestnik* begin to appear frequently in the sources. The Pravosudie Mitropolich'e, probably of fourteenth-century origin, identifies the *namestnik* as an official of the Metropolitan.[182] In inter-princely treaties, beginning from the mid-fourteenth century, the *namestnik* is often mentioned, sometimes even as a judge.[183] Fifteenth-century documents cite the *namestnik* with great regularity, and occasionally identify his judicial duties as a continuation of long-established practice.[184] Consequently, neither the *namestnik*'s appearance in the Dvina code, nor his exercise of judicial duties at that time, constituted any novelty.

Exactly how the *namestnik* system of administration evolved out of the *put'*, if in fact it did, is not clear. It may be that the *namestnik*, whose name indicates that he acted as the prince's surrogate, exercised the duties and privileges of the prince with the latter's authorization. The association of the *put'* with collection of the tribute suggests that the original excursions of these officials were made only for the collection of taxes, joined perhaps with the exercise of judicial functions. Some trace of such a procedure is retained in several documents dating from the 1440s.[185] The texts are immunity charters issued by Grand Prince Vasilii Vasil'evich, Dmitrii Shemiaka, and the Mozhaisk Prince Ivan Andreevich. All refer to the village of Prisetskoe located in Bezhetskii Verkh, an object of contention in the Muscovite civil war early in the fifteenth century.[186] The charters include the promise, made general in succeeding immunities for the fifteenth century, that the princely *namestniki* would not dispatch their agents (*dvoriane*) into that settlement, nor judge the people resident there in any offenses except murder. Likewise, the circuit or traveling court (*proezdnoi sud*) of the princely *namestniki* was neither to enter that settlement nor extract provisioning costs from the residents.[187]

Although the specific indication of a traveling court is not met again in the surviving documents, the significance of the exemption from the rapacity of the prince's servitors remained. Immunity charters exhorted the rural and urban judges (*volosteli* and *namestniki*) not to send their officials into the immunized territory, nor to permit their officials to be provisioned by the area's residents. The immunities also called on the judiciary's servants to take no fees from local residents and not to enter the immunized territory for any reason whatever (*ni v"ezzhaiut k nim ni po chto*).[188]

By the fifteenth century the *namestniki* and their rural counterparts, the *volosteli*, were well ensconced in Muscovy's judicial apparatus. Like the *namestnik*, the *volostel'* was known long before his absorption into Muscovite administration. The 1229 Smolensk Treaty with the German towns identified the *volostel'* as a local official, while Iaroslav's Statute clearly associated him with judicial functions.[189] The Novgorod Judicial Charter also recognized a clerical variant, and Pskov law made only brief reference to the *volostel'*.[190] But already in the mid-fourteenth century the *volostel'* was regularly mentioned in tandem with the *namestnik* in Muscovite documents.[191]

The official incorporation of the *volostel'* into Muscovite administration is noticeable somewhat later. The Dvina Administrative Charter did not include the *volostel'* in its judicial apparatus, but a few years afterward he was recalled, along with the *namestnik*, as a church administrative official in the agreement between Grand Prince Vasilii Dmitrievich and Metropolitan Fotii.[192] The actual administrative division that was to be clarified by the 1497 Sudebnik was first enunciated in the Statutory Regulation on Murder (*Zapis' o dushegubstve*), evidently promulgated in the reign of Vasilii Vasil'evich.[193] Crimes committed in the villages and countryside were to be heard by the *volostel'*, and the cases forwarded to Moscow, either to the grand prince, or in his absence, to the chief *namestnik*.[194] Admitting the *volostel'* to judicial competency independent of the *namestnik* indicates that the *volostel'* had already found a niche in Muscovy's judicial administration before the accession of Ivan III, and demonstrates the drift toward a judicial hierarchy centered in Moscow.[195]

The 1497 Sudebnik codified this plan, establishing a pyramid of courts in which the power of decision was vested in few hands. The pinnacle of justice consisted of the grand prince's own court, or that composed of members of his immediate family.[196] The concentration of power was diluted only by admitting certain select judges to the highest level of authority, the "boyar court" (*boiarskii sud*). Judges not entrusted with this commission were enjoined against deciding slavery, theft, and murder cases.[197] The holders of full jurisdiction were selected from the service elite, from the boyars and *okol'nichie*. The preamble to the Sudebnik itself suggests that the code was created exclusively for these servitors, to guide them in the conduct of adjudication. The occasional characterizations of the judges support this notion.[198]

In addition to laying down schedules of compensation for services performed by the judges and support personnel, the Sudebnik also concerned itself with certain matters of procedure, including the most obvious, judicial integrity. The Sudebnik inveighed against bribery and the exercise of favoritism, though the compilers could not bring themselves to make the officials personally responsible for such offenses. The very first article, which prescribed a kind of ideal attendance at judicial litigation, also included a provision by which a judge or secretary was prohibited from accepting bribes and from using the courts to avenge his own losses or promote his own friendships. A repetition of the injunction, enlarging attendance at the litigation proceedings, failed, like its predecessor, to mention any sanction against those inclined to favor the rich and slight the poor. Support personnel also were adjured not to favor some litigants over others, and a similar concern provoked a regulation enjoining bailiffs from using hired replacements.[199] But ignoring these regulations evidently brought no penalty from the administration, at least if one is to judge by the texts themselves.

The ruining of the innocent, which the Pskov Charter declared to be so odious, obviously had not disappeared in Muscovite courts. Bribes continued to have their effect upon the conduct of summons and adjudication. The long and frequent provisions devoted to fee collection and regulation in the Sudebnik do nothing to dispel the notion that justice was still primarily a function of revenue gathering.[200] Evidently that spirit penetrated the entire system, inasmuch as the Sudebnik's compilers found it necessary to point out that the bailiffs not only were prohibited from taking bribes from the defendants, but also were warned against extracting or accepting bribes proffered by the judges themselves.[201] Plainly the judges were not above using their underlings to engage in profit-making schemes on the side. Failing that, they were equally prepared to accomplish in court what their out-of-court urgings could not, as the Sudebnik attests in its warnings against concocted court convictions.[202] The discretion of the bailiff in putting criminals on bond also was restricted. In order to reduce the bailiffs' attempts to gain extra cash, the Sudebnik's compilers found it necessary to adjure the bailiffs not to sell thieves before a proper trial was held.[203] Finally, where the personal interests of the judges or bailiffs did not interfere, those of the litigants and their witnesses did. In something of an afterthought, in a provision tacked on to the end of the Sudebnik, the code prohibited these last from negating the consequences of justice by the easy path of bribery.[204]

Still, despite all the imprecations against the play of mankind's meanest instincts, only the lying witness, once discovered, faced any sort of financial or physical punishment for yielding to the temptation of personal gain. But careful examination of the surviving court records shows that conflicting testimony was no guarantee of stimulating the state's pristine wrath.[205] Consequently, the practical effects of the regulations against corruption, however noble their intention, are difficult to gauge.

The attention paid by the Sudebnik to questions of bribery would seem to indicate that Muscovy was already well on the way to establishing a vertical legal structure in the late fifteenth century. In fact, however, the high-sounding phrases of the Sudebnik ring hollow in the records that survive from the early sixteenth century. The judicio-administrative changes instituted in the second third of the century demonstrate that the rapacity of the government's officials was not assuaged by the fee schedules so carefully worked out in the 1497 Sudebnik. The 1539 local government (*guba*) statute for Beloozero, for example, suggests that local residents had petitioned the grand prince about the ineffectiveness of his officers. The government inspectors sent to the scene in response to the petitions seemingly used the occasion to despoil the local citizens of what wealth remained. The same refrain was sounded in later documents pertaining to other districts of Muscovy.[206] A 1552 plan for reorganizing local government in the Dvina region refers to still another petition from the locals. In this case the government alleged that it had received complaints blaming the depopulation of the district on the misbehavior of its administrators, ignominiously lumped together with thieves, brigands, and recidivist criminals, all of whom the Sudebnik had decreed worthy of execution.[207] In other words, even the highmindedness of the Sudebnik did not remove those traces of the old system whereby justice was but another name for the generation of income for the officials involved.

Despite the failures, there are signs that a triadic system of justice was emerging. The transition is revealed most clearly in the insistence upon documentation and the role specialization that characterized the court hierarchy in Muscovy. To bring a defendant to trial it was necessary to acquire the consent of the prince's judge, either *namestnik* or *volostel'*, who, in turn, required the services of scribe, secretary, and sealkeeper in order to prepare the necessary summons. Finally, a bailiff was called to execute the order.[208] Litigation itself also stimulated paper production. The trial record, judgment charter, postponement documents, and default charters each generated fees for the copyist, signer, and sealkeeper.[209] Slavery documents represented another whole area of income production.[210] In short, not only judges but numerous assistants as well were interposed between litigants.

More direct evidence of the trend toward a vertical structure of legal institutions is contained in the Sudebnik's provisions for seeking out socially opprobrious elements. Accusation of theft would bring the bailiff to the door of anyone so accused, and only a clean reputation could spare him some unpleasantness at the bailiff's hands. Even then the accusation was sufficient to earn the supposed culprit the obligation to pay the costs of the suit.[211] Reliance upon the general estimate of the community is, of course, exactly that notion of community consent which plays such a large role in the execution of revenge and composition in societies dominated by lateral legal relations. But the activity of the bailiff, reflecting the state's interest in capturing and punishing criminals, is surely symptomatic of the change to vertical relations, of the introduction of a notion of felony. Although the responsibility to make the charge still lay with the offended parties, investigation and prosecution were undertaken by the state organs.[212]

It is most significant that the Sudebnik makes specific allowance for the imposition of sanctions, including physical sanctions, upon the convicted. Even in making an arrest, the bailiffs exercised force to apprehend and secure the accused. Examination was accomplished through torture, while the Sudebnik prescribed the ultimate sanction for theft, robbery, murder, arson, church theft, criminal slander (*iabednichestvo*) and recidivist crime. Conviction based on the results of the duel sometimes won the criminal less drastic punishment. Otherwise, only first-time thieves escaped death.[213]

That key aspects of procedure still depended upon the complainant makes clear that the state judicial institutions had not gone wholesale into the business of prosecuting and investigating crimes. Although the first steps in that direction were worked out in the Sudebnik, elements of horizontal relations continued to express themselves. Accusation, relying upon the old forms of reconciliation, reappeared in Muscovite law, though in different guise. In its classic form, the judicial duel required the litigants themselves to fight to determine the vindication of the innocent and conviction of the guilty. Alternatively, disputants could become reconciled before the contest. This form of conflict resolution, though modified to suit the technology and mood of the times, still harks back to the principles of the Russkaia Pravda, and limits the state judicial organs to the simple supervision of the process.[214] The numerous sixteenth-century references to the duel are ample indication of the weight still attached to the lateral resolution of conflict. Only after the verdict had been reached under these circumstances did the state apparatus step in to implement the sanction.[215]

The key figure in the entire judicial structure, so carefully erected by the Sudebnik's compilers on the basis of Muscovite practice of the preceding century, was the bailiff. The Sudebnik lists several names for him, some of which appeared in earlier texts. *Pristav* is recalled in six articles,[216] *nedel'shchik* in thirteen,[217] *dovodchik* in only two,[218] and *podvoiskii* and *pravedchik* in but one each.[219] These officials were heirs to that system of mediation developed in Novgorod and Pskov, but in Muscovy their duties were more clearly defined.

The *pristav* was the predominant agent in the Muscovite courts throughout the fifteenth century. Already the Dvina code had specified restrictions on his visits into that territory, the type of provision under which this official is most frequently met in immunity charters of the fifteenth century.[220] Immunization from the *pristav*'s visitations may be dated with certainty to at least the mid-fourteenth century in the inter-princely treaties, and continued to be expressed in the various exemptions given private landholders in the next century.[221] Exemption was made more systematic in the Beloozero Administrative Charter, according to which the *pristav*'s entry into that territory was limited to a single foray during Lent.[222]

Attempts at similar limitations were expressed in particular immunities issued in the course of the fifteenth century.[223]

The interest of the landholders in escaping the *pristav*'s activity suggests that his presence was not desirable. Chief among the objections to his coming was the cost. Local residents were required to provide him with food and provisions, and therefore authorities limited the time any *pristav* might spend at any one location.[224] But the persistence with which the landholders evidently sought, and, at any rate, were awarded immunization from *pristav* activity suggests an even more pressing stimulus. It may be that initially the *pristav*, like other early administrative officials, was still involved in revenue collection. One fourteenth-century entry in the chronicles confirms this view.[225]

But the majority of the surviving citations assign the *pristav* only police functions. Certainly he fulfilled what might be called custodial duties, maintaining persons under guard.[226] One citation even indicates that he maintained the accused in chains.[227] In executing court summonses the *pristav* had to complete bonding arrangements to guarantee court appearances. Bond duties were an outgrowth of the reason for the visit, namely, to summon the accused before the court, and it was evidently under this rubric that the limitation upon the *pristav* visits was issued. The landholders were interested in keeping their peasants away from foot-dragging litigation whenever possible.[228]

Of the other bailiffs recalled in the Sudebnik, the *dovodchik* and *pravedchik* are also met regularly in fifteenth-century texts. Like the *pristava*, they were prevented from troubling the immunity recipient with the promise that the prince would not send them into those territories.[229] They too were to receive provisioning at the hands of the local population, a factor that prompted the inclusion of specific exemption from their spending the night among the immunized residents.[230] Immunity holders also were spared the fee collections undertaken by the *dovodchiki* and *pravedchiki*.[231] Both officials were the obvious equivalents of the *pristava*, often taking their places in immunity grants.[232] Some later documents even provide direct equation of all three, along with the sixteenth-century variation, the *nedel'shchik*.[233]

Both the *pravedchik* and *dovodchik* appear exclusively in documents from northeast Russia.[234] The former derived his title from the verb *praviti*, "to rule" or "carry out." The name no doubt bore a general connotation at first, but later came to signify the execution of tasks associated with the collection of court fees and similar work.[235] The *dovodchik*'s name hints even more directly at his judicial status. *Dovod* signifies "clue" or "evidence" and implies that the *dovodchik* performed more of the activity of judicial investigation, but this interpretation seems extreme, at least for the fourteenth century.[236] More likely the *dovodchik* had his roots in the same task of revenue gathering. Kliuchevskii applied this conclusion with very little conviction to an argument whereby *dovod* was related to, or a corruption of, *dokhod* (income) and therefore tied to fee collection.[237] A more likely alternative is that the official was obliged (*v dovode*) to fulfill various occasional missions assigned him by the prince.[238]

By late in the fifteenth century these bailiffs were attached to the regular judicio-administrative apparatus. The Beloozero Administrative Charter of 1488, for example, assigned the urban *namestnik* two *tiuny* and ten *dovodchiki*—two for use in the town and eight for the rural districts. Each was apportioned a separate district, and denied the right to travel on official business outside that region. The normal allotment of bailiffs assigned the *namestniki* probably was somewhat fewer than ten, though there is no direct confirmation of that.[239]

The *nedel'shchik* mentioned in the 1497 Sudebnik became thereafter the dominant form of bailiff. Although known to some texts of the late fifteenth century, he appears more regularly in sixteenth-century materials, where he becomes identified specifically with the grand prince's courts.[240] Several documents identify him as a *pristav*, so that one may understand all the provisions of the Sudebnik as referring to the same kind of official, albeit under different titles. Herberstein's description of the *nedel'shchik*'s activity corroborates this general impression.[241]

The fact that the name of this official is derived from the word for week (*nedel'ia*) has given rise to speculation that connects the *nedel'shchik* with the *virnik* of the Russkaia Pravda. The latter, it is argued, had to complete his duties within a week, since his provisioning requirements were defined by the Short Pravda only for a week's duration.[242] However, the specific term *nedel'shchik* does not appear in any documents until the middle of the fifteenth century, by which time various other bailiff offices had already emerged. Nevertheless, the *nedel'shchik*'s name is connected with its etymological root, since these officers of the court served in alternate weeks.[243] Like most Muscovite court officials, the *nedel'shchiki* were drawn from the middle service class who found in their office a means of increasing their financial resources.[244]

The basic income of the bailiffs was derived from fees taken for summoning defendants or witnesses, whether by walking (*khozhenoe*) or riding (*ezdnoe*). The Sudebnik, like other monuments of Muscovite administration, showed great concern for the bailiff's pay.[245] Even before departing on his mission of summons, the bailiff was guaranteed the appropriate fees. Presentation of litigants before the judge, arranging postponements for trials, and handling bond for the accused and accuser were counted among the bailiff's duties.[246] In all these matters bailiffs were held responsible for their charges, which may explain the Sudebnik's exhortations to the bailiffs to remain alert and immune to the inducements of bribes.[247]

The Sudebnik prescribes capital punishment in several articles,[248] but in only one is there any indication regarding the mechanics of its execution. Article eight prescribed that the grand prince's *tiun* and steward (*dvorskii*) were to carry out the sentence. Both officials themselves exercised judicial functions, so that it is unclear why they also would wield the instruments of punishment.[249] Bailiffs, however, did conduct torture sessions and therefore were familiar with the devices of coercion.[250] If the death penalty was carried out at all, the bailiffs, rather than the *tiun* or *dvorskii*, were the likely executioners.

Judicial Personnel and the New Legal Order

The development of a specialized staff of enforcement personnel brought Muscovy a new legal order. The court structure put together so carefully by the Sudebnik is a good example of the hierarchy so typical of vertical systems. At its head stood the grand prince and his intimates who held full rights of trial. In these courts alone could the final outcome of litigation be decided. This preserve of power was protected by a relatively intricate system that isolated authentic decisions from their specious counterparts. The line of authority from inferior courts to the courts of decision was direct. The rural *volosteli* and all those *namestniki* without the right of boyar court were immediately subject to the authority of the prince or his representatives, and consequently, trial records were constantly in transit from the provinces to the capital and back again.

In the spirit of the monopoly of such rights first expressed in Pskov and Novgorod, prospective litigants were obliged to state their complaints to government officials and request from them the bailiffs necessary to track down the offenders. Formal processes of document authentication guaranteed the government its monopoly over the exercise of judicial summons and trial, and thereby created still another vertical element in the orientation of legal relations. Although punishment sometimes consisted of nothing more than recognizing the litigant's loss, the state apparatus gradually took under its own control the exercise of sanctions, and, by simultaneously prohibiting various forms of assault, also effectively monopolized (in theory, at any rate) compensation for wrongs. Under these circumstances the state organs of arbitration were able to exert significant control over the various forms of mediation, at least to the extent that they could control events. Obviously, the reality of such a monopoly was strongly dependent upon the extent of actual control exercised by government institutions in the districts, especially those far removed from the center of power. The evidence extracted from the sixteenth-century sources indicates that the government's jurisdiction was not uniformly effective throughout the state, and the application of formal mediation likewise remained incomplete.

Lateral legal relations continued to exist, side by side with the provisions of the new order. As before, the judicial apparatus was essentially a passive one, relying upon wronged individuals or threatened communities to initiate proceedings. But once the complaint was lodged, state officials took cases under their exclusive authority. Except in cases where they restored to theft victims their lost property when that possibility existed, state officials arrogated to themselves summons, trial, and punishment. However, the only sure route by which the state organs may be said to have introduced, or even sought, evidence was their fortuitous discovery of *prima facie* evidence. It requires only a small leap to reach this stage from identical principles first adumbrated in the Russkaia Pravda. The difference in Muscovy was that the process now required the services of an official intermediary. It was not sufficient for the plaintiff to announce his discovery and await the return of stolen property. A bailiff was required to bring the accused to court, an institution which itself occupied an intermediary position between accuser and the accused. Completion of litigation demanded still more intermediaries—secretaries, scribes, and sealkeepers. In essence, triadic legal relations were constructed out of these components, and the juridical separation of plaintiff and defendant effected.

CHAPTER 5

Patterns of Evidence

The problem of identifying offenders and determining the bases of identification may be resolved in different ways corresponding to the type of legal structure from which redress is sought. As one might expect, under the dominance of customary norms testimony bears an informal character where it is demanded, and often is omitted altogether in questions of delict. Where used, testimony depends to a large degree upon the witness's reputation in the community rather than upon questions of fact as construed in vertical legal systems. Community consensus suffices to determine the accuracy of an accusation and its retribution (revenge).[1] But this kind of testimony becomes increasingly inadequate in more heterogeneous societies where the system of consensus is more difficult to maintain. Consequently, one may expect in vertical systems more frequent reliance upon strictly delimited notions of fact and less reliance upon a person's standing in the community.[2]

At the same time, the significance of oral evidence is gradually eroded by the attempt to systematize and record various transactions, processes that provide a material base for questions of fact. Where formerly it was sufficient to rely upon the community wisdom and memory, documents now suspersede traditional values and displace the role of community elders in relating how things used to be. Furthermore, the documents themselves become identified with the existing political power, which appropriates the exclusive right to issue and confirm these records. Such an arrangement has the happy consequence of providing income for officials of the system by mandating specific fees for compilation, recording, and authenticating the myriad documents associated with various transactions. Piecework pay relieves the central treasury of full responsibility for supporting court functionaries, and allows for their multiplication at minimal costs, still further extending the outreach of the central apparatus.

A crucial step in this process is the introduction of some means of authenticating genuine records of the hierarchy, and thereby distinguishing them from other compositions that might compromise the factual base of litigation. This gives rise to such modern appurtenances of legal procedure as signatures and seals. Each represents an attempt to make the document unique to the particular circumstance to which it pertains, and thereby hinder the efforts of those determined to upset the process of ascertaining matters of fact. Again, this task results in employing still more officials who protect the instruments of verification. The entire process of differentiation in the work force becomes most pronounced in the elaboration of the power hierarchy itself. Scribes, sealkeepers, and their colleagues increasingly become a requisite part of legal procedure, just as the various instruments of enforcement accompany the development of sanctions.[3]

The introduction of such a neat system is, of course, resisted in illiterate societies. The meaning of a piece of paper, even with curious markings of special significance, cannot compare to the value of an observation made by a respected member of the community. Resistance may be expected to be most prolonged in just those areas where the power hierarchy has not effectively made its presence felt. Here character reputation will enjoy a much longer life as a basis of litigation.

The transition from informal to formal modes of evidence is perhaps the clearest example of the growth of the law in medieval Russia. At the dawn of the thirteenth century, accusation and ordeals served as substitutes for judicial review. Evidence went no further than the willingness of kinsmen or relatives to vouch for the accused. Questions of fact depended upon the memories of a community's eldest and most esteemed residents. Only gradually did informal proofs yield their place to the evidence of documents and testimony of fact. By the end of the fifteenth century, official Muscovy highly valued paper records and recognized the desirability of factual testimony. Certainly the triumph of formal proofs was hardly complete, but the law had acknowledged the need for change, and change there would be.

Testimony

Changes in the institution of testimony are representative both of the prolonged life of customary means of gathering evidence and of official attempts to introduce evidentiary innovations. The witness of medieval Russia, met most often under the name *poslukh*, was responsible for listening, as his name suggests. He was essentially a witness of reputation rather than any kind of eyewitness, a function described by another word altogether (*vidok*).[4] Even more clearly, the *poslukh* functioned as a representative of the community, who, by attending the conclusion of an agreement, formalized the pact.[5] The term was used this way in the Primary Chronicle, the Efrem

Kormchaia, the Questionary of Kirik, two Novgorod birch bark charters, and numerous other medieval texts.[6]

Often it has proved convenient for scholars to identify the *poslukh* as an eyewitness (the modern Russian *svidetel'*). But the legal process outlined in the Russkaia Pravda makes such an understanding impossible. The confrontation procedure (*svod*), described in both redactions of the Pravda, demanded only the participation of the complainant, who publicly lodged his accusation, and the accused, who sought to escape blame.[7] There was little room for introducing evidence, nor were there means of making that evidence palatable to judges, since litigation seems to have been conducted without judges. Either the complainant was satisfied or he was not.

The wording of the confrontation procedure makes clear the presumption that both parties would participate in reaching a rapid and just conclusion to the complaint. However, if either litigant were dissatisfied, testimony could play a role. Procedure dictated that a man accused of theft as a result of possessing stolen property had to identify the person from whom he had purchased the goods. Should memory fail him, the testimony of two freemen or the customs man (*mytnik*) was necessary to confirm his story.[8] The two freemen, like the customs man, obviously were witnesses of the sale, and in that sense could verify the facts even though they are not identified directly as witnesses. But the remaining provisions have given rise to more difficulty. In an apparent redundancy, the text calls on the buyer who forgot his seller to introduce witnesses to take the oath on his behalf (*to iti po nem' tem" vidokom" na rotu* [emphasis added]). Some redactions specify that the witnesses be from the market (*vidokom" na t"rgu na rotu*).[9] Consequently, in terms even more definite than those in the preceding section, the Pravda indicates that witnesses were present at the conclusion of the purchase/sale, and could, therefore, identify the seller. Some have attempted to explain the apparent repetition by suggesting that the two freemen and the customs man were identified subsequently by their functional name (*vidoki*) and put to the oath to strengthen their original testimony further. As a result, the term *vidok* could be used to represent anyone who witnessed such an agreement.[10]

A subsequent provision in the Expanded Pravda reproduces the same situation, but utilizes different terminology. When the confrontation led to another territory, it was discontinued and the person currently under accusation was required to produce witnesses or the customs man (*poslukhi liubo mytnika* [emphasis added]) before whom the goods were purchased.[11] These witnesses are clearly the same persons who attended the conclusion of an agreement, and therefore could verify it. In this sense they may be described as witnesses of fact, present at the event.

The apparent confusion of terms may be explained by reference to another regulation of the Pravda. The Short Pravda outlined the procedure for assault cases in which the victim was marked by bruises or blood. Witnesses to the fight are all identified as *vidoki*. But a clarification in the second part of the Short Pravda allowed that a man so bruised and bloodied did not have to produce a *poslukh* to support his claim.[12] The usual reading of these provisions makes some attempt at equating the two forms of testimony denoted by different terms. But the Expanded Pravda utilized both terms to summarize the legal options, and coincidentally elucidated the distinction in terminology. According to the Expanded Pravda, a man who claimed to have been beaten, but who bore no marks of the engagement, was to bring forward a *vidok* whose testimony was to be compared with his own, word for word. Evidently, the *vidok* was one who actually witnessed the fight, and testified to its course, participants, and so on. The second section of the same article allowed that the instigator, even though physically harmed, must pay for his offense, despite the assistance proffered by *poslusi*. Clearly the latter offered no factual testimony.[13]

If one compares this section with the other references to *poslusi* in the Russkaia Pravda, it becomes clear that the *poslusi* were simply character referents, whom Western medievalists know as compurgators, or those in attendance at the conclusion of an agreement. For example, a man accused of murder could escape conviction and the responsibility for paying the bloodwite if he could summon to his defense seven *poslusi*, while some privileged persons could escape with as few as two such witnesses.[14] The difference in numbers between the privileged and the ordinary sloggers only emphasizes the social overtones of the testimony. Besides, nowhere are the *poslusi* called upon to substantiate any particulars regarding the homicide.

The fickle quality of testimony is reinforced elsewhere in the Pravda. In one instance, a man unfortunate enough to be accused of murder and unable to produce any *poslusi* could turn the tables and accuse the accuser of the crime, thereby evening the score and making them both eligible for an ordeal.[15] As demonstrated above, as many as seven such witnesses could be demanded, but here, without even one, the accused might fare as well as his accuser under the searching eye of the red-hot iron. This is, of course, a logical reaffirmation of the essential equality between litigants observable in horizontal systems like that of the Pravda.

The affirmative nature of the role of the *poslusi* is endorsed in other provisions relating to trade matters. The Short Pravda envisions a situation where a trader victimized by his partner attempts to retrieve his share of the goods from his reluctant cohort. Here the Pravda prescribed the gathering of twelve men before whom the contest was to be heard. The magical number of twelve has mesmerized succeeding scholars, who find it easy to see a jury here.[16] But comparison with a similar provision in a Novgorod treaty demonstrates that these men were simply the representatives of the community known as *poslusi*, who saw to it that the norms of justice were upheld in the litigation before them.[17] In neither citation, nor indeed elsewhere in the texts, are the *poslusi* called upon to render a verdict or enforce a decision against the loser. They were obliged only to be present during the course of litigation.[18]

At the conclusion of agreements, *poslusi* also were expected to be present, but merchants sometimes were freed from this obligation. Suits over small sums could be resolved by one of the principals taking the oath. For large sums the testimony of those who witnessed the transaction could resolve the case. Should the lender have omitted the precaution of acquiring *poslusi*, his loss could be blamed solely on his own stupidity.[19] Slavery and loan contracts entailed the same requirements.[20] In all these cases the lexicon and meaning are uniform. The *poslusi* were simply present at the conclusion of agreements, heard the oral contract (hence their name), and could therefore serve to verify the stipulations.

The significance of these witnesses was immeasurably greater in an illiterate society than in a record-keeping milieu. In the former they were required, in effect, to memorize the provisions of an agreement, and on demand recall the particulars. This mnemonic ability is not unusual in illiterate societies.[21] Marc Bloch acutely noted the same propensity in medieval Europe, where illiteracy and custom succeeded in evicting written law almost entirely from adjudication. Memory, rather than paper, played the leading role in evidentiary matters, so that children, who could be expected to remain on earth longer than adults, often appeared as witnesses.[22] In Russia witnesses were drawn from the outstanding members of the community, respected on account of age, social position, or wealth. Furthermore, only freemen could perform this task. Should a trustworthy slave induce a freeman to accuse another freeman of a crime, the daring accuser could pay for his bravado if the charge were not proven.[23]

Verification testimony resembling that of the Russkaia Pravda is repeated in Smolensk law. The 1229 Smolensk Treaty with Riga and the German merchants refused to admit the testimony of a single witness in international suits. Both a German and a Russian were required to complete the proceedings, thereby avoiding the national partisanship that might emerge from simple attestation. An identical provision was included in the project for a successor to the 1229 treaty.[24] The law of the northwestern city-republics of Pskov and Novgorod continued this tradition. Both codes use only the word *poslukh* to identify a witness. Unfortunately, only part of the Novgorod Judicial Charter survives, so that key aspects of testimony in Novgorod remain unknown. However, even from the scant references to the *poslusi*, it is certain that they performed in Novgorod the same verification duties that they fulfilled earlier. As before, slaves were refused the right to testify. Likewise, the accused had the right to confront the witness who had accused him, and the witness who failed to appear in order to support his original testimony precipitated dismissal of the case.[25] It was the absence of testimony rather than its nature that decided the case.

As noted below, the Novgorod Charter exhibits some preference for written evidence, so that the role of witnesses there might well have changed somewhat from that outlined in the Russkaia Pravda. Pskov law, which shared many principles with the law of its sister city, Novgorod, reveals the same preference for written materials, but testimony continued to be informal. In land litigation, for example, the Pskov Charter describes the conditions under which one could justify claims to a particular plot. Having cultivated that land for four or five years, the defendant was to produce four or five neighbors who were to affirm his claims as truth before God (*kak pravo pred bogom*), especially the claim that the plaintiff had not initiated litigation against the defendant over this land during the years he had cultivated it. It is true that the provision does not specifically refer to the neighbors as *poslusi*, but there can be no doubt that the Pskov neighbors, like earlier *poslusi*, served simply to affirm possession, to vouch for warranty.[26] Surviving examples of Muscovite land litigation require the same duties from witnesses, still identified as *poslusi*.

Other articles of the Charter support the contention that testimony in Pskov remained informal. In a stipulation which parallels that for litigation over land, the code prescribed that a tenant-farmer (*izornik*) who disputed the claims of a landlord could help his case by referring to four or five outsiders (*liudi storonnie cheloveki 4 ili 5*) who were to speak as though directly before God (*kak priamo pred bogom*). The landlord was under obligation to produce similar supporting testimony, although it would seem that in no case was the testimony decisive. Ultimately, one of the litigants was to take the oath, thereby ending the case.[27] Inherited land that fell into dispute also could be purged of counterclaims with the aid of witnesses. Either neighbors or outsiders to whom the land and its history were known (*a i susedom budet vedomo, ili storonnym liudem*) could support the claim of the defendant that the land was acquired by inheritance. As before, witnesses were to imagine themselves in the presence of the Almighty when giving their deposition, but the inclusion of the qualification of knowledge is strongly reminiscent of the Muscovite judgment charters, where such phrasing assumes an almost formulaic insistency.[28]

Still another Pskov reference suggests that the witnesses had to have been present at a crime. The first section of the article required of them that they had seen the assault (*a tot boi mnogy liudi videli v torgu ili na ulitsy, ili v piru* [emphasis added]), the qualification demanded of the *vidoki* in the Russkaia Pravda. The witnesses were required to confirm a statement of fact, in this case, that the accused beat the plaintiff. Should they so testify, conviction would immediately ensue. But conversely, the victim could initiate proceedings with as few as one *poslukh*—as opposed to a *vidok*—in which case the suit could be resolved through a duel.[29] It may be that the difference in the two eventualities centers upon the number of witnesses rather than the type of testimony, but a comparison with earlier usage indicates that the *poslukh* offered testimony different from that of witnesses of fact.

Other provisions of the Pskov Charter reinforce this conclusion. For example, no prejudice was to be attached to a suit in which the defendant did not refer to a witness. The law goes so far as to eliminate the witness of the plaintiff if the defendant did not produce one. Likewise, the defendant could make short shrift of the plaintiff's witness simply by accusing him of complicity in the crime.[30] In these cases the plaintiff was expected to refer to a particular person to whom he had announced the crime (*iavil [l]i komu*) committed against him, and the witness was expected to confirm not the accusation, but that the plaintiff had described the assault to him (*shto bityi iavlial boi svoi*). After all this, it was decided only that the defendant was to choose the method whereby he wished to vindicate himself—by duel or through the cross. Although the court did undertake a kind of interrogation of witness and plaintiff alike, the questioning was not directed to the facts of the allegation. Witness and plaintiff both were asked only where they had eaten and where they had spent the night.[31] Consequently, although the failure of a witness to appear guaranteed that the litigant who referred to him would lose, a witness's deposition did not guarantee the result of a case and did not serve as any kind of final proof. Testimony in Pskov, as in later Muscovy, was a kind of necessary preliminary without which litigation could not continue.[32]

The tenuous nature of testimony by *poslusi* is substantiated still further by the reluctance of witnesses to appear at court. For one thing, the law imposed upon the witness demands so stringent that they could only diminish incentives. For example, if a witness appeared and testified, he was expected to match the claims of his party exactly. Failing to parrot the allegation of his sponsor, the witness would invalidate his own testimony. Furthermore, if all this was not sufficient discouragement to the fulfillment of civic duty, the prospect of supporting one's testimony with life itself may have rendered the exercise of civic virtue totally unpalatable. In both Pskov and Muscovy, a witness could be challenged to a duel by the accused who, under certain circumstances, could hire a replacement. The witness was afforded no similar relief.[33]

The Muscovite 1497 Sudebnik altered this circumstance only slightly. The new code did exempt women, children, the elderly, the crippled, and church people from taking part in a duel for the purpose of authenticating their testimony, but it was still true that the lot of a witness was not an especially happy one. As before, failure to appear at court to give testimony had its penalties, but now this lapse could lead to the witness himself being assessed for the sum at issue.[34] Although the wording of the Sudebnik is not so specific as its Pskov predecessor, it seems clear that the *poslukh* was obliged to repeat his party's claims verbatim (*a poslukh ne govorit pered sudiiami v ystsevy rechi*).[35] After all this, when the reluctant witness had dragged himself to court with the bailiff's help and had spewed out the memorized text, thereby saving himself from court costs and the wrath of his party, he still had to face the prospect of passing into eternity because of his testimony. The opposition could choose to fight it out on the dueling field, a solution fraught with danger for the civic-minded witness. Procedure also permitted the opposition to discount completely the witness's testimony simply by placing the disputed goods at the cross, once all had gathered at the dueling field.[36] Though this eventuality surely brought the witness considerable psychic relief, it must have caused him consternation as well, inasmuch as he had already gone through a good deal which was quickly dismissed.

The Sudebnik also continued the old usage of *poslusi* as attesters to agreements of purchase and sale. In regulations recalling the Russkaia Pravda, Muscovite law required that the possessor of stolen goods identify the witnesses present at the purchase so as to avoid his own seizure for theft. But once again the significance of the testimony is open to doubt, as the accused could succeed in removing suspicion even if he had no witnesses. He needed only sufficient bravado to take an oath.[37]

In other respects, however, Muscovite law introduced considerable change in the nature of testimony, orienting it increasingly toward statements of fact. In particular, the Sudebnik's compilers inveighed against the bribing of court officials and witnesses, and instructed witnesses to describe truthfully only what they had *seen*. False testimony was to be penalized by assigning the perjurer to pay the suit costs himself.[38] Despite the obvious insistence in this article upon factual evidence, the code employed the old term *poslukh*. But the two articles devoted to testimony offered in connection with purchase/sale agreements abandoned the old term. Instead, the first simply prescribed the testimony of two or three "good men" to whom the matter was known (*a budet liudem dobrym dvema ili trem vedomo*). This requirement of knowledge is reminiscent of the terms of Pskov law on land litigation and of their reappearance in the judgment charters on the same subject in Muscovy.[39] But the other article that deals with witnesses to agreements introduced an entirely new term—*svidetel'*, the apparent equivalent of the *vidok* of the Russkaia Pravda. The variable that distinguishes this article from its predecessor on the same subject is the place of the agreement. Purchase/sale arrangements completed on foreign soil (*na chiuzhei zemli*) were to be verified by two or three "good people" (*dobrye liudi*) before whom the deal had been consummated. Their testimony relieved the accused of the necessity of resorting to the oath, an eventuality pursued in the absence of such witnesses. The witnesses, however, were not called *poslusi*, as in earlier centuries, but *svideteli*, witnesses of fact.[40]

This distinction had no immediate impact on Muscovite law. The 1550 Sudebnik utilized the basic testimony provisions of the 1497 Sudebnik without a corresponding borrowing of the particular term by which the latter distinguished witnesses of reputation from those of fact.[41] Furthermore, the cases of land litigation that filled the coffers of Muscovy's officialdom in the fifteenth and sixteenth centuries failed to observe the arduous qualification that the Sudebnik placed before them. Most often the documents identify witnesses as *poslusi*, and their names are attached to the document.[42] Later the witnesses were required to sign the papers in question, thereby further strengthening the authenticity guarantees for the document.[43] But this procedure was in no way firmly established, even by the time of the Sudebnik. In the judgment charters of the late fifteenth, and early sixteenth century, several variations were used to indicate that representatives of the community were present at the hearing of the case.

One type of attester were the *sudnye muzhi*, the men of court required to be in attendance at court proceedings. The attendees sometimes were called upon to verify the transcript when one of the litigants denied the accuracy of the court record at the final stages of adjudication before the grand prince (*doklad*).[44] We have no evidence that the men of court ever refuted the trial record, but their role was clearly parallel to that of the *poslusi* of earlier decades. This is especially manifest in the passive role they played during the arguments germane to the facts of the case. The court inquired only as to the accuracy of the trial transcript. Both the Beloozero Charter and the 1497 Sudebnik prescribed that the so-called "good men" (*dobrye liudi*) be in attendance at the court sessions of princely officials.[45] These people who enjoyed respect in the community very likely were the same ones that the Sudebnik identified by their court function.

Another variant of the *poslukh* in the judgment charters of Muscovy was the *znakhar'*, sometimes translated as eyewitness.[46] The root is derived from the word "to know" (*znat'*), hence, one who knows.[47] This meaning is enforced by the constant intoning of the judges in the judgment charters: "To whom is the matter known?" The litigants respond that "the matter is known" to their witnesses, Ivan and Fedko.[48] These *znakhari* presented their evidence with great conviction, usually relying on memory. They were expected, as one litigant phrased it, "to know and remember."[49] The claims to phenomenal memory seem to have had little effect on the outcome of the case, regardless of the fantastic spans of time of which the *znakhari* claimed to have personal knowledge. It was not unusual for the witnesses to assert their ability to recall events thirty, forty, sixty, or eighty years in the past.[50] Some daredevils even tried to outdo these significant memories. One *znakhar'* claimed to recall "from birth one hundred and twenty years," and went on to point out that he had heard the relevant information from his father.[51] The practice of claiming to have the information through one's relative was not restricted to such exorbitant claims. In another case a witness claimed to have heard from his father about the founding of a church. His cohort claimed to have gleaned the same data from his grandfather. The judge tried to direct them both to the relevant question, namely whose land was it? Both had to confess that they did not know.[52]

The inadmissibility of hearsay evidence, at least its implied inadmissibility, flies in the face of other aspects of testimony. For one thing, the *znakhari* were always organized into parties, each side having a suitable number of spokesmen for its point of view, and only rarely did witnesses contradict their favored litigant.[53] In some cases the *znakhari* are actually identified as parties, dubbed with the name of their litigant, a clear reference to their partisan role.[54] Certainly the *znakhari*, however they were identified, were expected to contradict the depositions of their counterparts grouped with the opposing litigant. It requires no sophistication in logic to deduce that both sides could not have presented accurate testimony over the same questions of fact.

If one looks carefully at the formulas in which the depositions are couched, other doubts over the factual nature of testimony may arise. Along with the seemingly precise estimates of their mnemonic abilities, witnesses often resorted to vague descriptions of the length of time the land in question had been worked by their candidate. Most often they were reduced to observing simply that "from olden times" (*izstariny*) so-and-so had worked these lands.[55] In view of the incredible memory claims, perhaps such fudging will not cause surprise, but it is quite likely that the terminology points to the customary nature of the testimony itself.

The time references in the testimony of the *znakhari* are repeated in still another variation on their role. Sometimes witnesses were described primarily in terms of their many years of residence in the area under dispute—*starozhil'tsy*, "long-time residents."[56] Several surviving case records affirm that the *starozhil'tsy* were the equivalent of the *znakhari*, fulfilling the same function.[57] Like the *znakhari*, they were expected to know the status of the land in question, and the history of its transfer and any squabbles that may have arisen about it. When necessary, they were called upon to pace off the borders of the territory—all this prior to the completion of the cadasters. Even after the regularization of land records, the demarcation of borders, which preceded examination of the cadasters, remained an integral part of adjudication.[58]

Another characteristic of these witnesses is the emphasis placed upon their standing in the community. When not called "knowing ones" (*znakhari*), long-time residents (*starozhilt'sy*), or men-at-court (*sudnye muzhi*), witnesses were identified as "good men" (*dobrye liudi*) or the "best men" (*luchshie liudi*) in the community. Clearly these are the good men and true who played leading roles in the inquisitory process known in England and in various places on the Continent in the early medieval period.[59] Although in Muscovy the Beloozero Charter first prescribed their presence at trials, the "good men" seem to have fulfilled a similar function much earlier in Smolensk, and in a somewhat different role, they also appear in early Novgorod documents.[60] But the coincidence of *dobrye liudi* with *znakhari* is supported by several Muscovite documents which equate them both in name and function. The questions asked them are identical to those asked of the *znakhari* ("to whom is it known?"), and like their equivalents, they fulfilled attestation functions at the completion of such documents as purchase agreements even from late in the fourteenth century.[61]

Each category of witness described above could be asked to supply specific factual information, over and above the seemingly formulaic response they gave in their partisan testimony. The most obvious case of such a request arose in the course of determining boundaries when the witnesses themselves were asked to lay out the borders.[62] But even here there was no apparent limit to the contradictions. Should the witnesses march off mutually contradictory borders, the documents merely record the boundaries so delimited, and the decision is referred to the judge at the review hearing (*doklad*).[63]

In summary, it is clear that the *poslusi* were witnesses of hearing, both in respect to their attendance at the conclusion of contractual agreements (at first no doubt oral) and with respect to the estimate they gave of a member of a community. Their parallels, the *dobrye liudi* and *sudnye muzhi*, also were required to attend court to legitimize the proceedings and verify the court record. The testimony offered by the *znakhari* and *starozhil'tsy* reflects the other phase of medieval Russian testimony—partisan support. The formulaic nature of their questioning was matched by an equally formalized testimony that relied mainly upon notions of community respect and social tradition. The accuracy of personal, firsthand testimony was minimized by exorbitant claims of memory, often vitiated by vague references to antiquity. Finally, the judge found no difficulty in accepting into the record two sets of conflicting testimony to be forwarded to the court of decision. The important thing was to include such witnesses (without whom one's case could not be considered complete), regardless of the number of fully certified documents introduced into evidence.[64] In short, eyewitness testimony, as represented first by *vidoki* and later by *svideteli*, played a relatively minor and certainly subordinate role in early Russian litigation. The partisan, consensual testimony denoted by the term *poslushestvo* evidenced both widespread usage and longevity.[65] The persistence with which traditional testimony continued to reign in litigation, despite the forthright attempts by the Sudebnik's compilers to introduce more factually based testimony, is a tribute both to the prolonged dominance of customary legal norms, and to the reluctance that greeted legal reform in Muscovy.

The informal nature of testimony in early Muscovy is emphasized by another parallel phenomenon. Like many traditional societies in which the official resources for controlling antisocial behavior are inadequate to the task, Muscovy relied upon consensual estimates of the community in order to identify criminals. At its worst, community questioning served to further character assassination, since members of the community, upon questioning by official pollsters, could designate which of their compatriots they regarded as socially unredeemable. Certainly Muscovy knew character assassins, but the general import of the investigation was to identify people who did not fulfill the usual obligations in a society dominated by custom.

Persons identified in the inquisitorial process are known in the surviving texts as "known evil people" (*vedomye likhie liudi*), individuals who evidently were criminal recidivists.[66] The characterization itself is sufficient to indicate the consensual nature of their reputation. The adjective *vedomoi* ("known") is of course extracted from the same root used by the judges to introduce testimony (*komu to vedomo?*), and serves to strengthen the suspected link between the two kinds of testimony. The frequent mention of recognized evildoers includes at least one case where these black sheep were grouped with criminals engaged in slander for profit. This case from 1509 calls for the execution of such an evil fellow (*likhoi chelovek*) as a thief, murderer, slanderer (*iabednik*), or "known evil person."[67]

The *iabedniki* were professional slanderers who specialized in laying charges of criminal conduct at the doors of innocent victims.[68] These calumniators enjoyed a temporary field day in the 1440s in Novgorod, when such accusations led to the immediate death of the accused and the appropriation of his earthly goods by his accusers.[69] A variation saw the *iabednik* hound his opponent by repeatedly initiating suit over the same disputed sum, itself inflated.[70] The more diabolical practitioners of this art evidently attempted to incriminate their enemies in offenses as serious as murder by throwing a disinterred corpse into the yard of the unsuspecting citizen, who shortly thereafter found himself the subject of a murder suit.[71] Similar diversions were practiced with respect to robbery cases.[72]

There can be no doubt that both accusations could stick. The *vina*, the homicide fee, relied upon just such physical evidence.[73] Likewise, proof in robbery and theft cases comprised the physical evidence of the theft, the stolen property itself (*polichnoe*).[74] But even in the absence of such tangible proof, it cannot be doubted that unsuspecting citizens branded as criminals were put through the mill on the most flimsy account. The 1497 Sudebnik, for example, found it desirable to include a section instructing interrogation personnel in the technique for evaluating the testimony of a thief. If during interrogation (torture?) the thief should accuse someone, one need only determine if the newly accused was previously *charged* with theft. In the presence of additional information (slanderer's testimony?), a person so named could be tortured on accusation of theft. Were there no previous allegations against his reputation (that is, he had managed to avoid stimulating the envy of his neighbors), he was put on bond pending an investigation of his reputation (*obysk*).[75]

Opportunities for doing in one's neighbor through this system did not diminish in the sixteenth and seventeenth centuries. The so-called general investigation (*poval'nyi obysk*) was often prescribed by the government, and permitted investigators to go through communities taking down accusations lodged against any freeman, serf, or slave.[76] References to the "known evil men" continue to appear in documents of the time. As before, the community was expected to turn over to the state for punishment any social deviants.[77]

The older equivalent of *iabednichestvo* was *poklep* (false, unproven accusation).[78] Both terms are used in one Muscovite document as the basis for sending princely bailiffs in quest of criminals,[79] but *poklep* is known even from the Russkaia Pravda. A person who fell under suspicion by this means could vindicate himself with the aid of seven *poslusi*, who certainly were nothing but character referents. Also reminiscent of *iabednichestvo* is a provision of the Russkaia Pravda that freed the commune (*verv'*) from payment of the bloodwite if a body turned up on its territory and no one knew the victim.[80] No doubt the Pravda was principally concerned with the death of outsiders, but our knowledge of defamation suggests the possibility of concern with false accusation as well. An unidentified corpse was exactly the means by which slanderers in Muscovy had connived against innocents. Perhaps it was not accidental, then, that the Russkaia Pravda, in the article immediately succeeding that discussing unidentified cadavers, provided penalties for slanderers. In the worst of circumstances, when the accused found himself under suspicion and could convince none of his friends to vouch for him, the Pravda allowed him to purge himself of the taint of wrongdoing by resorting to ordeals, though surely that was an undesirable alternative.[81]

The overwhelming bulk of the information indicates that Muscovy was slow to develop a notion of factual testimony. Instead, the surviving trial records sound the litany of partisan declarations based solely upon social station. Testimony continued to operate within traditionally informal modes that were poorly adapted to the heterogeneity which increasingly characterized Muscovite society. It is inconceivable, therefore, that Byzantine legal norms could fail to exert some influence on this form of evidence. "You judges, judge the words and not the heart," intones the Pravosudie Mitropolich'e. "What proceeds from the mouth of a man [should constitute] a trial."[82] In contrast to the traditional forms developed in secular Russian law, church law brought Byzantine refinements of judicial examination that sought to establish the factual basis of the testimony being offered.

The Zakon Sudnyi liudem, true to its Byzantine roots in the Ecloga, devoted considerable attention to the question of testimony.[83] Both redactions and each of the major recensions include an article which restricts the evidence of those who testified only to that which they had heard. Whereas the Short Redaction concluded that the testimony of a nobleman (*zhiupan*) was admissible even if hearsay, the Expanded text permitted the testimony of princes (rather than *zhiupany*), but cautioned the judge not to listen to the testimony if the witnesses themselves had not been present to observe at firsthand the events in question.[84] The same attitude of diligence surfaces in another long article inserted in both redactions of the Zakon Sudnyi. Here the judge is urged to examine the testimony of witnesses (*poslusi*) with patience and diligence, and to seek genuine witnesses who feared God, held no prejudices, and who testified only on account of a fear of God and his justice. Court was not to be held without such witnesses.[85]

The importance of this concept in the legal milieu of medieval Russia is difficult to overestimate. The reliance of judges on the formulaic testimony of character witnesses is one of the standard and unifying features of early Muscovite secular court procedure. But churchmen were fortified with Biblical as well as secular precedent for more factually based testimony. The Merilo Pravednoe, a guide designed for church courts, included two extracts from the Old Testament which outline precautions reminiscent of those built into the Zakon Sudnyi. Judges were urged to examine the witnesses who stand before God, the clerical hierarchy, and the judges.[86]

But not all the features of testimony envisioned in the Zakon Sudnyi adhere to the new model suggested by Byzantine law. In the same article in which the judges are urged to try the motives of those who testify, the text also imposed numerical limits on witnesses. The Short Zakon provided for eleven witnesses (*poslusi*) in large suits, and from three to seven in smaller suits. The Expanded Redaction stipulated one to eleven *poslusi* in large suits, and no fewer than three and no more than seven in less expensive suits. These figures have long puzzled historians of Slavic law, who have been unable to determine why specified numbers of witnesses of fact should be required.[87] Given the general context of Slavic legal norms, it is clear that these are not at all witnesses of fact, but simply the character witnesses which figure so prominently in other documents of this period.

What significance the allotted numbers had is difficult to decide. The procedure implied here was clearly distinct from that which predominated in medieval Russian secular courts. "The judge has the authority," the text admonishes, and before him the witnesses (*poslusi*) were to speak and lay out their information. Not only did the judge not have the power of decision in medieval Russian secular courts, but witnesses were not expected to establish questions of fact. Consequently, by penalizing those who give false information while under oath, the evidentiary regulations of the Zakon Sudnyi stand out in bold relief from the reality of medieval Russian secular jurisprudence. Finally, the codifier's interest in isolating the motives of witnesses remained unknown to secular law before the great Muscovite codifications.[88]

The issue of the number of witnesses is mentioned again in another section of the Zakon Sudnyi liudem. In the course of describing the appropriate procedure in slander cases, the text advises the judge not to hear any such case unless there were many witnesses (*svideteli*). Should the litigants not produce witnesses (*poslusi*), the judge was to order into action some form of ordeal upon which the loser was condemned.[89] Part of the interest of this article is the apparent confusion of the two varieties of witness—*svidetel'* and *poslukh*. But the text specifically distinguishes the two. In the first place, the judge is advised to conduct his hearing before many *svideteli*, but the litigants are to produce *poslusi* if they wish to avoid the results of God's justice.[90] There seems little difficulty in admitting that the *poslusi* here serve the same function of supplying evidence of good repute regarding particular litigants. Attendance of the *svideteli*, on the other hand, who were not witnesses to the offense, was required to see to it that those inclined to slander did not practice their profession against the judge as well, and thereby undermine the standing of the judiciary. The same function was executed in Muscovy, Pskov, and Novgorod under various names.

But the interest of churchmen in testimony was considerably more rigorous than these few provisions indicate. In a series of articles that appear exclusively in the Expanded Zakon Sudnyi, the text outlines the procedures appropriate to the construction of a will, and among them, includes an instruction on witnesses.[91] Like the testator, the witnesses (*poslusi*) were called upon to be in "healthy and whole mind"; robbers (*razboinitsi*), drunkards, thieves, or those who harbored evil designs against the testator were not admissible. Not only does the phrasing about the sound mind recall the surviving Muscovite testaments, but the indication of the quality of the testimony serves to underline the church's general interest in evidence.[92] In fact, the question of evaluating testimony was the subject of a separate article of the Expanded Zakon Sudnyi. The judge was cautioned to investigate carefully all *poslusi*, and prescribe trial by "God's justice," an eventuality not to be feared by those who constantly walk in the Law of God and bring joy to their God, rejoicing with the angels.[93]

Of course, the church did not simply propound its views on witnesses for wills and testaments alone. Witnesses were an important ingredient in the orderly conduct of the church's own business, as numerous documents from the early Muscovite period suggest. For instance, it served the church's sense of order to have "good witnesses" (*dobrye svideteli*) present at the installation of someone into the priesthood. Likewise, an individual's claims to conversion could find support in the confirmation of a *poslukh*.[94]

The first of these regulations was included among the decisions enacted at the Vladimir Council of 1273 which also authorized the new Kormchaia Kniga. In listing the various antisocial occupations that rendered a candidate unfit for service in Christ's church, the assembled hierarchs grouped perjurers (*rotnitsi*) with drunkards, thieves, and rapists. So serious an offense was perjury that the clerics deemed it necessary to spell out its exact nature, and proceeded to list other criminals whose behavior was equally odious—murderers, usurers, and their ilk.[95] That the violation of oaths was a significant concern is reflected in still another list of offenses contained in a fifteenth-century episcopal lesson. Along with the murderers went perjurers, liars, and those who practiced *kleveta* (slander by false accusation) and violated their oaths (*rota* and *kliatva*).[96]

Those familiar with clerical interest in perjury elsewhere in medieval Europe will hardly be surprised by the vituperation evident here.[97] But the interest of the Russian church in matters of testimony was even more sustained than these few regulations indicate. The copyists and compilers of the various juridical collections saw fit to include sizable portions of Byzantine legislation devoted to the same subject. Though our manuscript copies of these regulations seem to be fairly late texts—fifteenth- and sixteenth-century manuscripts—the tradition of their copying in early Russia almost certainly stretches back to the thirteenth century, when so much legal compilation took place. The most controversial collection is the Knigi zakonnye which included, along with other extracts from Byzantine law, the twenty-seventh title of the Procheiros Nomos.[98] The entire title is devoted exclusively to matters of testimony, and all the Byzantine provisions are reproduced in the Knigi zakonnye. The Slavonic text is not, however, a simple translation of its predecessors, inasmuch as the order of the articles was changed and several similar provisions from the fourteenth title of the Ecloga were added.[99]

Although no other texts are known that reproduce all the contents of the Knigi zakonnye, separate reproductions of various parts do exist. Of interest here is the copying of the chapters "On Witnesses" (*O poslusekh*) in a sixteenth-century miscellany bearing the title "Canons of the Holy Fathers" (*Pravila Sviatykh Ottsov*). These provisions were joined with articles denouncing the Latins, the Donation of Constantine, the Questionary of Kirik, the Statutes of Princes Vladimir and Iaroslav, and other juridical works extracted from the Kormchie.[100] Another sixteenth-century miscellany with somewhat different contents nevertheless includes the same abstracts from the Knigi zakonnye.[101]

Pavlov long ago argued that the Knigi zakonnye were constructed in the twelfth or thirteenth century, and recent study has suggested that the manuscripts in which the Knigi zakonnye are reproduced may spring from as early as the fourteenth century.[102] But even if these dates seem too early, the existence of manuscripts at least from the fifteenth century must be recognized.[103] It was precisely at this time that secular Muscovy was busying itself with redefining the notions of testimony that had reigned in preceding centuries.

The mere existence of these collections does not indicate that they necessarily played any direct part in the reform of Muscovite law, but their presence does suggest the church's general effort to introduce Byzantine values into the juridical life of medieval Russia.[104] In addition, manuscript marginal notes urging attentiveness hint at the practicality of the provisions enunciated in the manuscripts.[105] The contents of the other miscellanies that contain the chapters on testimony also suggest that these evidentiary norms were applied, at least in clerical courts.[106]

The potential contribution of the codex devoted to testimony was enormous. In wording reminiscent of the Zakon Sudnyi liudem, the text calls for reliable witnesses, and urges rejection of evidence found credible simply because of the high social station of the witness.[107] Witnesses who were not known to the principals were to be subjected to especially careful examination.[108] With respect to contradictory testimony the judge was advised to determine who were the trustworthy witnesses and to punish those who testified wrongfully for evil ends. A series of regulations covered the process of determining the reliability of the testimony secured. As above, contradictions were not tolerated, and the judges were to evaluate the worth, faith, and morals of witnesses.[109]

Perhaps most significant is the prohibition against hearsay testimony: "Witnesses shall not testify according to hearsay, saying we heard this . . . from someone. . . ."[110] Not only was hearsay testimony a fact of life in Muscovy, and this regulation therefore quite pertinent to the current situation in secular courts, but the article itself is a very close rewording of the provision on testimony which found its way into the 1497 and 1550 Sudebniki. The injunction against hearsay testimony is repeated elsewhere. The text counsels against listening to those who have heard something from the witnesses, and insists instead that the witnesses themselves be present at court where they may be questioned. The judge was cautioned to ascertain the motivation of witnesses, whether they stood to gain by their testimony, and whether they were friends or enemies of the litigants. Only then were they permitted to testify. The judge was also to determine whether they responded carefully and honestly to the queries. Where the testimony of witnesses conflicted, the legislator offered the sage counsel that the majority is not always right, and that the worth of testimony depends upon the motives of the witnesses.[111]

A large portion of the texts on testimony is devoted to the qualifications of witnesses, a feature only weakly developed in early Russia. The Zakon Sudnyi liudem had cautioned the court against accepting testimony from children against their parents, and from slaves against their lords.[112] The Pravosudie Mitropolich'e permitted children to testify against their father, but refused to admit their testimony in his behalf.[113] The codex on witnesses repeated the injunctions against a slave's testimony and child-parent accusations.[114] In addition, the law excluded from testifying those convicted and imprisoned for previous offenses.[115] A separate article refused the right of testimony to minors, slaves, lecherers (*bludniki*), the deaf, and sons still under parental authority.[116] The man who had testified once against someone was denied an encore, presumably to remove prejudice. The same reasoning may have influenced the decision to prohibit freedmen from offering testimony against their former lords.[117] Social snobbery may explain the reluctance to grant a hearing to the impoverished, strictly defined according to the value of their possessions.[118] Enforced testimony, extorted confession, and partisan evidence all were prohibited.[119] Fear of prejudiced testimony likely played a role in limitations imposed upon testimony provided by a single witness.[120]

Not only is the sheer bulk of these regulations impressive, particularly in the context of the general lack of secular attention to testimony, but also noteworthy is the manifest attempt to sort out factual and fanciful testimony. Despite their stated intention to obtain factual information, Muscovites apparently felt no qualms in using torture to increase the volume of testimony. Furthermore, the image of an active judiciary, inquiring into the motives of one witness, the age of another, and the prejudice of a third, contrasts starkly with the impassive judiciary portrayed in surviving Muscovite trial records.

Church documents reveal some ambivalence over testimony by members of the clergy, perhaps because of the dangers of perjury. The Zakon Sudnyi liudem in its Expanded redaction equated a priest's testimony with that of twelve of his fellow citizens.[121] The Pravosudie Mitropolich'e refused to permit priests, abbots, and deacons to testify except in cases pertaining to another abbot, priest, or deacon. Somewhat more generously, the Pravosudie permitted a monk to testify on behalf of his abbot if the subject of litigation touched upon his monastery.[122]

"On Witnesses" passively permitted clerical testimony, but betrayed some anxiety over its quality. Perjury by a priest or deacon was punished by removing him from his service for three years, during which time the villain was confined to a monastery. If he testified falsely regarding matters of conscience (*grekhovne i vine*), he was consigned to legal tortures. A similar destiny awaited lesser church officials who perjured themselves, though they were deprived of their church rank permanently. Churchmen with grievances against their brothers were to approach the bishop on the matter, and in the absence of a bishop, address the archepiscopal assistant (*namestnik*) who would conduct the litigation.[123]

Other provisions outlined procedure for having the witness swear to his testimony.[124] No similar requirement appears in other church texts, although the Pravosudie Mitropolich'e had permitted a witness whose reputation was maligned to challenge the claim.[125] For extremely grave criminal charges, *svideteli* (as opposed to *poslusi*) themselves had to be present to testify; their depositions alone were not acceptable. By the same token, for certain cases depositions could be sent to courts in other towns. This article is of special interest because it is clearly adapted from the Byzantine precedent. But in place of the proviso for the confirmation of the testimony before the provincial eparch or in Constantinople before the Sacred Tribunal, this reworking allowed the giving of such testimony before judicial lieutenants (*namestniki*) in the hinterland and before princely judges in the main town.[126]

Even a superficial review of these stipulations demonstrates that Muscovy had far to go to incorporate clerical evidentiary norms into the reality of secular judicial practice. Not only may one question the application of the prohibitions against enforced testimony, a favorite Muscovite device, and the regulations restricting evidence from minors, but partisan testimony, prohibited in Byzantine law, was the very backbone of Muscovite litigation. While injunctions against the testimony of slaves were not new with church law, the exhortations to examine carefully potential witnesses were well directed to the passive judges who operated in early Muscovy. Nevertheless, the available evidence indicates that while these instructions may have had some impact upon Muscovite codifiers, who wrote some of these principles into the Sudebniki, the church's laws on testimony had little actual bearing on the conduct of secular litigation. Muscovite trial records reveal very little initiative on the part of the judges, and virtually no interrogation, which is presumably what the Zakon Sudnyi liudem meant when it urged *istiazanie* upon the judges. Equally vain was the call to protect a defendant from having to testify against himself. Muscovy, rife with the slander of the *iabedniki* and their predecessors, took every suspicion as a basis for further investigation. Two slanders were the virtual equivalent of any piece of hard proof.

Even in Muscovy the credibility of testimony continued to depend upon the maintenance of traditional consensus. In a society that was becoming increasingly heterogeneous, however, consensus was difficult to maintain. It may be that the church's anxiety over perjury was motivated in part by a recognition that increased mobility, both physical and social, was undermining the restraints on false testimony built into the old system. What is certainly true is that character testimony remained dominant, essentially unchallenged by the more sophisticated set of evidentiary norms adopted by the church and directed to its secular counterpart. While the Sudebnik gave lip service to factual testimony, the credibility of witnesses continued to be appraised on the basis of long years and the presumed knowledge of tradition that age brought. Litigation utilized witnesses only as part of a formula without which no case was complete. The witness remained essentially a guarantor to warranty, both in attesting purchase/sale agreements and in warranting the character of litigants. But in neither case was testimony sufficient in itself.

Ordeals

Ultimate reliability, like sanctions, initially depended upon the interference of divinities. Therefore, in medieval Russia as in many traditional societies, ordeals played a large role. The Russkaia

Pravda knew various ordeals, and prescribed them for cases where there was insufficient evidence. As noted above, the defendant who could produce no witnesses was permitted to turn the tables on the accuser. Both then were tried by iron ordeal.[127] Similarly, when the stolen goods themselves were not discovered, the accused could be forced to yield to a variety of trials, depending upon the value of the suit. While trial by hot iron was clearly the most fearsome and, presumably therefore, the most effective device in ferreting out the truth, water and a simple oath had their place.[128] A cynic might observe that the accused who successfully avoided being burned by the iron might well deserve his vindication, even more than his contemporaries believed. But the reality must have been considerably more painful for those accused, often on the flimsiest of pretexts. It was possible for a man to be subjected to the iron on the basis of suspicion alone. Were the accused fortunate enough to be acquitted by the iron's justice, he was entitled to no compensation from those who so freely flung the accusation his way. Only when such an accusation was based upon a slave's word was the victim rewarded for his suffering at the iron.[129]

The use of water as a form for determining the reliability of the witness or litigant seems to have been rare, if one may judge from its single mention in the Russkaia Pravda.[130] By contrast, the use of the oath (*rota*) seems to have grown throughout the period under review here, especially with the development of trade relations. Suits over money on loan required an oath either from the witnesses corralled for support or from the principal, should he have been so naive as to conclude the agreement without witnesses.[131] The penchant to trust one's partner led to other situations where the principals themselves had to resort to oaths to clarify their relationship. In one case, the purchaser of stolen goods, having forgotten from whom he had purchased them, could take an oath to substantiate his claim that he himself did not commit the theft.[132] Similar professions of innocence were extracted from those who unwittingly aided a runaway slave or those who took the slave as their own, ignorant of his real master.[133]

The oath was also featured in assault cases. The Pravda allowed the foreign Varangians to take an oath to purge themselves of suspicion in cases where natives had to produce eyewitnesses (*vidoki*).[134] A variation of the same procedure was included in the Novgorod Treaty of 1187-1189. In disputes between Varangians and natives, either party could successfully refute the charge by taking the oath in the presence of twelve witnesses (*poslusi*). Assault charges also could be overthrown by the party who, by casting lots, won the right to take the oath.[135]

Novgorod developed a distinctive view toward the oath, requiring the kissing of the cross in fidelity to the town's judicial document, the Novgorod Charter. While one may admit a certain ceremonial character in this practice, even an element of formulaic ritual does not diminish the fact that the litigant who refused to make such an act of obedience to the laws of Novgorod was presumed guilty. Even though substitutions were permitted for women, the ceremony itself was indispensable. Witnesses found themselves in the same situation.[136]

Although Pskov law became more sophisticated under the influence of notions of written evidence, many of the provisions concerning the oath nevertheless show a great resemblance to the Russkaia Pravda. In matters of storage and loans, for example, where there were no witnesses to the transaction, the principals could resolve the matter by resorting to the oath, although other alternatives existed.[137] Land litigation fell under the same rubrics, the oath serving as one of the means of establishing the facts of the case.[138] Landlord-tenant and master-apprentice disputes, inheritance suits, and even assault and arson cases all could go the route of oath-giving.[139] The alternatives open in all these cases allowed the litigants to place the goods before the cross or go to the dueling fields.[140] The oath was greatly preferable to such life-ending alternatives as the duel, which may explain the strict scheduling established for oath-giving.[141] It seems likely that oaths were popular for the very reason that they proved ineffective—they could be violated with impunity, a condition that may have stimulated the church's outcry against false testimony and oath-breakers.[142]

Pskov law developed the oath in tandem with the duel, and thereby strengthened the role that the latter was to play in Muscovite law. To be sure, the duel was known earlier, but the Pskov Charter made unprecedented use of this form of trial.[143] Fifteenth- and sixteenth-century mentions of the duel were likewise not rare, but the citations have not deterred scholars from assuming that dueling was little used, despite the 1497 Sudebnik's detailed treatment of the fees and procedures for the duel's conduct.[144] Even the testimony of foreigners visiting Muscovy in the sixteenth century has not convinced skeptics of the actual application of this mode of proof.[145] Although the church had long opposed the use of the duel, the persistence with which it appears in the record suggests the ineffectiveness of this campaign.[146]

The Sudebnik did not totally ignore the earlier forms of "God's justice," permitting the use of the oath and the placing of disputed goods before the cross, as had been done in Pskov. But the absence of other kinds of proof led to the introduction of unusual means.[147] The duel, tied as it was to the fees of the officials, was adumbrated in detail, and the schedule of fees explicitly announced in the Sudebnik, a practice that had no parallel in the other forms of extraordinary justice.[148]

None of the forms of "God's justice," however, served to increase the sophistication of evidence introduced into Muscovy's courts. Violation of the oaths may be presumed to have been widespread, given the history of their enforcement in medieval Russia.[149] Whether the ordeals by water or iron were more effective is harder to judge with less information, but their disappearance suggests their ineffectiveness. Likewise, permission to substitute professional fighters for litigants and certain categories of witnesses lent a ludicrous aspect to the judicial duel. The wealthiest and strongest often achieved a legal victory that had no relation to the reliability of evidence.[150]

However ineffective these forms may have been in getting at the truth in matters of litigation, it is certain that they contributed to the creation of a large staff of personnel charged with carrying out the arrangements. The Expanded Russkaia Pravda sketched basic fees for dueling, but only with the 1497 Sudebnik was the entire framework set out in detail. The conduct of the duel was charged to the secretary (*d'iak*) and the ranking judge (*okol'nichii*), though the warnings against the crowds of supporters imply that more supervisory personnel may have been necessary.[151] Even the administration of the trials by water and iron suggests an elementary contingent of officials skilled in carrying out their specialties.[152]

With respect to the sophistication of evidence, however, none of this shows any particular advance. The use of oral testimony was confined to what proved to be essentially character testimony, despite the attempts manifest in the Sudebnik and elsewhere to introduce witnesses of fact. The oath, like other forms of ordeal, originally may have operated effectively within a society still bound by a strong consensus. But the oath was rapidly converted into an instrument by which the most trifling testimony was sanctified, a development that the frequent church protests confirm. The association of oaths with the cross, a central element in Russian oathgiving, was sufficient stimulus for clerics to urge upon the princes a more factual form of testimony, at about the same time as the Western church was abandoning the water and iron ordeals.[153] But the church's nudgings—in Russia they were no more than this— had little effect. Church courts themselves, however, presumably did operate on the principles extracted from Byzantine law, and in that way offered unspoken condemnation of the inadequate forms of proof admitted by secular courts.

Physical Evidence

Opportunity for the state courts to exercise their powers of judgment unimpaired by the inadequacies of testimonial evidence was concentrated in cases where direct implicating evidence was present. This type of adjudication is one of the few constants during the entire medieval period. The circumstance of incriminating evidence was examined by several articles in both the Short and Expanded Russkaia Pravda,[154] and was adumbrated in detail throughout early Muscovy.[155] Direct evidence of theft, the stolen property itself, was known in the Pravda as *tatebnoe*, etymologically linked to the word for thief.[156] Although Muscovy utilized a different word, the meaning was identical. *Polichnoe* (stolen goods) were those materials "recovered from a dwelling, from [defendant's] safekeeping: and if something is found in a courtyard or in a deserted dwelling, and not in [anyone's] possession, it [shall not constitute] material evidence [of theft or brigandage]."[157]

Some Muscovite documents, it is true, seem to identify *polichnoe* as a particular judicial fee,[158] but the majority of citations isolate *polichnoe* as the material evidence upon which the investigative procedure was based. Initially investigation was accomplished through confrontation (*svod*) by which the owners themselves pursued the thief. The same technique was used to involve the entire community in the pursuit of criminals (*sled*), and in Muscovite documents also was linked both to seizing the thief and recovering the stolen property.[159] Later cases involved the prince's officials more directly, though the meaning attached to the material evidence was the same.[160] Even in the face of growing domination by the prince's officials and the arrogation of criminal cases to princely jurisdiction, other members of the community still sometimes brought the evidence to court against the criminals.[161] Muscovite legislation formally adopted the essential principles that had governed litigation brought about by material evidence.[162] So entrenched did the distinction between material evidence and other forms of trial become that in at least one case *polichnoe*, like homicide, was regarded as a separate jurisdiction.[163]

Direct evidence played a similar role in homicide cases. A discovered corpse implicated in homicide those people on whose land the cadaver lay.[164] Precisely this circumstance entitled the prince to his fee (*vina*) when the killer either was not discovered or was not given up by local residents.[165] Whereas other homicide cases were based upon accusation and could be refuted either by witnesses or ordeals, the secret homicide, as Pollock and Maitland dubbed it, brought no one to justice.[166] Gradually these homicides fell under the authority of Muscovite officials, but numerous sixteenth-century Muscovite documents retain reference to the *vina* and the community's responsibility for explaining homicide.[167] With regard to direct physical evidence, as with testimony, later Muscovy gives no signs of having altered substantially its understanding of the function of evidence.

Written Evidence

Nevertheless, there was a real change in the rules of evidence between the thirteenth and fifteenth centuries. It is tempting to examine that change exclusively by means of the 1497 Sudebnik, so many of whose provisions are devoted to the composition, signing, and authentication of written documents. But the origins of this development are considerably older, and as with other aspects of medieval Russian rules of evidence, clerical influence was at work here, too.

As in much of Europe, in Russia it was the testament that first introduced documentary evidence to the law. The testament itself, if indeed it may be called that at the outset, was not so much a will as a post-obitum gift. Like Anglo-Saxon documents of the same genre, the medieval Russian testaments are simply evidential documents that confirmed oral testaments. And in Russia as in Anglo-Saxon England, the drift toward written wills owes its energy to the intervention of churchmen, who found in inheritance a jurisdiction much more easily penetrated than other zones of the law.[168] With the earliest mention of the old term for a testamentary disposition (*riad*), the tentacular arms of the church are already discernible.[169] But the role of the clergy was to become more pronounced. The earliest of the extant Pskov testaments, dating from the thirteenth century, includes one of the features that became standard in similar documents of a later era—the presence of priest or other churchman at the composition of the document.[170] Early Muscovite testaments reveal even stronger influence of the church and church law. One of the most telling signs of this effect is a phrase inserted into the preamble of wills, according to which the testator affirmed that he was of sound mind (*svoim tselym umom*), phrasing reminiscent of the instructions included in the Zakon Sudnyi liudem, itself mimicking Byzantine law on the subject.[171]

In accordance with the rules developed in the Zakon Sudnyi, testators regularly affirmed their faith in the Triune God, and strove to avoid selecting drunks, robbers, and the like as witnesses.[172] In this last task the testator was aided by the advice and recommendations of the clergy in attendance. Often priests, monks, and deacons served as witnesses, and frequently churchmen even did the actual writing of the document and affixed the appropriate seals to early wills.[173] Even the call for a conscientious executor, one who had nothing to do with the rabble of this world, sometimes was satisfied by use of a cleric.[174] But the hint of church prompting is more pronounced in documents that describe a procedure doubtless employed in all such testaments. We are told by one testator, for instance, that "by my head sat my spiritual father, Abbot Nikon" while the will was composed.[175] With the sinner approaching the only Just Judge, the priest at hand was in a perfect position to offer his insights into the best procedures for assuring a happy outcome to this earthly travail.[176]

Historians familiar with the role of the medieval European church in the rise of written testaments will find nothing astonishing in the church's activity in medieval Russia. Even the most cynical observer will allow that on the surface, at least, the church was interested in the fate of men's souls, and seized life's last moments to direct a sinner's attention to God. It was, of course, exactly in those last moments that the medieval Christian composed his testament, oral or written, so that the participation of the clergy was quite natural. The medieval inclination to use the deathbed to wash clean a life of sin inevitably brought the confessor into contact with the testator. This, too, was not unique to Russia. The English church, for example, so effectively welded together the notions of confession and testament that soon after the Norman Conquest it was already said that to die intestate was to die unconfessed. It was not substantially different elsewhere in Europe.[177]

Despite the laudable preoccupation of clerics with the pious dimensions of their deathbed duties, the material impact of the association of churchmen with their confessees cannot be denied. Testaments in Russia, as in much of Europe, became an extraordinarily productive source of clerical income by virtue of donations to church institutions. Gifts to churches and monasteries were part of every testament, whether carried out immediately on the testator's death or subsequently by the heirs in accordance with wishes of the deceased.[178] None of this took place without the knowledge of clerics, as the surviving documents prove. Churchmen's names abound in the witnessing, writing, signing, and sealing of such gift charters.[179]

In view of its enormous collection of written law, it should not prove surprising that the church should sponsor the move toward written evidence. The church hierarchs were the heirs of Byzantine legal norms, and could be expected to promote the virtues of Byzantium's codes, which were oriented to the use and value of written forms of evidence.[180] At least in Pskov and Novgorod, where written norms in medieval Russia seem to have developed first, the archepiscopal church and its nomocanonical collections wielded more than passing influence on the conduct of justice.[181]

The Pskov code itself is testimony to the trust in written evidence. Judges were expected to consult the document.[182] Pskov jurisprudents allowed that the code could require adjustment with the passage of time, and therefore it included a provision allowing changes in the law.[183] As in later Muscovite procedure, the winning litigant was awarded a copy of the court decision, which, like all authorized and legally binding documents, was represented by a duplicate in the archive at the Holy Trinity Cathedral. Documents not so registered with the authorities were not sufficient grounds upon which to base later claims.[184] Pskov law even provided for the inevitable appearance of forged documents, and devised rules to guide officials confronted with such a dilemma. Documents were evidently firm support for obligations contracted, and Pskov courts countenanced no interference with the relations defined in them.[185]

It is not surprising that the Pskov code contains a considerable body of inheritance law, not disassociated from the church's pretensions. The dying man who orally donated his goods in the presence of priest or outsiders could rest assured that his disposition would be carried out. In general, the old custom of oral testaments must have remained widespread in Pskov, since their occurrence was anticipated by the city's code. But it may be deduced from the same information that the writing of wills was becoming more frequent, a condition that led the compilers to distinguish between written and unwritten testaments.[186]

Our knowledge of Novgorod documentation is not so complete, but from what remains it is clear that similar principles were at work there. Litigation over land, for example, was ended by the presentation of a document to the winner, thereby providing a base for subsequent legal claims.[187] Similar documents accompanied criminal suits, those decided by a hearing as well as by default.[188] The latter could be avoided by one's presence at the hearing, a stipulation made easier by arrangements specified in court summonses.[189] Finally, the Novgorod Charter itself served as a kind of ideal source of written law, the authority of which was reinforced by the requirement that litigants swear by it.[190]

Despite the trend toward written judicial documents in Pskov and Novgorod, it was only in Muscovy that a writing society emerged in full flower. Whereas both Pskov and Novgorod had prescribed a wide array of documentation for various stages of litigation, only in Muscovy did this practice reach into the administrative and judicial structure itself, leading to job specialization in the process. Furthermore, despite the tendency toward written documentation that the Pskov and Novgorod codes display, there is precious little extant evidence of the application of this intention.[191] Later in Muscovy, on the other hand, the regulations of the codes and administrative charters are supplemented by a sizable amount of surviving case material.

One of the essential elements of Muscovite court procedure was the default judgment, a decision based solely upon the failure of one of the litigants to appear. This was already known in Novgorod and Pskov, and was institutionalized in the Dvina Charter of 1397 and the Beloozero Charter of 1488.[192] The 1497 Sudebnik laid down specific rules for the issuance of such documents, and took into account the financial needs of those responsible for composing default judgments.[193] Default records were impracticable unless some schedule for court appearances was formalized. This, too, was already part of the law of the northwestern city-republics. In Muscovy, the trial-date charters (*srochnye gramoty*) were the work of the secretaries and scribes who composed them, and the bailiffs who delivered them, and the Sudebnik shows great solicitousness for their wages.[194] The prince's officials were also responsible for composing documents defining relations between lord and slave, though the issuance of such materials was guarded carefully. Once again the officials were guaranteed their due, but it is more interesting to observe some of the refinements built into these regulations.[195] Slave manumissions, for example, were valid only if issued by the upper echelon of officials (those with *boiarskii sud*) and accompanied by the signature of the secretary. Any other manumissions were disallowed, except if the former master himself had written the liberating document with his own hand.[196] Surviving records represent numerous other paper variations—purchase/sale agreements, donation charters, border resolutions of property disputes, and many others.

The crowning piece in this paper architecture was the judgment charter, the record of litigation itself. This document did not appear alone, but was introduced in conjunction with the "transcript" of litigation—*dokladnyi spisok*. This innovation was necessary because of the nature of the court structure outlined in the Sudebnik. Some of the prince's judges were not empowered to decide certain cases deemed too significant (mainly types of criminal cases).[197] In addition, many "hearings" were conducted by temporary judges, especially in land litigation where the judge was present on the land under dispute.[198] All the proceedings were written up, and the transcript was forwarded to the appropriate judge. The resulting document was to bear the official seals necessary to prove its validity.[199]

At this point (what was known as *doklad* in Muscovy) the trial record was read in the presence of the litigants, who were asked to vouch for its accuracy. On that basis the judge was to render his decision, and send the case back to the first judge. This man was then responsible for seeing to it that the winning side received a copy of the entire process, known as the judgment charter (*pravaia gramota*). The Sudebnik used two occasions to enumerate the fees involved in this procedure alone.[200]

The value of such records is that they present in some detail both the procedure of litigation and some of the legal reasoning, neatly encapsulated in the decision rendered by the *doklad* judge. Enough study of these documents has been done to reveal the essential trends and makeup of litigation, but one may yet examine with profit the role of written evidence in the decisions.[201]

The very fact that such records were kept is itself an indication of the predisposition of the authorities toward written evidence, only one aspect of the broadened appeal of documentation in Muscovy.[202] Of more interest and utility, one may observe in the judgment charters the importance of written evidence in litigation. The surviving documents are skewed somewhat in favor of church institutions, especially the monasteries, whose recordkeepers seem to have done the most efficient job of preserving legal texts.[203] But even allowing for this distortion, the church seems to have been involved in the shift to written evidence very early. In the Pravosudie Mitropolich'e, which originated in the northern lands in the fourteenth century, there are references to both the judgment charter and the trial record. According to one provision, the winning litigant was to receive and keep a charter (*gramota*), and by the other, episcopal judges were to present themselves before the bishop, and not simply send a copy of the trial.[204]

This is not to suggest that even in church circles the adoption of written evidence immediately and totally displaced the witness. On the contrary, often the introduction of documentary evidence was only the prelude to the presentation of the men of the community to whom the matter was known. This served to placate the essentially illiterate population, who, as litigants, rarely had such documents; when they did possess these marvels of adjudication they often found themselves outgunned by the monastery's representatives. Certainly the monasteries most consistently introduced documents in support of their cases.

Although most of the surviving judgment charters belong to the last two decades of the fifteenth century and the first decade of the sixteenth, there is evidence that such forms of documentary proof were highly valued much earlier. Even in the first half of the fifteenth century there were a number of cases where we know from the judge's rationale that the victory was earned through the use of paper evidence. For example, a case dating from 1435-1447 records that the Kirill-Beloozero Monastery introduced immunity charters as proof of its possession of disputed territory. After the judge had read the appropriate provisions, he announced that, because of these documents, the monastery (represented by its elder) was vindicated ("and by reason of these charters . . . [the judge] gave judgment in favor of elder Ignatii").[205] Such a sophisticated verdict is unusual in early Muscovy's court records, and it may be no accident that this examination took place under the Beloozero Prince Mikhail Andreevich.[206]

The absence of documents did not always hinder the case of a litigant, although this sometimes happened, even quite early.[207] More often the case procedure involved presentation of documents, but rarely to the exclusion of witnesses. The church was known to be obviously well-armed with documents. For example, the judges often asked the litigants, in a kind of formulaic questionary, why they considered the land under litigation their own. After the response, it was often the judge's practice to ask what kinds of documents the litigant had, a question almost always directed to the monastery's representative. Then, even with the documents introduced, the judge asked to whom the matter was known (*komu to vedomo*)—that is, what witnesses did the monastery have.[208] For the peasants, the request for documents frequently was omitted altogether, and the judge moved right on to determine if there were witnesses.[209]

It seems that the peasants harbored considerable misgivings over the church's uncanny ability to win contests with these paper "proofs." In one case, for instance, the peasants managed to drag into court an immunity charter against the typically well-prepared monastery, which had come fortified with a judgment charter, among other documents. The peasants, having heard their case destroyed by the record of proceedings in the judgment charter, denied that such a trial as there described ever took place. The judge reminded them that the document as supplied was provided with a seal and contained the names of the *sudnye muzhi* present at the proceedings. This failed to convince the plaintiffs, who countered that "what [the clerics] wanted, they wrote." Though the judge did not dispute this observation, the monastery was awarded the decision.[210]

The monasteries also took advantage of the cadastral books that made their appearance late in the fifteenth century. These tax books contained references to land rights which litigants could draw upon to support their cases. There are numerous examples of the monasteries' use of this proof,[211] but the peasants again give the impression of dealing with a large unknown. In several instances they attempted to seize the initiative and themselves referred to the tax books, though this clever tactic did not bring the intended results.[212] Even in the sixteenth century, some contestants could not reconcile themselves to the immutability of the records so entered in the state tax books.[213]

This does not say that the monasteries always had their way in court so long as they had paper in their hands. Though a skeptical view of fifteenth-century literacy and Muscovite jurisprudence may suggest just such a situation, there were cases where the churchmen were not above trying to dupe the judges, only to be rebuked. In one case, for example, the representatives of the Ferapontov Monastery, for once finding themselves without the necessary documents, introduced the donor rather than the gift charter. The donor, in his turn, produced a gift and purchase/sale document to prove his right to give the land to the monastery. The judge allowed the charters to be read into the court record, but then objected that they were only copies and lacked some information important to the authentication of their contents—no witnesses were named nor were the names of the secretaries included. At the decision hearing (*doklad*) still more documents were introduced by the donor, but the seals were discovered to be specious, a factor taken into account in rendering the verdict.[214] But even without documents the monasteries continued to press their claims, often asserting that the relevant papers had been destroyed by fire.[215]

In general, the picture that emerges from these charters is a sad one for the peasants. The church, if it did not itself institute the move toward such written evidence, surely profited from it more consistently than did the peasants. Occasionally, the latter might register their stubborn resistance, denying whatever might appear in the paper magic of their opponents. But their pathetic attempts at counterattack did not appreciably change the direction of litigation in Muscovy. When peasant litigants did try to introduce evidence, it was often handled clumsily.[216] In one case, for example, the Simonov Monastery of Moscow had introduced a purchase/sale agreement to justify its claims to some particular land, and the opposition, not to be outdone by the well-prepared churchmen, claimed to have a will that proved its side of the case. Alas, the will was in the keeping of the monastery which was eager and willing to produce it. Not unexpectedly, it was of no help to the litigating peasants, who lost the case.[217] The miracle of paper was such that a monastery's own elder could offer no more convincing explanation to an inquisitive judge than this: we once had the desired document, but "because of our sins we lost that charter."[218]

The cement to this paper edifice was the development of the means of verifying written forms of evidence. Again, the church seems to have had its foot in the door. In order to provide for checks between copies and the original, it was necessary to store copies in a safe place, a task easily and early fulfilled by the church. Certainly in Pskov, and perhaps in Novgorod as well, it was necessary to have a copy of all official records in the central cathedral in order to have the documents recognized as authentic. Subsequently the Muscovite princes created a central archive for themselves, but it is not difficult to see here the educative arm of the church. Although in the northwestern lands churchmen were advising officials about the composition and preservation of such pieces of material evidence, except for the documents derived from the Beloozero principality there is no parallel information from the Muscovite princes themselves until well into the fifteenth century.

The clerical stimulus toward written records is also discernible even in terminology. Kliuchevskii, among others, noted that the words for secretary (*d'iak*), scribe (*pod'iachii*), and even the document itself (*gramota*) all reveal Greek roots.[219] Vladimir's Statute in one redaction includes the term for secretary in the list of church people immunized from state interference.[220] Sergeevich indicated that the term *d'iak* had replaced the older native word (*pisets*—a writer) in the fourteenth century.[221] Certainly it is clear from the fourteenth-century testaments of the Moscow grand princes that *d'iaki* already were in the personal employ of the princes, and in fact probably were enslaved to them.[222] The surviving documentation implies that at least for the fifteenth century the emerging princely administration was well-staffed with various clerks. Even here, however, a solid sprinkling of church secretaries is noticeable. The Metropolitan had his own secretaries,[223] as did the monasteries[224] and archbishops.[225] Numerous documents also were written by priests and "priests' sons" (*popovichi*) who took advantage of their literacy.[226] Other records reveal that many churches in the late fifteenth century had their own secretaries, as well as priests and sextons.[227] None of this proves the influence of the church in the shift toward paper records, although the fact that clerical copyists seem to have flourished early—in the fourteenth and early fifteenth centuries—and in private transactions suggests some evolutionary process.[228]

Eventually the secretaries came to fulfill exclusively the role of signing documents, thereby aiding in eliminating forgeries. A similar function was executed by seals (*pechati*) attached to completed transactions. The obvious importance of the seals is best shown in the comments of monastic copyists who, upon entering the documents into the copybooks, made note of the condition of the seal.[229] Cases survive where clerics themselves attached their own seals, but already in the fourteenth century the Moscow princes not only used royal seals, but seem to have developed a special official charged with affixing the mark—the *pechatnik*.[230]

The use of seals was known much earlier. The Greko-Rus' treaties showed their authenticity with oaths and attached seals.[231] Both the Novgorod and Pskov Judicial Charters provided for verification with seals, the latter permitting the seal of the archbishop to serve as the prince's equivalent.[232] In addition to the juridical references, several hundred seals, most detached from documents, survive from the pre-Mongol period alone.[233] Only two of these belong to the tenth century, and like most of the early seals, resemble coinage.[234] The majority of surviving seals from the eleventh century shows strong signs of Byzantine, probably clerical, influence. Not only are there seals of metropolitans and bishops, but there are even princely seals with Greek inscriptions.[235] Late eleventh- and early twelfth-century seals of the princes were written in Slavonic, although the message and accompanying depictions continue to show strong clerical influences.[236]

Of all the surviving seals dating from the tenth to early thirteenth centuries, less than eight percent remain fastened to the original record.[237] The earliest still attached to a document belongs to the twelfth century and the remainder to the thirteenth. The oldest and most disputed document of this type is the gift charter issued by Grand Prince Mstislav Vladimirovich and his son to Novgorod's Iur'ev Monastery.[238] The seal itself has fallen from the document, and the most recent examinations that have sought to tie a separated seal with this charter have yielded contradictory results.[239] Two thirteenth-century documents, likewise from Novgorod, are actually still adorned with seals—both represent treaties. The seals are similar, and reflect Byzantine influence to the extent that the inscription is Greek, the depiction is Greek (Athanasius the Great, Archbishop of Alexandria), and the saint represented on the obverse is also Greek (St. Theodore Stratilates).[240] Similar Christian inscriptions decorate a Pskov thirteenth-century seal also affixed to a document.[241] Although Soviet scholars have emphasized the pre-Christian origins of the early Russian seals, the bulk of the data shows a clear reliance upon Greek patterns.[242]

Consequently, the particular use to which seals were put in verifying juridical acts may be tied directly to clerical precedent. To be sure, their use was secularized, especially in Novgorod and Pskov, so that Muscovy's final elaboration of the system was already several steps removed from its church roots. Not only did the Novgorod and Pskov Charters develop distinct procedures for the use of seals, but even the fifteenth-century treaties by which Novgorod sought to stave off annexation bear these distinguishing marks.[243] Only with the 1497 Sudebnik did Muscovy codify the duties of the sealkeeper and his role in authenticating juridical documents. A seal was to be attached to judgment charters,[244] trial records,[245] default judgments,[246] warrants,[247] and slave manumissions.[248] Other documents of private law also were dignified with various seals, whose presence could affect litigation.[249]

Evidence and the Law

The uses of evidence changed demonstrably between the Russkaia Pravda and Muscovy's 1497 Sudebnik. Although some traditional elements remained, it is clear that partisan testimony succumbed to the same processes that undermined two-party confrontations. The increased complexity of social relations that grew out of Muscovy's drive toward statehood doomed the old consensual norms of evidence and weakened the acceptability of oral agreements. Part of the trend toward obsolescence no doubt sprang from the efforts of the princes to provide for a growing staff of civilian servitors. This intention may explain in part the elaborate prescriptions for paper evidence long before more traditional modes of proof actually yielded their place.

At the forefront of the shift stood churchmen and their own law. The call for factual testimony from witnesses first appeared in Russia in clerical texts. The earliest use of written agreements also seems to be tied primarily to churchmen. Not only did the church play a significant role in protecting and preserving paper evidence, but clerics were closely connected with the entire process of writing. We know of their role in wills and gift charters, and of the etymological connection between the Greek church and the terms by which secretaries and scribes came to be known in Muscovy. Similar clerical importance is revealed in the move toward authentication of documents. Finally, it was the church, personified in medieval Russia by its various institutions, that profited most consistently from the new evidentiary trends.

The impact of these changes was gradual. Certainly Muscovite adjudication, even by the early sixteenth century, did not show either a complete shift to factual testimony or the triumph of paper evidence. Traditional proofs died slowly. But a change in legal thinking had clearly taken place, and this alteration was felt in state as well as church circles. Its most immediate effect was to provide further stimulus toward the creation of more intermediaries between litigants. In this way the law was rationalized and bureaucratized.

CHAPTER 6

Medieval Russian Society and Legal Change

Medieval Russian legal development raises significant questions about early Russian society and its role in altering the law. On the one hand, the persistence of traditional legal formulations, especially outside the urban environments of Novgorod and Pskov, strongly suggests that the society which utilized that law was experiencing no fundamental changes to which the law had to respond. In fact, the thirteenth-century Russkaia Pravda, by comparison with the European so-called barbarian codes of the early Middle Ages, seems relatively antique and unaffected by principles of Roman law such as had altered Germanic law.[1] The comparison implies that late medieval Russian society, like its early Germanic counterparts, was relatively traditional, and demanded no political hierarchy.

However, as the preceding analysis demonstrates, medieval Russian law does give evidence of certain fundamental changes. Although the transition was gradual, by the end of the fifteenth century judicial sanction, a concept alien to earlier customary norms, had become firmly implanted in the law. At the same time, the appearance of judicial personnel and the trend described above in principles of evidence meant that a judicial hierarchy was in place and that the law itself was being rationalized. Both consequences suggest a more complex form of social ordering.

The exact tempo of the law's growth is difficult to trace, for reasons pointed out earlier. In rough terms, however, it seems clear that the first basic alterations in the legal order originated with the prince, and codification of these changes ultimately emerged in the first code of the centralized Moscow principality. That is, political authority was undoubtedly a vital force in legal change in medieval Russia. It is impossible, however, to attribute all the changes noted in this study to the prince's initiative alone. For one thing, much of the precedent for revitalizing principles of evidence belongs to the city-republics of Pskov and Novgorod, where in late medieval times the prince was little more than a figurehead. Furthermore, as many historians have pointed out, the presence of large numbers of clergymen, trained in canon law and practicing that law in clerical courts in Russia, could hardly have failed to have had its impact upon native customary law. Indeed, the peculiar conditions under which medieval Russian law survives—almost exclusively in clerical compendia—suggest at least that the church was closely associated with the changing law.

In short, two routes to legal change are possible. On the one hand it may be that the internal ordering of Russian society altered sufficiently in three centuries to require that the legal system adapt itself to new demands. While no absolute correlation between social structure and legal systems has yet been identified, there are strong indications that particular legal institutions are often associated with particular social orders.[2] At the same time, medieval Russia did not develop its law in isolation from external influences. The northwestern cities had fairly regular contact with foreign merchants, and the Byzantine-trained clerics gradually increased the number of their outposts throughout Russia.

Both factors, then, external and internal, merit closer inspection. At the outset it is important to recall the nature of medieval Russian legal change. In the first place, changes were gradual and not completely triumphant even in early Muscovy. Outside the urban centers, and especially in rural areas far removed from the political apparatus, law retained its traditional formulations. Secondly, the changes that did occur were intimately connected with the political structure. One of the chief developments was the multiplication of the prince's officials and the duties of those officials. The growth of the law, therefore, was most visible in the increased participation of the prince's underlings in judicial process. Finally, changes in the law were both procedural and substantive. In other words, the alterations were not simply minor adjustments or technical corrections. On the contrary, they struck at the heart of the old system, and in doing so struck at old Russian society as well.

The Role of the Church in Russian Legal Change

Nowhere in medieval Russia was the conflict between traditional behavior patterns and innovation more pronounced than in the struggle of paganism with Christianity. Despite the official tenth-century baptism with which Vladimir had inaugurated Russia's Christianization, pagan practices continued to challenge Christian teaching for centuries thereafter. Even in the cities where Russian Christianity had its beginnings, the conquest of traditional religion was neither swift nor direct.

Christianity's competitors left few records of their own with which one might reconstruct their dogma. Instead, paganism's detractors have supplied the main outlines of the diffuse practices that governed the lives of most medieval Russians. It is clear, for example, that a native fertility cult enjoyed a lively practice despite Christian condemnation. The twelfth-century Questionary of the Novgorod deacon Kirik points out that at that time food sacrifices were still being made to the fertility gods *Rod* and *Rozhanitsy*, and a fifteenth-century church text alludes to the same practice.[3] The parallel animistic cults also are known through various redactions of Vladimir's Statute. Some intractable types prayed in wooded groves, by water deemed sacred, and beneath grain sheds, in spite of the threat of clerical prosecution.[4]

Native Russian religion also had other, more definable characteristics. Church courts tried to deal with the priesthood of pagan religion which anchored much of the opposition to the new faith. Sorcerers, seers, and witches all felt the hot pursuit of the clerics. The seers (*volkhvy*) were perhaps the most infamous. One indication of the allegiance they commanded was their leadership of an abortive eleventh-century rebellion.[5] Evidently the seers performed a kind of shamanistic role. Some texts charge them with dissecting birds for the purpose of divining the future, and in another church document, it seems to be the seers who are castigated for using the entrails of reptiles and wild beasts as omens.[6]

The pagan priesthood was also associated with other magical practices. Some texts accused the seers of demon worship, probably because they attempted to ward off sickness and evil with special charms. Naturally the clerics protested strongly, and upbraided those who sought cures through the offices of God's enemies. Furthermore, those addicted to pagan practices were to be cured through special purgation techniques devised by churchmen. Nevertheless, as late as the sixteenth century many evidently still sought the aid of the witches and sorcerers.[7]

Although the ingredients of the charms and potions are not known, it may be that disinterred corpses played some role in the sorcerers' machinations. Certainly the church felt a strong sense of responsibility in overseeing a person's departure from this world. The hope of the redeemed was a resurrection, so that the Orthodox clergy often reminded believers to express confidence in the life everlasting and to avoid shedding tears for the dead.[8] Nevertheless, churchmen showed a special interest in the proper burial of their flock. The Questionary of Kirik, for example, prohibited burial after sundown, and urged those who found bones of the dead lying exposed to inter them.[9]

However, the church's interest in burial was more substantial than theology alone may indicate. Both redactions of the Zakon Sudnyi liudem and most redactions of Vladimir's Statute mention the seriousness of grave robbery, and assign jurisdiction over this offense to church courts.[10] Although grave robbery may be linked to motives of personal enrichment,[11] the religious associations of death suggest that the use of mortal remains for anti-Christian ends is at least as plausible. The practice of unearthing the remains of deceased relatives, whose bones then occupied a place of honor in the peasant house, was evidently widespread among the Eastern Slavs. Ultimately, the implements associated with the exhumation then played a role in other family celebrations such as marriage.[12]

Witchcraft seemingly served purposes opposite to those of the sorcerers. Church texts accuse the witches of poisoning, though of course this was not an offense exclusively practiced by witches and sorcerers. The Canons of Il'ia make clear that wives sometimes practiced this act upon unloved husbands,[13] but there are indications that murder by poisoning was associated particularly with the pagan witches. Rostislav's Statute, by which the Smolensk episcopacy was established, confines its list of church jurisdictions almost exclusively to matters commonly of clerical interest—marriage, divorce, church desecration, and the like. But despite the fact that homicide was certainly subject to the rules of secular law, the statute also claims jurisdiction over cases of murder by poisoning.[14] While this correlation implies the religious nature of poisoning, Iaroslav's Statute makes the connection more specific. In prescribing a fine to be given to the Metropolitan, the Statute listed those eligible: "And if a wife will be a sorceress or wizard or seer or witch or poison-maker . . . , the Metropolitan shall not be deprived of six grivny."[15] Finally, the letters written by Metropolitan Fotii to the churches in Novgorod and Pskov early in the fifteenth century identify poisoning and potion preparations with "evil old women" (*likhie baby*). Fotii urged the righteous to teach these women the error of their ways, and, failing this, to drive them out of the community.[16]

The collision between the traditional, pagan order and the norms of Christianity came out most clearly in the differing views of marriage. The churchmen were horrified to learn that the Drevliane, one of the tribes of early medieval Russia, conducted themselves "in a wild way, living like beasts," without marriage. Instead, they abducted the girls of their choice and at a ceremony by the water appropriated them as mates. Other tribes, the Radimichi, Viatichi, and Severiane, likewise earned the reproaches of the chronicler who likened their existence to ordinary beasts, since they, too, seem to have ignored marriage. During the course of festival celebrations (*igrishcha, pliasaniia*), men selected women who appealed to them, even if the alliances proved temporary. According to the Christian chronicler, these pagans confirmed their ignorance of God by taking several wives, thereby "making a law unto themselves." Only the Poliane among the early tribes were singled out for praise since they, unlike the others, practiced marriage and showed reverence for kinsmen.[17]

Although these observations are placed in the chronicle narrative in an undated section, it is certain that the practices described here lingered long after Christianity had officially displaced paganism in Russia. One of the most repeated complaints voiced by the clerics was their lack of success in inducing the natives to accept the Christian view of marriage, and to permit the church to conduct the ceremony. The canonical texts of Metropolitan Ioann II, which belong to the late eleventh century, include a pessimistic assessment of this problem. As Ioann tells it, only boyars and princes came to the church to be married. Consecration and marriage among ordinary folk had made no headway whatever because the chief competition, the festival dances, continued to dominate marriage arrangements.[18]

That medieval Russian brides and bridegrooms did not feel compelled to secure the church's consent for their union does not in itself provide much information. Much the same reluctance characterized West European medieval lovers.[19] But it was not simply a case of informal marriages contracted without the assistance of clergymen. Rather, marriages were consummated through bride abduction and other pagan consecrations. Both Iaroslav's and Rostislav's Statutes proscribed the abduction-rapes, indicating that the custom was still known at least in the twelfth century.[20] How the actual operation was carried out is not exactly known, but already late in the eleventh century the clerics were alerted to the fact that the festivals of traditional pagan society were orgies of dancing and drinking which served only as the preliminaries to promiscuous sexual relations.[21]

Marriages also were effected through more formal modes in pagan religion. The 1273 Vladimir Church Council heard it reported that in the Novgorod region brides were still being conducted to the water's edge where presumably the marriage was sanctified.[22] The church statutes also claim that elements of ancestor and fertility cults—principally the cutting of cheese—solemnized other marriages.[23]

Even Muscovite church texts bear witness to the p ɔlonged popularity of the traditional marriage forms. The early fifteenth-century pastoral letters of Metropolitan Fotii complain that Orthodox marriage remained foreign to the folkways of many Russians:[24]

> And [regarding] those who live with their wives despite the law, without the priestly blessing . . . , teach them and lead them to Orthodoxy; with the blessing they should be married [*poimalisia*] to their wives; if they wish to live without that blessing, separate them, and you priests, do not receive them.

Those who persisted in disobeying, who, in effect, lived in fornication, were labeled pagans and heretics, and the redeemed were urged to disassociate themselves from them.[25] Another fifteenth-century episcopal lesson complains about "unnatural carnal sins" and the "imitation of heterodox customs" which included fornication, sodomy, drunkenness, and marriage with close relatives.[26] Finally, a sixteenth-century text devoted to marriage remarks that the heretics still did not marry according to the law.[27]

In short, the clerics' attack upon traditional marriage customs had not gone well. Centuries after Vladimir had imported the new religion, much of Russian native religion remained unaffected. The frequent bleating about rape, fornication, adultery, and bigamy—offenses definable only within the context of uniform marriage procedures—underlines the ineffectiveness of the Christian assault on customary practice.[28] Not surprisingly, the clerics had similar difficulties with notions of divorce and incest.[29] Both touched directly upon the traditional methods of marriage and in the process intruded upon kinship definitions as they were accepted by the general populace. In all these matters, then, one can perceive the distinct potential contributions of canon law to the legal and social milieu of early Russia. But even allowing for the implicit exaggeration in clerical accounts of pagan excesses, it is difficult to escape the conclusion that the church did not wage an especially effective struggle against the traditional order.

The limited results achieved by churchmen were in no way the result of formal constraints imposed upon the clerics' enthusiasm. The medieval Russian princes had little hesitation in allowing churchmen to indulge themselves in their battle with social traditionalism. Consequently, in its inroads against native morality, the church felt no drag from secular interference. On the contrary, the princes actively intervened to lend the clergy assistance. Not only had they sponsored the importation of Christianity, but the princes were also interested in erasing the competing loyalties of traditional social structures. Therefore the financial and legal aspects of clerical activity found their guarantors in the persons of the Russian princes.

The church received two kinds of support—financial and juridical. Initial authorization for church revenue came from Vladimir himself, the Christianizer of Old Russia. Upon completion of the Church of the Holy Mother of God in Kiev, Vladimir pledged a tenth of his own income for the church's support.[30] Exactly when the principle of the tithe was extended to all the Russian lands is not clear, but most redactions of Vladimir's Statute contain a generalized formula of income guarantee, a development that must have occurred sometime in the twelfth century with the compilation of the Statute's archetype.[31] This broadened income base would thus have coincided with the early growth of church landholding, which took place with the first grants to monasteries in the twelfth century. However, since the big push in church landholding did not occur until the fourteenth century, the compilers of Vladimir's Statute devised means of providing additional revenues for church institutions.[32] Sometime late in the twelfth or early in the thirteenth century the bishop was assigned the duty of supervising the various measuring devices connected with trade conducted within town limits.[33] Discharging this duty not only increased the church's visibility, but also provided needed supplementary income in the form of fees extracted for performing this service.

In addition to income, the church also required a formal definition of its jurisdictional rights in order to undertake the fight against paganism. These guarantees, too, were written into the princely statutes. Vladimir's Statute, for example, threatened with eternal damnation those who violated the church's right to conduct trials and those who interfered with church people "in all towns ... and in those parishes and districts where there are Christians."[34] Iaroslav's Statute, for its part, introduced church jurisdiction by outlining clerical court competence in divorce proceedings in all towns; other provisions of the Statute considerably enlarged clerical jurisdiction in numerous aspects of family law. Again, based upon recent textual analysis, these jurisdictional assignments seem to have originated in the thirteenth or early fourteenth century.[35] At about the same time church courts also were firmly established in both Pskov and Novgorod, judging by the sizable role allotted to these courts in both cities.[36] The increase in church landholding in the fourteenth and fifteenth centuries meant that clerical jurisdiction multiplied itself several times over, and gradually penetrated the extremes of the Russian territories. Granted immunity from secular interference by special agreements with the ruling princes, church lands became minor principalities where canonical texts presumably dominated judicial procedures. In short, the church succeeded in establishing a broadly based network of courts operating at the local level where they could exert maximum influence upon the traditional legal formulations and courts of the countryside.[37]

Long before this took place, however, the church had asserted for itself a role in the administration of justice. The Primary Chronicle includes a vignette which describes the bishops' attempts to help Vladimir curb crime. In urging stronger action against robbers and murderers, the bishops advised Vladimir that he was "established by God for punishing evil [ones] and for showing mercy to the good."[38] The precise dates and origins of this narrative, discussed in detail above, are not firmly established. Indeed, it is doubtful that the event ever actually took place. What cannot be doubted, however, is that the tale accurately reflects the clerics' views on the church's moral right to participate in the administration of justice.

The same theme was struck in legal texts. Both redactions of the Zakon Sudnyi liudem include a passage urging upon the prince the high calling of administering justice.[39] Hegumen Feodosii gave more direct exhortations to Prince Rostislav Mstislavich: "God commanded you to walk in justice on this earth, and to conduct trials in justice and to rely upon [literally to stand on] the kissed cross [*v krestnom tselovanii*] and to care for the Russian lands."[40]

Despite such exhortations and the considerable assistance the church received in its struggle with native custom, the clergy could claim little success in its endeavors. The old lure of large kinship configurations, traditional community celebrations and customs gave way before the church's soldiers only slowly. Whatever other changes may have occurred in medieval society, much remained unchanged in spite of the clergy's best efforts.

Nevertheless, there are signs that the church did play some role in advancing legal change in old Russia. Its interest in the family provided a natural lever for asserting clerical claims to inheritance jurisdiction, and in this area of the law the church did make a serious contribution. The signs of clerical impact, however, are indirect rather than direct. For although the church was in possession of

Byzantine inheritance law, there is little trace of the clergy's interest in forcing that law upon secular codifiers.[41] To be sure, clerical legal texts attempted to appropriate jurisdiction over inheritance, first in Vladimir's Statute and then later and somewhat more cautiously in the Expanded redaction of the Zakon Sudnyi liudem.[42] But in general the church's case for adjudication rights was weak. Not only did the Expanded Russkaia Pravda contain a large complex of regulations devoted to inheritance, but subsequent secular codes prolonged secular claims to exclusive control over inheritance litigation.[43] Consequently, it was not Byzantine law that guided late medieval Russian jurists in deciding such disputes.

However, while church courts never fully won the right to try cases over disputed inheritances, it was canon law that framed the written testamentary instrument. The priest who sat by the testator's head was in an enviable position to affect the testament, especially with the prospect of eternity looming before the eyes of the dying man.[44] With the outcome assured, the clerics in attendance could introduce procedural peculiarities common in Byzantine practice. The chief trophy of this interaction was the will itself. Written rather than oral, subscribed to before the Triune God and a host of literate clerics, these medieval testaments were instrumental in introducing new notions of evidence.

The church was well suited to its role as sponsor of written evidence. It had at its disposal a large reservoir of clerks, and furthermore, church law itself was written law and showed a pronounced preference for written evidence.[45] It was only natural that clerics involved with legal compilations should strive to introduce norms of written law and evidence. Direct confirmation of that sort of campaigning is lacking. But the indirect information is telling. The numerous cases analyzed above establish that church institutions and their officers were the first to profit regularly by written evidence in early Muscovite litigation. To the untrained peasants who tangled in court with paper-laden monastics, the entire event was unintelligible. Only the clerics found no mystery here. Even in the city-republic of Pskov the church's hand is detectable in the shift to paper evidence. It was the archepiscopal cathedral that served as the repository for all official documents in Pskov, and failure to register an agreement there rendered any contract void.

The emergence of entirely new principles of testimony bears even stronger traces of clerical input. The extract from Byzantine law, "On Witnesses," pointedly argued for more rational forms of proof. Although no record survives which attributes the shift in medieval Russian testimony to canonical law, that conclusion is not difficult to accept. It was precisely the same clerical perspective that earlier in Western Europe had helped to rationalize secular courts, particularly with respect to the introduction of written evidence.[46] The crowning achievement of the clerics' campaign in the West was the 1215 Lateran Council, which eliminated the ordeal from court procedure.[47] Although the new rules governing written testimony on the Continent did not mark the complete victory of rational evidence, the church's role in stimulating the shift is beyond question.[48]

In Russia the parallel is not exact. For one thing, while the European courts gradually phased out most ordeals, Russia retained the ordeal in various shapes well into Muscovite times, and only occasionally did churchmen raise their voices against particular variants of the law's wager.[49] Testimony and written evidence, however, did receive special attention in Muscovy. By 1497 the Muscovite prince employed a full staff of bureaucrats to dispense documentary proof, and at the same time he adjured witnesses to relate only that which they themselves had seen. Of course decreeing did not make it so, and informal irrational proofs continued to wield great influence in Muscovite courts.

That the Russians did not duplicate the wide-ranging shift toward more rational modes of proof which characterized late medieval European jurisprudence is not difficult to explain. The activity of legal scholars at the great medieval universities of Bologna and Paris had revived Roman and canon law as part of the larger reacquaintance with classical tradition. But in Russia there was no equivalent scholarly interest in the law before the seventeenth century.[50] Consequently, the Russian church's influence could not have had the same impact on developing legal institutions as its counterpart in Western Christendom.

Furthermore, not only were there no schools of law where principles of evidence might be discussed, but the churchmen in medieval Russia who were conversant with the law brought with them not so much Roman as Byzantine law. The distinction was a significant one. The Slavs, first introduced to written law through the brutal provisions of the Ecloga, obtained Roman law only at some remove. The Isaurian Ecloga was a self-proclaimed repudiation of Roman law and reflected rather more the talion preferences of the Isaurian emperors than any Roman legal tradition.[51] The Macedonian Procheiros Nomos, an improvement upon the Ecloga, although hardly a substantial return to classical Roman jurisprudence, was the other complete secular Byzantine code introduced into Russia before the eighteenth century.[52] Neither code was the equivalent of Justinian's compilations, and neither was especially true to Roman roots. Therefore, while the church did import particular novels of Justinian and some later emperors, Russian law could not expect to find a sustained, learned understanding of Roman law among the Byzantine and Byzantine-trained clergy who ministered to the flock in medieval Russia.

As a result, while it is clear that the church contributed to the change in medieval Russian law, it is just as clear that it was not the chief agent of that change. On the one hand, it is certain that churchmen occupied positions from which they might have exerted influence upon secular rulers to adapt the law to conform with principles of Roman and canon law. In a few areas—inheritance and testimony—there are unmistakable traces of clerical influence. From an early time church officials were using and advocating written testamentary instruments, and before anyone else did so churchmen were using written evidentiary forms in litigation. In all this clerical input is clearly traceable.

But in Russia, unlike Western Europe, the growth of the law is not attributable in any significant degree to the conscious efforts of clerics to rationalize the whole of the legal structure. The Russian churchmen had among them no one to equal Peter the Chanter, no one to examine the rationality of ordeals and to attempt to reconcile contemporary judicial procedure with classical practice.[53] Furthermore, the Roman inheritance that filtered into Russian judicial texts was significantly altered from the Justinianic texts that played an important role in the revival of Roman law in the West. Instead the medieval Russian jurists were faced with Byzantine alterations—rarely to the benefit of the law. Even as late as 1649 Russian secular law borrowed chiefly Byzantine maimings rather than Roman procedure for the revisions of Muscovite law. In other words, while the church and church legal collections played some role in legal change, developments within medieval Russian society itself must have accounted for much of the growth of the law in the thirteenth, fourteenth, and fifteenth centuries.

Society and Legal Change

As the church's experience with pagan religion makes clear, medieval Russian society was not especially open to change. Contrary to what some would have us believe, Christianity did not early succeed in opening any mortal wounds in traditional society. Furthermore, the sustained popular resistance to innovation indicates that it was not as a result of society's own dramatic realignment that legal change appeared in medieval Russia. Quite the opposite: even late in the fifteenth century some aspects of judicial procedure seem hardly distinguishable from their thirteenth-century antecedents. Signs of a new order were present and even were institutionalized in law, but common perceptions of the law remained unchanged.

The striking distinction between official and popular conceptions of the law is itself descriptive of the type of change introduced. In much the same fashion as Christianity had come to Russia, the new legal system was imposed upon Russian society forcefully from above. Just as the church was Vladimir's creature, the vertical legal order was the result, gradual to be sure, of princely intrusions into the realm of customary law. As proof of this contention one need only examine the relatively static nature of Russian social organization in the thirteenth, fourteenth, and fifteenth centuries and contrast it with the dramatic changes in princely administration.

Two principal viewpoints on medieval Russia's social order predominate in the historical literature. Most historians of late imperial Russia, especially the so-called state school, argued that early Russia was fundamentally a customary society in which informal social bonds were far stronger than the formal ties of political or economic institutions. Chief spokesman for the state school historians was S. M. Solov'ev who argued that clan (*rod*) relations dominated Russian society right up to the twelfth century. The succeeding three or four centuries, which Solov'ev regarded as a transitional period, saw only a slow ebbing of the role of kinship in regulating social intercourse in the face of a growing state order.[54]

In spite of the apparent belittling of the state order, Solov'ev's argument relied rather heavily upon the history of princely relations recorded in the Primary Chronicle. The repeated scenario of the clan elder sitting on the Kievan throne and lesser kinsmen occupying less prestigious capitals throughout the Russian land served as the chief evidence for the theory of clan relations.[55] But even if the princes' penchant for shifting capitals accurately reflects the prevalence of a kinship hierarchy, it says very little about the social structure of the remainder of the population.

To remedy this deficiency, Solov'ev took note of another entry in the Primary Chronicle which characterized the society of the Eastern Slavs: "Each lived with his own clan (*rod*), separately, in their own places [sic], [and] each had his own clan (rod)." Unfortunately, this description, part of the introductory section of the chronicle, remains unconfirmed by any subsequent references in the chronicle text. No matter, because for Solov'ev the dubious analogy of princely behavior was sufficient basis to extend the clan principle to medieval Russian society at large.[56]

Soviet historians, with few exceptions, depict a far different society. It is now customary to read in Soviet historical studies that Russian society of the thirteenth century was characterized by feudal fragmentation.[57] Ultimately this assessment has social consequences, but the premise upon which the conclusion rests is political: some sophisticated state structure, once active, had by the thirteenth century already receded. In place of state structures, wide-ranging private institutions are said to have carried on the functions of government. Meanwhile social relations reached the level of complexity at which class antagonism and exploitation became highly visible. Several decades ago, B. D. Grekov offered what has since become the standard explanation of these matters. Already in the ninth century, he asserted, a full-fledged state structure was in existence, a condition that allowed a suitable time for the development of feudal relations several centuries later.[58]

In other words, medieval Russian society already was characterized by considerable social and economic differentiation and labor specialization. Far from being a relatively small, tradition-bound agrarian social structure, early Russia was a thriving, increasingly urban, and highly adapted society. Even though agriculture still predominated in the economy, the appearance of class relations and economic exploitation is to most Soviet historians vividly manifest from the available sources. Allusions to slave-holding are quickly brushed away—medieval Russia was closer to European societies exactly contemporary with it than it was to any traditional society.[59]

It is difficult to escape the impression that the two viewpoints describe totally different societies. To some extent they do. The materials used most often to justify Soviet historical judgments are drawn from medieval urban archaeology.[60] Transposing these data to the society at large and using urban phenomena to explain difficult passages in the written record is a genuine temptation, but surely not all of medieval Russian society resembled Novgorod.[61] The theory of clan relations seems equally bankrupt on face of the evidence so far adduced to support it. Solov'ev's typology runs roughshod over the distinctions that clearly did emerge in the medieval period between town and country. One cannot fault Solov'ev for not knowing what archaeology has only recently revealed, but it is time to revise the generalized conception of medieval Russian society.

Careful analysis of legal norms and structures shows that neither of the two prevailing images of early Russia warrants confidence. On the one hand, there are explicit clues that Russia had not really entered the late Middle Ages in tandem with the rest of European society. As late as the beginning of the thirteenth century effective judicial intermediaries remained unknown to the law, and satisfaction continued to depend upon the initiative of those directly wronged. In place of the hard evidence demanded later in the period, traditional forms of character reference persisted in determining the community's reaction to deviant behavior. Even revenge justice had only recently been expunged from the legal codes. All this, far from representing the legislative initiative of the Kievan princes, reflects customary legal norms. There is no reason to doubt that customary law held sway earlier in Kievan history as well.

On the other hand, there are signs that at least in parts of the Russian lands the law was indeed changing, presumably in step with the society it served. Particularly in the growing towns of northwest Russia, law became increasingly separated from the popular consciousness and embarked instead on a new course. Rationality was added to its procedures, and simultaneously sanctions were substituted for the compliance once guaranteed by the social homogeneity of the group. Particularly marked was the more frequent use of written documents as evidence. External influence, especially through the agency of the church, also had greater sway in the towns than in the countryside, where change came more slowly.

The usual approach to medieval Russian social history is to proceed directly to analyze the terms of social distinction in the legal codes. But the outcome of that effort, repeated countless times with identical and hopeless results, needs no restatement.[62] Still, there are some allusions to social organization that do deserve attention. The Russkaia Pravda uses several terms—*mir, verv'*, and *v'rvnaia*—to refer to rural communal organizations, and also recalls another term, *zemlia* or land, in discussing the limits of theft investigations. Each term demonstrates that its territorial meaning was not far removed from more traditional concepts of kinship and social organization.

The *verv'* has provoked a good deal of speculation.[63] As noted above, it had special obligations in homicide suits. The duty to find the killer fell upon any *verv'* within whose territory a corpse was found. The only alternative was to pay the prince a fee which released the community from further obligations in the matter, and therefore afforded protection to one of the community's members were he the killer.[64] Although the texts are less clear on subsidiary duties, it seems fairly certain that the *verv'* also represented a kind of mutual guarantee for its members, paying for their escape from legal consequences and most likely, as compurgators, swearing to their integrity in actual trials.[65] But upon what basis the *verv'* was organized is not clear.

Soviet historians are inclined to see in this institution a form of social organization based simply upon territorial limits. Support for their view is drawn not from regulations governing the activity of the *verv'* itself, but from others of the Pravda's provisions which deal with theft investigations (*sled*). The search for stolen property was in fact defined within geographical limits. Similar to the English hue and cry, pursuit of the thief in Russia was incumbent upon all local citizens. If the search led to a village (*selo*), and the inhabitants of that village refused to pursue the thief, they themselves could be held liable for all costs of the theft. On the other hand, should the investigation lead to a deserted place where there was no settlement, then no one was assessed for costs.[66]

But, for all the superficial similarities to the English hundred, no one knows what the *verv'* really was. Clearly in the time of the Pravda's compilation it had a certain territorial definition. But because the word disappeared from the language soon thereafter, there is no reliable etymology to explain its origins. Instead there are two shaky attempts. The first fits neatly into a territorial definition. A few medieval literary texts mention a *verevka*, an unspecified unit of measurement.[67] While it is true that the term, more usual for sixteenth- and seventeenth-century Muscovy, does appear in one fifteenth-century document, *verevka*'s correspondence to *verv'* is hardly compelling.[68] A second etymology imposes a similar strain on one's credulity. Already in the middle of the nineteenth century someone had noticed that the South Slavic term which denoted a relative, *v'rvnik*, greatly resembled the Russkaia Pravda's *verv'* or *v'rvnaia*.[69] But for almost a half century afterwards no one else paid any attention to this observation.

The implication of the association of the two terms was that the *verv'* might have been more than a territorial designation. In origin, at least, it might have been organized on principles of kinship. This realization prompted several attempts to compare the Russkaia

Pravda's *verv'* with the *zadruga*, a patriarchal extended family still observable in contemporary South Slavic society. But bridging several centuries and numerous subcultures as they did, the first historians who ventured into this field of comparative social history were understandably reluctant to claim very much for their findings.[70] The comparison proved only that it was possible for a sizable kinship organization to operate from a given territory.

Only with examination of South Slavic kin terminology itself could the comparison prove more fruitful. A late medieval legal codex provides that substantive comparison. Poljica, a small territory on the Dalmatian coast under Venetian domination in the late Middle Ages, compiled a collection of local laws sometime around the fifteenth century. One of the regulations refers to a *vrv'* as a descending line of heirs who as a general rule recognized no division of the land they mutually worked. While no other duties known to be incumbent upon the *verv'* of the Russkaia Pravda appear in the Poljica codex, the possibility that the *verv'* did have kinship roots is tantalizing.[71] But in itself, this etymology of the *verv'* is far from convincing.

However, traces of kinship are also detectable in other local units known from the sources. Like the *verv'*, *zemlia* appears in the Russkaia Pravda as a geographical or jurisdictional limit. The confrontment procedure (*svod*), in which a theft victim attempted to trace the disposition of his stolen goods, depended upon the towns through which the regressing questioning led throughout the territories or lands (*po zemliam*).[72] The precise limits denoted by these words are not obvious, however, since a subsequent article directly specified that confrontment was not to be continued into another land (*v chiuzhiu zemliu*). If the thief were not discovered by the time the investigation reached the border, that is where the matter ended.[73] Reconciling the explicit prohibition against continuing confrontment beyond the "land" with the assertion elsewhere that confrontment in fact required vigorous prosecution throughout "the lands" is not easy. Evidently different concepts are at work here.[74]

The word for land (*zemlia*) appears in the medieval sources with some regularity.[75] The Primary Chronicle itself occasionally uses the term as a surrogate for "state" or political structure. For example, the Byzantine state is described as the Greek Land (*Gretskaia zemlia*), and the steppe peoples, the Polovtsy, are said to have inhabited the Polovtsy Land (*Polovech'skaia zemlia*).[76] At the same time the chronicler uses the term to describe particular configurations within the East European plain whose peoples took part in Kievan society. Hence, one of the central tribes, the Drevliane, are said to have had their own land, and Novgorod had its own land.[77] Are these, too, indications of independent polities, something akin to what we describe by the word state?

Certainly in a later period the term had political overtones. By the fourteenth century, northeast Russia had laid claim to the political mantle which the term *Russkaia zemlia* connoted.[78] But that the expression meant the same thing in earlier days is dubious. As Nasonov and others recently have shown, by the thirteenth century the term had two separate geographic meanings connected with the immediate Kievan region itself and the larger area of the southern principalities.[79] But the term also preserved a religious association. Well into the twelfth century the Moist Mother Earth (*zemlia*) remained part of the pagan religion. Consequently, the concept of the land was connected in general with ancestor veneration, particularly with the ancestral clan of the Kievan princes.[80]

Exactly the same connections with ancestor veneration penetrate the names of the various East Slavic tribes. Many of the denominations by which the Slavs are known in the Primary Chronicle clearly are patronymics derived perhaps from some eponymous ancestor. For example, the Radimichi and Viatichi got their names from Radim and Viatko who likely were worshipped as tribal ancestors.[81] Indeed ancestor veneration remained active. As late as 1294 some Russian princes themselves indulged in a very blatant form of ancestor worship, addressing prayers to their forebears despite the fact that the church had never canonized their princely predecessors.[82] Furthermore at least one of the eponymous tribes maintained social and political autonomy late in the twelfth century, so that it is not inconceivable that other, smaller units of social organization, like *zemlia* and *verv'*, could retain pagan associations that relied upon kinship ties even in the face of growing territorial importance.[83] Simply put, the geographic significance of both terms does not obliterate characteristics that had their origins in traditional society.

Few are the historians who will find that judgment easy to reconcile with their conceptions of medieval Russian society. But the truth is that for all the talk to the contrary, the idea of territoriality is developed very weakly in the Russkaia Pravda. Although the Pravda is extremely solicitous and attentive to questions of theft of movables, landed property received only oblique treatment.[84] In one article the code established a fine for those who destroyed border markers carved in trees, and in another examined the destruction of plowland divisions.[85] While it is easy to grant that these regulations point to some notions of real estate, it is not easy to determine whose borders were marked in this way.

Certainly the medieval Russian princes possessed their own estates well before the thirteenth century, the chief evidence of which is the Pravda's attention to estate officials who administered the prince's lands.[86] Somewhat less effective proof of the same proposition are the various indications of gifts made to church institutions by the medieval princes. Although these donations are invariably invoked by historians attempting to prove large-scale landownership, the few villages granted to monasteries in this way are quite insignificant.[87] Taken together with all the indications of traditional social organization persisting in medieval Russia, the Pravda's allusions to landed property are not convincing as demonstrations of large-scale landholding either by princes or the church.

If the borders alluded to in the Pravda refer to any lands besides those of the prince, it may be that they point to borders of local communities. Those social organizations mentioned in the Pravda offer no additional help in this matter. Besides the *verv'* and *zemlia* already discussed above, the only other community organization cited is the *mir*, referred to just once in the Short Pravda.[88] The *mir*, too, is rarely met in medieval sources, although it seems to have borne some territorial connotations. Numerous scholars have suggested that these varying community organizations, despite differences in regional terminology, were essentially identical with communal structures known from Muscovite sources.[89] As alluring as this explanation may be, there simply is no proof to support the comparisons.

Nonetheless, there is one medieval settlement type that does lend itself to substantive analogy with the communities cited in the Russkaia Pravda. Though not included in any legal text, the *pogost* was contemporary with the *verv'* and *mir*. Evidently it was known primarily in the northern Russian territories, since the *pogost* is first recalled in the Primary Chronicle's account of the conquest and administration of the Novgorod land in the middle of the tenth century. After her famous subjugation of the Drevliane who had killed her husband, Igor, Princess Olga established *pogosty* and tribute points (*dani*) along the Msta River. Besides demanding tribute (*dan'*) and taxes (*obrok*), Olga also specified hunting reserves which, together with the *pogosty*, remained in use at least until the time when the chronicle account was written.[90] Although vague, the phrasing of the text suggests that initially the *pogost* served as some kind of primitive administrative center where the princess's agents could conveniently collect the tribute.

Documents of a later period support this suggestion. The statutory charter of the eleventh-century Smolensk Prince Rostislav indicates that in Smolensk the *pogosty* did serve as tax collection centers. Likewise, the statute of the twelfth-century Novgorod Prince Sviatoslav Ol'govich required from each individual *pogost* a specific payment. And a thirteenth-century treaty of Novgorod mentioned collection of the tribute in connection with the *pogost*.[91] Finally, Vladimir's Statute, in outlining the territorial limits of clerical jurisdiction, listed a series of populated areas by which the document's compilers intended to encompass all possible combinations: "in all towns . . . and in the *pogosty* and in the villages where there are Christians."[92]

As Vladimir's Statute makes clear, the *pogost* was identifiable neither with a town nor a village, and consequently must have held a position that distinguished it from both. Most scholars are inclined to recognize this distinction in the peculiar commercial origins of the *pogost*. Etymologies play an important role here, since the root *gost-*, the conceivable stem of *pogost*, itself exists in noun form to denote a merchant or visitor.[93] Supplementary persuasion is provided by attempts to chart maps of the *pogosty*. The data so far presented indicate that almost all of these settlements were located along waterways, especially rivers and, to a lesser extent, lakes.[94]

Still, the leap from this information to the conclusion that the *pogost* was a medieval trading center, especially in the hinterland in the tenth century, is a big one indeed. While it is undeniably true that location along a river bank conferred many transportation benefits upon local residents, it is also true that communities with a relatively low level of agricultural technology likewise locate along river beds, especially in forested regions where the river plain makes cultivation easiest.[95] Only with the development of more sophisticated methods of tilling and clearing the land is it possible to think of spreading out into the forested regions. Furthermore, large-scale demographic shifts made possible by altered technology also may occur only if other bonds, such as kinship, which help cement traditional societies, have reached the point where they will admit such differentiation.

There is reason to believe, however, that the *pogosty* existed well before kinship ties had receded to the point where they would have allowed significant social differentiation. Some decades ago, S. B. Veselovskii suggested that the *pogosty* may have served as gathering places in connection with the conduct of pagan ceremonies and sacrifices, and that the natural drawing power of these spots in its turn encouraged merchants and princes to utilize the *pogosty* for collecting tribute and for dispensing justice.[96] Although Veselovskii offered no evidence to confirm his suggestion, archaeological data subsequently unearthed indicate that the *pogosty* were the sites of local cemeteries long before Christianity penetrated the hinterland. Nearby stood the small fortified refuge, the *gorodishche*, which likely served as the center for various cult ceremonies, especially those connected with the dead.[97]

In other words, the *pogost*, like the *verv'* and *zemlia*, shows characteristic traces of religion and kinship. Originally associated with ancestor worship, the *pogost* ultimately was assimilated by the new religion. In modern Russian the term survives to denote a parish, especially a parish cemetery.[98] The Christian overlay belongs to a later era when the *pogost*, deprived of its early pagan meaning, could retain only its old communal focus. Even in Muscovy, it was the parish refectory that served as the community center where communal elders (*starosty*) were elected, where taxes were apportioned, and where court hearings took place.[99] These are the vestiges of a social organization dependent upon neither prince nor church.

Examination of medieval rural social structures supports the suggestion advanced above that early thirteenth-century Russian society retained much of its traditional arrangement. Like the law which mirrors it, old Russian society gives little evidence of having entirely abandoned kinship as an organizing principle. Not only did the law explicitly recognize the rights of kinsmen in obtaining legal satisfaction and sharing legal responsibility, but the extant evidence, even though fragmentary, indicates persuasively that the basic units of social organization likewise had not lost their connections with tribal cults and ancestor veneration.

But having given traditional social structure its due, one must nevertheless admit that medieval Russian society was undergoing significant change in the thirteenth, fourteenth, and fifteenth centuries. As both the Pskov and Novgorod Judicial Charters demonstrate, city justice was coming into its own, and with its rise the traditional forms of ordeal, character witness, and attestation began to fade. Increasingly, responsibility before the law was guaranteed by impartial third parties and not by the informal restrictions of kinship.

The beginnings of that transition are already noticeable in the Russkaia Pravda. Many of the central regulations in the Expanded redaction are devoted to questions of trade, so that thirteenth-century Russia was alert to one source of its alteration.[100] But the urban codes are evidence not only that trade was waxing, but that a wholly new kind of social grouping was in the making. While the *verv'*, *pogost*, and even *zemlia* had associations with kinship, the city (*gorod*) was the symbol of a new order. Its origin was related primarily to economic needs, and its size was governed only by the potential lure of profit.

The literature on the growth of old Russian towns is substantial, and there is no need to review it here.[101] Two observations will suffice. In the first place, the number of Russian towns was never very great. Although the fourteenth-century "List of Russian Towns" includes 358 entries, the bulk of the towns listed there were not actually located within the central Russian lands; a few years after the list was compiled even fewer towns remained, since Lithuania took Smolensk and its surrounding territories. By the beginning of the fifteenth century there were ten genuine cities in the Russian lands on that list.[102] Even making allowances for various towns in northeast Russia that were not listed, the absolute number of medieval Russian towns was not great. In other words, Muscovy inherited a society that was still essentially agrarian. Realizing the dimensions of medieval urbanization may temper the more exaggerated claims as to the kind of social transformation medieval Russia experienced.

In the second place, those towns which did exist were not overpopulated. Of course, it is difficult to come up with any firm demographic data for towns which left no statistical records, but this has not dissuaded the adventuresome from making valiant stabs at estimating urban populations. Early thirteenth-century Kiev, we are told, had a population of 42,000; Moscow late in the fourteenth century is said to have had 20-30,000 citizens, and a century later, 30-40,000. Similar, if vaguer, claims are advanced for other medieval Russian towns.[103] Based upon rough calculations of housing units and arbitrary estimates of household size for the purposes of calculation, these numbers compel no final acceptance. But in spite of the unreliability of the figures, it is clear that medieval Russia had cities of growing populations.

Again, however, caution is in order before advancing too far with urbanization theory. In the first place, it was in the thirteenth century that the Mongol invasions struck at some of the largest of the Russian cities. Kiev, for example, after the 1240 sack appeared to papal envoys as a field strewn with bones.[104] Riazan', located just southeast of Moscow, was also leveled by the Mongol armies, and numerous other cities, including Moscow, felt the destructive hand of the invaders.[105] Undoubtedly the Mongol raids retarded urban growth, particularly along the southern frontier of the steppe, the Mongols' springboard into Russia.

However, it is important to note that the northern cities did not suffer quite so severely from the Mongol presence. Novgorod's famous thirteenth-century prince, Aleksandr Nevskii, negotiated his city's capitulation and thereby probably saved Novgorod from Kiev's fate,[106] an accomplishment much eulogized since then. Social change could thus proceed unimpeded in Novgorod and in its sister city, Pskov. The predictable result was that here social differentiation made more rapid headway, particularly among the commercial classes. In this light it seems no accident that the Novgorod and especially the Pskov Judicial Charters betray the earliest signs of moving away from the traditional legal order that prevailed in the Russkaia Pravda.

Because of conditions favorable to the preservation of the records of medieval Novgorod, a great deal is known about the city. The blizzard of particular archaeological reports covers everything from houses to shoes. It is certain that there, perhaps more than anywhere else in medieval Russia, occupational differentiation had become institutionalized, even though the urban population was not entirely divorced from agriculture.[107] The evidence of craft production in metals, glass, and pottery seems to point to fairly high levels of technology.[108] Although in itself the acquisition of new technology does not necessarily imply labor specialization, the written sources make that conclusion certain. Merchant corporations are known from early documents,[109] and the legal codes themselves identify master craftsmen who took in apprentices.[110] Even the existence of hired labor finds confirmation in the Novgorod Judicial Charter.[111] Furthermore, as the coin finds in Novgorod and other cities show, there was a money economy.[112]

In short, the carpenters, bridgebuilders, potters, smithies, and the rest were part of a population increasingly separated from the land on which the overwhelming bulk of medieval Russian society still labored. As the archaeology again demonstrates, even in the towns paganism did not yield at once to Christianity. But in the thirteenth and fourteenth centuries the missionary efforts of the Orthodox clergy netted genuine gains.[113] The rupture with ancestral places and religion, begun with the first physical migration from tribal lands, was sealed with the deepening of urban roots, and the townsmen proved not unreceptive to the claims of the new religion.

Meanwhile much of Russian society experienced no significant changes. The basic social division between free and non-free remained, but more subtle distinctions seem not to have penetrated rural society. The Pravda's few allusions to commercial matters are engulfed by innumerable regulations that detail agricultural concerns.[114] And tied to the land as he was, the medieval agriculturalist was still close to the soil which had nourished his ancestors and the way of life they had created. Consequently, not only did paganism remain strong, but the entire society stayed glued to traditional folkways and demanded no change in the law. Where kinship still served to help frame jural consensus, sanction was relatively useless. Compensation rather than punishment was the rule. Evidence, too, remained largely defined by customary usage, and as the surviving case sample illustrates, traditional procedure retained great vitality even in trials conducted by Muscovite judges in the sixteenth century.

Legal Change in Medieval Russia

In other words, the society which Russian medieval law had to service yields to no uniform generalization. It was a society in transition, but not everywhere changing at the same pace. One might think of it as a pastiche of cultures. Even the very approximate differences in development between city and countryside hide the numerous subcultures whose folkways remained unaffected for many years after the Mongols had gone. The several East Slavic tribes, their Finnic and Turkic neighbors who also settled within the boundaries of the emerging Muscovite state, all undoubtedly maintained an ethnic self-awareness that perpetuated traditional society and demanded no change in the law.[115] The prior claims of kinship and pagan religion resisted innovation, and thus the law remained in harmony with the society it served. As impervious to the new religion as the pagan Russians must have seemed, they could have been no less steadfast in fighting off alterations in the law. When churchmen fanned out into the countryside in the fourteenth century in search of pagan souls to redeem, they took with them the rudiments of written law. But neither enterprise—legal or redemptive—met with much initial success.

The towns proved to be a more suitable environment for introducing change. Urban residents were already uprooted from agrarian society, and had left behind their ancestral lands. Although their religion remained pagan, the newcomers had proven by their migration that they were susceptible to change. When confronted with the increasingly complex demands of business, with none of the informal guarantees that had operated satisfactorily in the hinterland, the townsmen perceived the utility of a legal order more suited to the heterogeneous, relatively specialized society which they now comprised. Then, too, the temporary (by rural standards) nature of urban citizenship meant that some of the traditional elements of testimony had to be abandoned. Even were kinsmen available to vouch for the honesty of a townsman, that avowal meant little to an itinerant merchant. Therefore the victory of documentary evidence, unprejudiced and portable, was virtually guaranteed.

The altered perspective of medieval townsmen also changed their perception of Christianity. From the very beginning the church in Russia was an urban phenomenon. Vladimir's forced conversion involved marching all Kiev's townsmen into the Dnepr River, and subsequent evangelization employed similar techniques to multiply rapidly the number of converts.[116] In spite of resistance the church's first converts were urban, and it is no surprise that the first churches and monasteries arose within city walls.[117] Before the fourteenth century Christianity had almost no impact outside the towns, and thus the clergy's cultural baggage—principally its law—could have had no importance in rural society.

Townsmen, however, saw the new church in a completely different light. From the first, written culture in Russia was Christian culture, and that identification proved a boon to churchmen busy composing wills that enriched the temporal church. But it also meant that the clergy could locate near the center of the changing social and legal order. Whether church law made inroads because social change demanded a system of law that the clergy happened to possess, or because the clergy themselves were active propagandists of their own law, matters little. The important fact to be observed is that the church with its sizable legal resources was firmly entrenched in the same environment that proved receptive to legal change. The victory of writing and rational testimony might have occurred without the churchmen, but surely their presence accelerated the process.

Nor was that acceleration restricted to the northwestern cities which early moved to some kind of republican government. The church's original victory was not only urban, but, equally important, it was gained through the prince's intervention. As scholars have often noted in explaining other aspects of the history of the church in Russia, the new religion was Vladimir's creation. It is barely conceivable that the link between prince and church fashioned at the outset of Kievan history could immediately have withered. The surviving sources suggest just the opposite. The extension of princely power was accompanied rather regularly by an extension of clerical power. The whole complex of princely statutes is nothing if not a compact of mutual aid.

As a result, while it is unlikely that either in town or country the church was the lever of legal change, it certainly must have acted the part of the fulcrum. As with its progress in converting the natives to the new religion, its impact upon the law was uneven. Late medieval Russia remained overwhelmingly agrarian, and therefore overwhelmingly pagan and customary. But the multi-ethnic amalgam which constituted Russian society at the dawn of the thirteenth century slowly and unevenly began to yield to the new demands of town life. Almost simultaneously customary law ceded its place to a new kind of law, primarily princely law.

The first signs of change in the bilateral nature of legal remedies were clearly due to the princes' initiative. The first monetary sanctions were attached to harms done to the princes' officials, while the decision to replace revenge with composition was embodied in the legislative fiat of Iaroslav's sons. It was the prince's official who gradually intruded into horizontal legal relations, and finally, with the advent of an entire staff of judicial officers, it was princely legislation that governed the validity of various forms of testimony and written evidence.

Neither urbanization nor political centralization affected all areas of medieval Russia. Consequently, the growth of the law was neither uniform nor universal. But a fundamental change had taken place. Even though sixteenth-century Russia in practice was still dominated by procedures of the old order, there was no turning back. The consolidation of the prince's power and the gradual elimination of all counterclaimants to political authority meant that there would be no further resistance to the extension of princely law. The third party had become an essential participant in the legal process.

LIST OF ABBREVIATIONS

AAE	*Akty, sobrannye v bibliotekakh i arkhivakh Rossiiskoi imperii Arkheograficheskoiu ekspeditseiu imperatorskoi Akademii nauk*
AFZ	*Akty feodal'nogo zemlevladeniia i khoziaistva XIV-XVI vekov*
AGR	*Akty, otnosiashchiesia do grazhdanskoi raspravy drevnei Rossii*
AI	*Akty istoricheskie, sobrannye i izdannye Arkheograficheskoiu kommissieiu*
AIu	*Akty iuridicheskie, ili Sob anie form starinnogo deloproizvodstva, izd. Arkheograficheskoi kommissii*
AN SSSR	Akademiia nauk SSSR
ARG	*Akty russkogo gosudarstva: 1505-1526 gg.*
ASEI	*Akty sotsial'no-ekonomicheskoi istorii severo-vostochnoi Rusi kontsa XIV-nachala XVI v.*
ChOIDR	*Chteniia v Obshchestve istorii i drevnostei rossiiskikh pri Moskovskom universitete*
DAI	*Dopolneniia k aktam istoricheskim, sobrannye i izdannye Arkheograficheskoiu kommissieiu*
DDG	*Dukhovnye i dogovornye gramoty velikikh i udel'nykh kniazei XIV-XVI vv.*
GBLOR	Moscow. Gosudarstvennaia ordena Lenina biblioteka SSSR imeni V. I. Lenina, otdel rukopisei
GIMOR	Moscow. Gosudarstvennyi istoricheskii muzei, otdel rukopisei
GPBOR	Leningrad. Gosudarstvennaia ordena trudovogo krasnogo znameni publichnaia biblioteka imeni M. E. Saltykova-Shchedrina, otdel rukopisei
GVNP	*Gramoty Velikogo Novgoroda i Pskova*
LGU	Leningradskii gosudarstvennyi universitet
MGU	Moskovskii gosudarstvennyi universitet
MP	*Merilo Pravednoe po rukopisi XIV veka*
NPL	*Novgorodskaia pervaia letopis' starshego i mladshego izvodov*
PR	*Pravda Russkaia*
PRP	*Pamiatniki russkogo prava*
PSRL	*Polnoe sobranie russkikh letopisei*
PSZ	*Polnoe sobranie zakonov Rossiiskoi imperii*
PVL	*Povest' vremennykh let*
RIB	*Russkaia istoricheskaia biblioteka*
RP	Russkaia Pravda
TsGADA	Moscow. Tsentral'nyi gosudarstvennyi arkhiv drevnikh aktov
ZSL	Zakon Sudnyi liudem

NOTES

Chapter 1

1. See, for example, Lawrence M. Friedman, who argues successfully that "major legal change follows and depends on social change" (*Legal System*, p. 270).

2. John Austin, *Lectures*, 1:175-77.

3. *Max Weber*, pp. 5-6, 16, 19, 27, 52-59, 67, 72, 83-84, 94, 96, 198-282.

4. Friedman, *Legal System*, p. 214.

5. Roscoe Pound, *Social Control*, pp. 18-22; Pound, *Spirit*, pp. 85, 139-42; Pound, *Introduction*, p. 47.

6. Hermann Kantorowicz, *Definition*, pp. 7, 12, 21, 79.

7. Hans Kelsen, *Pure Theory*, pp. 1, 11, 25, 30, 33-54, 106.

8. H.L.A. Hart, *Concept*, pp. 26-40, 77-96, 193-205. One attempt to apply Hart's system to analyzing a legal structure is Lloyd A. Fallers' study of Basoga law in Uganda (*Law*, pp. 11-14).

9. See Richard A. Falk, "International Jurisdiction," pp. 295-320; Michael Barkun, *Law*, pp. 16, 23, 36, 67-71.

10. Barkun, "Conflict Resolution," pp. 124-25; Barkun, *Law*, pp. 95-114.

11. Richard D. Schwartz and James C. Miller, "Legal Evolution," pp. 160-69; and Howard Wimberley, "Legal Evolution," pp. 78-83. Based upon a sample of ethnographic data extracted from the Human Relations Area Files, these studies suggest a correlation between social differentiation and legal change.

12. Barkun, *Law*, p. 23; *Max Weber*, pp. 89, 91-92, 96; Schwartz and Miller, "Legal Evolution," pp. 159-69.

13. For one objection to the evolutionary slant, see Friedman, *Legal System*, pp. 280-89. More on this question appears below.

14. Vilhelm Aubert, "Competition and Consensus," pp. 26-42.

15. William M. Evan, "Public and Private Legal Systems," pp. 169, 172, 182.

16. Sir Henry Sumner Maine, *Ancient Law*, p. 170.

17. For one survey of the bulky literature, see Laura Nader, Klaus F. Koch, and Bruce Cox, "The Ethnography of Law: A Bibliographical Survey," *Current Anthropology* 7 (1966) : 267-94.

18. Max Gluckman, *The Judicial Process Among the Barotse of Northern Rhodesia (Zambia)* (Manchester: Manchester University Press for the Institute for African Studies, 1955; 2d ed., 1967; 2d ed. rev., 1973); Gluckman, *The Ideas in Barotse Jurisprudence* (New Haven: Yale University Press, 1965); Gluckman, *Politics*, pp. 17-18; Gluckman, "The Reasonable Man," pp. 51-55, 127-31, 151-56. For some of the criticisms of

Gluckman's views, see Paul Bohannan, *Justice*, pp. v-viii; Bohannan, "Ethnography," pp. 401-18; Bohannan, "Differing Realms," pp. 33-42. Also see Gluckman, "African Jurisprudence," pp. 439-54; Gluckman, "Concepts," pp. 349-73; Gluckman, *African Traditional Law in Historical Perspective* (London: Oxford University Press, 1974).

19. Sally F. Moore, "Legal Liability," pp. 54, 73-74, 99-100.

20. See, for example, Elizabeth Colson, "Social Control," pp. 199-212.

21. E. Adamson Hoebel, *The Law of Primitive Man* (Cambridge, Mass.: Harvard University Press, 1961); Hoebel, "Law and Anthropology," pp. 835-54; Gluckman, *Politics*, pp. 81-168; A. N. Allott, A. L. Epstein, and Max Gluckman, "Introduction," pp. 1-81. Gluckman often reiterated his refusal to accept as legal those systems which have no institutions which he called forensic—elementary judicial institutions. See Gluckman, *African Traditional Law*, pp. 36-40. Still, Gluckman will admit as legal, i.e., brought into the public arena, self-help supported by group pressure.

22. Of the numerous titles in the literature, several stand out for their usefulness in comparative law. See Roy F. Barton, *Ifugao Law*, University of California Publications in American Archaeology and Ethnology, vol. 15, no. 1 (Berkeley, 1919); P. P. Howell, *A Manual of Nuer Law* (London: Oxford University Press for the International African Institute, 1954); Isaac Schapera, *A Handbook of Tswana Law and Custom*, 2d ed. (London: Oxford University Press for the International African Institute, 1955); A. L. Epstein, *Juridical Techniques and the Judicial Process: A Study in African Customary Law*, The Rhodes Livingstone Papers, no. 23 (Manchester: Manchester University Press, 1954); Leopold Pospisil, *Kapauku Papuans and Their Law*, Yale University Publications in Anthropology, no. 58 (New Haven, 1958); Pospisil, "The Nature of Law," pp. 746-55; Pospisil, "Multiplicity," pp. 1-4; Pospisil, "Social Change and Primitive Law," pp. 832-37; Pospisil, "Legal Levels," pp. 2-26; Pospisil, *Anthropology of Law: A Comparative Theory* (New York: Harper and Row, 1971).

23. A. S. Diamond, *The Evolution of Law and Order* (London: Watts and Co., 1951); Diamond, *The Comparative Study of Primitive Law* (London: The Athlone Press, 1965), where he significantly condensed his views. Most recently Diamond has supplemented his earlier work with new ethnographic data (*Primitive Law, Past and Present* [London: Methuen, 1971]).

24. Among the titles available to buttress the arguments advanced here, two will suffice to demonstrate the whole. A political anthropologist argues frankly for evolution from egalitarian societies to states—the former undifferentiated and based upon reciprocity, and the latter highly differentiated (Morton H. Fried, *The Evolution of Political Society: An Essay in Political Anthropology* [New York: Random House, 1967]). Another attempt to chart legal and social change is the work of Roberto Mangabeira

Unger who, while rejecting evolutionary schemes, posits the coordination of the growth of hierarchy and specialization at the expense of internal social bonds (*Law in Modern Society: Toward a Criticism of Social Theory* [New York: The Free Press, 1976], esp. pp. 49-57, 63, 137).

25. To my mind, Friedman summarizes this argument best (*Legal System*, pp. 142-43).

26. P. P. Howell noted that "scales of compensation for wrongs can be quoted by the older generation of Nuer with surprising consistency," even without any codified schedule (*Manual*, p. 25).

27. These characteristics have been noted in the synthetic studies as well as in the ethnographic reports on which the general works were based. See Hoebel, *Law*, pp. 82, 114, 137, 193, 216-18; Hoebel, "Three Studies," p. 427; Gluckman, *Politics,* pp. 188-89; Gluckman, "African Jurisprudence," p. 444; Barkun, *Law*, p. 128. For more specifics, see Ernest Wallace and E. Adamson Hoebel, *The Comanches*, pp. 210-12; K. N. Llewellyn and E. Adamson Hoebel, *The Cheyenne*, p. 73; Barton, *Ifugao*, pp. 94-95; Howell, *Manual*, pp. 28, 31-32; Hilda Kuper and Leo Kuper, "Introduction," p. 8; Pospisil, *Kapauku Papuans*, pp. 259-61; Pospisil, "Multiplicity," p. 3; Pospisil, "Legal Levels," pp. 22-23; Bohannan, "Theories of Homicide," pp. 30-31; Fallers, *Law*, p. 70.

28. Hoebel, *Law*, p. 114; Barton, *Ifugao*, pp. 94-95; Howell, *Manual*, p. 28. Numerous other examples may be cited, but it should be noted that Pospisil, in particular, has taken issue with this conclusion. On the basis of a case in which a Kapauku headman legislated approval of his own incestuous act, Pospisil deduced that legal systems interact with one another on different levels ("Social Change," pp. 833-35; "Multiplicity," pp. 2-3). On a broader statistical base Pospisil suggested a "functional" description of law, itself operative on different levels ("Nature," pp. 746-55). The theoretical framework recalls the efforts of Evan, described above.

29. See Bohannan, "Theories," p. 31; Jean la Fontaine, "Homicide," p. 94; Howell, *Manual*, p. 229. Several articles in Hilda Kuper and Leo Kuper, eds., *African Law: Adaptation and Development* detail the impact of Muslim, Continental Roman law, and British common law upon the customary legal systems of Africa. Also see Gluckman, *Ideas and Procedures*, passim.

30. See, for example, Schapera, *Handbook*, pp. 2, 12, 19, 46; Jan Vansina, "A Traditional Legal System," pp. 97-119; Gluckman, *Politics,* pp. 144-45. Fallers claimed that Soga society at the time he observed it was likewise vertically oriented (Fallers, *Law*, pp. 40-43; Fallers, "Customary Law," p. 614). However, the British judicial system evidently was imposed over Soga native courts more than fifty years before Fallers arrived (Fallers, *Law*, pp. 58-59; L. A. Fallers and M. C. Fallers, "Homicide," pp. 66-67).

31. See M. G. Smith, "The Sociological Framework of Law," pp. 26-27; also see Kuper and Kuper, "Introduction," p. 20. One may add that societies experiencing political centralization need not demonstrate the

unicentric culture so prominent in Bohannan's analysis. In fact, it seems at least arguable that the very existence of multicentric cultures pushes society toward imposed uniformity. Codification of the law is only one way in which a society attempts to standardize legal satisfactions.

32. This is precisely what happened to the Nuer. Prior to British intrusion forty head of cattle redeemed a homicide. Subsequently the fee was increased to fifty cattle, ten of which went to the government as a fine (Howell, *Manual*, p. 48). Soga princes, chiefs, and headmen, under British rule became civil servants, collecting taxes and the like in a society where self-help was officially prohibited (Fallers and Fallers, "Homicide," pp. 68-69). Edward Westermarck noted that the Berbers paid part of the homicide bloodmoney to the Sultan, if they were loyal to him, or they paid a "fine" to the district governor. Were the tribe in rebellion, part of the bloodmoney might be given to the Berber chief so as to induce him not to assist the other party ("Blood-feud," pp. 363-64). Howell noted that in some cases the Nuer intermediary, the Leopard-Skin Chief, was entitled to a fee for his services in arranging and settling a homicide dispute, though it was not clear to the Nuer themselves whether his share was taken out of the settlement, or was counted over and above the total (*Manual*, p. 51, n. 1).

33. The Nuer, for example, found it difficult to comprehend why the British wanted to penalize a man by imprisonment after the accused had already made composition. Even more puzzling to them was the idea of punishing a man for an offense he had committed against a member of his own family. As the Nuer saw it, such an offender hurt himself, and was not liable to further prosecution. See the examples related by Howell, *Manual*, pp. 61, 235-36.

34. This explains in part the Nuer resistance to coercive sanctions (Howell, *Manual*, pp. 41, 235). Also see Elizabeth Colson, "Social Control," p. 205.

35. Richard G. Salem and William J. Bowers, "Severity," pp. 21, 37; Kuper and Kuper, "Introduction," p. 20.

36. Of the considerable literature I examined on this question, the vast majority has demonstrated that sanctions do not produce a generalized deterrent effect. That the existence of such sanctions reinforces social norms is just the obverse of saying that most people abide by laws that accurately reflect norms within the jural community. The crucial factor with respect to the deterrent effects of sanctions is the perception of these penalties by social deviants. See Johannes Andenaes, "The General Preventive Effects," pp. 957-66; Andenaes, "General Prevention," pp. 191-92; Franklin Zimring and Gordon Hawkins, "Deterrence," p. 113; Salomon Rettig, "Ethical Risk Sensitivity," pp. 587-88. This being so, some have suggested a typology for crime and deterrence where one may correlate a deviant's commitment to crime with the type of deviance by which he will be affected (William J. Chambliss, "Types of Deviance," pp. 712-13). The

argument over the relationship between deviance and sanctions is summarized in a competent article by Richard D. Schwartz and Sonya Orleans ("On Legal Sanctions," pp. 64-87). The vast literature is surveyed by Theodore G. Chiricos and Gordon P. Waldo, "Punishment and Crime," pp. 200-217. All the literature and consideration of problems associated with deterrence theory appear in Franklin E. Zimring and Gordon J. Hawkins, *Deterrence*, passim.

37. See Bohannan's summary of the African reception of a particular type of homicide—killing witches, adulterers, or thieves caught stealing (Bohannan, "Patterns of Murder," pp. 233-34).

38. This is what Max Weber described as formally irrational legal systems (*Max Weber*, pp. 51-52, 77-78, 81, 89).

39. For an interesting study of the use of the oath, see Hugo Huber, "Ritual Oaths," pp. 41-49. The North American Plains Indians also made wide use of the purgatory oath (Wallace and Hoebel, *The Comanches*, p. 228; Llewellyn and Hoebel, *The Cheyenne*, pp. 151-52). A variation on the fire theme is the practice of the Ifugao, who required that accused and accuser unhurriedly lift stones out of boiling water (Barton, *Ifugao*, p. 96). Numerous variants exist in a great range of societies. See Hoebel, *Law*, pp. 266-74. John M. Roberts suggests that oaths and similar autonomic ordeals are associated with "somewhat complex cultures where they perform important functions in the maintenance of law and order in the presence of weak authority and power deficits" ("Oaths," p. 207). Also see Allott, Epstein, and Gluckman, "Introduction," p. 35.

40. This process is recorded fairly well in Fallers' study of Soga courts. While various ordeals formerly had served to decide cases, the British outlawed these practices. Composition and retaliation yielded to fines, imprisonment, and whippings. Finally, case books of judicial litigation became incorporated into Soga practice. All that is missing here is the presence of statutory law, especially since Fallers insists that the Soga did not even utilize previous judicial precedent to settle litigation (Fallers, *Law*, pp. 40-70; Fallers, "Customary Law," pp. 613-14).

41. On the role of memory in pre-literate societies, see Hoebel, *Law*, p. 251. Many ethnographers have noted that the principles of behavior were well known within the jural community, even without written statutes. See, for example, Howell, *Manual*, p. 25; Epstein, *Juridical Techniques*, p. 36; Fallers, *Law*, p. 313. Part of this easy facility with the law no doubt springs from social homogeneity (Smith, "The Sociological Framework," p. 26). The first appearance of legal codes, by their very nature, has not proven easy to observe. One study of the introduction of such codes offers useful insights into comparative legal studies (Dan Fenno Henderson, "Promulgation of Tokugawa Statutes," pp. 9-25).

42. *Max Weber*, p. 84; Robert Redfield, *Primitive Law*, pp. 5-9; Kuper and Kuper, "Introduction," p. 20. Diamond phrased it more aptly:

"Changes in society call for changes in the law, and [at this stage] there is a central authority to make them" (*Evolution*, pp. 138-39).

43. See Hoebel, *Law*, pp. 87, 114, 139; Wallace and Hoebel, *The Comanches*, pp. 232-34; Fallers and Fallers, "Homicide," p. 69; la Fontaine, "Homicide," pp. 96-97; Barton, *Ifugao*, p. 76; Westermarck, "Blood-feud," pp. 362-65; Colson, "Social Control," pp. 199-205; Fallers, *Law*, p. 56; Howell, *Manual*, p. 27. Composition often exists as an alternative to retaliation, and has been observed at some point in most of the illustrations just cited. Howell devoted considerable space to arguing that composition scales among the Nuer served only as formulas through which negotiations reached a settlement (*Manual*, pp. 25-57). On the relation of damages to other legal notions, see Schwartz and Miller, "Legal Evolution," pp. 160, 166-67.

44. For example, see Hoebel, *Law*, pp. 82, 114, 137, 193, 216-18; Pospisil, *Kapauku Papuans*, pp. 260-61; Wallace and Hoebel, *The Comanches*, pp. 210-12; Llewellyn and Hoebel, *The Cheyenne*, p. 73; Barton, *Ifugao*, pp. 95-125; Howell, *Manual*, pp. 28, 31-32; Gluckman, *Politics*, pp. 188-89; Gluckman, "African Jurisprudence," p. 444. Also see Schwartz and Miller, "Legal Evolution," pp. 165-67.

45. See, for example, Fallers, "Customary Law," pp. 605-16; Fallers, "Changing Customary Law," pp. 139-44; Howell, *Manual*, p. 229; la Fontaine, "Homicide," p. 94; Bohannan, "Homicide," p. 31. One may chart an interesting variation on this theme in Mongol law (V. A. Riasanovsky, *Customary Law*, p. 94).

46. Howell, *Manual*, pp. 61, 229, 235-36; Colson, "Social Control," p. 205; Schapera, *Handbook*, pp. 48-49.

47. Elizabeth Colson has observed, for example, that the Tonga show mixed loyalties among the various groupings to which they belong, so that the role of kinship may diminish with respect to other kinds of loyalties ("Social Control," pp. 199-212). Gluckman has enlarged upon this idea somewhat, showing the relationship between the decline in the importance of kinship and the undermining of the feud (*African Traditional Law*), pp. 29-31). Also see Moore, "Legal Liability," p. 71.

48. Schwartz and Miller, "Legal Evolution," pp. 160, 167.

49. Nevertheless, there are valiant attempts. See, among others, J. M. Wallace-Hadrill, "The Blood-feud of the Franks," pp. 459-87; D. A. Bullough, "Early Medieval Social Groupings," pp. 3-18; Lorraine Lancaster, "Kinship in Anglo-Saxon Society," pp. 230-50, 359-77.

50. See D. S. Likhachev, *Tekstologiia*, pp. 60-88.

Chapter 2

1. These figures are based on data compiled by E. I. Kolycheva (*Kholopstvo*, p. 203) and updated by later manuscript discoveries. See Ia.

N. Shchapov, "Russkaia Pravda," pp. 70-72. For a list of previously examined copies, see PR 1:55-59; V. P. Liubimov, "Novye spiski," pp. 840-62; A. A. Zimin, "Novye spiski," pp. 323-30; Ia. N. Shchapov, "Novoe o spiskakh," pp. 209-11; Shchapov, "Novye spiski," pp. 100-103.

2. V. O. Kliuchevskii, *Sochineniia*, 1:211-12. Recently it has been suggested that civil law first entered the Kormchaia in Novgorod because there the clergy wielded considerable civil power (Shchapov, *Vizantiiskoe*, p. 223). There is no specific evidence to support this conjecture.

3. For an explanation of the term, see P. Ivan Žužek, *Kormčaja*, pp. 7-13. A similar etymology was offered by Baron G. A. Rosenkampf (*Obozrenie*, pp. 67-68).

4. A brief discussion of the nomocanons may be found in H. J. Scheltema's article in the *Cambridge Medieval History* where the appropriate literature is cited (H. J. Scheltema, "Byzantine Law," pp. 61-62).

5. I. I. Sreznevskii, "Obozrenie," pp. 15-45; Žužek, *Kormčaja*, pp. 21-24; Shchapov, *Vizantiiskoe*, pp. 53-55. The Efrem text, itself incomplete as it survives, was published by V. N. Beneshevich (*Drevneslavianskaia kormchaia XIV titulov bez tolkovanii* [St. Petersburg, 1906-1907]), and completion of that redaction under the direction of Iu. K. Begunov and Ia. N. Shchapov is now under way. The latter also has published a brief description of the redaction's history (Shchapov, "O sostave," pp. 207-15). Also see Mikhail Benemanskii, *Zakon Gradskii*, pp. 29-35.

6. GIMOR, Synod Collection, no. 227. For a brief paleographic description, see T. N. Protas'eva, ed., *Opisanie*, 1:95; M. V. Shchepkina, T. N. Protas'eva, L. M. Kostiukhina, V. S. Golyshenko, "Opisanie," p. 145; S. P. Obnorskii, *O iazyke*, passim.

7. Shchapov, *Vizantiiskoe*, pp. 67, 91, 96-100; Shchapov, "Retseptsiia," pp. 124-26; Shchapov, "Nekotorye," p. 265.

8. Specifics of this chronology have long been disputed. A. S. Pavlov initiated the debate with his assertion that a Slavonic Kormchaia, dependent upon Byzantine precedents, was in use in Russia already in the tenth century. Pavlov further hypothesized that a second nomocanon was translated into Slavonic from Greek during Iaroslav's reign, so that the clergy was equipped with both the Scholasticus Nomocanon and the so-called Photian Nomocanon in Fourteen Titles. For evidence of the first, Pavlov referred to the Ustiug Miscellany, and for the latter to the Efrem Kormchaia (*Pervonachal'nyi*, passim; *Kanonicheskoe*, pp. 114-17). These conclusions initially found support in the work of another eminent church historian, a contemporary of Pavlov, N. S. Suvorov (*O tserkovnykh nakazaniiakh*, p. 111; *Konspekt*, p. 39). In other words, Suvorov attempted to undercut somewhat the significance of Byzantine law, suggesting instead a heavy element of Catholic influence on particular components of the Kormchaia (*Sledy zapadnokatolicheskogo tserkovnogo prava v pamiatnikakh drevnego russkogo prava* [Iaroslavl', 1888]; *K voprosu o zapadnom vliianii na drevnerusskoe pravo* [Iaroslavl', 1893]). The implications of western influ-

NOTES TO CHAPTER 2

ence were unacceptable to Pavlov, who presumed to lead the critique of Suvorov's findings (*Mnimye sledy katolicheskogo vliianiia v drevneishikh pamiatnikakh iugoslavianskogo i russkogo tserkovnogo prava* [Moscow, 1892]). A concise summary of the debate was published by N. K. Nikol'skii ("K istorii," pp. 110-24). Also see N. Suvorov, *Uchebnik*, pp. 165, 187-90; Kirill Mysovskii, "Drevnee russkoe pravo," pp. 189-96; "O pervonachal'nom sostave," pp. 541-47; "Ob osnovaniiakh," pp. 311-23. Recent work on this topic suggests an origin in Russia of the Syntagma in Fourteen Titles sometime late in the eleventh century (R. G. Pikhoia, "K voprosu," p. 309). Shchapov's thorough analysis of the Kormchaia's contents does not prove the document's time of arrival in the Russian lands, but taken together with the sum of other evidence seems persuasive (*Vizantiiskoe*, pp. 101-102).

9. Other copies include GIMOR, Uvarov Collection, no. 124; GBLOR, f. 303, no. 207; GBLOR, f. 247, no. 268; GPBOR, f. 717, no. 1056/1165; GPBOR, F. II. 250. These copies are described by Shchapov ("O sostave," pp. 209-12), and Žužek includes a cursory examination (*Kormčaja*, pp. 21-22), excluding GBLOR, f. 247, no. 268. For a detailed description of the last, see Ia. N. Shchapov, "Novyi spisok kormchei Efremovskoi," pp. 258-76.

10. GBLOR, f. 256, no. 230. See Sreznevskii, "Obozrenie," pp. 113-34; V. E. Ushakov, "Ustiuzhskaia," pp. 20-40. On the history of the revisions of the Efrem redaction, see Shchapov, *Vizantiiskoe*, pp. 104-15.

11. Pavlov, *Pervonachal'nyi*, pp. 16-24; Pavlov, *Kanonicheskoe*, pp. 114-16; Sreznevskii, "Obozrenie," p. 134; Shchapov, "Nekotorye," p. 268.

12. RIB 6:85-86. Incidentally, Shchapov has recently demonstrated that this council took place in summer or early autumn 1273, and not 1274 as is usually supposed (*Vizantiiskoe*, p. 184).

13. Žužek, *Kormčaja*, p. 35; Shchapov, *Vizantiiskoe*, pp. 146-50.

14. Žužek, *Kormčaja*, pp. 29-38; Sreznevskii, "Obozrenie," pp. 12, 47-84; Shchapov, *Vizantiiskoe*, pp. 117-19.

15. The most recent count found nearly forty copies, about thirty of which survive in various Ukrainian, Belorussian, and Russian copies (Shchapov, *Vizantiiskoe*, p. 117; Shchapov, "Retseptsiia," p. 126). Also see Žužek, *Kormčaja*, p. 49, although in evaluating Žužek's figures one must remember that he compiled his information without ever seeing any manuscript in the U.S.S.R. (ibid., pp. 2, 46). One manuscript of the Serbian redaction, at some point divided and separated, has recently been matched with its missing half (Ia. N. Shchapov, "Pervonachal'nyi sostav," pp. 140-47).

16. See Žužek, *Kormčaja*, pp. 52-56; Shchapov, *Vizantiiskoe*, p. 153. Žužek also lists the contents of the printed Kormchaia (*Kormčaja*, pp. 64-106).

17. Sreznevskii, "Obozrenie," pp. 12, 85-112. On the history of its

compilation, see Ia. N. Shchapov, "K istorii teksta," pp. 295-301; Shchapov, "Nekotorye," pp. 266-67; Shchapov, *Vizantiiskoe*, pp. 163-72; Žužek, *Kormčaja*, pp. 38-41. For a recent attempt at dating its compilation, see V. L. Ianin, "O date," pp. 287-92.

18. Shchapov, "K istorii teksta," pp. 297-99; Shchapov, *Vizantiiskoe*, pp. 206-209. For a description of the Lukashevich Kormchaia, see Ia. N. Shchapov, "Sobranie rukopisnykh knig," p. 9.

19. GIMOR, Chudov Collection, no. 4; GIMOR, Synod Collection, no. 132. See Ia. N. Shchapov, "Varsonef'skaia," pp. 93-101; Shchapov, "K istorii teksta," pp. 295-301; Shchapov, *Vizantiiskoe*, pp. 163-65; Sreznevskii, "Obozrenie," pp. 111-12.

20. See, for example, Shchapov, "Varsonof'evskaia," pp. 96-100; Shchapov, *Vizantiiskoe*, pp. 213-17.

21. Shchapov, "K istorii teksta," pp. 297-98; Shchapov, *Vizantiiskoe*, pp. 209-13.

22. The first to appreciate the significance of the Kormchaia was Nikolai Kalachov, "O znachenii kormchei," pp. 3-8.

23. PR 1:123-33.

24. A copy of this text may be found in PRP 1:244-46; and Shchapov, *Drevnerusskie*, pp. 22-24.

25. GPBOR, f. 728, no. 1173. See PR 1:137.

26. GPBOR, F. II. 119, described in PR 1:181-82.

27. See Žužek, *Kormčaja*, pp. 42-45. For particular sixteenth-century variations of the Kormchaia, see Iu. K. Begunov, "Kormchaia Ivana Volka Kuritsyna," pp. 141-59; N. A. Kazakova, "K izucheniiu," pp. 345-49.

28. The Chudov Kormchaia combined the Novgorod Kormchaia text with the Merilo Pravednoe, another complex of legal materials which is discussed in detail below. The oldest extant Kormchaia of this type is GIMOR, Chudov Collection, no. 167. See PR 1:204-205 and *ZSL kratkoi*, pp. 18-19.

29. M. N. Tikhomirov, *Issledovanie*, pp. 88-90; PR 1:89-103.

30. N. V. Kalachov first listed the contents according to the oldest extant text ("Merilo Pravednoe," pp. 28-36). Also see MP, pp. vi-xiii. For the text of the Pravda, see PR 1:104-17; MP, pp. 665-89. On the text devoted to church people, see MP, p. 664; RIB 36:40-53. For the history of this last text, see Ia. N. Shchapov, "Pravilo," pp. 72-81.

31. GBLOR, f. 304, no. 15. See MP, pp. v, xiv; PR 1:89; Tikhomirov, *Issledovanie*, p. 88, 90-97; Tikhomirov, "Vossozdanie," p. 181; Tikhomirov, "Zakon," p. 206; *ZSL kratkoi*, pp. 7-26; Kalachov, "Merilo Pravednoe," p. 28.

32. GIMOR, Synod Collection, no. 525; GIMOR, Synod Collection, no. 524; GPBOR, f. 351, no. 145/1222. The deviant manuscript is GBLOR, f. 173.I, no. 187. For a description of the first two manuscripts, see Protas'eva, *Opisanie*, 1:165-67. All the manuscripts are described in *ZSL kratkoi*, pp. 56-57 and Tikhomirov, *Issledovanie*, pp. 89-90. Also see PR 1:99-103.

33. Tikhomirov, *Issledovanie*, p. 89; Tikhomirov, "Zakon," pp. 205-206; Tikhomirov, "Vossozdanie," p. 181.

34. See MP, pp. 2-3.

35. Basic manuscripts of this type are surveyed in PR 1:203-14. The contents of this arrangement are discussed by Tikhomirov, *Issledovanie*, pp. 108-25.

36. TsGADA, f. 135, no. 383 (formerly V. 1. no. 1). For description of the contents and a discussion of the dating, see Tikhomirov, *Issledovanie*, pp. 143-47; *ZSL prostrannoi*, pp. 31-33; PR 1:277; *Russkie dostopamiatnosti*, 2:iv; and L. V. Cherepnin, ed., *Gosudarstvennoe drevlekhranilishche*, pp. 155-57.

37. NPL, pp. 477-509. See Tikhomirov, *Issledovanie*, p. 148.

38. Nikolai Kalachov pioneered this approach (*Predvaritel'nye*, pp. 89, 93, 94, 96, 104, 109, 112).

39. *Ustav sviatogo velikogo kniazia Vladimira o tserkovnykh sudakh i o desiatinakh*, ed. V. N. Beneshevich (Petrograd, 1915); later republished in RIB 36:1-72. Beneshevich's work on Iaroslav's Statute was prepared for press, but never published. The proofs with corrections are now part of Beneshevich's archive collection housed in Arkhiv Akademii nauk SSSR (Leningrad), f. 192, op. 1, no. 35, fols. 22-42, 54-71, 81-88; fols. 43-45 list fifty-five manuscripts which Beneshevich used for the first three redactions of the planned edition. In his 1921 report on the work, Beneshevich indicated that part of his work on Iaroslav's Statute indeed was published in RIB 36 as pp. 109-20. The printer's proofs for these pages are still in the archive collection (fols. 54-59). See V. N. Beneshevich, "Avtoreferat," p. 184. Also see V. N. Beneshevich, ed., *Sbornik pamiatnikov*, 1:59-89, where the basic texts of the Statutes of Vladimir and Iaroslav appear.

40. S. V. Iushkov, *K istorii drevnerusskikh iuridicheskikh sbornikov (XIII v.)* (Saratov: Gosudarstvennoe izdatel'stvo, 1921). Part of the reason that the booklet was neglected on publication was that it was published in a provincial city during the Civil War. Mentioned in a brief review together with Stratonov's work on the Short Pravda, the booklet was almost ignored by A. E. Presniakov (*Kniga i revoliutsiia* 2, no. 1 [1921]:47).

41. See S. V. Iushkov, *Izsledovaniia*, pp. 27-48; Iushkov, "Russkaia Pravda," pp. 72-77; Iushkov, *Russkaia Pravda*, pp. 34-55. For a recent appraisal of Iushkov's contribution, see A. A. Zimin, "Iz istoriografii," pp. 275-82.

42. Iushkov, *Izsledovaniia*, pp. 29-48; Iushkov, *K istorii*, pp. 1-8, 16-27; Iushkov, "Russkaia Pravda," pp. 75-77.

43. Iushkov, *K istorii*, p. 3; Iushkov, *Izsledovaniia*, pp. 28-29. Iushkov gives a much more complex description of this process in *Russkaia Pravda*, the basic conclusions of which are summarized on pp. 54-55. On the *Pravilo zakonno*, see Shchapov, "Pravilo," pp. 72-81.

44. Iushkov, *K istorii*, p. 3; Iushkov, *Izsledovaniia*, pp. 28-29.

45. Iushkov, *K istorii*, pp. 20-23; Iushkov, *Izsledovaniia*, p. 34. A slightly different version appears in Iushkov's *Russkaia Pravda*, pp. 34-43.

By Iushkov's calculations, the Collection of Princely Statutes represented a church collection, and the Russkaia Pravda a secular collection (*Izsledovaniia*, pp. 34, 36).

46. Iushkov, *K istorii*, pp. 23-25; Iushkov, *Izsledovaniia*, pp. 32, 36-40; Iushkov, "Russkaia Pravda," pp. 75-76; Iushkov, *Russkaia Pravda*, pp. 34-37.

47. See MP, p. 664.

48. Iushkov, *K istorii*, pp. 25-26; Iushkov, "Russkaia Pravda," pp. 76-77.

49. MP, p. 140, where the contents of the Collection of 30 Chapters are listed. The moralizing literature precedes this division of the manuscript. See Iushkov, *K istorii*, pp. 15-16, 26-27; Iushkov, *Izsledovaniia*, p. 32; Iushkov, "Russkaia Pravda," pp. 75-76.

50. Iushkov, *K istorii*, pp. 15-16; Iushkov, *Izsledovaniia*, p. 32; Iushkov, "Russkaia Pravda," p. 76; Iushkov, *Russkaia Pravda*, p. 55.

51. Ia. N. Shchapov's dissertation for the Candidate's degree ("Tserkov' kak feodal'naia organizatsiia v drevnei Rusi v X-XII vv.," Cand. diss., Moscow, 1964) was devoted to the study of the text history of the princely charters, excluding only Iaroslav's Statute. The dissertation served as the basis for a later book, supplemented by materials on Iaroslav's Statute (*Kniazheskie ustavy i tserkov' v drevnei Rusi XI-XIV vv.* [Moscow: Nauka, 1972]). The same material was used to produce a raft of smaller studies of manuscripts connected with the princely statutes. The major work of this series was devoted to the text history of Iaroslav's Statute ("Redaktsiia," pp. 481-513). A critical edition of the princely statutes and certain other legal texts appeared somewhat belatedly (*Drevnerusskie kniazheskie ustavy [XI-XV vv.]* [Moscow: Nauka, 1976]).

52. Ia. N. Shchapov, "K kharakteristike," p. 177.

53. Ibid., pp. 179, 184. For differing estimates of the origin of the Sophia First Chronicle, see M. D. Priselkov, *Istoriia*, pp. 150-52; A. A. Shakhmatov, *Obozrenie*, p. 155; D. S. Likhachev, *Russkie letopisi*, pp. 312-13.

54. NPL, pp. 477-508; Shchapov, "K kharakteristike," pp. 180-82. Elsewhere Shchapov asserts that the article on dishonor usually appears in a complex of juridical monuments, one of whose components is the Concordance, rather than Expanded, redaction of the Zakon Sudnyi (*Drevnerusskie*, p. 197).

55. V. N. Tatishchev, *Istoriia*, 2:75, 77, 239 (n. 225), 241 (n. 240). See the drafts of this project, published by S. N. Valk ("Tatishchevskie," pp. 628-57). For a discussion of Tatishchev's frustration, see S. N. Valk, "Russkaia Pravda XVIII v.," pp. 125-30; Valk, "Tatishchevskie," p. 610.

56. Valk, "Russkaia Pravda XVIII v.," pp. 135, 139-40.

57. Ibid., pp. 140-41. The successful matching of the Krestinin copy with GIMOR, Museum Collection, no. 798, was the achievement of M. N. Tikhomirov ("Krestininskii spisok," pp. 398-400).

58. This edition does not name Boltin as editor, but Valk has successfully demonstrated Boltin's role. See Valk, "Russkaia Pravda XVIII v.," pp. 141-49; Valk, "Boltin," pp. 650-56. A recent textual study of this edition suggests that Boltin used two copies of the Expanded Pravda unknown to us—one copy each from the Obolensk-Karamzin type and from the Museum type (A. L. Nikitin, "Boltinskoe," pp. 53-65).

59. Valk, "Russkaia Pravda XVIII v.," pp. 149-50. Cf. N. M. Karamzin, *Istoriia*, 2:30-44. Karamzin mentions his discovery of the Synod and Pushkin texts in the appended notes (for example, n. 65, p. 27).

60. *Russkie dostopamiatnosti*, 1:17-58 (the text itself appears on pp. 28-58); *Sofiiskii vremiannik*, 1:111-29.

61. This work originally was published in German, and later appeared in Russian translation as *Drevneishee russkoe pravo v istoricheskom ego raskrytii*, trans. I. Platonov (St. Petersburg, 1835). For a discussion of Ewers's relation to the publication of the Russkaia Pravda, see S. N. Valk, "Russkaia Pravda XIX v.," pp. 194-202.

62. G. A. Rosenkampf, *Obozrenie*, pp. 10-11, 149-50. A summary of Rosenkampf's work appears in Valk, "Russkaia Pravda XIX v.," pp. 214-20.

63. Valk, "Russkaia Pravda XIX v.," pp. 220-38.

64. *Russkie dostopamiatnosti*, 2:10-142. The Zakon Sudnyi liudem appeared on pp. 143-220, and Iaroslav's Statute on Bridges on pp. 287-315.

65. Valk, "Russkaia Pravda XIX v.," pp. 242-44.

66. Nikolai Kalachov, *Tekst*, p. i. Valk also claimed that Kalachov had used fifty copies ("Russkaia Pravda XIX v.," p. 250). However, in preparation for the Soviet Academy edition of the Pravda, V. P. Liubimov, counting copies actually used by Kalachov, could find only forty-six ("Ob izdanii," p. 302).

67. Kalachov, *Predvaritel'nye*, pp. 89, 93, 94, 96, 104, 109, 112; Valk, "Russkaia Pravda XIX v.," p. 251.

68. Kalachov, *Tekst*, pp. 1-5 (Academy copy), 6-20 (Trinity), 21-42 (Karamzin), and 43-48 (Obolenskii). An index of terms and names, a table comparing the article enumeration of the Synod copy in relation to the other copies of the edition, and samples of the handwriting of each copy are appended. *Tekst* was reprinted in 1847, 1881, and 1889.

69. V. I. Sergeevich, "Russkaia Pravda," pp. 1, 7-20, 40; Sergeevich, *Lektsii*, pp. 37-75.

70. V. I. Sergeevich, *Russkaia Pravda*, pp. vi, xiii, 1-34. This edition was greeted with some skepticism, but received hearty applause from P. N. Mrochek-Drozdovskii ("Novoe izdanie," pp. 1-32). Mrochek-Drozdovskii's own work was probably the most significant contribution in the interim between Kalachov and Sergeevich. See his *Izsledovaniia*, nos. 2, 4 (Moscow, 1881, 1885), and "Izsledovaniia," pp. 1-245.

71. L. K. Goetz argued for the ancient origins of the Pravda most

carefully in a four-volume study and translation of the Pravda, which appeared in German between 1910 and 1914. For reactions to this attempt, see M. F. Vladimirskii-Budanov, "Das russische," pp. 1-24; A. Presniakov, "Goetz," pp. 153-67; Aleksandr Filippov, "Russkaia Pravda," pp. 164-216; Filippov, "Iz inostrannykh," pp. 311-37; M. A. D'iakonov, "Prof. Dr. Goetz," pp. 232-52.

72. A. I. Iakovlev, ed., *Russkaia Pravda*, p. 3.

73. E. Chernousov, "K voprosu," pp. 303-22; N. A. Maksimeiko, *Opyt*, pp. 114-206; D. Golenishchev-Kutuzov, *Russkaia Pravda i Vizantiia* (Irkutsk, 1913).

74. For example, N. A. Maksimeiko, "Russkaia Pravda," pp. 382-95.

75. A. I. Sobolevskii, "Dve redaktsii," pp. 17-23; I. A. Stratonov, "K voprosu," pp. 385-424; D. M. Meichik, "Russkaia Pravda," pp. 78-100.

76. A. I. Iakovlev, L. V. Cherepnin, eds., *Russkaia Pravda po spiskam Akademicheskomu, Troitskomu i Karamzinskomu* (Moscow, 1928). Also see V. P. Liubimov, "Ob izdanii," p. 307, where Liubimov complains that Iakovlev and Cherepnin used Kalachov for their edition. Liubimov's article also suggests that Grekov in 1918 republished Sergeevich's edition, but the list of Grekov's works contains no such credit ("Spisok nauchnykh trudov B. D. Grekova," *Akademiku Borisu Dmitrievichu Grekovu ko dniu semidesiatiletiia. Sbornik statei* [Moscow: AN SSSR, 1952], p. 22).

77. Liubimov, "Ob izdanii," p. 304; Liubimov, "Paleograficheskie nabliudeniia nad Troitskim," pp. 109-14. The notation on p. 109 is that this was abstracted from "a report read 6 March 1929 at the subcommittee for the preparation of an edition of the Russkaia Pravda by the Archeographic Commission of the Academy of Sciences." Liubimov's work was under way as early as 1924, however. See the report of his activities given before the Sector on Russian history, 15 December 1924 (*Uchenye zapiski instituta istorii Rossiiskoi assotsiatsii nauchno-issledovatel'skikh institutov obshchestvennykh nauk* 3 [1929]:391).

78. E. F. Karskii, ed., *Russkaia Pravda po drevneishemu spisku* (Leningrad: AN SSSR, 1930); variants used for this edition are listed on pp. 22-24. For previous editions see I. I. Sreznevskii, *Paleograficheskii snimok*, pp. 1-26; and N. A. Marks, ed., *Russkaia Pravda po Sinodal'nomu spisku* (Moscow, 1910).

79. S. V. Iushkov, ed., *Rus'ka Pravda. Teksti na osnovi 7 spyskiv ta 5 redaktsii* (Kiev: Ukrains'ka akademiia nauk, 1935), pp. iv-vii; texts appear on pp. 1-178.

80. Liubimov, "Ob izdanii," pp. 307-12.

81. B. D. Grekov, ed., *Russkaia Pravda po spiskam Akademicheskomu, Karamzinskomu i Troitskomu* (Moscow-Leningrad: Ogiz, Sotsekgiz, 1934); Grekov, ed., *Pravda Russkaia. Uchebnoe posobie* (Moscow-Leningrad: AN SSSR, 1940); *Pamiatniki istorii Kievskogo gosudarstva IX-XII vv.*, ed. G. E. Kochin (Leningrad: Sotsekgiz, 1936), no. 23.

82. M. N. Tikhomirov, "Russkaia Pravda," pp. 138-55.

83. M. N. Tikhomirov, *Issledovanie o Russkoi Pravde* (Moscow-Leningrad: AN SSSR, 1941). The title page and binding incorrectly identify the author as N. N. Tikhomirov.

84. M. N. Tikhomirov, *Posobie*, pp. 39-46 (Academy Short Pravda), 49-74 (Trinity Expanded Pravda), 113-19 (Abbreviated Pravda), 127-29 (Pravosudie Mitropolich'e), 125-26 (fragment associated with Zakon Sudnyi liudem).

85. N. A. Maksimeiko, "Moskovskaia redaktsiia," pp. 127-62.

86. V. P. Liubimov, "Paleograficheskie nabliudeniia nad Akademicheskim," pp. 156-61.

87. *Pravda Russkaia*, ed. B. D. Grekov, 3 vols. (Moscow-Leningrad: AN SSSR, 1940-1963): vol. 1, *Teksty*; vol. 2, *Kommentarii*; vol. 3, *Faksimil'noe vosproizvedenie tekstov*. See Liubimov, "Spiski," pp. 11-54.

88. S. V. Iushkov, "Russkaia Pravda," pp. 72-89 and *Russkaia Pravda*, pp. 27-200. Iushkov had the misfortune to try to write good history in a highly politicized environment. His 1950 study got him into trouble in some quarters because he failed to make sufficient bows to Marx and Lenin. Worse, he was accused of having anti-Marxist conceptions of history (P. P. Epifanov, "K voprosu," pp. 93-104). Epifanov even had the gall to declare that Iushkov's work bore a "falsely scientific character," a proposition which he based on Stalin's vacuous venture into linguistics (ibid., p. 104).

89. PRP 1:71-232.

90. G. L. Geiermans, "Tatishchevskie," pp. 163-74; Valk, "Tatishchevskie," pp. 607-57; Valk, "Boltin," pp. 650-56; Nikitin, "Boltinskoe," pp. 53-65. Also see S. L. Peshtich, *Russkaia istoriografiia*, 1:249-50.

91. Among linguistic studies, see A. M. Selishchev, "O iazyke," pp. 57-63; A. S. Oreshnikov, "K voprosu," pp. 121-30; Oreshnikov, "K istorii," pp. 151-55; Henrik Birnbaum, "On Old Russian," pp. 115-40 (reprinted with slight changes in Birnbaum, *On Medieval Writing*, pp. 234-59). For an ideological examination, see I. U. Budovnits, "O stat'e 12," pp. 197-201. Some of the worst examples of this approach belong to the pen of L. V. Cherepnin. See, for example, the nadir of his work, "Russkaia Pravda," pp. 89-99. Cherepnin could be forgiven such labors, considering the era of the article's appearance, but recent versions are only slightly less galling. See L. V. Cherepnin, "Obshchestvenno-politicheskie," pp. 128-278. Deprived of the heaviest of ideological overlays, historico-textual analysis has yielded some useful data, as M. D. Priselkov's long review of the Academy edition of the Pravda proved ("Zadachi," pp. 238-50).

92. N. L. Rubinshtein, "Drevneishaia," pp. 3-10; M. O. Kosven, *Semeinaia*, pp. 133-60. A. A. Zimin participated in two creditable examinations of the Pravda. With A. G. Poliak, Zimin celebrated the tricentennial of the Ukraine's "reconstitution" with Russia ("Znachenie Russkoi

Pravdy," pp. 116-22). In addition to examining the Pravda's relationship to the law of Poland, Lithuania, Novgorod, and Pskov, Zimin and Poliak here laid the groundwork for Kolycheva's later study of slavery on the basis of the Pravda. In another article, Zimin attempted to reconstruct the history of the Short Pravda ("K istorii," pp. 155-208). For examples of reprintings of the Pravda, see *Khrestomatiia po istorii SSSR s drevneishikh vremen do kontsa XV v.*, ed. M. N. Tikhomirov (Moscow: Sotsekgiz, 1960), pp. 194-229; *Sbornik dokumentov po istorii SSSR dlia seminarskikh i prakticheskikh zaniatii*, ed. V. V. Mavrodin, et al., 10 vols. to date (Moscow: Vysshaia shkola, 1970-), 1:131-45.

93. George Vernadsky, ed. and trans., *Medieval Russian Laws*, pp. 26-56. Vernadsky's translations often miss the mark, as for example, his translation of article 14 of the Short Pravda: "He must produce two bails [to guarantee that he will come] within five days" (*To poruchnika za piat' dnii*). Other examples are cited below.

94. Vladimir V. Gsovskii, "Medieval Russian Laws," pp. 152-58; Samuel Kucherov, "Indigenous," pp. 257-82; Oswald P. Backus III, "Legal Analysis," pp. 283-90; Darrell P. Hammer, "Character," pp. 291-95. Two studies devoted to the interrelationship between Roman law and the Pravda also appeared, both ill-advised (V. V. Gsovskii, "Roman Private Law," pp. 363-75; Darrell P. Hammer, "Russia," pp. 1-13).

95. See especially Marc Szeftel, "La condition," pp. 375-430; Szeftel, "Le Statut," pp. 635-56; Szeftel, ed. and trans., *Documents*, pp. 21-115. Szeftel also includes translation and commentary on the Pskov Judicial Charter, and the Statutes of Vladimir, Iaroslav, Vsevolod, Sviatoslav, and Rostislav (ibid., pp. 117-213, 229-45, 247-65, 267-80, 281-86, and 287-99 respectively).

96. Michel Laran and Jean Saussay, eds., *La Russie*, pp. 41-45 (Short Pravda), pp. 45-48 (parts of the Expanded Pravda).

97. See Tikhomirov, *Issledovanie*, pp. 220-24; Szeftel, "La condition," pp. 375-430; Iu. G. Alekseev, "Chastnyi akt," pp. 125-41; Alekseev, "Naimit i gosudar'," pp. 22-29.

98. See V. I. Picheta, "Litovskii statut," p. 24; *The Lithuanian Statute*, pp. 2-12.

99. Sergeevich, *Lektsii*, p. 75; Sergeevich, "Russkaia Pravda," p. 40.

100. PRP 2:124-26; GVNP, no. 28; *Pamiatniki istorii Velikogo Novgoroda i Pskova*, no. 43; M. F. Vladimirskii-Budanov, *Khristomatiia*, 1: 108-12; *Smolenskie*, pp. 20-52.

101. PRP 2:54, 58.1; *Smolenskie*, p. 18. For two accounts of the possible relation between the various texts, see PRP 1:54-56 and *Smolenskie*, p. 62.

102. *Smolenskie*, pp. 20, 25, 30, 35, 39, 45; a detailed paleographic description of the individual manuscripts appears on pp. 52-62.

103. Editors of *Smolenskie* try to connect this text to events preceding the 1229 Treaty (pp. 13-17), but the opposite chronology must prevail (see

PRP 2:55-56), a view that is supported by the legal change examined below.

104. Some scholars have insisted that the Novgorod Charter consisted of only those forty-two articles now known to us—the first twenty-four as an independent complex later supplemented by the remainder. See P. N. Mrochek-Drozdovskii, "Glavneishie," pp. 119-21; Mrochek-Drozdovskii, "Pamiatniki," p. 50; V. N. Latkin, *Lektsii*, pp. 37-38; B. M. Kochakov, "Novgorodskaia," pp. 11-13. For a contrasting view, see M. F. Valdimirskii-Budanov, *Obzor*, pp. 95-96; L. V. Cherepnin, *Russkie feodal'nye arkhivy*, 1:374; and PRP 2:210.

105. One of the early studies of the Novgorod Charter disputed the contention that Moscow exercised any influence at all on Novgorod law (Fedor Panov, "Izsledovanie," pp. 255-57). For a description of the manuscript, see Cherepnin, *Russkie feodal'nye arkhivy*, 1:334-42. The Novgorod Charter was first published by Karamzin (*Istoriia*, 5:159-62 [n. 404]), and shortly thereafter in AAE 1, no. 92. Other documents from this manuscript appear in AAE 1, nos. 87, 90, 91, 93, 94. Several twentieth-century publications also included the Charter. See Vladimirskii-Budanov, *Khristomatiia*, 1:200-216; *Pamiatniki istorii Velikogo Novgoroda i Pskova*, no. 39; PRP 2:212-18.

106. Estimates of the Charter's dates vary somewhat. For arguments supporting an origin in the mid-fifteenth century, see Mrochek-Drozdovskii, "Pamiatniki," p. 50 and "Glavneishie," pp. 117-21; Vladimirskii-Budanov, *Obzor*, p. 95; Sergeevich, *Lektsii*, p. 31; A. N. Filippov, *Uchebnik*, pt. 1, p. 129. D. Ia. Samokvasov suggested compilation in the mid-fifteenth century, and a 1471 copying (*Drevnee russkoe pravo*, p. 239). Kochakov supported a 1446 compilation ("Novgorodskaia," pp. 10-11) and S. V. Pakhman a 1471 origin (*Istoriia*, 1:222). The most complex reconstruction attempt comes from L. V. Cherepnin, who posited redactions of 1385, 1422, and 1446/7, and the 1471 version which was oriented toward Moscow's power squeeze of Novgorod. See Cherepnin, "Sostav," pp. 222-53 and *Russkie feodal'nye arkhivy*, 1:373-96.

107. The manuscript of the complete text is now housed in the Library of the Academy of Sciences (Biblioteka Akademii nauk [Leningrad], otdel rukopisei, 34.2.31). For a detailed description, see *Opisanie rukopisnogo otdela*, pp. 328-32. Also see B. B. Kafengauz, *Drevnii Pskov*, pp. 328-32; and Iu. G. Alekseev, "Paleograficheskie nabliudeniia," pp. 70-79.

108. Karamzin, *Istoriia*, 5:158-59 (n. 404). For examples of later editions, see Evgenii Bolkhovitinov, *Istoriia*, 1:45-47; AAE 1, no. 103.

109. *Pskovskaia Sudnaia Gramota sostavlennaia na veche v 1467 godu*, ed. M. S. Vorontsov (Odessa, 1847).

110. F. N. Ustrialov provided a translation, detailed notes and glossary of terms (*Izsledovanie Pskovskoi Sudnoi Gramoty 1467 goda* [St. Petersburg, 1855]). I. E. Engel'man was first to propose in detail a complex

history of composition for the Charter, stretching from Aleksandr Nevskii to 1467 (*Sistematicheskoe izlozhenie grazhdanskikh zakonov soderzhashchikhsia v Pskovskoi sudnoi gramote* [St. Petersburg, 1855]). The essential outlines of these views were already suggested by Nikolai Kalachov in his review of the 1847 edition ("Pskovskaia," pp. 165-78).

111. The title was changed slightly: *Pskovskaia Sudnaia Gramota (1397-1467 gg.)* (Odessa, 1868). As an example of the influence of this edition, see Vladimirskii-Budanov, *Khristomatiia*, 1:148-90.

112. *Pskovskaia Sudnaia Gramota*, ed. N. D. Chechulin (St. Petersburg: Imperatorskaia arkheograficheskaia kommissiia, 1914).

113. P. E. Mikhailov, "Novye dannye," pp. 132-42; Mikhailov, *Iuridicheskaia priroda zemlepol'zovaniia po Pskovskoi sudnoi gramote* (St. Petersburg, 1914).

114. M. K. Rozhkova, *K voprosu o proiskhozhdenii i sostave Pskovskoi Sudnoi Gramoty* (Leningrad-Moscow: Kniga, 1927).

115. L. V. Cherepnin and A. I. Iakovlev, "Pskovskaia," pp. 255-59; L. V. Cherepnin, "K voprosu," pp. 203-31; B. B. Kafengauz, "O proiskhozhdenii," pp. 295-326; Cherepnin, *Russkie feodal'nye arkhivy*, 1:408-47; I. D. Martysevich, *Pskovskaia sudnaia gramota: Istoriko-iuridicheskoe issledovanie* (Moscow: MGU, 1951); I. I. Polosin, *Pskovskaia sudnaia gramota, Uchenye zapiski Moskovskogo gosudarstvennogo pedagogicheskogo instituta imeni V. I. Lenina*, kafedra istorii SSSR, vol. 65, no. 3 (Moscow, 1952); Kafengauz, *Drevnii Pskov*, pp. 112-37; Alekseev, "Paleograficheskie nabliudeniia," pp. 79-103.

116. *Pamiatniki istorii Velikogo Novgoroda i Pskova*, no. 77; Martysevich, *Pskovskaia*, pp. 134-95; Polosin, *Pskovskaia*, pp. 11-51; PRP 2:286-324; Cherepnin and Iakovlev, "Pskovskaia," pp. 237-54.

117. See, for example, B. B. Kafengauz, "Pskovskie," pp. 28-48 and "O pskovskikh," pp. 132-39. These articles also appear in reworked form in Kafengauz, *Drevnii Pskov*, pp. 7-35. Martysevich's monograph pounds heavily on the same theme (*Pskovskaia*, pp. 49-89). An interesting exception to this rule is the work of M. M. Isaev, "Ugolovnoe pravo Novgoroda," pp. 126-42.

118. On Pskov's relations to Novgorod, see A. I. Nikitskii, *Ocherk*, pp. 88-105.

119. An entire segment of the Pskov Judicial Charter, articles 109-20, constitutes a basic reworking of norms of the Russkaia Pravda, a factor that has helped fuel debate on the relative age of this section. See Cherepnin and Iakovlev, "Pskovskaia," pp. 258-59, 296-97; Kafengauz, "O proiskhozhdenii," pp. 308-309. Zimin, among others, observed that traces of the Russkaia Pravda were detectable in other portions of the Pskov Charter as well (PRP 2:375; also see pp. 341, 352, 356, 360, 367-69, 373, 377, 379).

120. See Cherepnin, *Russkie feodal'nye arkhivy*, 1:334-42.

121. Karamzin, *Istoriia*, 5:86-87 (n. 244); AAE 1, no. 13;

Vladimirskii-Budanov, *Khristomatiia*, 1:140-47; *Pamiatniki istorii Velikogo Novgoroda i Pskova*, no. 58; GVNP, no. 88; PRP 3:162-64; A. I. Iakovlev, ed., *Namestnich'i*, no. 1.

122. See V. N. Bernadskii, *Novgorod*, pp. 218-19.

123. Iakovlev, *Namestnich'i*, nos. 2-16. The 1488 Beloozero Administrative Charter also appears in PRP 3:170-74, along with later texts in PRP 4:188-97. A list of the administrative charters appears in PRP 4:222-23.

124. TsGADA, f. 135, no. 384 (formerly V. 1. no. 3). See Cherepnin, ed., *Gosudarstvennoe drevlekhranilishche*, p. 157; and *Sudebniki XV-XVI vekov*, pp. 14-16.

125. Baron Sigismund von Herberstein, *Notes*, 1:102-104. Herberstein's Latin text is reproduced in *Sudebniki XV-XVI vekov*, pp. 31-32.

126. See *Sudebniki XV-XVI vekov*, p. 111.

127. *Zakony velikogo kniazia Ioanna Vasil'evicha i Sudebnik tsaria i velikogo kniazia Ioanna Vasil'evicha s dopolnitel'nymi ukazami*, eds. Konstantin Kalaidovich and Pavel Stroev (Moscow, 1819; 2d ed., Moscow, 1878), pp. 1-17; AI 1, no. 105.

128. *Sudebniki Ioanna*, pp. 1-11; Vladimirskii-Budanov, *Khristomatiia*, 3d ed., 2:82-107. Forty copies of the 1550 Sudebnik are known. See *Sudebniki XV-XVI vekov*, pp. 113-31.

129. M. V. Klochkov, *Ukazatel' slov i vyrazhenii vstrechaiushchikhsia v Sudebnikakh 1497, 1550 i 1589 gg.* (Iur'ev, 1902); *Sudebniki Ioanna*, p. 51.

130. *Sudebniki XV-XVI vekov*, pp. 13-108. The first Soviet edition appeared in *Sudebniki Russkogo gosudarstva*, ed. N. Dobrotvor (Gor'kii: Gor'kovskii gosudarstvennyi pedagogicheskii institut imeni M. Gor'kogo, kafedra istorii SSSR, 1939). This volume concentrates on such things as the "progressive" nature of the 1497 Sudebnik (p. 10) or the influence of Pokrovskii on Iushkov's views of the Sudebnik (p. 9). See also S. I. Shtamm, ed., *Sudebnik 1497 goda* (Moscow: Gosiurizdat, 1955); PRP 3:345-416.

131. Horace W. Dewey, "The Sudebnik of 1497," Ph.D. diss., University of Michigan, 1955; Dewey, "The 1497 Sudebnik," pp. 325-38; Dewey, *Muscovite Judicial Texts*, pp. 7-21. A number of other articles touch on matters relating to the Sudebnik. See, for example, Horace W. Dewey, "Defamation," pp. 109-20; Dewey, "Trial by Combat," pp. 21-31; Horace W. Dewey and A. M. Kleimola, eds. and trans., *Russian Private Law*, pp. 28-204.

132. Marc Szeftel, "The Sudebnik of 1497," pp. 547-52; Szeftel, "Le Justicier," pp. 531-68.

133. S. V. Iushkov, "Sudebnik," pp. 1-46. For an example of the methods of text criticism applied to the Sudebnik, see Cherepnin, *Russkie feodal'nye arkhivy*, 2:280-386.

134. On dating, see Szeftel, "Sudebnik," p. 548; *Sudebniki XV-XVI vekov*, p. 15. On the contents, see Szeftel, "Sudebnik," p. 550; Dewey,

"1497 Sudebnik," p. 325. Dewey suggests that some omissions may be due to inexperience on the part of its compilers (p. 336), while Iushkov explained the Sudebnik's imperfect contents by suggesting that each local area had its own legal collection which the 1497 code supplemented ("Sudebnik," p. 38). Dewey's explanation, that the Sudebnik simply provided a "framework within which customary law could operate," seems most consistent with the continued copying of the Pravda ("1497 Sudebnik," p. 337).

135. Critics will add that the Pravda also survives in numerous seventeenth- and several eighteenth-century copies. But these represent a small fraction of all extant copies, and in that way emphasize their deviation from the usual survival odds of manuscripts. Besides, later copies frequently contain significant changes; this is especially true of copies of the Abbreviated redaction.

136. Sobolevskii, among others, espoused the opposite view ("Dve redaktsii," pp. 20-23).

137. See Presniakov, "Goetz," pp. 158, 166. Recently M. B. Sverdlov has attempted to revive arguments for the Short Pravda's antique origins. Noting similarities between the Short Pravda and the Germanic barbarian codes, Sverdlov deduces that the former must therefore be of the same vintage as the latter. The argument is not persuasive. One might observe, however, that the Pravda and the Germanic codes reflected similar social structures. See Sverdlov, "K istorii," pp. 135-59.

138. See Vladimirskii-Budanov, "Das russische," pp. 19-20; Tikhomirov, *Issledovanie*, pp. 35-40.

139. Goetz tried to abandon this labeling. See Presniakov, "Goetz," pp. 158, 166.

140. See Tikhomirov, *Issledovanie*, pp. 70-74; PRP 1:105-106; I. Ia. Froianov, *Kievskaia*, p. 101. This does not exclude the possibility that a fifteenth-century copyist inserted terms contemporary with him, thereby changing the linguistic value of the Short Pravda. A variation of this view is presented by Oreshnikov, who argues that the Expanded Russkaia Pravda in its oldest copies preserves certain peculiarities not reflected in later copies of the Short Pravda ("K voprosu," p. 122). Selishchev, on the other hand, demonstrated the presence of a number of archaic, South Slavic terms and grammatical patterns in the Short Pravda ("O iazyke," pp. 58-63). Most recently Ladislav Matejka has noted the penetration of Slavonisms into the later, rather than earlier, copies of the Expanded Pravda ("Diglossia," pp. 186-97), although where this leaves linguistic datings of the Pravda is not clear to me. Professor Matejka was kind enough to provide me with a copy of this paper prior to its publication.

141. At a minimum, the Expanded Russkaia Pravda consists of two statutes identified by both the headings and separate chapter indications in some copies. For example, see the Trinity copy where the first section (*Sud Iaroslavl' Volodimerich'*) is identified as chapter 28, and the second section

(*Ustav Volodimer' Vsevolodicha*) is marked as chapter 29 (PR 3:43, 53; MP, pp. 665, 677). More detailed examination of the text suggests that other layerings may rest within the Expanded Pravda—for example, sections devoted to inheritance and slavery.

142. See Tikhomirov, "Vossozdanie," pp. 173-84. Not only did the Pravda become part of the Kormchaia Kniga in northeast Russia, but copies of the Pravda themselves show increasing use of Old Church Slavonic, a telltale sign that clerics were doing the copying (Matejka, "Diglossia," pp. 193-95).

143. Liubimov, "Spiski," pp. 35-42; Tikhomirov, *Posobie*, p. 18; Tikhomirov, *Issledovanie*, pp. 166-81.

144. Texts appear in PR 1:281-92, 299-317. For commentary on the manuscript errors, see PR 1:51-52, 278-79.

145. The Synod copy does contain, however, a unique arrangement of articles (PR 1:123-33). See A. S. Oreshnikov, "O sinodal'nom spiske," pp. 52-54; PR 1:121-22. For a linguistic study of that same copy see S. P. Obnorskii, "Russkaia Pravda," pp. 749-76.

146. Tikhomirov originally proposed that Simeon of Tver' served as the compiler of the Merilo ("Vossozdanie," pp. 181-82), but later backed off from that position somewhat (MP, pp. v, xiv). Also see Tikhomirov, *Posobie*, p. 17; Tikhomirov, *Issledovanie*, pp. 88-89; Liubimov, "Paleograficheskie nabliudeniia nad Troitskim," pp. 109-14; PR 1:89.

147. GPBOR, F. II. no. 119. For manuscript description, see PR 1:181-82; on the origins of this recension, see Tikhomirov, *Issledovanie*, pp. 137-38.

148. See PR 1:137. Tikhomirov argued for a late fourteenth-century origin on the basis of terminology reminiscent of Novgorod's literature on the *Strigol'nik* heresy (*Issledovanie*, pp. 139-40). More recently, Shchapov has rejected this basis for dating the Sophia Kormchaia, using instead the Tale on the Bulgarian and Serbian Patriarchates to suggest a date in the 1420s-1460s ("Iuzhnoslavianskii," pp. 211-13).

149. Tikhomirov proposed an origin early in the fourteenth century (*Issledovanie*, pp. 119-22), but the large extant manuscript base of this Kormchaia, the bulk of whose copies belong to the late fifteenth and early sixteenth centuries, suggests an origin later than Tikhomirov admits. See GIMOR, Uvarov Collection, no. 791/556; GIMOR, Chudov Collection, no. 167; and PR 1:203-205.

150. Tikhomirov, *Issledovanie*, p. 127; Liubimov, "Spiski," p. 51.

151. St. Stephen of Perm' (1340-1396) represents an excellent example of this direction of Orthodox activity. See George P. Fedotov, *Russian Religious Mind*, 2:230-42. Also see A. V. Kartashev, *Ocherki*, 1:239-44. Ia. N. Shchapov has observed the connection between the expansion of state power and church missionary activity ("Tserkov' i stanovlenie," p. 63).

152. Recently H. W. Dewey and A. M. Kleimola have summarized

these debates with some surprising conclusions (*Zakon*, pp. v-xxii). Also see A. M. Kleimola, "Law," pp. 17-27.

153. GIMOR, Synod Collection, no. 132; GIMOR, Chudov Collection, no. 4; GBLOR, f. 256, no. 230. The texts appear in *ZSL kratkoi*, pp. 35-59, 115-54.

154. GBLOR, f. 304, no. 15. See *ZSL kratkoi*, pp. 55-64, 157-67; MP, pp. 252-62.

155. *ZSL kratkoi*, pp. 67-100, 171-77.

156. NPL, pp. 488-507; *ZSL prostrannoi*, pp. 44-78, 217-39.

157. TsGADA, f. 135, no. 383 (formerly V. 1. no. 1); *ZSL prostrannoi*, pp. 31-43, 175-214.

158. GBLOR, f. 98, no. 245; GPBOR, f. 717, no. 412/968/858. These texts, among others, serve as variants in *ZSL prostrannoi*, pp. 57-78. Also see GPBOR, f. 588, no. 1572; PSRL 16:289-304.

159. *ZSL prostrannoi*, pp. 22-27. For reproduction of the texts, ibid., pp. 81-135.

160. Several studies of the relationship between the Ecloga and the Short ZSL appeared early in the twentieth century. See, for example, T. Florinskii, "Drevneishii pamiatnik," pp. 418-26; Haralampi Oraschakoff, "Ein Denkmal," pp. 251-54. The same point of view, however, has been argued in more detail with better technique. See Venelin Ganev, *Zakon*", pp. 58-87, and the appended tables which compare the readings of the basic copies and redactions with the Ecloga. A likewise competent comparison of the Ecloga with the Expanded ZSL was done by Theodor Saturnik (*Příspěvky*, pp. 143-64). Also see M. Andreev, "Iavliaetsia li?" p. 11. One of the earliest salvos in the debate over Byzantine influence was fired by Georgi G. Gubidelnikov, who argued that the Short ZSL was highly influenced by the Byzantine, rather than the Slavonic, version of the Ecloga ("Zakon"," pp. 150-54, 156).

161. The bulk of this literature is by Josef Vašica, who has argued for a Czech origin of the Short Zakon. See his "Origine," pp. 154-74; "Jazyková povaha," pp. 521-37; "K lexiku," pp. 61-66; and "Kirillo-Mefodievskie," pp. 12-33.

162. This is the point of view first developed by Suvorov in the late nineteenth century. More recently, Vašica, whose works are listed above, has continued to expound this line of interpretation. Also see Heinrich Felix Schmid, "La legislazione," pp. 395-403; Vladimir Prochazka, "Le Zakon" Sudnyj Ljud'm'," pp. 359-75, 112-50; Dewey and Kleimola, *Zakon*, pp. viii-ix.

163. S. V. Troitski, "Apostol," pp. 38-51; Troitski, "Sv. Mefodii kak zakonodatel'," pp. 83-141; Troitski, "Sviatoi Mefodii ili Bolgarskii kniaz'?" pp. 117-26.

164. See Mikhail Andreev, "Sur l'origine," pp. 331-44; Andreev, "Iavliaetsia li?" pp. 6-9, 13-18; Ganev, *Zakon*", pp. 7-25; Andreev, "K"m v"prosa," pp. 17, 35-37. Andreev ("K"m v"prosa," pp. 18-30) took the

NOTES TO CHAPTER 2   211

lead in attacking Vašica, who responded in kind, relying largely upon linguistic data ("K otázce," pp. 1-19).

165. *Sofiiskii vremiannik*, 1:130-48; *Russkie dostopamiatnosti*, 2:143-220; Sreznevskii, "Obozrenie," pp. 200-207, with variants from the Ustiug and Synod copies.

166. Georgi T. Danailov, "Edin" pametnik", " pp. 3-59 (texts of the Short ZSL on pp. 20-24 and Expanded ZSL on pp. 26-38); S. S. Bobchev, "Edin" pametnik"," pp. 613-45 (text of Short ZSL on pp. 634-43). The other titles in the literature are cited by Ganev (*Zakon*", pp. 144-57).

167. *Rus'ka Pravda*, pp. 137-68; NPL, pp. 488-507.

168. *ZSL kratkoi; ZSL prostrannoi*; Ganev, *Zakon*" (printed in only 500 copies).

169. Rosenkampf, *Obozrenie*, pp. 118, 134-52; Kalachov, *Predvaritel'nye*, pp. 245-48; Pavlov, *Pervonachal'nyi*, pp. 24, 94-100.

170. Pavlov and Suvorov debated at length the issue of Western influence on the penalties assigned by the Zakon Sudnyi. See Suvorov, "O sledakh," pp. 5-6; Suvorov, *Sledy*, pp. 3-90, 130-59; Suvorov, *K voprosu*, pp. 155-275; Suvorov, *Uchebnik*, p. 190; Pavlov, *Mnimye*, pp. 50-107. Suvorov seems to have gotten the better of the argument. See Nikol'skii, "K istorii," pp. 116-21; *ZSL kratkoi*, p. 25.

171. Iushkov was confined to observing the presence of the Zakon Sudnyi in the company of the Russkaia Pravda, while denying the influence of the former on the latter (*Russkaia Pravda*, pp. 37-43, 54, 93-119, 368-69).

172. Tikhomirov, *Issledovanie*, pp. 143-55; Tikhomirov, *Posobie*, pp. 125-26.

173. L. V. Milov, "Novoe," pp. 51-63; Milov, "K istorii teksta prostrannoi," pp. 65-78; Milov, "K istorii teksta kratkoi," pp. 97-101. Milov also participated with Tikhomirov in the preparation of the texts of the Zakon Sudnyi for publication in *ZSL kratkoi* and *ZSL prostrannoi*. Shchapov's work is less directly tied to the Zakon. See his *Kniazheskie*, pp. 78, 248-49; "K kharakteristike," pp. 175, 180, 185; "K istorii teksta," pp. 295, 297, 299; "Varsonof'evskaia," p. 93; "Nekotorye," p. 269.

174. Reproduced in PRP 1:244-46 and RIB 36:12-24. On dating, see Protas'eva, *Opisanie*, 1:96; Shchapov, *Kniazheskie*, p. 39.

175. PVL 1:85.

176. Beneshevich found eighty-five copies of the Statute and ninety-one copies of its relatives (*Pravilo o tserkovnykh liudiakh, Riad i sud*, and *Sii liudi sbornyia*). Additional copies from foreign sources also were published in RIB 36. Shchapov's recent exhaustive edition includes more than two hundred copies (*Drevnerusskie*, pp. 12-84).

177. See, for example, PRP 1:237.2, 244.2; Shchapov, *Drevnerusskie*, pp. 15, 16, 18, 19, 21, 22, 30, 37, 42, 46, 54, 60, 69, 72, 76.

178. The text was even incorporated into the records of the 1551 Church Council (*Stoglav*, pp. 132-34); Shchapov, *Drevnerusskie*, pp.

49-59. The question of the Statute's trustworthiness separated Pavlov, who supported the Statute's authenticity, from Suvorov, who did not. See Pavlov, "K voprosu," pp. 72-73 and "Istoriia," p. 500 (where Pavlov agreed that the regulations may have belonged to Grand Prince Vladimir, but were only compiled in the form of a Statute in the thirteenth century); Pavlov, *Mnimye*, pp. 122-48; Pavlov, *Kanonicheskoe*, pp. 133-37. Suvorov suggested that the Statute originated only in the fourteenth century, the period to which the oldest extant copy may be traced. See Suvorov, *Sledy*, pp. 175-214; *K voprosu*, pp. 296-324; *Uchebnik*, pp. 193-94; "O sledakh," p. 6. Suvorov's position was developed by V. Markov ("Vopros," pp. 136-47, 335-41). The same questions had been raised before. See the anonymous article, "Ustavy v. k. Vladimira," pp. 422-45; Kirill Mysovskii, "Drevnee russkoe pravo," pp. 210, 139-72, 266-301. The general historiography is surveyed by Shchapov, *Kniazheskie*, pp. 13-26.

179. *Ustav sviatogo velikogo kniazia Vladimira o tserkovnykh sudakh i o desiatinakh* (Petrograd, 1915), republished in RIB 36:1-72. The basic texts were included in Beneshevich, *Sbornik pamiatnikov*, 1:59-77. Numerous copies had been published separately, and all are cited in Shchapov, *Drevnerusskie*, pp. 13-14, 16, 17, 20, 22, 26-28, 35-36, 42, 46, 50, 60, 62-63, 68-69, 72, 75.

180. S. V. Iushkov, *Izsledovanie po istorii russkogo prava. Vyp. 1: Ustav kn. Vladimira* (Novouzensk, [1926]). Beneshevich in his 1921 report on the publication of Vladimir's Statute indicated that Iushkov was waiting, even in 1921, to publish his work ("Avtoreferat," p. 183).

181. Oleksandr Lotots'kyi accused Beneshevich of ignoring Ukrainian manuscripts which he supposed to be older and presumably more reliable than the Muscovite and Novgorodian manuscripts upon which Beneshevich's edition was based ("Tserkovnyi ustav," pp. 7-44; *Ukrains'ki dzherela*, pp. 204-33). More recently, Shchapov claims to have pursued Lotots'kyi's suggestion, examining manuscripts in L'vov and Kiev, but to no avail. According to Shchapov, all such manuscripts he discovered represented only copies of the Novgorod and Muscovite manuscripts (*Kniazheskie*, pp. 24-25).

182. PRP 1:237-54; Shchapov, *Kniazheskie*, pp. 28-135; Shchapov, "Tserkov' kak feodal'naia organizatsiia," pp. 76-318; Shchapov, *Drevnerusskie*, pp. 12-84.

183. PVL 1:85.

184. The existence of such a charter is Shchapov's deduction, based on the mention of the Princess Anna (d. 1011) in the Statute. This conclusion also fits Shchapov's understanding of the layering to which the statute was submitted in the years of its compilation. See his charts in "Tserkov' kak feodal'naia organizatsiia," p. 115 and *Kniazheskie*, p. 37. The argument is summarized in *Kniazheskie*, pp. 115-27.

185. This runs counter to Shchapov's attempts to place the Statute's archetype in the twelfth century (*Kniazheskie*, pp. 127-28; "Tserkov' kak feodal'naia organizatsiia," p. 314), but I find in his arguments very little to

NOTES TO CHAPTER 2

overcome the bald fact that the new, so-called "Russian" Kormchaia omitted this historic document.

186. PRP 2:212.1, 213.8-9, 215.26-27, 287.2; 1497 Sudebnik, 59.

187. PRP 2:39.2, 41.6, 41-42.7, 162.2, 163.5-7, 164.8, 165.14-15.

188. Shchapov, *Kniazheskie,* pp. 38-40, 44-48; Shchapov, "Tserkov' kak feodal'naia organizatsiia," pp. 128-30. For the texts, see Shchapov, *Drevnerusskie,* pp. 21-62.

189. PSRL 21.1:118-19; see Shchapov, *Drevnerusskie,* pp. 81-84.

190. Shchapov, *Kniazheskie,* pp. 69-73; Shchapov, "Tserkov' kak feodal'naia organizatsiia," pp. 175-87; Shchapov, *Drevnerusskie,* pp. 62-68.

191. Shchapov, *Kniazheskie,* pp. 73-98; Shchapov, "Tserkov' kak feodal'naia organizatsiia," pp. 138-70; Shchapov, *Drevnerusskie,* pp. 68-72. The oldest complete manuscript is GPBOR, f. 588, no. 234, a sixteenth-century text; two other incomplete manuscripts are older (Library of the Arad Episcopacy [Rumania], no. 21; Khar'kov Historical Museum, inven. 21129). For description, see Shchapov, *Drevnerusskie,* pp. 68-69; Shchapov, *Vizantiiskoe,* pp. 270-71.

192. Shchapov, *Vizantiiskoe,* pp. 210-12; Shchapov, *Kniazheskie,* pp. 56-57, 62, 67-68.

193. Shchapov, *Kniazheskie,* pp. 49-52; the text is reproduced in Shchapov, *Drevnerusskie,* pp. 72-74.

194. Shchapov, *Kniazheskie,* p. 102; Iushkov, *Izsledovaniia,* p. 105.

195. Pavlov again proposed a kind of compromise, refusing to award Iaroslav authorship of the Statute, but admitting the practical application of the regulations in the tenth and eleventh centuries ("Istoriia," pp. 504-507). Also see Pavlov, *Mnimye,* pp. 148-59; Pavlov, *Kanonicheskoe,* pp. 137-39. Originally Suvorov did not question the utility of Iaroslav's Statute (*O tserkovnykh nakazaniiakh,* pp. 277-80), but his later works reflect considerably more skepticism (*Sledy,* pp. 222-34; *K voprosu,* pp. 365-79; *Uchebnik,* p. 194). Also see Markov, "Vopros," pp. 343-44.

196. Beneshevich, "Avtoreferat," p. 184. The proofs were certainly completed, and some printed copies were actually made (Arkhiv AN SSSR, f. 192, op. 1, no. 35; the printed sheets for pp. 109-20 are on fols. 54-59).

197. Shchapov, "Redaktsiia," pp. 481-513. Evidently Shchapov also prepared a detailed description of the copies of the Statute, a paper he intended to publish in *Arkheograficheskii ezhegodnik za 1963 god* (see "Redaktsiia," p. 483, n. 2), but to my knowledge it was never published separately. The information now is in print, however, in the new edition (Shchapov, *Drevnerusskie,* pp. 85-139).

198. Shchapov, "Redaktsiia," p. 492; Tikhomirov, *Issledovanie,* pp. 107-25.

199. Shchapov, *Kniazheskie,* p. 207; Shchapov, "Redaktsiia," p. 493. For the text, see Shchapov, *Drevnerusskie,* pp. 116-20, where the Academy recension appears as variants to the Frolov recension.

200. Shchapov, *Kniazheskie,* p. 202; Shchapov, "Redaktsiia," pp.

494-95; Shchapov, "K kharakteristike," pp. 174-80. For the texts of the two confirmation charters, see Shchapov, *Drevnerusskie*, pp. 182-85.

201. Shchapov, *Kniazheskie*, p. 203; Shchapov, "Redaktsiia," pp. 495-96; all the copies and the text of this recension are included in Shchapov, *Drevnerusskie*, pp. 120-25.

202. Rival Metropolitans claimed legitimate succession between 1375-1377, and again 1416-1420. There were several other minor skirmishes between would-be Metropolitans as well.

203. GPBOR, f. 717, no. 9/1086, fols. 106-10v. See Shchapov, *Kniazheskie*, pp. 203-206; "Redaktsiia," p. 493; and *Drevnerusskie*, pp. 121-25, where this copy appears as variants to the Bal'zerov recension.

204. NPL, pp. 481-85; Shchapov, *Drevnerusskie*, pp. 93-99; Shchapov, *Kniazheskie*, pp. 220-21. Two rubles did not equal twelve grivny. In Moscow, a ruble was worth ten grivny, and in Novgorod the same ruble was worth thirteen grivny. The different reading here is probably the result of the copyist's efforts to include figures from two different copies of the Statute. On money equivalencies, see V. L. Ianin, "Den'gi," pp. 331, 342.

205. Shchapov, *Kniazheskie*, pp. 208-15; Shchapov, "Redaktsiia," pp. 506-10. On the characteristics of the Chronicler of Periaslavl'-Suzdal' see Shakhmatov, *Obozrenie*, pp. 119-27; Likhachev, *Russkie letopisi*, pp. 435-37. The Statute's text appears in Shchapov, *Drevnerusskie*, pp. 103-107.

206. Shchapov, *Kniazheskie*, pp. 216-19; Shchapov, "Redaktsiia," pp. 502-503; for a list of copies and the text, see Shchapov, *Drevnerusskie*, pp. 85-91.

207. Shchapov, "Redaktsiia," p. 504; *Kniazheskie*, pp. 215-19. The text is printed in PRP 1:265-72, and Shchapov, *Drevnerusskie*, pp. 91-93.

208. Shchapov, *Kniazheskie*, pp. 211-14; Shchapov, *Kniazheskie*, pp. 99-103.

209. Shchapov, *Kniazheskie*, pp. 221-26; Shchapov, "Redaktsiia," pp. 486-87, 496-98; Shchapov, *Drevnerusskie*, pp. 127-36. Another copy of marginal utility for present purposes is the Ustiug redaction, a generalizing version of the Statute incorporated into a late sixteenth-century chronicle (Shchapov, *Drevnerusskie*, pp. 138-39; *Ustiuzhskii letopisnyi svod*, pp. 41-42).

210. Shchapov, who attempted to fix Iaroslav's Statute to a time frame close to the eleventh century, is reluctant to admit any application of the Statute in the fourteenth and fifteenth centuries. The main evidence on which he bases this skepticism is the absence of direct indication of the Statute's application, and the appearance of a reworking of the Statute in the Ukraine, the so-called *Svitok Iaroslavlia* (*Kniazheskie*, p. 315). The logic of this conclusion escapes me. There are few indications of the Statute's application at any time, including the eleventh century when Shchapov supposes the Statute arose. If a reworking of the Statute means

something, why does the widespread copying of the Statute in the northeast not indicate anything? The fact is that no copies whatever exist from anytime before the fifteenth century.

211. Dating of this statute is disputed, since the document itself bears no date. See Shchapov, *Drevnerusskie*, pp. 140-45; PRP 2:39-42; *Smolenskie*, pp. 75-80; *Pamiatniki istorii Kievskogo gosudarstva*, no. 32 (dated to 1150); DAI 1, no. 4. Shchapov discusses the manuscript as well as the document's contents ("Smolenskii ustav," pp. 37-47; *Kniazheskie*, pp. 136-50; "Tserkov' kak feodal'naia organizatsiia," pp. 14-38) and argues that Rostislav's Statute coincided with the establishment of the Smolensk episcopacy in 1137, so that the date 1157 in "Tserkov' kak feodal'naia organizatsiia," p. 57, must be an error. Unaccountably, L. V. Alekseev assigns the Statute an origin in 1136, despite his allusions to Shchapov and others as his source ("Ustav," pp. 85-86). Still, Alekseev's effort to chart the geography of the Statute is a most innovative attempt to fix the Statute in space and time. For a sharp contrast in quality, see N. N. Usachev, "Gramoty," pp. 15-17.

212. This similarity led Shchapov to conclude that the Smolensk Statute and Vladimir's Statute had a common source which belonged to the eleventh or early twelfth century (*Kniazheskie*, pp. 37, 121-25).

213. Consequently the Statute survives in the company of three other documents outlining and confirming the Smolensk episcopacy's privileges. See Shchapov, *Drevnerusskie*, pp. 140-46.

214. PRP 2:162-65. A. A. Zimin proposed that the document actually was compiled only in the fourteenth century ("Ustavnaia," pp. 123-31; PRP 2:161). Earlier, S. V. Iushkov had suggested a thirteenth-century origin ("Ustav," pp. 405-24). V. L. Ianin supported the idea of an origin in the late thirteenth century (*Novgorodskie posadniki*, pp. 89-93). Shchapov has proposed the most complex history of the text, which he regards as a Novgorodian falsification of Vladimir's Statute that was compiled sometime late in the thirteenth century and subsequently supplemented (*Kniazheskie*, pp. 169-77; *Drevnerusskie*, p. 153). The most extensive study of the Statute is due to G. Barats ("Kritiko-sravnitel'nyi razbor," pp. 165-211, 127-63).

215. NPL, pp. 485-88; for lists of copies and the text, see Shchapov, *Drevnerusskie*, pp. 153-58.

216. For a photographic reproduction and edition of the Synod text, see M. N. Tikhomirov and M. V. Shchepkina, *Dva pamiatnika*, pp. 18-24, 28-30. Also see PRP 2:118-19; Shchapov, *Drevnerusskie*, pp. 147-48. For commentary, see Shchapov, "Tserkov' kak feodal'naia organizatsiia," pp. 39-41, 75; Shchapov, *Kniazheskie*, pp. 150-65; Pavlov, "Istoriia," pp. 508-11. For the description of the other copy of the Statute, a fifteenth- or early sixteenth-century text, see Shchapov, "Novyi spisok Novgorodskogo ustava," pp. 395-98.

217. For the first edition, see S. V. Iushkov, "Pravosudie," pp. 115-

20. The manuscript is described in detail by M. N. Tikhomirov, who also published a photographic reproduction of the Pravosudie itself ("Pravosud'e," pp. 32-55). The text has subsequently been published several times. See Shchapov, *Drevnerusskie*, pp. 207-11 for the text and a listing of other places where it may be found.

218. Cherepnin, *Russkie feodal'nye arkhivy*, 2:25-29; Tikhomirov, *Posobie*, pp. 127-29; PRP 3:438-40; Tikhomirov, "Pravosud'e," p. 44. Most recently Shchapov has endorsed Tikhomirov's last view on the basis of the manuscript's convoy and contents (*Drevnerusskie*, p. 208).

219. For an English translation and commentary on the Farmer's Law, see W. Ashburner, "The Farmer's Law," *Journal of Hellenic Studies* 32 (1912):68-95.

220. Pavlov discusses the earlier editions and their inadequacies ("Knigi," pp. 4-8). For reactions to Pavlov's edition, see F. I. Uspenskii, "Drevneishii pamiatnik," pp. 300-313; V. G. Vasil'evskii, "Knigi," pp. 317-51; A. Sobolevskii, "Knigi," pp. 352-58. Also see V. Chernov, "K voprosu," pp. 429-34; PRP 1:258; Shchapov, *Kniazheskie*, pp. 210, 249-51; Shchapov, "Redaktsiia," pp. 502-503.

221. Pavlov, "Knigi," pp. 16-17. Recently Shchapov has endorsed Pavlov's dating ("Prokhiron," pp. 50-51). The basic manuscript is fifteenth-century in origin. Other manuscripts reproduce portions of the Knigi, some of which are discussed below. See Pavlov, "Knigi," pp. 8-9.

222. Both marital and evidentiary regulations appear in GBLOR, f. 209, no. 156, fols. 101-106. Also see GPBOR, F. II. 251, fols. 91-93v., which reproduces the regulations on testimony from the Knigi.

223. See N. I. Tiktin, *Vizantiiskoe pravo kak istochnik Ulozheniia 1648 goda i novoukaznykh statei* (Odessa, 1898).

CHAPTER 3

1. Schwartz and Miller, "Legal Evolution," p. 166. Also see Richard D. Schwartz, "Social Factors," pp. 471-91.

2. See Redfield, *Primitive Law*, pp. 8-9; Barkun, "Conflict Resolution," pp. 124-25; Barkun, *Law*, pp. 67, 71, 109.

3. Redfield, *Primitive Law*, p. 13; Barkun, *Law*, p. 36; Gluckman, *Politics*, p. 87. Mark Kosven, in a remarkable book for its time, charts a model for the impact of economic change on the early stages of legal development (*Prestuplenie*, pp. 32-36, 68-80, 130-32). Also see Gluckman, *Politics*, pp. xv, xxi, 40-41, 45-46, 48-49, 66-67, 83, 87. A more generalized discussion of the social and economic characteristics associated with legal change may be found in Diamond, *Comparative Study*, pp. 17-22.

4. See Gluckman, *Politics*, p. 141; Barkun, *Law*, pp. 16, 147; Schwartz and Miller, "Legal Evolution," p. 166.

NOTES TO CHAPTER 3

5. Despite his reliance on the role of coercion, E. Adamson Hoebel introduced several detailed examples of just this sort of community censure (*Law*, pp. 263-64). Hoebel's definition notwithstanding, his chapter devoted to "The Trend of the Law" gives an interesting characterization of legal evolution and the development of sanctions.

6. Of course this view is disputed by most Soviet historians, but a conscientious reexamination of Kievan society suggests that agriculture in the twelfth century was still weakly developed, princely income was drawn mainly from hunting, and revenge still operated in the context of clan relations (Froianov, *Kievskaia*, pp. 13-99). The northern territories, such as Novgorod and Pskov, suffered less under the Mongols, a factor that may have contributed to their later, relatively more rapid social progress. See V. N. Bernadskii, *Novgorod*, p. 16.

7. Short RP, 1; Expanded RP, 1. The Abbreviated Pravda, almost certainly a later compilation, reduced the list of eligible avengers to the members of the immediate biological family (father, sons, and brothers). See PRP 1:197.1.

8. For a sampling of the literature on this matter, see PR 2:246-54. It may be that the prescribed avengers did not exhaust the potential for recriminations, inasmuch as the list did not include women. See Vladimirskii-Budanov, cited in PR 2:24. However, Kosven has argued that women are among the first omitted from such procedures (*Prestuplenie*, p. 29). Exceptions to the general mediocrity of the literature include the work of Kosven (*Prestuplenie*, pp. 19-27; *Semeinaia*, p. 68) and Froianov (*Kievskaia*, pp. 25-26, 33-43). A less sophisticated work of the nineteenth century that still deserves attention is the study of A. A. Sukhov, "Obychno-narodnye," pp. 44-116, 35-44.

9. Expanded ZSL, 69, a regulation drawn from Exodus 21:23-25.

10. This took place only after some time. The 1497 Sudebnik ordered thieves executed (articles 8, 10, 13), and the 1550 Sudebnik mirrored these provisions (articles 52, 55, 56, 60). The 1649 Ulozhenie revealed a greater dependence on talion. Theft, for example, earned the perpetrator the loss of his ear in 1649, but by 1669 the same offense resulted in the loss of fingers, hands, and feet, depending upon the conditions of the crime. See PRP 6:384-85; PSZ 1, no. 441.8, 9, 15, 17.

11. PVL 1:97.

12. Expanded RP, 2.

13. The persistence of revenge despite the Iaroslavichi is argued most persuasively by Froianov. He points out that the aorist verb form (*otlozhisha*) used in the provision suggests the reformers' intention to abolish revenge, whereas the perfective (*otlozhili*) would have denoted the moment of actuality (*Kievskaia*, pp. 39-41). Mrochek-Drozdovskii used various chronicle readings to demonstrate that revenge remained in practice well after the inclusion of redemption in the Russkaia Pravda (*Izsledovaniia*, pt. 2, appendix 1, pp. 1-15), a suggestion supported by the revisions in the cir-

cle of revengers permitted in the Abbreviated Pravda (PRP 1:197.1). A similarly skeptical view on the effectiveness of the abolition of revenge was offered by M. M. Isaev, "Ugolovnoe pravo Kievskoi Rusi," p. 164.

14. Short RP, 1; Expanded RP, 1. Similar principles appear in the 1229 and 1270 Smolensk treaties (PRP 2:58.1, 72.2-3). See Kosven, *Prestuplenie*, pp. 45-46, 79-80.

15. Already the laws of Ethelbert (560-616) mention the principle of composition, but in the laws of Edmund (939-946) the homicide was subject to feud only if his kindred did not produce full compensation within twelve months (*English Historical Documents*, 1:392-93). See Pollock and Maitland, *History*, 2:450-51; Julius Goebel, Jr., *Felony*, pp. 21, 38.

16. Expanded RP, 3.

17. Short RP, 1; Expanded RP, 1, 3.

18. PRP 2:58.1, 72.2-3.

19. Expanded RP, 4. The assumed etymology of *vira* is based upon the Latin root for man (*vir*) (Vasmer, *Etimologicheskii slovar'*, 1:318). This kind of evidence has stimulated a continuing debate over the existence of Germanic influence on Old Russian law. One original etymology was suggested early in the nineteenth century by I. Diev, who tried to deduce *vira* from the Greek root for weight and *dikaia* from the Greek verb meaning "to throw" ("O virakh," pp. 66). According to Nikolai Kalachov, *dikaia* was derived from the same term applied to vacant land (*dikaia zemlia*), and later was transferred to the *vira* paid by all ("Ob ugolovnom prave," p. 354). Kosven believed that *dikaia* indicated the voluntary nature of the community's payment (*Semeinaia*, p. 138). Other opinions are surveyed in PR 2:276-81.

20. Expanded RP, 5, 7-8.

21. See Nikolai Lange, *Izsledovanie*, p. 125; Tikhomirov, *Posobie*, p. 162; Diev, "O virakh," pp. 58-59; F. Depp, *O nakazaniiakh*, p. 60. The main viewpoints are cited in PR 2:290-93.

22. Tikhomirov, *Posobie*, p. 164; G. E. Kochin, *Materialy*, p. 295; Mrochek-Drozdovskii, *Izsledovaniia*, pt. 2, p. 252.

23. Expanded RP, 35.

24. Expanded RP, 83, 84 (*to na potok, na grabezh' dom iego, peredi pagubu isplativshiu, a v protse kniaziu potochiti i* [emphasis added]).

25. PRP 2:60.6. It is not clear that the prince's complaint was based on an actual delict, since the phrasing indicates simply that the prince's anger was kindled.

26. PRP 2:73.7.

27. PRP 2:60.4, 73.5. The Novgorod Treaty of 1189-1199 also prohibited the imprisonment of debtor merchants (PRP 2:126.13).

28. NPL, pp. 26/211 (*pototsisha [v] Kyevu k Vsevolodu K"stiatina Mikul'tsitsa*), 72 (*Kniaz' zhe iskovav, potochiia v Pereiaslavl'*), 295/450 (*i izymav Nemtsov i Chiud i iskovav ikh, potochi v Novgorod a sam poide na Chiud*); PSRL 1.2:301 (*potochi Mstislav kniaz' polot'skye Tsriugorodu*

s zhenami i detmi); PSRL 15:326 (*i iat' Stanimira Dernovicha s synom s Nezdilom, i okovav potochi, i tovara poima bes chisla i opiat' pusti ikh*). Also see PSRL 4:197 and 15:382.

29. I. I. Sreznevskii, *Materialy*, 2:1291-92.

30. PSRL 2:319. See L. K. Goetz, cited in PR 2:296.

31. PR 1:149, 152, 159.

32. PR 1:149, n. 7.

33. PRP 1:197.3.

34. One may note in passing the omission of a large portion of articles 7 and 8 in the Archeographic version (PR 1:301).

35. PR 1:196.83. Recently L. V. Milov has suggested a similar understanding for *potochiti* in the Slavonic translation of the Ecloga. Unfortunately, this interesting observation is based upon a kind of inverted deduction. The translation of the Ecloga in the Merilo Pravednoe used the term *zatochiti* (MP, p. 382) where originally the Ecloga had prescribed exile. Milov supposes that *potochiti* was the transitional translation ("O drevnerusskom," p. 148).

36. V. I. Dal', *Tolkovyi slovar'*, 3:928, 934; Vladimirskii-Budanov, *Obzor*, pp. 277-78.

37. Confrontation was the procedure basic to recovery of lost and stolen property. See Short RP, 14; Expanded RP, 35. The significance of confrontation as a manifestation of horizontal legal relations is discussed below in Chapter 5.

38. Short RP, 13; Expanded RP, 34. The prince's horse was protected by a fee exactly double the figure that defended an ordinary man's animal (Short RP, 28; Expanded RP, 45). See Froianov, *Kievskaia*, pp. 58-59.

39. Exactly the same process took place in Western law (Goebel, *Felony*, pp. 26-27, 53, 65, 87, 93-94). But European law did not exercise a monopoly over communal responsibility. Fifteenth-century Ottoman law, like the older Russkaia Pravda, held local communities responsible for locating murderers and other criminals. Failure to identify the culprit meant that the community had to pay the compensation. Alternately, the community could rid itself of the obligation and the criminal simply by declaring him notorious, whereupon the accused was banished (Uriel Heyd, *Studies*, pp. 106, 117-18, 134). All this while revenge and composition were still widely practiced.

40. Goebel, *Felony*, pp. 10, 147, 206-207. In Russia it is certain only that the bloodwite collector received a portion of the total (Expanded RP, 9, 10).

41. Expanded RP, 3. Also see, among others, ARG, no. 18; AFZ 1, no. 223; AFZ 2, nos. 62, 63, 79, 87, 103, 149, 171, 226, 231, 232, 302, 317, 367; AFZ 3, nos. 11, 14, 37, 48, 5 (appendix numeration); ASEI 2, nos. 108, 217, 497; ASEI 3, nos. 25, 27, 92; PRP 3:162.1, 172.14.

42. Expanded RP, 19.

43. Short RP, 1, 19, 22, 23; Expanded RP, 1, 3, 12. The same princi-

ple was part of the Smolensk text for a successor treaty to that of 1229. Here the prince's steward and emissary were protected by twenty silver grivny, where one silver grivna equaled four grivny of kuna (PRP 2:72.3, 75.21). Also see the Novgorod Treaty of 1189-1199 (PRP 2:125.2).

44. The literature is abstracted in PR 2:132-38.

45. Expanded RP, 3. The provisions are identical to those of article 1, but draw more argument as a result of some nebulousness in the text. The earliest symptom of vertical legal relations among the Franks, the *bannus*, was observed in connection with royal control over the army. Court favorites were among the first to benefit from special protection (Goebel, *Felony*, pp. 46-49). Also see Salic law, where murder of a man in the king's service cost three times more than the killing of any other free Frank (*Select Historical Documents*, p. 182 [xli.1,3]).

46. PRP 2:72.3. The precedent appears in the Novgorod Treaty of 1189-1199 (PRP 2:125.2).

47. Expanded RP, 5. Presniakov first speculated that the prince received the bloodwite and a head fee for princely personnel (*Lektsii*, 1:216). In another work Presniakov seemed to be unconvinced of this explanation, although his understanding of the prince as the victim was the same (*Kniazhoe pravo*, pp. 265-66). Also see Presniakov's review of Goetz's work on the Pravda ("Goetz," p. 162).

48. The *riadovnik*, *smerd*, and male slave (*kholop*) were each protected by a five-grivna payment. A female slave (*raba*) was defended by a six-grivna fee, and domestic tutors and handicraftsmen by twelve-grivna fees (Short RP, 25-27; Expanded RP, 14, 16, 17). On the other hand, a prince's page (*otrok*), groom, and cook were protected each by a forty-grivna sum (Expanded RP, 11, 15).

49. Expanded RP, 88. One may note here that the principle of distinguishing a woman's wergeld from a man's was not uniform in medieval Europe. In England, for example, the worth of a free woman was identical to that of a free man (Pollock and Maitland, *History* 2:437). Salic law increased a woman's wergeld in consonance with her ability to bear children (*Select Historical Documents*, p. 177).

50. Article 1 of both redactions of the Pravda provided for the wergeld only under the formula "If a man kills a man...." Article 3 of the Expanded Pravda (which outlines the *dikaia vira*) provided the fee schedule for that community "in which the body [literally, the head] lies" (*v ch'ei zhe vervi golova lezhit'*).

51. Short RP, 19. The meaning of the phrase *v obidu* has been debated at length. See PR 2:133-38. The punitive nature of this payment contrasts with the division of the bloodwite permitted in cases of the *dikaia vira* as outlined elsewhere in the Russkaia Pravda (Short RP, 20; Expanded RP, 3-6).

52. Short ZSL, 18; Expanded ZSL, 20; PRP 3:174.23. The term was also known later. See 1550 Sudebnik, 24; 1589 Sudebnik, 36.

53. PVL 1:42.

54. Sreznevskii, *Materialy*, 2:502-504; Mrochek-Drozdovskii, *Izsledovaniia*, pt. 2, pp. 212-17; Tikhomirov, *Posobie*, pp. 156-57; Kosven, *Prestuplenie*, p. 36; B. O. Unbegaun, "Le 'crime,' " pp. 203-204.

55. See ASEI 2, no. 166; PRP 1:95.

56. Professor Kleimola has kindly pointed out to me the correlation of this regulation with a provision in the Expanded Zakon Sudnyi that allowed the immediate dispatch of dogs who had done damage by burrowing into storage structures (Expanded ZSL, 51).

57. See, for example, PRP 1:96.

58. Short RP, 20; Expanded RP, 3. Vernadsky's translation ("in a highway attack") is most unfortunate. He repeats the error in the equivalent provision of the Expanded Pravda (*Medieval Russian Laws*, pp. 31, 36).

59. See, for example, AFZ 1, nos. 1a ("They came, lord, against the Metropolitan's village, against Novaia, with many people by *razboi*, yea, lord, they did beat and pillage us"), and 222 ("Having come ... against us by *razboi*, yea us ... they did beat and pillage"); Sreznevskii, *Materialy*, 3:21. Mrochek-Drozdovskii claimed that the term originated with revenge, hence its association with homicide (*Izsledovaniia*, pt. 2, pp. 251-52, appendix, pp. 144-62).

60. PRP 2:58.1 ("And if they kill a free man, then give up the *razboiniki*, as many as there will be; if there will be no *razboiniki*, then give ten grivny of silver for the head [*za golovu*]"). Despite the usual distinction made between murderers and *razboiniki*, even some later cases persist with this identification (AFZ 3, nos. 300 ["*razboiniki* killed her husband"], and 307 ["*razboiniki* killed two (*pomeshchiki*)"]). Also see AGR 1, no. 45.

61. Kalachov, "Ob ugolovnom prave," p. 322. The confusion may be alleviated somewhat by Horace Dewey's identification of *razboiniki* with professional criminals ("Muscovite *Guba* Charters," p. 288). Felony, too, early fell from the list of emendable crimes. For a discussion of the evolution of a similar term (felon) in English law, see Pollock and Maitland, *History*, 2:464-70.

62. A distinction between murderers who killed by stealth or as a profession and those who committed homicides recompensable through wergeld has also been observed in medieval English law. See Thomas A. Green, "Societal Concepts," pp. 669-70; J. M. Kaye, "Early History of Murder," pp. 368-70; Goebel, *Felony*, p. 53.

63. Short RP, 3-8; Expanded RP, 40. While article 40 of the Expanded Pravda provides for a twelve-grivna fee, article 38 of the Short Pravda mentions no figure. Killing any free man presumably required payment of forty grivny (Short RP, 1; Expanded RP, 1).

64. Pavlov, "Knigi," p. 63 (article 4); MP, p. 643 (article 3). See Kliuchevskii, *Sochineniia*, 1:210; Meichik, "Russkaia Pravda," p. 87; Golenishchev-Kutuzov, *Russkaia Pravda*, p. 30. A survey of pre-

revolutionary literature on this question and a rousing rebuttal to claims of Byzantine borrowings may be found in Chernousov, "K voprosu," pp. 303-22.

65. Expanded ZSL, 63. Cf. Ecloga 17.45.

66. Exodus 22:2-3; Expanded ZSL, 72. See Saturnik, *Příspěvky*, p. 159 (article 64 by Saturnik's calculations). The same passage in a different, more lucid translation appears in the Merilo Pravednoe in the Extracts from Mosaic Law (MP, p. 243). The mysterious *pod"kopanie* is omitted here. It seems significant that the majority of the texts cited by Sreznevskii which use the term *pod"kopati*, absent in the Merilo Pravednoe, are Biblical texts which connect this word with cases of theft—two from the Ostromir Gospel (Sreznevskii, *Materialy*, 2:1058). The only other text in which the term is used is the same chronicle entry which contains the narrative on *razboi*, Vladimir and the bishops (PVL 1:86). That passage is examined in more detail below.

67. PRP 1:103, 156.

68. In the Short Pravda, the twelve-grivna figure appears often in torts (articles 4, 8, 17). The murder of the prince's estate foreman (article 24) and slave tutor (article 27) were punished by a twelve-grivna payment. A similar system prevailed in the Expanded Pravda (articles 13, 15, 17) where property loss cases also were punished by exactions of the same dimensions (for example, articles 71-74, 79).

69. This includes homicides of various categories of the dependent population (for example, Expanded RP, 13, 15, 17).

70. The immunity charters issued by the grand prince and appanage princes began the limitation of judicial rights sometime in the fifteenth century. The formula extending such immunities to the recipients excluded homicide. See, for example, ASEI 1, no. 29; ASEI 2, no. 45; AFZ 1, no. 230. For a comprehensive study of the gradual restriction of judicial immunities, see Zlotnik, "Immunity Charters," pp. 113-64.

71. PRP 3:427.12. The reference to Byzantine law is encapsulated in the expression *Gradskii zakon* by which the Procheiros Nomos was known in medieval Russia.

72. 1497 Sudebnik, 8, 9; PRP 2:287.7, 8.

73. PRP 2:172.10. A similar expression was used in the 1497 Sudebnik (articles 7, 38). *Prodazha* generally represented a fine (PRP 1:148), although there is some question about this designation (Sergeevich, *Lektsii*, p. 306; Isaev, "Ugolovnoe pravo Kievskoi Rusi," p. 166). This matter is discussed in more detail below. *Kazn'* denoted physical punishment, though not necessarily any particular type. See, for example, PSRL 25:278 ("Seize them all and punish them [*kazniti*] and beat them with the knout and cut off their hands and sever their legs and for others cut off their heads" [1462]).

74. See Iakovlev, *Namestnich'i*, nos. 5, 1-5, 7 (second numeration).

75. Expanded RP, 3-5, 8; PRP 3:162.1. If the ten rubles reflect a

Novgorod currency of an earlier century, the ruble must equal one silver grivna (PRP 3:188). In that case, the fee would equal the forty-grivna payment prescribed in the Pravda (one silver grivna equaled four grivny of kuna—PRP 2:58.1). However, the 1397 Dvina code is a long way from twelfth-century Novgorod or thirteenth-century Smolensk. According to Ianin, Novgorod rubles of 1399, for example, were computed at thirteen grivny of kuna, and fifteen grivny of kuna in the thirteenth century—170.1 and 196.2 grams of silver respectively. The forty grivny of the Russkaia Pravda equaled 1,962 grams, the same as ten Novgorod rubles of the thirteenth century (Ianin, "Den'gi," pp. 326-31).

76. PRP 3:172-73.14; ASEI 3, no. 25.20, 27.15; ARG, no. 18; Iakovlev, *Namestnich'i*, nos. 4, 7, 8, 10, 11, 13, 14, 16.

77. ASEI 2, nos. 108, 217. Both charters are from mid-fifteenth-century Beloozero, and use the Novgorod ruble, equal to two Muscovite rubles. Also see AFZ 2, nos. 62, 63, 79, 103, 149, 171, 226, 231, 232, 302, 317, 367; AFZ 3, nos. 11, 14, 37, 5 (appendix). The same fee is recalled in a few seventeenth-century documents (AFZ 2, no. 48; ASEI 3, no. 92—two rubles). The two-ruble bloodwite also is mentioned in a document from the Tver' region (AFZ 2, no. 87), evidently as a result of adopting the Novgorod currency terminology. Moscow imposed its own system on Novgorod by the treaties which preceded Novgorod's annexation (PRP 2:250.15, 256.7). The bloodwite is often recalled in immunities by way of excusing the recipient from paying it (for example, ASEI 2, no. 497; ASEI 3, nos. 13, 21; AFZ 1, no. 223).

78. The *sled* was a method of pursuing criminals by the local population (Expanded RP, 77). Those who refused to permit the pursuers to cross local boundaries in order to continue their search, and who refused to join the posse, faced punitive action. Several fifteenth-century documents recall the *sled*, pointing the finger at reluctant citizens (AFZ 1, nos. 230, 233). Both the *sled* and the *obysk*, the investigation of citizens in order to seek out criminal offenders, were prescribed often by the Ulozhenie (21.35, 36, 39, 42-44, 60). Despite the objections of Vladimirskii-Budanov (*Obzor*, p. 538), it seems likely that the institution devolved from older communal responsibilities (Sergeevich, *Lektsii*, pp. 473-74). For a survey of these investigative forms, see Nikolai Lange, *Drevnee russkoe sudoproizvodstvo*, pp. 115-22. As noted below, the inquisitorial examination of the citizenry has its parallel in Western medieval European law. See Pollock and Maitland, *History*, 1:142, 151-52; 2:642.

79. See PRP 1:246.15, 261.27; PRP 2:39.2, 39-40.3, 102.

80. PRP 2:117. The sum proposed by Sviatoslav was 100 grivny of new kuna. On the value of this grant, see Shchapov, *Kniazheskie*, pp. 158-65.

81. Short RP, 42; Tikhomirov, *Issledovanie*, p. 72.

82. Expanded RP, 9, 10. Cf. PRP 2:301-304. Regarding the sixty-grivna payment of the Short Pravda, Zimin has observed that most of the

digits of that unspecified series (*60 griven i 10 rezan i 12 veveren*) were carried over to the Expanded Pravda (articles 9, 10) as supplementary payments (*virniku 8 griven, a 10 kun perekladnaia, a metelniku 12 vekshi, virniku 16 griven i 10 kun i 12 vekshi*), albeit in different monetary units (PRP 1:143).

83. Expanded RP, 107. Most scholars do not count this a fee paid to the *virnik*. After that the unanimity wanes (PR 2:689-90).

84. Short RP, 42; Expanded RP, 9, 10, 107. One explanation allowed that the small fee went to the *virnik*, while the twenty percent collection from the *vira* went to the prince (Depp, *O nakazaniiakh*, p. 41). Lange, on the other hand, believed that the eight- and sixteen-kuna sums were extracted from the defendant; the nine kuny were taken from the plaintiff, who thereby expressed his gratitude for assistance rendered by the prince's official (*Izsledovanie*, p. 92).

85. NPL, p. 104; PSRL 5:87; PSRL 7:266; PSRL 15:27.

86. For example, PVL 1:85-87; NPL, p. 167; PSRL 9:67; PSRL 15:119; PSRL 25:367.

87. PVL 1:83, 85-86. Presumably this was the origin of Vladimir's Statute. See Shchapov, *Kniazheskie*, pp. 126-27.

88. This line of argument is reminiscent of other parts of the Primary Chronicle. See, for example, the moralizing that the chronicler directed toward Sviatopolk, who, thinking to seize power alone (1015), revealed his ignorance of divine intervention in this world, for "God gives power to whom he wishes; he establishes tsar and high prince, [and] to whom he wishes he gives [power]" (PVL 1:95).

89. The addition in the Novgorod Chronicle is interesting. Although the bishops first protested to Vladimir about the old style of punishment, and recommended the divine order of sanctions, the Novgorod chronicler records that Vladimir, restoring the *vira*, lived "according to the arrangement of God, his grandfather and father" (NPL, pp. 167, 553 [emphasis added]). The Primary Chronicle does not include the divine prescription, nor could it, since the bishops had argued for abolition of the bloodwite. Of the several deductions one might make from this slip, at least one fits in with the argument advanced here. Even when Vladimir clearly returned to the primitive practice of his forefathers, the religious chronicler, in the spirit of eulogizing Vladimir that penetrates the entire chronicle entry, could not refrain from heaping praise on the saintly prince.

90. See A. A. Shakhmatov, *Razyskaniia*, pp. 1-3; Likhachev, *Tekstologiia*, pp. 448-49. There are signs, however, that the Laurentian and Hypatian accounts were copied from different sources. For example, the Laurentian and its copies omit some lines at the end of the tale which are present in the Hypatian and Novgorod First Chronicle (*da tako budi. I zhiviashche Volodimir*). The two texts also reverse word order in several places (*a dobrym na milovan'e / a na milovan'e dobrym* and *ot'niu i dedniu / dedniu i otniu*) and substitute words (*so ispytom / s ispytaniem*). I have

NOTES TO CHAPTER 3 225

reproduced the text and variants in an appendix to "Reconsidering Crime and Punishment in Kievan Rus'," *Russian History* 7(1980): 283-93.

91. Compare, for example, his assertiveness in demanding a Byzantine royal bride, a presumption not lightly entertained by the Byzantines (PVL 1:76).

92. A. A. Shakhmatov, *Povest' vremennykh let*, pp. 157-61, 383; Shakhmatov, *Razyskaniia*, pp. 159-61. George Vernadsky evidently was genuinely warmed by the story, comparing Vladimir to Tolstoy, both of whom Vernadsky imagined adopted a passive attitude to wrongdoers. On even less evidence, Vernadsky announced that this spirit was shared by many other Kievans as well (*Kievan Russia*, p. 73).

93. Sergeevich, *Lektsii*, pp. 303, 312. The issue is summarized by Vladimirskii-Budanov, who connects L. K. Goetz's work with Sergeevich's edition of the Russkaia Pravda ("Das russische," pp. 11-15). Also see Aleksandr Filippov, "Russkaia Pravda," p. 171; Kucherov, "Indigenous," pp. 276, 282.

94. Short RP, 42. The exception is Short RP, 20, which apparently describes the *dikaia vira* (although it is here called *virnoe*).

95. Expanded RP, 3-6, 8, 9, 11, 18-20, 30, 89, 107.

96. The single exception, noted above, is the 854 entry of the Novgorod First Chronicle which describes the modest exactions of the early Russian princes (NPL, p. 104).

97. PRP 1:33-34.13. Compare Short RP, 1 and Expanded RP, 1.

98. PRP 1:7.4.

99. The textual problems presented by the treaties are summarized briefly in PRP 1:4-5, and the literature is cited in PRP 1:69-70.

100. See, for example, Ecloga 17.45-50 and Procheiros Nomos 39.16, 79-80, 82-84. Divine agency was certainly on the minds of some of the chroniclers. The Novgorod First Chronicle, although relating that Vladimir returned to the old practice of collecting the bloodwite as had his father and grandfather, adds that this was a divine ordinance as well (NPL, p. 167). The Nikon Chronicle alters the tale to fit its theocratic aims, claiming that Vladimir began to execute criminals "according to divine law" (PSRL 9:67).

101. PRP 3:427.12.

102. 1497 Sudebnik, 8, 9, 39; Iakovlev, *Namestnich'i*, nos. 5, 1-5, 7 (second numeration).

103. PSRL 9:67.

104. Kosven, *Prestuplenie*, pp. 77-80.

105. Expanded RP, 11.

106. For parallels in medieval Europe, see Goebel, *Felony*, pp. 46-49.

107. Pollock and Maitland, *History*, 1:88, 2:487; *Laws of the Kings of England*, p. 265. There is some indication that an institution similar to the *murdrum* already existed in England under Canute, but the general

principle was known to Swedish law and to an early capitulary appended to the Lex Salica (Pollock and Maitland, *History*, 1:89). One may observe here some similarity between medieval English and Russian law in the rules of special procedure common to both which attempted to protect the interests of the monarch's foreign assistants. Compare, for example, William's rules on English-French suits with those of the Russkaia Pravda between Varangian and Novgorodian (*Laws of the Kings of England*, p. 233; Short RP, 10).

108. PRP 2:117; Ianin, "Den'gi," p. 326.

109. Shchapov has argued effectively that the village in question served as a collection point for the entire Onega region (*Kniazheskie*, pp. 158-65). A similar conceptualization emerges from the work of L. V. Alekseev on the twelfth-century Statutory Charter of the Smolensk Prince Rostislav ("Gramota Rostislava," p. 187; "Ustav Rostislava," p. 110).

110. Pollock and Maitland, *History*, 2:557.

111. The term denotes a fine in numerous later documents. See, for example, PRP 2:286.1, 289.27, 291.37, 293.52, 296.80, 298.96-97, 300.111; 1497 Sudebnik, 8, 53. According to Vasmer, *prodazha* is derived from *prodati* in the original sense of payment for something given to someone (*Etimologicheskii slovar'*, 3:372). See Sergeevich, *Lektsii*, p. 306; Sukhov, "Obychno-narodnye," p. 56; Isaev, "Ugolovnoe pravo Kievskoi Rusi," p. 166.

112. For example, PVL 1:143; PSRL 7:6; PSRL 9:120.

113. PSRL 7:91; PSRL 9:253-54; PSRL 20:130; PSRL 23:50; PSRL 25:85.

114. PSRL 10:230; PSRL 15.1:67.

115. See, for example, PSRL 11:8 and 15.1:84. Tver' citizens complained that Prince Vasilii Mikhailovich and his wife imposed on them a heavy burden of "dishonor payments, tortures, despoiling of property and *prodazhi* without mercy." The chronicles also contain the complaint about a *namestnik* of Ivan Mikhailovich dispatched in 1405 to Kashin where the official did much evil "by *prodazhi* and robbery." See PSRL 6:132; PSRL 8:77; PSRL 11:192; PSRL 20:221; PSRL 23:140; PSRL 24:170. In another case, the citizens of Luka were enraged by the offenses and *prodazhi* of the prince's *namestnik*. On judging the complaint, the prince determined that his official was indeed guilty, and obliged him to repay all the *prodazhi*. See PSRL 6:222; PSRL 20:336. For an example of treating the *prodazhi* like any revenue operation, see PSRL 4:250, 251.

116. The document containing what was thought to be the oldest reference to *prodazha* in a juridical act is now considered a forgery (ASEI 1, no. 1, p. 25). Despite what is argued here, the weakness of the very idea of sanction shows through in some of the threats aimed at violators of immunity grants. Those dating from the late fourteenth century (for example, ASEI 1, nos. 2, 5) promise the violators a place in judgment before God,

and only gradually did the prince himself promise to sanction deviants (ASEI 1, nos. 29-31, 40, 41). It is interesting to note that one of the documents uses a church term (*zapoved'*) to indicate a financial sanction (ASEI 1, no. 40). Cf. B. O. Unbegaun, "Russe et slavon," p. 178.

117. English law of approximately the same time likewise dispensed with emendations, but moved (in theory, at least) directly to afflictive sanctions (Pollock and Maitland, *History*, 1:576, 2:458-59).

118. Short RP, 3-7; Expanded RP, 23, 25, 27, 28, 68.

119. Short RP, 3, 6; Expanded RP, 26.

120. See, for example, PRP 1:148, 149; PR 2:65-68, 71-72, 339-40, 349.

121. Short RP, 2. The formula is significantly changed in the Expanded Pravda, and is discussed in detail below.

122. PRP 2:52.2.

123. PRP 2:72.4.

124. Expanded RP, 29.

125. See Sergeevich, *Lektsii*, p. 306. The word usually denoted a sanction in the Russkaia Pravda. See PRP 1:148-49. It is also known from Vladimir's Statute, Rostislav's Administrative Statute, the Pskov Judicial Charter, Beloozero Administrative Charter, and the 1497 Sudebnik. The matter is discussed briefly in PRP 2:330 and *Sudebniki XV-XVI vekov*, p. 56.

126. The testimony of the witness was to be examined to see that it matched exactly the plaintiff's complaint (Expanded RP, 29).

127. Expanded RP, 28 ("If someone cuts off a finger, [he must pay] 3 grivny [as a] fine and a grivna of kuna to [the victim] himself"), and 30 ("If [someone] strikes [a man] with a sword, but does not kill [him], then 3 grivny [as a fine], and a grivna for treatment to [the victim] himself for the wound").

128. See Expanded RP, 37, 38, 45, 46, 68, 80, 81, 84, 89, 121. *Prodazha* appears in other articles as well, although the designation there is by no means indisputable.

129. Expanded RP, 29.

130. Expanded RP, 23, 27, 30, 31. See Short RP, 4, which contains the parallel to Expanded RP, 23.

131. Short RP, 33; Expanded RP, 78. The Short version lists the *ognishchanin*, *tiun*, and *mechnik*, while the Expanded version defends only the *ognishchanin*. On the debate, see PR 2:198-204, 574-76.

132. PRP 2:300.11, 301.120.

133. On the relation of the Pskov Charter to the Russkaia Pravda, see Cherepnin, *Russkie feodal'nye arkhivy*, 1:431.

134. PRP 2:289.26, 292.48.

135. Short RP, 14, 16. Of course, the appearance of the defendant was not devoid of community support. Article 14 stipulated that the de-

fendant was to provide a guarantor should he not respond within five days. England had similar regulations (Pollock and Maitland, *History*, 2:163-65).

136. A recent observation, based on Lithuanian precedent, suggests that in Novgorod, at least, the owner did mark the property, if not the thief (I. P. Starostina, "K tolkovaniiu," pp. 171-74).

137. Expanded RP, 32, 34-36, 38-39.

138. Expanded RP, 32. Also see Short ZSL, 32 and Expanded ZSL, 36.

139. It may reasonably be supposed that the three-day interval was based upon some ideal time for communicating the summons and the accused's response. To my knowledge, no accurate records for estimating the distribution of news in early medieval Russia survive, but fifteenth-century English examples suggest wide variance in the distance coverable in three days (C.A.J. Armstrong, "Some Examples," pp. 444-53).

140. Expanded RP, 37. Also see Expanded RP, 35.

141. Expanded RP, 38. The parallel passage of the Short Pravda assigned a three-grivna composition (Short RP, 11).

142. Expanded RP, 36-37, 39.

143. PRP 3:162-63.5. Vernadsky's translation again falls short of the mark. Unaccountably, he omitted the article's last phrase which prescribed branding (*Medieval Russian Laws*, p. 58).

144. PRP 2:290-91.34, 292.46-47, 293.56. The Pskov Judicial Charter also prescribed that arsonists, thieves, and others could die for their crimes, while homicide evidently was sanctioned solely by a one-ruble fine (PRP 2:287.7-8, 293.52, 298.96-97).

145. See, for example, PRP 2:289.25, 293.54.

146. PRP 2:287.7-8.

147. Short RP, 12; Expanded RP, 33. Inexplicably, Vernadsky added to the Expanded article the judgment that the three-grivna payment was a fine, but there is no evidence for this (*Medieval Russian Laws*, p. 40). Specific blacklisting of horse thieves was not unique to the Pravda, but was often mentioned in other "barbarian laws." See, for example, Katherine Fischer Drew, *Burgundian Code*, pp. 91-92; Drew, *Lombard Laws*, pp. 116-18.

148. Short RP, 13; Expanded RP, 34. The principle is reinforced in still another provision on the same subject. Someone who ruined another's spear, shield, or clothes was responsible for the damage (Short RP, 18).

149. Short RP, 28; Expanded RP, 45. Both instances formulate the payments in a manner parallel to the obvious restitution provisions: "Then pay for it (*za n'*) three grivny, and for the others (*za inekh*) two grivny" (Expanded RP, 45). A similar principle was at work in Iaroslav's Statute where dishonor payments were phrased in the same way—*za sorom*—while the church took an additional fee (PRP 1:265-66.1, 266.2-3, 267.5).

NOTES TO CHAPTER 3

150. Expanded RP, 84.
151. Expanded RP, 35.
152. PRP 2:300.110.
153. Short ZSL, 24, 26; Expanded ZSL, 26-27, 30. These regulations have their parallels in other European "barbarian codes."
154. 1497 Sudebnik, 10, 62; 1550 Sudebnik, 55, 58, 87. The forms and ideals of punishment in medieval Russia and Muscovy were examined superficially in several nineteenth-century works. See Depp, *O nakazaniiakh*, pp. 15-71; A. Bogdanovskii, *Razvitie*, pp. 18-69; M. N. Stupin, *Istoriia*, pp. 10-22; A. G. Timofeev, *Istoriia*, pp. 66-80, 85-88. Most of these works simply list the various penalties, sometimes offering explanations of the origins of the punishments. Timofeev, for example, was inclined to link the appearance of afflictive sanctions with the "brutish" Tatars.
155. See 1497 Sudebnik, 8, 9, 11, 13, and 39, where execution was prescribed. The specific prohibition against selling impecunious criminals is contained in articles 8 and 39. The Sudebnik also forbade judges and bailiffs themselves to sell their charges (articles 35, 43). On later forced sale, see the 1550 Sudebnik, 55; cf. 1589 Sudebnik, 107, 182. Similar parallels may be observed between articles 56, 60, 61, and 71 of the 1550 Sudebnik and articles 108, 113, and 126 of the 1589 Sudebnik. See Horace W. Dewey and Ann M. Kleimola, "Coercion by Righter," pp. 156-67.
156. MP, p. 380 ("And against the thief who has stolen, the first official [*vlastel'*] has a choice, either there will be fines [*prodazhi*] or tortures [*muki*]"). Only two studies of this text have been published. L. V. Milov determined that the provision was inserted in the thirteenth or fourteenth century ("K istorii drevnerusskogo prava," pp. 55-59). I. I. Smirnov published a more detailed study in which he suggested, on the basis of terminology shared by the theft provisions and the Pravosudie Mitropolich'e, that the article was included in the Merilo Pravednoe sometime in the second half of the fourteenth century ("Ustavlen'e tat'by," pp. 488-99). For the most recent edition, see Shchapov, *Drevnerusskie*, pp. 198-99.
157. See, for example, Expanded RP, 29, 31, 32, 60, 72, 73.
158. Expanded RP, 30, 37, 38, 68, 78, 80, 81, 84, 89.
159. Cf. 1497 Sudebnik, 10.
160. PRP 2:286.1.
161. PRP 2:300.112.
162. PRP 3:426.5. On the other hand, article 24 of this same text provided for composition and a fine (PRP 3:428.24).
163. Expanded RP, 45-46; PRP 1:158. For a summary of the debate, see PR 2:396-403. Article 46 specifically allowed composition and doubled it because of the slave's status. See Vladimirskii-Budanov, *Khristomatiia*, 1:51-52; I. I. Smirnov, *Ocherki*, pp. 65-68.
164. Isaev, "Ugolovnoe pravo Kievskoi Rusi," p. 166.
165. PRP 3:428.24. On the history of *vina*, see P. N. Mrochek-

Drozdovskii, "Materialy," p. 17. Tikhomirov argued that *vina* was a Novgorodian term which replaced *vira* (*Issledovanie*, p. 165), but why it appears here in a non-homicidal action is not clear.

166. Short RP, 39; Expanded RP, 82; PR 2:219. See Short ZSL, 16, where damaging someone's woods earned the offender the duty to pay double the losses, and Expanded ZSL, 19, where the guilty party could be sold to pay the losses.

167. Short RP, 31; Expanded RP, 43, 83. Oreshnikov argues that the text of the Short Pravda intended to denote ten rather than eighteen criminals, and convincingly shows the common approach to the problem in the Pravda's two redactions ("K istorii," pp. 152-55).

168. PRP 2:302.1.

169. PRP 1:260.10, 268.12/8, 270.46. See Ecloga 17.41; Procheiros Nomos 39.18, 75. Ia. N. Shchapov thought that the arson provisions were inserted in the Statute only in the twelfth century ("K istorii sootnosheniia," pp. 179-180; "Ustav," p. 74).

170. Short ZSL, 17; Expanded ZSL, 17-19. These regulations tie arson offenses and their punishment to the individual's responsibility for the fire.

171. Short RP, 32; Expanded RP, 71, 72, 75, 76, 80. Beaver theft was punishable by payment of twelve grivny (Expanded RP, 69). For the economic significance of beekeeping, see Froianov, *Kievskaia*, pp. 56-57; and Froianov, "Kniazheskoe zemlevladenie," pp. 47-50.

172. Short RP, 35; Expanded RP, 79.

173. Short RP, 37; Expanded RP, 81. See Froianov, *Kievskaia*, pp. 56-57; Froianov, "Kniazheskoe zemlevladenie," pp. 46-52. For the most part, Froianov's work has been met with stony silence, so that it is difficult to gauge its effect. However, O. M. Rapov, with whom Froianov has come into direct conflict, has acutely observed that Froianov's views "lower to some degree the level of socio-economic and political development of the Old Russian State," and lead to a denial of feudalism and feudal property among the Kievan princes ("O nekotorykh aspektakh," p. 92).

174. Expanded RP, 70.

175. Expanded RP, 3, 7.

176. Short RP, 34; Expanded RP, 73.

177. Expanded ZSL, 55. Tikhomirov, in reconstructing the text, used the wording of the Pushkin copy (*naima* instead of *oranie*), though elsewhere he describes the Pushkin copy as generally inferior to the Archeographic, excepting the introductory articles (*ZSL prostrannoi*, pp. 8, 9, 12). No note is attached to explain Tikhomirov's choice. The same monument treats property destroyed by unrestrained animals (Expanded ZSL, 50).

178. PRP 3:162.4, 173.18.

179. 1497 Sudebnik, 62. This regulation, like that of the Beloozero Administrative Charter, cites the fine as a replacement for a ram, evidently the traditional border payment (see PRP 3:162.4).

NOTES TO CHAPTER 3   231

180. This viewpoint, while undoubtedly correct as the above discussion shows, has suffered from overkill by Soviet historians. See, for example, Cherepnin, "Obshchestvenno-politicheskie otnosheniia," pp. 134, 153, 157, 164, 169, 185-86, 199-203, 236, 251.
181. PRP 2:213.10, 215-16.28, 216-17.34.
182. PRP 2:213.8, 215.23, 216.33, 216-17.34. The development of judicial personnel is discussed in detail in Chapter 4.
183. PRP 2:291.37, 294.58, 295.64-65, 295.67, 296-97.82, 297.83.
184. PRP 2:287.7-8.
185. PRP 3:162-63.5.
186. PRP 3:172.10.
187. 1497 Sudebnik, 39.
188. 1497 Sudebnik, 10-11.
189. The relative inaccessibility of portions of Muscovy may be deduced from the haphazard way that administrative reform was undertaken in the mid-sixteenth century. See Iakovlev, *Namestnich'i*, no. 12; nos. 1-3, 5-7 (second numeration).
190. See PRP 3:173.19; 1497 Sudebnik, 12, 38-39; ASEI 3, nos. 25.10, 27.21; Iakovlev, *Namestnich'i*, nos. 4, 5, 7, 10, 12. See Goebel, *Felony*, pp. 70-74, 258.
191. This matter is discussed in more detail below. See 1497 Sudebnik, 10, 12-14.
192. PRP 3:162-63.5; 1497 Sudebnik, 8, 10, 12-14. Although Vernadsky noted in his introduction the practice of branding thieves as originating in the Dvina code, he omitted the appropriate provision in his translation (*Medieval Russian Laws*, pp. 12, 58). Branding criminals was known to the Byzantines as well (Pavlov, "Knigi," p. 55). On communal participation, see G. V. Demchenko, "K voprosu," pp. 153-75.
193. Charles R. Tittle and Charles H. Logan, "Sanctions and Deviance," pp. 378, 384, 386-87; Charles H. Logan, "General Deterrent Effects," p. 72; Charles R. Tittle, "Crime Rates," pp. 419-20, 423; Richard G. Salem and William J. Bowers, "Severity," pp. 35-36.
194. John C. Ball, "The Deterrence Concept," p. 353.
195. Charles R. Tittle and Alan R. Rowe, "Moral Appeal," p. 495; Schwartz and Orleans, "On Legal Sanctions," pp. 86-87; Rettig, "Ethical Risk Sensitivity," pp. 583, 587-88; Chambliss, "Types of Deviance," pp. 712-14; Salem and Bowers, "Severity," p. 37.
196. See 1497 Sudebnik, 8, 9, 12, 13; ASEI 3, no. 27. Mikhail Benemanskii attempted to derive this terminology from Byzantine roots, suggesting that the same criminals were known in the Knigi zakonnye as *imenitii razboinitsi* (*Zakon Gradskii*, pp. 163-65). Also see Pavlov, "Knigi," p. 65.
197. Salem and Bowers, "Severity," pp. 21, 37.
198. Kolycheva, *Kholopstvo*, pp. 202-206.

Chapter 4

1. Schwartz and Miller, "Legal Evolution," pp. 160, 168.
2. *Max Weber*, pp. 5, 19. But "a 'legal order' shall rather be said to exist wherever coercive means, of a physical or psychological kind, are available; i.e., wherever they are at the disposal of one or more persons who hold themselves ready to use them for this purpose" (p. 16).
3. *Max Weber*, pp. 6, 52, 67.
4. Gluckman, *Politics*, pp. 86-90, 141.
5. Barkun, *Law*, pp. 96, 109; Schwartz and Miller, "Legal Evolution," p. 160; Aubert, "Competition and Consensus," pp. 34-35.
6. Barkun, *Law*, p. 128; Hoebel, *Law*, pp. 114-16, 259, 266.
7. *Max Weber*, pp. 19, 24, 27, 74, 96. Weber also imputed to religion a certain "formalizing" tendency in legal development because of the limits of magical techniques (p. 77).
8. Barkun, *Law*, p. 151. Roscoe Pound recognized this some time ago (*Social Control*, p. 22).
9. Schwartz and Miller, "Legal Evolution," p. 166.
10. Hoebel, *Law*, p. 329. Hoebel's reliance on coercion is evident throughout this monograph, but is stated more bluntly in an early article: "The really fundamental *sine qua non* of law in any society is the legitimate use of physical coercion" ("Law and Anthropology," p. 843). In another work Hoebel says that "law without sanction is unthinkable" ("Three Studies," p. 424). Also see Jack P. Gibbs, "Definitions," p. 431. Gibbs specifically excludes revenge from notions of law "however regular the revenge and however improbable the retaliation" (p. 432).
11. Barkun, *Law*, p. 151.
12. *Max Weber*, p. 93. But Weber thought the prince's role vitiated by the intrusion of the popular folk-assembly.
13. Among the numerous pre-revolutionary studies, see, for example, Vladimirskii-Budanov's reaction to one attempt to excise princely legislative activity ("Das russische," pp. 1-24). Among Soviet scholars, S. V. Iushkov will serve to illustrate the point ("Russkaia Pravda," pp. 72-89).
14. A. E. Presniakov, *Kniazhoe pravo*, pp. 192, 290, passim. Even the communal elders (*starosty*) are ascribed to princely genius (ibid., p. 195).
15. For a typical argument of this position, see V. T. Pashuto, "Cherty," pp. 68-73.
16. The earliest mention of the *druzhina* in the Primary Chronicle appears under the year 941 (PVL 1:33; cf. PVL 2:287). The personal nature of this grouping is discussed by Sergeevich, who attributed the root of the term to the word meaning friends (*druz'ia*) (*Drevnosti*, 1:379). Also see Froianov, *Kievskaia*, p. 57; Presniakov, *Kniazhoe pravo*, pp. 225, 229.
17. Most discussions on the development of administrative officials are characterized by a tendency to generalize sixteenth- and seventeenth-century functions to earlier officials about whom little is known. M. V.

Shakhmatov, for example, determined that the bloodwite collector (*virnik*) was the direct parallel to the later Muscovite bailiff (*nedel'shchik*) (*Ispolnitel'naia vlast'*, 1:10).

18. Short RP, 19-23. Also see Short RP, 33.

19. Sreznevskii, *Materialy*, 2:603; Tikhomirov, *Posobie*, p. 157; Mrochek-Drozdovskii, *Izsledovaniia*, pt. 2, pp. 218, 117-35 (second numeration); Dal', *Tolkovyi slovar'*, 2:1156. Supplementary deductions then make of the *ognishchanin* a boyar or similarly distinguished member of society. See, for example, Sergeevich, *Drevnosti*, 1:359. To be sure, the *ognishchanin* several times appears in the chronicles in the company of the "younger retinue" (*grid'ba*). But he also appears with merchants, and no one would claim therefore that he was a merchant (NPL, pp. 219, 283).

20. NPL, pp. 32, 42, 73. Later chronicles simply reproduce these references. See Kochin, *Materialy*, p. 214.

21. Short RP, 33; Expanded RP, 78; PRP 1:95; Sergeevich, *Drevnosti*, 1:359-63.

22. See, for example, AFZ 3, nos. 37 and 48 where immunity recipients were freed from jurisdiction of *namestniki, volosteli*, and their *tiuny*.

23. PRP 2:68.34. The bailiff (*pristav*) could be dispatched on judicial missions either by the prince or his *tiun* (PRP 2:63.14).

24. PRP 1:245.5, 245.9, 246.14; PRP 2:163.5, 165.14.

25. PRP 2:215.25, 248.3, 250.24. In addition to the surviving cases where the grand prince's *tiuny* were judges (ASEI 1, no. 557; ASEI 2, no. 370; ASEI 3, no. 208), the 1497 Sudebnik includes several provisions which imply that other *tiuny* ranked with the urban and provincial judges (*namestniki* and *volosteli*). Article 40 permitted the *tiun* to provide judgment charters, and article 65 allowed him to split court fees with his superior (*namestnik*). Later Muscovite documents also identify *tiuny* as judges (AFZ 3, nos. 37, 68). The Pravosudie Mitropolich'e assigned the same dishonor payment for *namestnik* and *tiun* (PRP 3:426.2). Also see, for example, NPL, pp. 295/450, 322; PSRL 7:115, 150; PSRL 25:106, 134.

26. PRP 2:75.21; PSRL 7:80, 102.

27. Expanded RP, 110.

28. DDG, nos. 3, 4, 8, 12, 20, 28, 61, 80, 89.

29. 1497 Sudebnik, 66; see Kolycheva, *Kholopstvo*, p. 57.

30. This is one of the definitions suggested by Tikhomirov (*Posobie*, p. 170). The association implies that the *ognishchanin*, like the *tiun*, was a slave, but there is no direct confirmation of that.

31. Expanded RP, 11-13.

32. PRP 1:245.5, 246.14; PRP 2:163.5, 165.14. The single positive reference to the judicial activity of the *tiun* is contained in only one redaction of the 1229 Smolensk Treaty (D) (PRP 2:68.34). For general confirmation of the *tiun*'s development as non-legal sources portray it, see S. V.

Zavadskaia ("O znachenii termina," pp. 157-64), who demonstrates that *tiun* was equated with terms meaning curator, administrator, and judge.

33. Short RP, 42; Expanded RP, 9.

34. Kochin, *Materialy*, p. 46; M. A. Britsyn, *Iz istorii*, pp. 24-25. Despite the restrictions imposed by the sources, Britsyn depicts the *virnik* as one who "conducted investigation and trial on murder and collected fees for various criminal offenses." It is this kind of theorizing that led Shakhmatov to equate the *virnik*, whose fees were paid by the week, with the *nedel'shchik*, whose name is based on the word for week (*Ispolnitel'naia vlast'*, 1:10). Also see Mrochek-Drozdovskii, "Materialy," p. 19.

35. Expanded RP, 10. The size of the bloodwite—eighty grivny—indicates that princely personnel are under discussion here. Another article provides subsidiary fees payable by those lucky enough to escape the onerous bloodwite (Expanded RP, 20).

36. There is some discussion over *poliud'e*. A recent study describes it as a contribution from the free populace (Froianov, *Kievskaia*, pp. 116-17), but the more traditional views tie it to the payment of tribute (Sergeevich, *Drevnosti*, 3:187-88). On the *sud proezdnoi*, see PRP 2:249.11. Its mention in immunities denied these courts and their officials the right to extract "feeding" (*korm*) from the immunity recipient (for example, ASEI 1, nos. 165, 170). Mrochek-Drozdovskii suggested that the rounds of the bloodwite collector served to replace the judicial functions carried out in the *poliud'e* excursions (*Izsledovaniia*, pt. 2, p. 138).

37. Short RP, 42; Expanded RP, 74.

38. For example, PRP 1:143.

39. Sreznevskii, *Materialy*, 3:764-65. According to Britsyn, the term in Common Slavic originally denoted one who had no right to speak (*Iz istorii*, pp. 32-33). See PSRL 2:46, 218, 225. Arguments against the etymology offered here have so far failed to convince most philologists. See F. F. Kopechnyi, "K etimologii," pp. 54-61.

40. Expanded RP, 9, 11, 20, 74; Sreznevskii, *Materialy*, 3:764-65. As an example of the *otrok*'s military service, see PSRL 25:15.

41. Expanded RP, 9, 107. Vernadsky mistakenly altered the meaning of article 107 with his translation (*Medieval Russian Laws*, p. 53).

42. Tikhomirov, *Posobie*, p. 154. Also compare the 1189-1199 Novgorod Treaty (PRP 2:125.6). Mrochek-Drozdovskii, on the other hand, identified the *metel'nik* as the official name of the *otrok* entrusted with the mission of judicial police officer ("Materialy," p. 126). Szeftel described the *metel'nik* as a secretary who carved notes into boards (*Documents*, p. 103).

43. Expanded RP, 74.

44. Expanded RP, 9. On *perekladnoe*, see Tikhomirov, *Posobie*, p. 154.

45. The editors of PRP were so intent on demonstrating the scribal functions of the *pisets* that they suggested that the fee described as *za mekh*

("for fur / skin") actually indicated a reference to parchment (PRP 1:171). This view merely reproduced Sreznevskii's judgment which had, however, no other support than Sreznevskii's opinion (*Materialy*, 2:252).

46. On the origin and history of the term *d'iak*, see Kliuchevskii, *Sochineniia*, 6:232; Britsyn, *Iz istorii*, pp. 43-45. For examples, see ASEI 1, no. 199; ASEI 2, no. 274; ASEI 3, no. 351. Some documents of the late fifteenth and early sixteenth centuries depict the *pistsy* as judges in land cases (for example, ASEI 1, nos. 581, 658; ASEI 2, nos. 306-10, 338; ASEI 3, nos. 50, 105, 221 and 223; AFZ 1, nos. 114, 254, 258, 306). The early cadasters (*pistsovye knigi*) also were compiled by *pistsy* (Henry L. Eaton, "Cadasters," pp. 54-55).

47. PSRL 2:139.

48. PRP 1:58; PRP 2:293.50, 296-97.82.

49. PRP 1:87; Tikhomirov, *Posobie*, p. 154; Shakhmatov, *Ispolnitel'naia vlast'*, 1:9.

50. Short RP, 1; Expanded RP, 1.

51. Short RP, 33; Expanded RP, 78.

52. Expanded RP, 86. The term is not in evidence elsewhere in the sources (Britsyn, *Iz istorii*, pp. 29-30). V. V. Mstislavskii fantasized that the *mechnik* was a kind of public defender of communal rights, but this seems unlikely ("O poklepnoi vire," pp. 1-14). Sergeevich connected the *mechnik* with military tasks (*Drevnosti*, 1:425-26), an explanation supported by references in the Novgorod First Chronicle where "swordbearers" (*mechenoshi*) are recalled (NPL, pp. 64, 269). More recently Szeftel has suggested that the *mechnik* was charged with the physical execution of sanctions, an interpretation vaguely based on correspondence to the Latin and Greek equivalents offered by Sreznevskii (*Documents*, p. 42). Also see Mrochek-Drozdovskii, "Materialy," pp. 126-28.

53. Sreznevskii, *Materialy*, 1:798; Vasmer, *Etimologicheskii slovar'*, 1:508; PRP 1:177.

54. For example, see PSRL 7:81.

55. PSRL 7:89.

56. Kliuchevskii, *Sochineniia*, 6:148.

57. Expanded RP, 107. There is some confusion over the intent of this article since Vladimir's Statute seemingly appropriates to church courts all disputes over inheritance. See PR 2:691-93. Shchapov argues that in the course of the late medieval centuries the church came to control lower levels of inheritance adjudication ("K istorii sootnosheniia," pp. 175-77).

58. PRP 2:62-63.14, 65.22, 74.13.

59. PRP 2:80, 237. On citations of the *birich*, see Kochin, *Materialy*, p. 27. Muscovite references include ASEI 3, nos. 2, 13, 21.

60. PRP 3:165. Also found in GVNP, no. 84.

61. Shakhmatov, *Ispolnitel'naia vlast'*, 1:10-11. Britsyn is more cautious, noting that the source is unclear (*Iz istorii*, p. 38).

62. NPL, pp. 32, 58, 259; *Pistsovye knigi Obonezhskoi piatiny*, pp. 17-22, 24, 46; *Novgorodskie pistsovye knigi*, 2:148, 160, 193, 194, 197, 212-21, 223, 225-28, 232, 264-73; 3:152.

63. NPL, p. 486; PRP 2:162. A fifteenth-century birch bark charter seems to indicate that the *birich* delivered a court summons (A. V. Artsikhovskii, V. L. Ianin, *Novgorodskie gramoty na bereste* [*Iz raskopok 1962-1976 gg.*], pp. 66-68).

64. See PSRL 7:45 ("They sent the *podvoiskie* and *birichi* through the streets to shout it out"); PSRL 25:45 repeats the same wording; PSRL 25:177 ("From Novgorod do not summon them neither by *dvoriane, podvoiskie, sof'iane, izvetniki* or *birichi*."). A similar formula appears in a fifteenth-century immunity charter (PRP 2:199-200). The *sof'ianin* and *izvetnik* were peculiar to Novgorod (PRP 2:237). More on them below.

65. PRP 2:65.22/20.

66. PRP 2:215.23, 218.39. The first provision matches that noted above in grouping *podvoiskii, sof'ianin, izvetnik*, and *birich*. The second citation resembles the chronicle notation whereby the *birich* or *podvoiskii* was to shout out the announcement (PSRL 7:45).

67. PRP 2:215.23.

68. PRP 2:250.18. See Kochin, *Materialy*, p. 132.

69. PRP 2:237.

70. Short RP, 1. For a sample of the literature on the names mentioned here, see PR 2:32-57.

71. NPL, p. 58; 1497 Sudebnik, 8. Herberstein described persons who placed incriminating evidence at the homes of innocent persons, and then charged them with a crime (*Notes*, 1:103). Dewey thinks this a form of *iabednichestvo* ("Defamation," p. 113). Also see 1550 Sudebnik, 72; AAE 1, no. 257; AI 1, no. 165.

72. P. N. Mrochek-Drozdovskii, "O drevnerusskikh iabetnikakh," pp. 1-19; Britsyn, *Iz istorii*, pp. 33-35; Szeftel, *Documents*, p. 42. Also see AFZ 2, no. 71 ("My bailiffs (*pristavove*) enter [lands] on the basis of false accusations from *iabodniki* [sic] and they tie up and sell peasants").

73. A. V. Artsikhovskii and V. I. Borkovskii, *Novgorodskie gramoty na bereste (Iz raskopok 1956-1957 gg.*), pp. 56-58.

74. Kliuchevskii was persuaded that the word's origin was Germanic (*ambatt*), and therefore counted the *iabednik* a princely servitor whose duties gained him a bad reputation (*Sochineniia*, 6:191).

75. PRP 2:215.23. The term *sof'iane* is also used in the Statute on Bridges (PRP 1:207; PR 1:317, 390). A. Nikitskii suggested that the term designated the entire collective of servitors of St. Sophia, what he called the clerical regiment (*dukhovnyi polk*), and that various secular servitors were the individual components (*Ocherk*, pp. 191-92). A. V. Kartashev, on the other hand, visualized the *sof'iane* as the clergy attached to the archepiscopal cathedra (*Ocherki*, 1:188). Also see PRP 2:237; Kochin, *Materialy*, p. 336.

NOTES TO CHAPTER 4   237

76. The term seems to have originated with the Poles, and may have sprung from military functions as some have suggested (Britsyn, *Iz istorii*, p. 51; Shakhmatov, *Ispolnitel'naia vlast'*, 1:9). B. O. Unbegaun disputed this etymology, and suggested instead that the root was taken from *podvoj* which signified an entrance. Consequently, in a line of development that Unbegaun paralleled with the French *huissier*, the *podvoiskii* originally guarded the door, introduced newcomers, and finally executed judicial tasks ("La Fausse Évidence," pp. 335-39).

77. NPL, pp. 86, 317.

78. NPL, pp. 45/239, 71/280, 86/317. Also see PSRL 25:147, 177, 304-306, 315.

79. See, for example, PSRL 25:306 ("The Novgorodians gave against them *podvoiskii*-type bailiffs [*pristava*]").

80. PRP 2:215.23.

81. PRP 2:257.18.

82. PRP 2:188; GVNP, no. 279.

83. A. V. Artsikhovskii and V. I. Borkovskii, *Novgorodskie gramoty na bereste (Iz raskopok 1955 goda)*, pp. 25-26.

84. PRP 2:292.49, 295.64, 296.81.

85. PRP 3:163.9, 10.

86. PRP 2:199-200; AFZ 2, no. 25; 1497 Sudebnik, 64. A similar application of the *podvoiskii* took place in the Metropolitan's administration (AFZ 1, no. 298).

87. PRP 2:215.23, 289.25, 295.64, 296.81. Also see PRP 2:199-200.

88. Neither Pskov nor Novgorod law specifically assigned to the bailiffs implementation of sanctions. Novgorod provided only for the arrest of suspects (PRP 2:216-17.34). Pskov authorized the bailiff to investigate complaints, arrest the accused, and shackle them on need (PRP 2:293-94.57, 295.64, 295.65, 298.98). The Pskov Charter did, however, provide for execution of certain criminals, and the bailiffs were a likely source of fulfilling this commission. At any rate, of all the officials mentioned in the Pskov code, the bailiffs' job description most closely approximates the executioner's function.

89. Pollock and Maitland (*History*, 2:582) claimed that even thirteenth-century England had no professionals assigned exclusively to judicial duties, but that judgment has come under criticism. John P. Dawson found "a permanent court of professionals" already functioning in the 1190s, and by the thirteenth century the Court of Common Pleas and the King's Bench constituted professional courts (*History*, pp. 129-30).

90. PRP 2:215.23, 215.25, 289.25, 295.64, 296.81.

91. See M. N. Tikhomirov, *Krest'ianskie i gorodskie vosstaniia*, pp. 163-99.

92. NPL, pp. 125, 159, 166.

93. For example, NPL, p. 20: "Mstislav went from Novgorod to Kiev for the [Kievan] throne . . . and placed (*posadi*) his son Vsevolod on the

throne in Novgorod." Also see Sreznevskii, *Materialy*, 2:1227-30; Dal', *Tolkovyi slovar'*, 3:854-56.

94. Kliuchevskii, *Sochineniia*, 6:186.

95. See Ianin, *Novgorodskie posadniki*, p. 45. Lists of the Novgorod mayors are contained in the Novgorod First Chronicle (NPL, pp. 164-65, 471-72). For additions and corrections, see Ianin, *Novgorodskie posadniki*, pp. 15-44. Both Rostislav's Statute (PRP 2:42.7) and the *Rukopisanie* of Vsevolod (PRP 2:175.2) emphasize the role of the mayor in judicial matters. Zimin argues on the basis of some internal contradictions that the latter text actually belongs to the fourteenth century (PRP 2:174, 178). Ianin connects the appearance of the original text with the early thirteenth-century prince Vsevolod Mstislavich. In the fourteenth or late thirteenth century the *Rukopisanie* was reconciled with Vladimir's Statute (*Novgorodskie posadniki*, pp. 89-93; "K khronologii," pp. 60-68). Ia. N. Shchapov rejected Ianin's clever analysis, and suggested instead a late thirteenth-century origin for the *Rukopisanie* as a falsified document reflecting political struggles of that time. Only later did it undergo textual changes (*Kniazheskie*, pp. 169-77; *Drevnerusskie*, p. 153). Tikhomirov proposed the earliest origins—early in the twelfth century (*Krest'ianskie i gorodskie vosstaniia*, pp. 181-88).

96. PRP 2:212.2, 248.5, 253.12.

97. PRP 2:212.2-3, 248.4-5. More on the *namestnik* appears below.

98. PRP 2:214.20, 215.26, 248.5. The provision for representation of the community expressed in article 26 of the Novgorod Charter found a different expression in Muscovy (cf. 1497 Sudebnik, 24, 28).

99. The name is evidently derived from the size of the military unit, the thousand (*tysiacha*), which he commanded (Tikhomirov, *Posobie*, p. 170; Sreznevskii, *Materialy*, 3:1073-76).

100. Expanded RP, 53.

101. PRP 2:212.4, 212.5a, 213.8-9, 215.27, 215-16.28.

102. PRP 2:213.8, 215.27 ("The mayor and *tysiatskii* and archbishop's representative *and their judges* and other judges all are to kiss the cross and judge them in justice" [emphasis added]).

103. PRP 2:125.

104. PRP 2:135, 137.

105. PRP 2:248.6; NPL, pp. 472-73 for a list of *tysiatskie*.

106. PRP 2:212.3. On the Old Scandinavian origins of the term, see Britsyn (*Iz istorii*, p. 15).

107. PRP 2:248.3, 4. Article 4 limits to fifty the number of men attached to the *namestnik*, *dvoretskii*, and *tiun* in the prince's quarters in Novgorod.

108. PRP 2:215.25.

109. PRP 2:135.5, 135.7, 137.4, 138.14, 138.17, 139.4, 139.6, 139.14, 140.18, 140.26.

110. ASEI 1, no. 557; ASEI 2, no. 370; ASEI 3, no. 208; AFZ 3, nos. 37, 48; 1497 Sudebnik, 40, 65; PRP 3:172.9, 173.19.

111. PRP 2:286.3, 287.6. See B. B. Kafengauz, *Drevnii Pskov*, pp. 36-71.

112. PRP 2:300.109. The Pskov church remained under the jurisdiction of the Novgorod Archbishop, despite several attempts to create an independent bishopric (Nikitskii, *Ocherk*, pp. 207-26, 317-44). The Novgorod Archbishop was first elected in 1156 (Kartashev, *Ocherki*, 1:188).

113. PRP 2:286.4-5, 292.48.

114. See PRP 2:163.5.

115. PRP 2:212.5a, 213.6.

116. See, for example, PRP 2:215.25.

117. PRP 2:215.23, 216.29, 216-17.34, 218.40-41.

118. PRP 2:243. The nature of the name has induced some speculation about the *pozovnik* as a litigant (Britsyn, *Iz istorii*, p. 53; Cherepnin and Iakovlev, "Pskovskaia sudnaia gramota," p. 271). Although the term may have originated in the litigant's duty to seek out his opposite, the surviving texts which generalize the function of summons and attribute it to the *pozovnik* would seem to eliminate consideration of such a definition (PRP 2:215.23; ASEI 3, nos. 13, 21).

119. PRP 2:200 (reprinted in ASEI 3, no. 13). In another Muscovite text the *pozovnik* is used as a general term to designate *dvorianin, podvoiskii*, and others (ASEI 3, no. 21).

120. Sreznevskii, *Materialy*, 1:646-47; Mrochek-Drozdovskii, "Materialy," p. 53; Kochin, *Materialy*, p. 89. Vasmer inexplicably suggested a seventeenth-century Polish origin (*Etimologicheskii slovar'*, 1:489), but as V. D. Nazarov recently demonstrated, the *dvorianin* is known from the twelfth century ("*Dvor* i *dvoriane*," pp. 104-22).

121. Kochin, *Materialy*, pp. 83-89; Sreznevskii, *Materialy*, 1:645-46. On the judicial duties of the *dvoretskii* and relationship to the *dvorskii*, see Sergeevich, *Drevnosti*, 1:466-76.

122. The *dvor* is mentioned in the Short Pravda (38, 40) and Expanded Pravda (29, 58, 83, 100, 102, 103). The *dvorskii* is included in only one article of the Expanded Pravda (66) and the *dvorianin* in one supplementary article ("O muke," PR 1:341, 362, 390, 457).

123. See M. B. Sverdlov, "Dvoriane," pp. 54-59. The *dvoriane* and *deti boiarskie* became the main instruments of the military system established in late fifteenth-century Muscovy (Richard Hellie, *Enserfment*, pp. 25-29).

124. PRP 2:136.20, 138.20, 140.20. However, as noted above, at least occasionally the *dvorianin* did execute various court-assigned duties. One recently discovered birch bark charter, belonging probably to the twelfth century, indicates that even then *dvoriane* were sent on summons. As the text's editors point out, the case demonstrates that judicial norms of

the fifteenth century were at work two or three centuries earlier. But whether the insults detailed in the charter constituted a judicial case may be questioned. See Artsikhovskii and Ianin, *Novgorodskie gramoty na bereste (Iz raskopok 1962-1976 gg.)*, pp. 130-34.

125. Britsyn, *Iz istorii*, p. 49; Sreznevskii, *Materialy*, 2:1458-59; Dal', *Tolkovyi slovar'*, 3:1162-63.

126. PSRL 7:176, 192; PSRL 25:154, 162; ASEI 3, no. 190. Also see AFZ 1, no. 172.

127. PRP 2:140.29.

128. For example, DDG, nos. 2, 5, 7, 9, 11, 13, 17; AFZ 1, nos. 1, 6, 71, 103, 116, 145, 190, 193, 210, 233, 247, 257, 259, 280; ASEI 1, nos. 74, 92, 93, 98, 133, 219, 243, 246, 262, 265; ASEI 2, nos. 161, 174-76, 183, 201, 243, 315, 323, 324, 363, 385, 403, 410, 411; ASEI 3, nos. 55, 220, 225, 392, 393, 478.

129. NPL, pp. 422, 462; A. V. Artsikhovskii, *Novgorodskie gramoty na bereste (Iz raskopok 1952 goda)*, pp. 18-20. It is interesting to note that here the *pristav* parallels the *dvorianin*.

130. Shakhmatov, *Ispolnitel'naia vlast'*, 1:8; cf. DDG, no. 11 ("I shall not send my tax-collectors [*dan'shchiki*] nor my *pristava*").

131. PRP 2:215.25-26, 216.29, 216-17.34, 291.37, 293-94.57, 295.65-67, 296.76, 297.84, 298.98.

132. PRP 3:163.12, 168.8, 173.16, 173-74.22; 1497 Sudebnik, 32, 44, 45, 53, 63, 67. *Pristava* were not always assigned duties that were specifically judicial (Sreznevskii, *Materialy*, 3:1458-59).

133. PRP 2:215.25-26.

134. PRP 2:216.29.

135. PRP 2:216-17.34. Vernadsky was reluctant to translate the last section as an indication of actual sanction, but that conclusion seems inescapable (*Medieval Russian Laws*, p. 90).

136. It seems likely, for example, that the *pristav* carried out the documents setting court dates, though no officials are mentioned in the article which describes that process (PRP 2:215.24).

137. PRP 2:216.30, 218.41.

138. PRP 2:293-94.57, 294.59. Article 57 envisions exactly that process of false accusation by which the *iabetnik* or other bailiffs may have acquired their unsavory reputation.

139. PRP 2:295.65, 295.67, 298.98.

140. PRP 2:296.76, 297.84. After 1539, the *pristav* was joined at sales by the *guba* elder and "outside people"—those not connected with the litigants (PRP 2:296.76, 297.84).

141 PRP 2:291.37.

142. PRP 2:292-93.49, 295.64, 296.81, 295.66, 289.25.

143. PRP 2:294.59, 361. The *podverniki* were unique to Pskov (Britsyn, *Iz istorii*, p. 57). Vernadsky describes them as porters, certainly an error (*Medieval Russian Laws*, p. 73).

NOTES TO CHAPTER 4   241

144. PRP 2:292-93.49, 295.64, 296.78, 296.80-81.

145. PRP 2:295.64.

146. PRP 2:298.98. The *pristav* was specifically cleared of homicide accusations in such an eventuality.

147. PRP 2:295.65, 295.67, 296.80, 292-93.49.

148. PRP 2:214.3. The confrontment procedure (*svod*) known to the Russkaia Pravda and later Muscovy constituted a logical antecedent to this requirement.

149. The allusion to a written document (*riad*) stems chiefly from the provisions on inheritance (Expanded RP, 50, 92, 99, 110). But despite the controversy this subject has generated (see PR 2:634-39), a written contract in any of these cases is unlikely, if only because the Pravda devotes little attention to the secretary (Expanded RP, 74). A related argument has arisen over the *riadovnik / riadovich* (Short RP, 25; Expanded RP, 14), a name probably derived from the *riad* (PR 2:166-70).

150. Vasmer, *Etimologicheskii slovar'*, 1:560.

151. PRP 2:213.8, 213.12, 214.21, 216-17.34, 217.35.

152. PRP 2:213.8, 215.24, 216.30-31, 218.40.

153. PRP 2:214.13. See PRP 2:235 on the *pozov*.

154. The thirteenth-century treaties of Novgorod with its princes contained specific restrictions on the issuance of documents by the latter (PRP 2:135.5, 138.12, 139.4).

155. PRP 2:289.25, 296.79.

156. PRP 2:296.79, 297.83.

157. Pskov law did provide for executions, but who performed them is not clear. The *pristav*, involved in matters of arrest and detention, seems the most likely candidate (PRP 2:216-17.34, 298.98).

158. Perhaps the most famous example of this type of excursion was Igor's ill-fated attempt to collect his fees twice in one season, an act of rapacity that earned him his death and the Drevliane who killed him the revenge of Ol'ga (PVL 1:39-40; PSRL 2:42-46). The account of the Byzantine Emperor Constantine Porphyrogenitus even uses a Greek transliteration of the Russian term (*De Administrando imperio*, p. 63). Debate has arisen over the relationship between *poliud'e* and the *dan'*. Kliuchevskii, among others, contrasted the two (*Sochineniia*, 6:200-201). Most recently, I. Ia. Froianov has offered a much more complex distinction whereby the *dan'* constituted a tribute payment from the heirs of the subject tribes in early medieval Russia, and *poliud'e* represented a voluntary contribution from the free population (*Kievskaia*, pp. 113-18, 121-25; "Danniki," pp. 33-34).

159. ASEI 3, no. 1.

160. DDG, no. 11.

161. DDG, no. 20; also see DDG, no. 16.

162. Helen M. Cam, *Hundred*, pp. 54, 89-95, 163; William Alfred

Morris, *Medieval Sheriff*, pp. 13-14, 30, 67-68, 98, 104, 111, 241, 280; Helen M. Jewell, *English Local Administration*, pp. 87-95, 185.

163. Jewell, *English Local Administration*, p. 22; Pollock and Maitland, *History*, 1:530; Cam, *Hundred*, p. 118; Dawson, *History*, p. 129.

164. Cam, *Hundred*, pp. 132-35; Morris, *Medieval Sheriff*, pp. 8-9, 115, 189, 191; Jewell, *English Local Administration*, pp. 25, 46.

165. Morris, *Medieval Sheriff*, pp. 34-37, 53, 61, 63, 67, 111; Helen M. Cam, *Liberties*, p. 28.

166. See, for example, P. D. King, *Law*, p. 52, for a description of Visigothic royal servants.

167. For example, DDG, nos. 12, 16, 20.

168. DDG, nos. 2, 4, 12, 17.

169. ASEI 1, no. 224; ASEI 2, no. 326; ASEI 3, nos. 69, 73, 74, 107, 279. References to *putnye boiare* also appear in fourteenth-century documents (DDG, nos. 11, 13). A. K. Leont'ev, in a discussion focusing on the origins of the chancellery system, insisted that the *put'* constituted only personal missions carried out by the prince's underlings, inasmuch as no organized system of administration had yet been worked out (*Obrazovanie*, p. 27).

170. PRP 3:179; Kliuchevskii, *Sochineniia*, 6:193. Sergeevich tied the term to the notion of the right to hunt and thereby extract income from the territory (*Drevnosti*, 1:413-16).

171. The first uses of *prodazha* are discussed above in Chapter 3. See, among other citations, PSRL 7:91, 9:253-54, 10:230, and 11:8.

172. Canute laid special charge on the reeves to avoid bribe-taking (Morris, *Medieval Sheriff*, pp. 11-12), and by the thirteenth century, sheriffs, bailiffs, and justices were sworn not to do wrong for favor, hate, gifts, or promises (Jewell, *English Local Administration*, p. 34). The Muscovite prince, Vasilii Dmitrievich, proposed in the 1397 Charter for the Dvina Land to amerce officials of his who excessively taxed his subjects (article 13). The 1488 Beloozero Charter also threatened with punishment those who overstepped the bounds of avarice which the law allowed in soaking the local population (article 23), but no means of carrying out these threats was defined. The 1497 Sudebnik *begins* with a prohibition against bribe-taking (article 1), which reflects poorly on fifteenth-century Muscovy's justices. One may note in passing that the Pskov Judicial Charter included several injunctions designed to protect the integrity of the local courts (articles 3-5). Here, as in later Muscovy, however, there already existed a schedule of fees payable for the services of scribe, bailiff, and judge.

173. The significance of the assembly's demise as well as the role of the clergy in Moscow's rise were pointed out by Sergeevich (*Drevnosti*, 2:33-50, 623-58). The church's role in the rise of Moscow has become a regular feature of the literature. See S. M. Solov'ev, *Istoriia*, 2:562-94;

Kliuchevskii, *Sochineniia*, 1:265-70, 2:23-29; A. E. Presniakov, *Obrazovanie*, pp. 121-41, 290-92, 307-17, 352-72, 449-56.

174. PRP 3:163.6.

175. PRP 3:162.1, 162.3, 162-63.5. The last regulation is reminiscent of article 80 of the Pskov Judicial Charter (PRP 2:296.80).

176. PRP 3:162, 164.15 (and concluding protocol).

177. The early history of the *namestnik* administration is surveyed by Ivan Beliaev ("O sude namestnich'em," pp. 289-304) and Ivan Andreevskii (*O namestnikakh*, pp. 5-32).

178. PRP 1:245.14. Also see PRP 2:163.5 for a similar concern.

179. Shchapov, *Kniazheskie*, p. 39; Tikhomirov and Shchepkina, *Dva pamiatnika*, p. 19. For representative citations, see Sreznevskii, *Materialy*, 2:301-303.

180. Expanded RP, 114. Cf. PR 1:360, 388. The usual term in these passages is *posadnik* (for example, PR 1:116, 162, 177).

181. PR 1:345-46, 365-70. E. I. Kolycheva observed similar reflections in slavery law of the same period (*Kholopstvo*, pp. 202-206).

182. PRP 3:426.2. On the fourteenth-century origin of the Pravosudie Mitropolich'e, see Tikhomirov, "Pravosud'e," pp. 43-44; Tikhomirov, *Posobie*, p. 127. The association of the *namestnik* with the Metropolitan depends upon the argument that identifies the Pravosudie as a document compiled for the Metropolitan.

183. DDG, nos. 2, 6, 9, 11, 13.

184. For example, DDG, no. 45 (ca. 1444): "Our *namestniki* judge in those courts even so as it was before this. . . ." Nevertheless, little specific information about the *namestniki* survives from the period before the fifteenth century. See A. A. Zimin, "Namestnicheskoe upravlenie," pp. 271-90.

185. ASEI 1, nos. 165, 170, 179, 304.

186. Iu. V. Got'e, *Zamoskovnyi krai*, pp. 372-73. Possession of Bezhetskii Verkh was disputed between Novgorod and Moscow in the fourteenth century. Although Moscow allegedly annexed Bezhetskii late in that century, Novgorod still regarded it as its own in the fifteenth century. Tver' also made claims on the region (Bernadskii, *Novgorod*, pp. 215-18, 246, 250). The issuance of charters by a succession of contending parties during the civil war lends a hazardous coloring to the information in the documents.

187. Almost involuntarily one recalls the English justices in eyre who at one point made excurses into the countryside once every seven years (Pollock and Maitland, *History*, 1:544).

188. For example, AFZ 1, nos. 71, 86, 88, 97, 98, 123, 133, 145, 173, 210, 212, 213, 230, 233, 264; ASEI 1, nos. 131, 224, 236; ASEI 2, nos. 49, 66, 79, 92, 140, 164, 191, 199, 212, 228, 232, 245, 265, 266, 321, 360, 363, 364, 386, 391, 397, 415, 426, 448, 466, 473, 475, 476, 480.

189. PRP 2:68.36; Shchapov, *Drevnerusskie*, pp. 90, 92, 99, 103, 114, 120, 124-25. It is worth pointing out that church *volosteli* are more prominent in Iaroslav's Statute than the Metropolitan's *namestnik* in the Pravosudie Mitropolich'e.

190. PRP 2:217.36, 292.48.

191. DDG, nos. 2, 6, 9, 12, 13, 15.

192. PRP 3:422.7.

193. On dating the *Zapis' o dushegubstve*, see Cherepnin, *Russkie feodal'nye arkhivy*, 2:351-52; I. I. Smirnov, "Sudebnik 1550 goda," p. 313; PRP 3:199-200; A. L. Khoroshkevich, "K istorii," pp. 193-203; G. V. Semenchenko, "O datirovke," pp. 53-58.

194. PRP 3:168-69.9.

195. Sergeevich, *Lektsii*, pp. 221-22.

196. 1497 Sudebnik, 21, 24.

197. 1497 Sudebnik, 1, 20, 38, 40, 43.

198. For address to boyars, see 1497 Sudebnik, 2, 3, 6, 16, 17; on the *okol'nichie*, articles 4, 5, 6, 7. Article 21 equates the fees of the court of the grand prince's family with those who hold the right of boyar jurisdiction (*boiarskii sud*). The code's procedural character has stimulated debate on the document's juridical significance, especially in view of the Sudebnik's overwhelming preoccupation with judicial fees. Dewey explains these matters by the Sudebnik's arrangement whereby subjects are examined in the order of the ranks of the officials concerned with each of these functions ("1497 Sudebnik," pp. 321, 325-26). Also see PRP 3:374-75.

199. 1497 Sudebnik, 1, 31, 33, 34, 38. Also see article 35 where the bailiffs are adjured not to sell thieves.

200. Fees or payments are mentioned in thirty-six of the Sudebnik's sixty-eight articles (Dewey, "1497 Sudebnik," p. 325).

201. 1497 Sudebnik, 33.

202. 1497 Sudebnik, 19.

203. 1497 Sudebnik, 35.

204. 1497 Sudebnik, 67.

205. A false witness, once discovered, was subject to payment of the costs of the suit and damages (ibid.). For examples of conflicting testimony, see ARG, no. 10; Ann M. Kleimola, *Justice*, pp. 43-45.

206. PRP 4:176 ("[And you further petition that] you were caused great losses by our investigators . . ."). The inclusion of this phrasing in all but one of the local reform charters of the early sixteenth century has stirred some doubts about the authenticity of the petitions. N. E. Nosov suggests that petitions had been written, but that the government generalized those few actually received and applied them to regions where no petitions were in fact written (*Ocherki*, pp. 238-42). For later cases, see PRP 4:179; DAI 1, no. 31.

207. PRP 4:188-89; 1497 Sudebnik, 8, 9.

208. 1497 Sudebnik, 26, 28, 31. There is no hint here of the bailiff

NOTES TO CHAPTER 4   245

serving the warrant in the company of the defendant, a practice known in Pskov (PRP 2:298.98).

209. 1497 Sudebnik, 15, 16, 22, 24, 26-28, 36, 40, 45. All these documents are surveyed in Dewey and Kleimola, *Russian Private Law*, pp. 28-32, 41-48.

210. 1497 Sudebnik, 17, 40, 41, 43.

211. 1497 Sudebnik, 8, 12.

212. The Muscovite investigation bears a strong resemblance to the English medieval *inquisitio* or jury of accusation. While the Englishmen were expected to point out those soiled by *fama publica*, the Muscovite citizens attested to the criminal reputation of miscreants among them (Pollock and Maitland, *History*, 1:142). The implications of the inquest for Muscovite justice are discussed in more detail in Chapter 5.

213. 1497 Sudebnik, 8-11, 13, 34-36, 38. No records of actual executions are extant, but Western visitors to Muscovy in the sixteenth and seventeenth centuries relate the practices of physical sanction and capital punishment in sufficient detail to suggest that felons in fact were executed, at least periodically. See Giles Fletcher, *Of the Russe Commonwealth*, pp. 52-53; Adam Olearius, *The Travels of Olearius*, pp. 229-32.

214. 1497 Sudebnik, 4-7.

215. Among the sixteenth-century references to the duel, see ASEI 1, no. 651; ASEI 2, nos. 336, 407; ASEI 3, nos. 25, 27, 50, 223, 375, 377, 390; AFZ 1, nos. 1a, 2a, 222; AFZ 3, no. 23; ARG, nos. 18, 230, 255. Cf. 1497 Sudebnik, 7, 38.

216. 1497 Sudebnik, 32, 44, 45, 53, 63, 67.

217. 1497 Sudebnik, 4-7, 26, 28, 29, 31, 33-37.

218. 1497 Sudebnik, 38, 45.

219. 1497 Sudebnik, 50, 64.

220. PRP 3:163.12.

221. DDG, nos. 2, 5, 11, 13 ("do not send your *pristava*"); cf. ASEI 1, no. 92 ("do not give a *pristav* against them") and AFZ 1, no. 1 ("[We shall] not send to those [who live in the settlement] tax collectors nor *pristava*"); GVNP, no. 3.

222. PRP 3:173.22.

223. For example, ASEI 1, nos. 74, 219, 243, 278; cf. ASEI 3, no. 27.25.

224. See, for example, PRP 173.22.

225. PSRL 25:212.

226. NPL, pp. 422, 463; PRP 3:428.24.

227. Unsuccessfully, however. See PSRL 25:266 ("[Fedor Basenok] having inveigled his *pristav* [into freeing him], then escaped from his chains and fled. . . .").

228. PSRL 25:306 ("The Grand Prince . . . ordered . . . his *pristava* to put them on secure bond"). See, among others, ASEI 1, nos. 219, 245, 278; ASEI 2, no. 243.

229. DDG, nos. 2, 5, 11, 27, 40, 45, 52, 56, 58; AFZ 1, nos. 264, 283; ASEI 1, nos. 139, 175, 189, 197.

230. AFZ 2, no. 21 ("and the *dovodchiki* are not to spend the night among them"); PRP 3:170.4.

231. For example, ASEI 1, nos. 31, 76, 101, 131, 139, 189, 197, 218, 221, 236; ASEI 2, nos. 49, 76, 92, 98, 140, 153, 164, 191, 199, 212, 222, 232, 265, 321, 323, 349, 360, 364, 382, 391, 415, 466, 475; AFZ 1, nos. 71, 88, 97, 123, 145, 193, 212, 230, 251, 283.

232. For example, AFZ 1, no. 264; ASEI 1, no. 197.

233. See AIu, no. 21. The complainants requested a *pristav* but received a *dovodchik* whose performance proved inadequate. They then received a *nedel'shchik* from the Moscow grand prince.

234. Britsyn, *Iz istorii*, pp. 43-45, 48. Both are mentioned often in the Novgorod cadastral books (Kochin, *Materialy*, pp. 98-99).

235. Shakhmatov, *Ispolnitel'naia vlast'*, 1:18; S. B. Veselovskii, *Feodal'noe*, p. 273; Sreznevskii, *Materialy* 2:1361-62.

236. Veselovskii, *Feodal'noe*, p. 273; Shakhmatov, *Ispolnitel'naia vlast'*, 1:17-18. Britsyn follows this lead so far as to say that the *dovodchik* carried out the investigation of crimes (*Iz istorii*, p. 43).

237. Kliuchevskii, *Sochineniia*, 6:507. See AAE 1, nos. 234, 257 (*poshlinnye liudi*).

238. Kliuchevskii, *Sochineniia*, 6:158.

239. PRP 3:170.3; Veselovskii, *Feodal'noe*, p. 273.

240. ASEI 1, nos. 345, 500, 595, 607, 607a, 647; ASEI 2, nos. 239, 416, 426; ASEI 3, nos. 55, 84, 172, 372, 377, 390, 475, 478; AFZ 1, nos. 1a, 2a, 98, 162, 222; AFZ 2, nos. 171, 226, 356, 367. See Scott J. Seregny, "The *Nedel'shchik*," pp. 168-78.

241. AFZ 1, no. 280; AIu, no. 21; ASEI 2, no. 426; ASEI 3, no. 478; Herberstein, *Notes*, 1:106.

242. Short RP, 42. See Shakhmatov, *Ispolnitel'naia vlast'*, 1:10.

243. 1550 Sudebnik, 47. See Kliuchevskii, *Sochineniia*, 6:198; I. D. Beliaev, "O vyvoze," p. 113.

244. Shakhmatov, *Ispolnitel'naia vlast'*, 1:26. Evidently the same reliance on the middle service class held true for the sixteenth-century officials of the reform administration. See Nosov, *Ocherki*, p. 338.

245. 1497 Sudebnik, 29, 30, 44; PRP 3:163.8, 173.16, 173.22.

246. 1497 Sudebnik, 31, 36.

247. 1497 Sudebnik, 33-35.

248. 1497 Sudebnik, 8-11, 13, 39.

249. In addition, the juridical competency of the *tiun* is implied in many immunity charters (for example, ASEI 1, no. 552; ASEI 2, no. 370; ASEI 3, no. 208). A. A. Zimin alleges that the *dvoretskii* was a judge even in the fifteenth century ("O sostave," p. 181).

250. 1497 Sudebnik, 14, 34.

Chapter 5

1. This principle has been well documented for traditional societies. See Gluckman, *Politics*, pp. 190-93; Hoebel, *Law*, p. 88.

2. Traditional societies are generally dominated by the aged, wealthy, and successful. See Wallace and Hoebel, *The Comanches,* pp. 211, 213; Llewellyn and Hoebel, *The Cheyenne Way*, p. 73; Hoebel, *Law*, pp. 73, 82, 114, 137, 193, 216, 218; *Max Weber*, pp. 90-92.

3. Examining the process of legal rationalization and labor specialization was one of Max Weber's main contributions to our understanding of the process of legal change (*Max Weber*, pp. 96, 210, 224, 351).

4. Sreznevskii, *Materialy*, 2:1237-39; Kliuchevskii, *Sochineniia*, 6:216-18; Vasmer, *Etimologicheskii slovar'*, 3:340. Vladimir Prochazka has suggested an evolutionary development of the term *poslukh*, according to which the Slavic understanding of the *poslukh*, as reflected primarily in the Zakon Sudnyi liudem, was derived directly from Byzantine law ("Po-sluch"," pp. 231-51). This much seems true, as the discussion below demonstrates, but the transition from reputation testimony to testimony of fact took much longer than Prochazka indicates. For more on the distinction between *vidok* and *poslukh*, see Vasilii G. Demchenko, *Istoricheskoe izsledovanie*, pp. 6-18, 54-56; PRP 1:88; Szeftel, "La condition," p. 378.

5. N. Diuvernua, *Istochniki prava*, p. 194.

6. PVL 1:171; Beneshevich, *Drevneslavianskaia kormchaia*, p. 194; RIB 6:62.28; A. V. Artsikhovskii, *Novgorodskie gramoty na bereste (Iz raskopok 1958-1961 gg.)*, pp. 61-66, 76-77. One birch bark charter names God as an attestor (Artsikhovskii and Ianin, *Novgorodskie gramoty na bereste [Iz raskopok 1962-1976 gg.]*, p. 115).

7. Short RP, 14, 16; Expanded RP, 35-39.

8. Expanded RP, 37.

9. Synod and Trinity IV (PR 1:125, 332).

10. PR 2:379-80. Nikolai Lange in particular supported this interpretation by criticizing the copies' punctuation (*Izsledovanie*, pp. 230-32).

11. Expanded RP, 39. The phrasing of this article has produced some confusion. What other territory may be alluded to here is not at all clear. Similar regulations developed in pre-Conquest England, where prejudice attached to any purchase not consummated in the populated centers. The function of witnesses was to vouch to the warranty of purchase (Pollock and Maitland, *History*, 1:58-59).

12. Short RP, 2, 30.

13. Expanded RP, 29. Vernadsky, by translating both terms synonymously, mistakenly suggested that the second witnesses, *poslusi*, proved that the complainant had started the fight (*Medieval Russian Laws*, p. 39).

14. Expanded RP, 18. Also see Short RP, 10. Those privileged by requiring only two witnesses were the Varangians and Kolbiagi. The ques-

tion of their identity has stimulated a large debate which is not especially relevant to this study. A recent investigation has suggested some novel conclusions (A. G. Kuz'min, "Ob etnicheskoi prirode," pp. 54-83).

15. Expanded RP, 21. This is one case where Vernadsky's translation seems preferable (*Medieval Russian Laws*, p. 38). Most other scholars suggest that the clause in question (*a ist'tsia nachnet' golovoiu klepati*) refers simply to the original accusation (PR 2:335-37). The difficulty is that *istets'* is in the accusative, and the succeeding clause suggests an ordeal for both litigants (*to ti im pravdu zhelezo*).

16. Short RP, 15. The Archeographic copy lists *12 mouzha* (PR 1:79). Vernadsky perceives a jury here (*Medieval Russian Laws*, p. 29), as does Szeftel (*Documents*, pp. 45-46), among others. Part of the impetus for discerning a jury here is the parallel that the twelve men provide with medieval English law. For example, a tenth-century law of Aethelred prescribed an inquest before twelve thegns (*Laws of the Kings of England*, p. 65). The number of jurors in England varies, however, so that the magic of the twelve men of medieval Russia has little power to connect them with their English counterparts. Pollock and Maitland, associating the jury's origin with the *inquisitio* of the Franks, seem inclined to attribute the jury to the Normans, despite other native English precedents (*History,* 1:140-43). But more recent assessments of the evidence suggest that some revision of the classic interpretation is in order. See, among others, Doris M. Stenton, *English Justice*, pp. 1-21; Dawson, *History*, pp. 120-21.

17. PRP 2:126.10. The editors of PRP offer the suggestion that these twelve men constituted the communal court of the eleventh century (PRP 2:130).

18. Both on the Continent and in England the selection of reputable members of the community who were obliged to witness commercial transactions was already formalized very early (Pollock and Maitland, *History*, 1:141; *English Historical Documents*, 1:399).

19. Expanded RP, 47-49, 52.

20. Expanded RP, 50, 110.

21. See Hoebel, *Law*, p. 251.

22. Marc Bloch, *Feudal Society*, 1:109-14.

23. Expanded RP, 31. The boyar's steward (*tiun*), a member of the slave elite, was permitted to testify. In minor cases the near-slave (*zakup*) was also accepted as a witness if there were no alternatives (Expanded RP, 66). The communal elders (*startsy gradskie*) exemplified similar socially valued attributes, so that they probably often served as witnesses. See V. V. Mavrodin and I. Ia. Froianov, "Startsy gradskie," pp. 29-33.

24. PRP 2:61.8, 73.9.

25. PRP 2:214.22, 217.35. However, a slave was permitted to testify against another slave.

26. PRP 2:287.9.

27. PRP 2:293.51. According to the editors of PRP, *izorniki* were in-

NOTES TO CHAPTER 5   249

debted peasants attached to the land (PRP 2:352-53). A. D. Martysevich translated the term as "(dependent) agriculturalist" (*Pskovskaia*, pp. 157, 161). Szeftel repeats nearly every opinion voiced in the literature, then settles on "laboureur" (*Documents*, pp. 188-90, 217). The most detailed study was done by Kafengauz who identified the *izorniki* as indebted feudally dependent peasants ("Pskovskie izorniki," pp. 28-48). While the *izornik* in some way certainly was dependent, there is no reason to believe that he was "feudally" dependent.

28. PRP 2:293.55. See A. M. Kleimola, "Formulae and Formalism," pp. 360-61.

29. PRP 2:289.27.

30. PRP 2:289.23-24.

31. PRP 2:288.20. A similar provision of the Novgorod Charter required only that the witness swear to the truth of his allegations—namely that the individual he identified was a thief, robber, brigand, arsonist, or slave. No attempt was made to ascertain the nature of the testimony (PRP 2:217.36). Reputation inquiry had a long life in Muscovy.

32. The Novgorod law discussed above (PRP 2:217.35) may be explained with reference to these observations. The failure of a witness to appear was not so much indicative of the bankruptcy of a charge as it was a violation of the necessary preliminaries for judicial review. Without a witness a litigant could not move on to the next step—the ordeals and a decision.

33. PRP 2:289.21-22.

34. 1497 Sudebnik, 50, 52.

35. 1497 Sudebnik, 51.

36. 1497 Sudebnik, 48. It is not clear that the dueling actually was carried out. See Kleimola, *Justice*, pp. 61-66; Dewey, "Trial by Combat," pp. 23-26; Herberstein, *Notes*, 2:104-105; Lloyd E. Berry and Robert O. Crummey, eds., *Rude and Barbarous Kingdom*, p. 34.

37. Expanded RP, 37; 1497 Sudebnik, 46, 47. On similar use of oaths in traditional societies, see Hoebel, *Law*, p. 247; *Max Weber*, p. 78.

38. 1497 Sudebnik, 67.

39. 1497 Sudebnik, 46; PRP 2:293.55. Examples from Muscovite judgment charters appear below.

40. 1497 Sudebnik, 47.

41. 1550 Sudebnik, 15-19, 93, 99; 1497 Sudebnik, 67.

42. For example, ASEI 1, nos. 4, 10, 11, 12. The phrasing (*na to poslusi*) indicates simply that they were present at the conclusion of the agreement.

43. For example, ASEI 1, no. 114 (1434-45). Among others, see AFZ 1, nos. 58, 61, 63, 64.

44. For example, ASEI 1, no. 607; ASEI 3, nos. 172, 251. Also see 1550 Sudebnik, 69; 1589 Sudebnik, 123.

45. PRP 3:173.19; 1497 Sudebnik, 38. It is worth noting that the at-

tendees are identified by position within the countryside's commune, an institution that did not share the enthusiasm for legal reform generated in Moscow.

46. Dewey, *Muscovite Judicial Texts*, p. 89.

47. Sreznevskii, *Materialy*, 1:993; Vasmer suggests that this was a taboo name (*Etimologicheskii slovar'*, 2:101).

48. For example, ASEI 1, nos. 340, 397, 421; AFZ 1, no. 103.

49. *U nas znakhorei . . . te, gospodine, sia znaiut i pomniat . . .* (ASEI 2, no. 229).

50. This matter is discussed by Ann M. Kleimola ("Muscovite Judgment Charters," pp. 45-48) and G. E. Kochin (*Sel'skoe khoziaistvo*, pp. 395-96).

51. ASEI 2, no. 481. It would seem that he was not believed, inasmuch as his party lost the suit, though the judge did not say why. The incident recalls Marc Bloch's observations on the predominance of customary law in medieval Europe, where children often appeared as witnesses since they could be expected to live longest. In order to aid the young in the recollection of august legal transactions, their elders resorted to boxing them on the ear, enforced baths, and other extraordinary events (*Feudal Society*, 1:114).

52. AFZ 1, no. 249.

53. See, for example, ASEI 1, nos. 431, 594; ASEI 3, no. 208.

54. See, for example, AFZ 1, no. 103. The representative of the Metropolitan's peasants, Serapion, gave his name to his side's *znakhari*, Serapionovye, and the prince's man, Larivonka, did the same for his side, Larivonkovye.

55. For example, ASEI 1, nos. 521, 524, 571, 583.

56. The *starozhil'tsy* are discussed in detail by Kochin (*Sel'skoe khoziaistvo*, pp. 395-426).

57. ASEI 1, no. 607; ASEI 3, no. 208.

58. See, for example, ARG, no. 77. The tax books were first compiled late in the fifteenth century (Eaton, "Cadasters," p. 57).

59. Pollock and Maitland, *History*, 2:642; Goebel, *Felony*, p. 74; Bloch, *Feudal Society*, 2:369; King, *Law*, p. 113; Cam, *Liberties*, pp. 50-52.

60. PRP 3:173.19; PRP 2:68.34; NPL, pp. 22-24, 508.

61. AFZ 1, no. 103; ASEI 1, no. 2; ASEI 2, no. 404.

62. Kleimola describes this process admirably ("Muscovite Judgment Charters," pp. 183-85; *Justice*, pp. 37-41).

63. ARG, nos. 10, 134.

64. For example, ASEI 1, no. 523; ARG, nos. 40, 194.

65. ARG, nos. 194, 255. Both introduce a distinction between testimony (*poslushestvo*) and an investigation (*obysk*).

66. Horace Dewey has suggested the role of recidivism and its reflection in "reputation testimony" ("Muscovite *Guba* Charters," pp. 284,

287; *Muscovite Judicial Texts*, p. 87). It has been proposed that this whole idea was drawn from Byzantine law, but the notion of specific, documented recidivism is out of the question here, given the state of Muscovite record keeping in the fifteenth and early sixteenth centuries (Benemanskii, *Zakon Gradskii*, p. 165). The emphasis on reputation brings to mind similar practices known in various traditional societies (Gluckman, *Politics*, pp. 190-94). Pollock and Maitland discuss this process as a predecessor of the jury of presentment, since the locals neither directly accused nor gave witness. Rather, they gave "voice to common repute" (*History*, 2:642).

67. ASEI 3, no. 27.

68. The cases are summarized by Dewey ("Defamation," pp. 109-20). A similar view is expressed in *Sudebniki XV-XVI vekov*, p. 54. The early history of the term is more confusing, but the general consensus is that the *iabednik* was some kind of princely official (PRP 1:87; Tikhomirov, *Posobie*, p. 174; Mrochek-Drozdovskii, "O drevnerusskikh iabetnikakh," pp. 1-19). Also see Artsikhovskii and Borkovskii, *Novgorodskie gramoty na bereste (Iz raskopok 1956-1957 gg.)*, pp. 56-58.

69. NPL, p. 425.

70. Kalachov, "Ob ugolovnom prave," p. 324; Lange, *Drevnee russkoe sudoproizvodstvo*, p. 92.

71. *Sochineniia Ivana Peresvetova*, pp. 179-80.

72. Dewey, "Defamation," p. 113.

73. The term *vina* replaced the older usage known in the Russkaia Pravda (*vira*). It represented a fee payable by the community when a corpse was discovered and no murderer apprehended (Tikhomirov, *Issledovanie*, p. 165; PRP 3:172.14). Iaroslav's Statute used the term in a more general sense (PRP 1:269.27, 270.42, 270.44-45, 270.47, 270.49, 271.53).

74. PRP 3:172.11.

75. 1497 Sudebnik, 14.

76. On the *poval'nyi obysk*, see 1649 Ulozhenie, chapters 10, 20, 21 (PRP 6:112-15.161-62, 117.175, 353-54.95, 389.35).

77. For example, AFZ 1, no. 192; AFZ 3, nos. 23, 27, 63, 65; ASEI 3, no. 27. See Expanded RP, 4-8.

78. Sreznevskii, *Materialy*, 2:1106-1107; Mrochek-Drozdovskii, *Izsledovaniia*, pt. 2, p. 233; G. Fogel', "O poklepnoi vire," pp. 137-38.

79. AFZ 2, no. 71.

80. Expanded RP, 18-19.

81. Expanded RP, 20-22.

82. PRP 3:427.10.

83. *ZSL kratkoi*, pp. 24-25; Saturnik, *Příspěvky*, pp. 144-52, 156, 157, 165. Prochazka uses these same regulations to argue the evolution of testimony in medieval Russia, though with results somewhat different from those presented here ("*Posluch*'," pp. 231, 246-51).

84. Short ZSL, 22; Expanded ZSL, 25.

85. Short ZSL, 2; Expanded ZSL, 9.

86. MP, pp. 251-52; GBLOR, f. 173.I, no. 187, fol. 293. These articles are lifted from Deuteronomy 19:16-19.

87. The nature of these witnesses was discussed in detail in a prolonged debate between two prominent nineteenth-century historians of canon law. See Suvorov, *Sledy*, pp. 38-81; Pavlov, *Mnimye sledy*, pp. 80-99; Suvorov, *K voprosu*, pp. 242-46.

88. Expanded ZSL, 9.

89. Short ZSL, 2; Expanded ZSL, 2.

90. The reading is corrupted in the Pushkin copy and absent in the Archeographic copy of the Expanded Redaction. "It is not fitting for the prince and judge to listen without many witnesses . . ." (*ZSL kratkoi*, p. 104).

91. Expanded ZSL, 83.

92. For an example of comparable phrasing in Muscovite testaments, see ASEI 1, nos. 11, 108 (*svoim tselym umom*).

93. Expanded ZSL, 41.

94. RIB 6:91, 62.28.

95. RIB 6:90-91.

96. RIB 6:851.

97. Pollock and Maitland, *History*, 2:541-43.

98. Pavlov, "Knigi," pp. 1-92.

99. Pavlov, "Knigi," pp. 4, 85, 90. Also see MP, pp. 142-62.

100. GBLOR, f. 209, no. 156. For a description of the manuscript, see *Opis' sobraniia rukopisnykh knig P. A. Ovchinnikova*, p. 33. Shchapov believes that miscellanies of this type must have been compiled no later than early in the fifteenth century (*Kniazheskie*, pp. 106-109). His attempt to tie this particular manuscript to Polotsk is ingenious, but not proved.

101. GPBOR, F. II. 251, fols. 91-93v. For a description of the manuscript, see *Otchet imperatorskoi publichnoi biblioteki za 1905 g.* (St. Petersburg, 1912), pp. 124-33. The contents of this collection are repeated in a seventeenth-century manuscript (GPBOR, XVII. no. 178) described in *Otchet imperatorskoi publichnoi biblioteki za 1886 g.* (St. Petersburg, 1889), pp. 80-90.

102. Pavlov, "Knigi," pp. 16-17. Vasil'evskii suggested an even earlier appearance of these articles in Slavonic translation ("Knigi," pp. 324-25), while Sobolevskii accepted a later date, and ascribed the appearance of the Knigi zakonnye in Russia to South Slavic influence of the fourteenth and fifteenth centuries ("Knigi," pp. 355-56). Shchapov has proposed a fourteenth-century origin (*Kniazheskie*, p. 109).

103. Pavlov, "Knigi," pp. 8, 9.

104. According to Maksimeiko, the fact that in some copies of the Kormchaia the Byzantine chapters On Witnesses immediately preceded the Russkaia Pravda must have brought about changes in the Pravda's own provisions on testimony ("Moskovskaia," pp. 138-39).

105. For example, GPBOR, F. II. 251 bears several notations of a copyist or later reader urging that attention be paid to particular provisions on a witness's motives and quality of testimony (fols. 92-92v.).

106. Both manuscripts add articles devoted to testimony given by clerics (GBLOR, f. 209, no. 156, fols. 105-106; GPBOR, F. II. 251, fol. 93v.).

107. *O poslusekh*, 1 (all citations given according to Pavlov's division into articles of the Knigi zakonnye).

108. Ibid., 2, 7.

109. Ibid., 4, 10.

110. Ibid., 6.

111. Ibid., 11, 12, 14.

112. Likewise, the testimony of a slave against a freeman was suspect. Only when the object of the testimony and the witness both were slaves could such testimony be accepted, although even here under conditions of torture (*ispytanie*) (Short ZSL, 20; Expanded ZSL, 22).

113. PRP 3:428.27.

114. *O poslusekh*, 16, 19, 21, 27-28.

115. Ibid., 17, 21.

116. Ibid., 25. Majority in this case was attained only at age twenty (ibid., 17). Cf. Short ZSL, 20 and Expanded ZSL, 13.

117. *O poslusekh*, 16, 22.

118. Ibid., 15.

119. Ibid., 18, 23, 24, 29. Pskov law, too, tried to curb partisan boisterousness at court (PRP 2:294.58).

120. *O poslusekh*, 26.

121. Expanded ZSL, 57.

122. PRP 3:427.23, 428.28.

123. *O poslusekh*, 31-33.

124. Ibid., 5. Cf. Ecloga 14.7.

125. PRP 3:427.18.

126. *O poslusekh*, 8-9.

127. Expanded RP, 21. On references to the iron ordeal, see Mrochek-Drozdovskii, "Materialy," pp. 68-71.

128. Expanded RP, 22. Iron was decreed for suits with value of more than one-half gold grivna, water for those over two silver grivny, and oaths for the rest. See Sergeevich, *Lektsii*, pp. 453-54; Vladimirskii-Budanov, *Obzor*, pp. 524-25. Pollock and Maitland indicate that the outcome of the iron ordeal was not by any means guaranteed. Among their evidence for this conclusion is a register of judgments from a thirteenth-century Hungarian monastery which claimed about even odds for escaping conviction from the iron. However, Pollock and Maitland go on to point out, in what they assume to be support of their position, that English procedure in some cases gave the appellee the choice between bearing the iron himself or per-

mitting the accused to bear it (*History*, 2:599). On the face of it, the choice implies no prejudice, but a more skeptical reading of this provision suggests that its enforcement could produce results not unlike those allegedly contained in the Hungarian register. Worldly-wise litigants tried to guarantee that the other fellow experimented with divine intervention, while the faithful undertook the trial themselves. The results depended therefore not so much upon the iron, as upon the attitudes litigants brought to the ordeal. No exact description of the iron ordeal survives from Russia, but the doom of Aethelstan on its application no doubt provides a close approximation ("Medieval Legal Procedure," pp. 12-13).

129. Expanded RP, 85, 87. The difficulties of enduring trial by iron are indicated by the Smolensk-German treaties of the thirteenth century. The guest merchants in each of the towns were not to be put to this test without their permission (PRP 2:61.9, 73.10).

130. Expanded RP, 22. The water ordeal was applied often in Russia to suspected witches. See Russell Zguta, "The Ordeal by Water," pp. 222-24. The logic of the water ordeal appears in Hincmar's neat capsulization ("Medieval Legal Procedure," p. 11).

131. Expanded RP, 47, 49, 52.

132. Expanded RP, 37.

133. Expanded RP, 115, 118.

134. Short RP, 10; Expanded RP, 31. It seems likely that this provision arose in connection with the events of 1015, when Iaroslav attempted to topple his father, Vladimir, from his sovereignty over the Novgorod land, where Iaroslav ruled with his father's authorization. Iaroslav hired the Varangians to assist him in his enterprise, but the local citizens found the imported soldiers offensive. See NPL, pp. 168-69, 174-76; Cherepnin, "Obshchestvenno-politicheskie," pp. 131-39.

135. PRP 2:126.9-10. The editors of PRP argue that the lots determined who had the right to place his witnesses before the court (PRP 2:129), but the phrasing (*rote shed*) is singular, as is that employed for the casting of lots, and suggests that the litigant went through the oath.

136. PRP 2:214.14-19.

137. The principal alternatives were the duel and placing the disputed sums before the cross (PRP 2:288.17-18, 289-90.28, 290:29, 298.92, 300.107). Drunks were released from responsibility (PRP 2:300.114).

138. PRP 2:299.104, 299-300.106.

139. PRP 2:293.51, 293.55, 297-98.90, 298.91, 298.95, 299.102, 299.105, 301.116.

140. PRP 2:288.17-18, 288.20, 289-90.28, 290.29, 298.91-92, 299.101, 299.105, 300.107.

141. PRP 2:298.99. It is worth emphasizing that the Pskov code often observes that these methods of establishing the truth were to be used only in the absence of the more tangible evidence of witnesses and documents

NOTES TO CHAPTER 5

(PRP 2:293.51, 293.55, 298.94, 299.104). In the same way, suits based upon uncertified notes fell under the purview of the regulations governing the administration of the oath. "Uncertified note" is Vernadsky's translation of the term *doska*—board—and seems consistent with the verification procedures described in article 32 (*Medieval Russian Laws*, pp. 67-68).

142. B. A. Romanov, *Liudi i nravy*, 1st ed., p. 175; 2d ed., p. 134; H. W. Dewey and A. M. Kleimola, "Promise and Perfidy," p. 336. The ineffectiveness of Christian oaths in a society which was still largely pagan ought cause no surprise.

143. For earlier citations, see PRP 2:61.10, 73.11. The Pskov Judicial Charter mentioned the duel in articles 10, 13, 18, 20, 21, 28, 36, 37, 92, 101, 107, 117, 119. A complete survey of the prescription and use of the duel in medieval Russia may be found in Marc Szeftel, "Le Jugement," pp. 267-93.

144. PRP 2:249.10; PRP 3:204.4; AFZ 1, nos. la, 2a, 117, 222, 259, 261, 306; ASEI 1, nos. 257, 340, 582, 628, 651; ASEI 2, nos. 296, 334, 336, 375, 407, 409, 411, 414; ASEI 3, nos. 22, 27, 50, 223, 364, 375, 377, 390; ARG, nos. 10, 230, 255. See Cherepnin, *Russkie feodal'nye arkhivy*, 2:247. Dewey, although doubting the actual practice of the judicial duel, noted the further development of provisions devoted to duels in both the 1550 and 1589 Sudebniki ("Trial by Combat," pp. 23, 26). Older studies indicated that the sixteenth century witnessed the "flowering of duels." See K. F. Kalaidovich, "O poedinakh," pp. 13-21; I. Beliaev, "Pole," pp. 46-48. By contrast, it appears that in fourteenth-century Western Europe the duel had already nearly passed out of use (George Neilson, *Trial by Combat*, p. 16).

145. Herberstein, *Notes*, 2:104-105; Berry and Crummey, *Rude and Barbarous Kingdom*, p. 34; Staden, *Land*, p. 16. Kleimola suggested that the duel was simply a formulaic ingredient of the court case ("Formulae and Formalism," p. 372).

146. The evidence is summarized by Szeftel, "Le Jugement," pp. 288-93. Also see 1497 Sudebnik, 49, 52, by which clerics were exempted from dueling. A similar rule existed in Pskov (PRP 2:291.36).

147. 1497 Sudebnik, 47-48, 58.

148. 1497 Sudebnik, 4-7, 68. Payment out of armor was also known in Pskov (PRP 2:291.37). The Expanded Pravda did make provision for fees for those who administered the oath (article 109).

149. See Fedotov, *Russian Religious Mind*, 1:287-95; Dewey and Kleimola, "Promise and Perfidy," pp. 327-41.

150. See Staden, *Land*, p. 16. Women, children, cripples, the elderly and the ill, as well as churchmen, could hire substitutes (PRP 2:291.36; 1497 Sudebnik, 49, 52). In England, clerics escaped battle only after 1176 (Neilson, *Trial by Combat*, p. 46). The use of champions evidently was prevalent in early medieval Europe where the wealthy were able to

monopolize all the best combatants, and thereby doom poor litigants to inevitable judicial defeat (James B. Thayer, "The Older Modes of Trial," p. 67, n. 1).

151. Expanded RP, 107; 1497 Sudebnik, 68. Herberstein mentions the crowd of unruly spectators (*Notes*, 2:105).

152. Expanded RP, 22, 109.

153. Pollock and Maitland, *History*, 2:599.

154. Short RP, 14, 16, 21, 38; Expanded RP, 3, 19, 22, 32, 34, 35, 37, 38, among others. Also see PRP 3:162-63.5.

155. PRP 3:162-63.5, 172.11; PRP 2:294.60; PRP 3:427.13, 427.17, 427.21; GVNP, no. 20; 1497 Sudebnik, 13.

156. Short RP, 38; Expanded RP, 37.

157. PRP 3:172.11. The translation is Dewey's (*Muscovite Judicial Texts*, p. 4). Also see ARG, no. 18. The origin of *polichnoe* may nevertheless belong to the Russkaia Pravda, one of whose provisions uses the term *litso* to denote stolen property (Expanded RP, 34; PRP 1:153). The same term bearing the same meaning also appears in the Lithuanian Statute of 1529, one of whose sources included the Russkaia Pravda (see *The Lithuanian Statute*, p. 191).

158. For example, ASEI 3, nos. 309 (*s vinoiu i polichnym*), 311 (*s polichnym i poshlinami*), 314 (*s vinoiu i s polichnym i so vseiu poshlinoiu*), 315, 316, 322, 324, 325, 328, 329, 333, 354, 355, 360, 361, 369, 388, 389; ASEI 1, no. 474 (*s sudom i s polichnym*).

159. Expanded RP, 77; ASEI 1, no. 516; AFZ 1, nos. 230, 233.

160. For example, AFZ 3, no. 57. Also see ASEI 2, nos. 133, 256; ASEI 3, nos. 25.18, 27.17.

161. ASEI 2, no. 458 (*i muzhi polichnoe polozhili*); AGR 1, no. 45.

162. 1497 Sudebnik, 13, 14.

163. ASEI 1, no. 475 (*sud i polichnoe i dushegubstvo*).

164. Expanded RP, 3.

165. PRP 1:246.15; PRP 2:39.2; PRP 3:162.1, 172.14; A. V. Artsikhovskii and V. I. Borkovskii, *Novgorodskie gramoty na bereste (Iz raskopok 1953-1954 gg.)*, pp. 48-49; and the same authors' *Novgorodskie gramoty na bereste (Iz raskopok 1955 goda)*, pp. 31-33.

166. For example, Expanded RP, 7, 18, 19; Pollock and Maitland, *History*, 2:487. The English parallel, the *murdrum*, is only a more famous equivalent of the *dikaia vira* of early Russia, as discussed in Chapter 2.

167. PRP 3:162.1, ASEI 2, nos. 108, 217, 497; ASEI 3, nos. 25, 27, 92; AFZ 2, nos. 62, 64, 77, 84, 99, 144, 166, 228, 236, 316, 333, 409; AFZ 3, nos. 11, 37, 48, app. 5; ARG, no. 18.

168. Sergeevich, *Lektsii*, p. 422; Vladimirskii-Budanov, *Obzor*, pp. 408-409; P. I. Beliaev, "Pervichnye formy," pp. 138-72. See H. D. Hazeltine's preface to Dorothy Whitelock, ed., trans., *Anglo-Saxon Wills*, pp. viii, xiii, xxiv.

169. Expanded RP, 92. Allusion to clerical intervention appears in

NOTES TO CHAPTER 5

the article's provision for the "soul's portion" of the estate. *Riad*, by the way, was not exclusively used to denote testaments. Some citations manifestly tie the term to any kind of agreement (PRP 1:6, 262, 271; PRP 2:72, 75, 188-89; Expanded RP, 110), and in one case (Expanded RP, 99), it is not at all clear that the testament was written.

170. PRP 2:278. Also see two clerical testaments from the twelfth and thirteenth centuries (GVNP, nos. 103, 105).

171. Expanded ZSL, 83 ("arrange [your] estate while healthy and of sound mind [*tselym umom*]"). Cf. Procheiros Nomos 21.2. See ASEI 1, no. 11. A variant (*svoim tselym umom i razumom*) is introduced in some later testaments (ASEI 1, no. 108; ASEI 2, no. 168). Some wills use still another variation (*svoim tselym umom i v svoem smysle*—ASEI 2, no. 361).

172. Expanded ZSL, 83, 84. See, for example, ASEI 1, no. 11 ("In the name of the Father, Son, and Holy Ghost, be it known that I, Patrikei, a servant of God, departing this world . . .").

173. For example, ASEI 1, nos. 108, 228, 253. On writers of these testaments, see ASEI 1, no. 11; ASEI 2, no. 361; ASEI 3, no. 100. For seals, see ASEI 1, no. 108; ASEI 2, nos. 168, 361; ASEI 3, nos. 67, 67a, 68.

174. Expanded ZSL, 82. Cf. ASEI 2, no. 361.

175. ASEI 1, no. 11. Variants of the same formula are found in ASEI 1, no. 253; ASEI 2, nos. 87, 168, 361, 474.

176. The dying testator was reminded of his immediate future, and advised to care first for his soul, and only then for his children and wife (Expanded ZSL, 82-84).

177. Charles Gross, "The Medieval Law of Intestacy," p. 120; Pollock and Maitland, *History*, 1:128, 2:356. This doctrine led to some extreme results. See the story in Pollock and Maitland regarding the twelfth-century confessor who failed to reach the dying man in time (ibid., 2:357-58).

178. For an example of the latter, see ASEI 2, no. 40 ("Be it known that I, Marfa Danilova, in accordance with the instructions of my husband, my lord, have given to the house of the Most Pure Virgin . . . Witnessed by my spiritual priest Semen").

179. For example, ASEI 2, nos. 40, 47, 54, 153a, 342. Exactly this phenomenon was operative elsewhere, as Hazeltine notes (Whitelock, *Anglo-Saxon Wills*, p. xxiv).

180. E. E. Lipshits discusses the Byzantine propensity to use paper and its effect upon litigants (*Ekloga*, pp. 10-11).

181. PRP 2:212.a, 212.1, 213.8, 286.a, 291.38.

182. PRP 2:286.4, 296.77.

183. PRP 2:300.108.

184. PRP 2:287.12, 287-88.14, 288.19, 290.30-32, 291.38, 296.75.

185. PRP 2:287.13, 294.61, 295.73, 295-96.74, 296.79, 299.103a.

186. PRP 2:288.15, 293.55, 297.88-89, 298-99.100.

187. PRP 2:213.7, 213.11-12.

188. PRP 2:216.33, 218.39-40. In Novgorod a default judgment was called *obetnaia* (PRP 2:242).

189. PRP 2:216.31, 217.36.

190. PRP 2:217.36, 218.38.

191. The only attempt made to trace the legal consequences of the birch bark documents is the work of L. V. Cherepnin, *Novgorodskie berestianye gramoty*, pp. 36-112, 317-80.

192. PRP 3:163.9, 173-74.22; PRP 2:213.8, 216.33, 218.40, 293.50, 296.82; Artsikhovskii and Borkovskii, *Novgorodskie gramoty na bereste (Iz raskopok 1955 goda)*, pp. 10-11; Artsikhovskii and Borkovskii, *Novgorodskie gramoty na bereste (Iz raskopok 1956-1957 gg.)*, pp. 77-78; Artsikhovskii, *Novgorodskie gramoty na bereste (Iz raskopok 1958-1961 gg.)*, pp. 61-66.

193. 1497 Sudebnik, 25, 27.

194. 1497 Sudebnik, 26.

195. 1497 Sudebnik, 17, 20.

196. 1497 Sudebnik, 18, 42.

197. 1497 Sudebnik, 18, 20, 38.

198. For examples of the *proezdnoi sud*, see ASEI 1, nos. 165, 170, 179, 304. There also were instances of a different kind of temporary judge, as examined by P. I. Beliaev, "Spetsial'noe naznachenie sudei," pp. 1-16.

199. 1497 Sudebnik, 16, 24.

200. 1497 Sudebnik, 22, 40.

201. Nearly all the recent work on this subject has been done by Ann M. Kleimola ("Muscovite Judgment Charters [*Pravye Gramoty*] of the Fifteenth Century," Ph.D. diss., University of Michigan, 1970; "Formulae and Formalism," pp. 355-73; *Justice in Medieval Russia*, pp. 1-93; with Horace W. Dewey, *Russian Private Law*, pp. 41-211). Also see Cherepnin, *Russkie feodal'nye arkhivy*, 2:226-52; Horace W. Dewey, "Judges and the Evidence," pp. 189-94; D. M. Meichik, *Gramoty XIV i XV vv.*, pp. 28-54.

202. The beginnings of this process are described briefly by Eaton, "Cadasters," p. 57.

203. Whether this was the result of the monasteries' stone walls or a consequence of the fact that the churchmen were the winners, and hence, preservers, of an inordinate number of such documents, remains to be discovered.

204. PRP 3:427.19-20. The reading in article 19 (*tat'* or *dati*) is disputed, but the latter makes more sense. See a photocopy of the relevant passage in M. N. Tikhomirov, "Pravosud'e," p. 52.

205. ASEI 2, no. 90.

206. Regrettably we know little about Mikhail Andreevich himself, except that he sided with Vasilii II during the civil war and gradually ceded all power over his appanage in the years of the reign of Ivan III. The ultimate cession is confirmed in his testament, which is also interesting for the

solicitousness Mikhail showed for the courts protected by immunity grants he had given (". . . My lord, the Grand Prince, granted that after my death he would not violate my courts . . . and that my sovereign, the Grand Prince, after my death would not violate my grants [of privilege], so that after my death my people would not weep" [DDG, no. 80, pp. 310-11]).

207. For one such case, see ASEI 2, no. 358.

208. ASEI 1, nos. 523, 607; ASEI 2, nos. 229, 401, 481; AGR 1, nos. 20, 23.

209. See, for example, ASEI 2, no. 401.

210. ASEI 2, no. 406 (*chto sebe khoteli, to pisali*). The reasons for the victory included the refusal of the peasant witnesses (*znakhari*) to support the claims of their side.

211. For example, ASEI 1, nos. 585-89.

212. ASEI 2, no. 296. The plaintiff even introduced a written complaint which was duly read into the record. This case does not have the decision appended, so we are deprived of the results. The judge did criticize the inconsistencies in the plaintiff's suit, and it seems unlikely that he won. Also see ARG, no. 77.

213. AGR 1, no. 15. The plaintiff lost because his land was not found in the books, but it may also be significant that he had no *znakhari*.

214. ASEI 2, no. 333.

215. ASEI 1, no. 590; ASEI 2, nos. 368, 374, 381, 383; ASEI 3, no. 221.

216. For example, ASEI 1, no. 582. In this case the peasants claimed to have a document, but when the judge requested it, they could not provide it. They underminded their own case by claiming that they gave away the document in question, and furthermore, could not remember what was written in it. We are informed in the decision that they lost the case because they did not place the document before the judge. Also see AGR 1, no. 16. Here the litigant admitted to losing his own copy, but he disputed the accuracy of the monastery's copy. Ultimately he reversed himself and became reconciled to the monastery's version. Also see ASEI 3, no. 105.

217. ASEI 2, no. 387.

218. ASEI 2, nos. 286, 288.

219. Kliuchevskii, *Sochineniia*, 6:232.

220. PRP 1:238.8; Shchapov, *Drevnerusskie*, pp. 16, 19, 20, 21. The text does not omit the look-alike word for deacon (*d'iakon*) or deaconness (*d'iakonovaa* or *diakonitsa*), which indicates that this was no simple textual confusion.

221. Sergeevich, *drevnosti*, 1:560 (the text reproduces an obvious misprint [IV instead of XIV] to indicate the century of the replacement).

222. For example, DDG, nos. 1, 4. For a survey of the early structure of the *d'iak* administration and an inventory of some of the first *d'iaki* known to us by name, see A. A. Zimin, "D'iacheskii apparat," pp. 219-86.

The listing for the fifteenth century, at any rate, is not complete, as comparison with the likewise incomplete index of S. B. Veselovskii shows (*D'iaki i podiachie*, pp. 4, 19, 24, 38, and passim).

223. AFZ 1, nos. 29, 243; ASEI 1, nos. 251, 253; ASEI 2, nos. 352, 354, 359, 361, 381; ASEI 3, nos. 5, 67, 67a, 68, 100, 404.

224. AFZ 1, no. 243; ASEI 1, nos. 255, 256, 272, 284, 304; ASEI 2, nos. 238, 246, 263, 268, 290 (fol. 25), 491. An archmandrite's secretary also was known (ASEI 2, nos. 377, 472, 474), as were ordinary *inoki* (ASEI 2, nos. 29, 63) and *cherntsy* (ASEI 2, nos. 8, 25, 26, 32, 33, 36, 47, 54, 57, 71, 84, 85, 87, 89, 100, 104, 114, 119, 144, 145, 148, 153a, 178, 208, 215, 231, 343, 387).

225. AFZ 1, no. 303; ASEI 2, nos. 183, 234, 280, 291, 302, 315, 331.

226. ASEI 2, nos. 2, 3, 7, 27, 34, 35, 62, 72, 73, 81, 83, 86, 116, 184, 187, 226, 276, 385a, 434.

227. Many of these secretaries held fields on church land. See *Novgorodskie pistsovye knigi*, 1:71, 160, 177, 399, 449, 451, 457, 470, 497, 612, 640, 652, 698, 708, 739, 756, 791, 864; 2:123, 132, 172, 198, 203, 263, 321, 393, 401, 422, 442, 461, 469, 498, 499, 513, 707, 736, 762, 784, 826, 872. The frequency of Greek names among the secretaries is interesting, though not unexpected. See, for example, in the above listing those who are named Feofilat, Feofilatko, Dorofeiko, Ofonasko, Ofonas, Vafromii, Elizarko, and so on. According to V. K. Chichagov, by the fifteenth century, if not earlier, Greek personal names had become not at all unusual (*Iz istorii russkikh imen*, pp. 11-28).

228. For example, ASEI 2, nos. 2, 3, 7, 8, 25-27, 29, 32-36, 47, 54, 57, 62, 63; ASEI 3, no. 5. A complete inventory of all the persons who executed the copying of surviving documents is clearly desirable, but not immediately foreseeable. Such a listing could provide a handy index to the kinds of documents copied by clerics and the periods during which this activity flourished.

229. For example, ASEI 1, nos. 7, 15, 108, 168, 169, 178; AFZ 2, nos. 2, 16, 19, 39, 98.

230. For examples of clerics' seals, see DDG, nos. 8, 71. On the *pechatnik*, see PSRL 25:196; Sergeevichi, *Drevnosti*, 1:550.

231. The seal is mentioned specifically as authenticating the 971 Treaty (PRP 1:59.4), though a reference to the practice of authenticating documents with seals was included in the 944 Treaty (PRP 1:32.2a). The latter citation also provided for seals and documents, though not necessarily combined (PRP 1:31.2 ["Whereas previously ambassadors brought gold seals and merchants silver (seals), now your prince has ordered that documents be sent to our Imperial Highness"]). See E. I. Kamentseva and N. V. Ustiugov, *Russkaia sfragistika*, p. 41.

232. PRP 2:213.8, 214.21, 215.24, 216.30, 296.82.

233. V. L. Ianin, *Aktovye pechati*, 1:155.

234. Ibid., 1:166, 249; Kamentseva and Ustiugov, *Russkaia sfragistika*, p. 63.

235. Ianin, *Aktovye pechati*, 1:14-33, 44-59, 168-79, 286-87.

236. Ibid., 1:67-75, 87-131, 187-91, 193-216, 291-92, 294-314.

237. Ibid., 1:5.

238. GVNP, no. 81.

239. The historiography is summarized by Ianin, who rejects the usual identification of the seal (*Aktovye pechati*, 2:16-21). Kamentseva and Ustiugov do not find Ianin's argument persuasive (*Russkaia sfragistika*, pp. 66-68).

240. GVNP, nos. 3, 29. The seals (nos. 380.1, 382.1) are described by Ianin (*Aktovye pechati*, 2:8-11, 159-60, 302-303). Athanasius was Iaroslav's Christian name.

241. Ianin, *Aktovye pechati*, 2:160; Kamentseva and Ustiugov, *Russkaia sfragistika*, pp. 81-82.

242. Ianin, *Aktovye pechati*, 1:155; Kamentseva and Ustiugov, *Russkaia sfragistika*, pp. 40-41, 62. An important series of exceptions are the seals of Ratibor and those bearing the inscription *D'neslovo* (Ianin, *Aktovye pechati*, 1:60-64, 75-86).

243. PRP 2:251.25, 255.a, 258.24.

244. 1497 Sudebnik, 15, 22, 23, 40.

245. 1497 Sudebnik, 16, 24.

246. 1497 Sudebnik, 25.

247. 1497 Sudebnik, 28.

248. 1497 Sudebnik, 17, 40.

249. See, for example, ASEI 2, nos. 333, 406.

Chapter 6

1. Numerous examples spring to mind. The Lombards under Rothair in the seventh century first obtained a written codification of their customary law. Although far more detailed than the Russkaia Pravda, Lombard law contains governing principles and several particular articles similar to those of the Russkaia Pravda. Composition is the prevailing mode of satisfaction, and only occasionally does the king's own interest in justice become obvious. Even so, Rothair was conscious of his own role in promulgating the law, as the preface to his collection indicates. By the time Liutprand undertook a revision of Lombard law early in the eighth century the king himself conceived the laws, studied and promulgated them. Likewise the king's treasury makes a conspicuous appearance in legal remedies, and procedure too has changed significantly. By the middle of the eighth century, King Ratchis and his judges viewed themselves as intermediaries between rich and poor, and urged appropriate conduct upon Lombard judges (see Drew, *Lombard Laws*, passim). A roughly similar chronological alter-

ation is observable in Alamannic and Bavarian law (*Laws of the Alamans*, passim). Closer contact with Roman law had more dramatic consequences in barbarian law. The Burgundian code, the product of compromise between barbarian and Roman law late in the fifth and early in the sixth centuries, contains much of the compensation prescriptions, but corporal sanctions are equally manifest (Drew, *Burgundian Code*, passim). More clearly Roman is the (Visigothic Code, essentially a seventh-century compilation (*Visigothic Code*, passim). These examples may easily be multiplied. For a useful, compact history of the interaction of Roman and Germanic law, see Paul Vinogradoff, *Roman Law in Medieval Europe* (Cambridge: Speculum Historiale, 1968). M. B. Sverdlov provides some useful comparisons between the Pravda and barbarian codes ("K istorii," pp. 142-45, 156-57).

2. Schwartz and Miller, "Legal Evolution," pp. 159-69; Wimberley, "Legal Evolution," pp. 78-83.

3. RIB 6:31.33; N. Gal'kovskii, *Bor'ba*, 1:153-83, 2:84-91.

4. PRP 1:245.6; Shchapov, *Drevnerusskie*, pp. 23, 31, 38, 43, 47, 56-57, 78. E. V. Anichkov discusses the possible placement of Perun's grove, as well as the general significance of groves, water, and grain sheds in pagan religion (*Iazychestvo i Drevniaia Rus'*, pp. 296-97, 324). A. Kotliarevskii claimed that Slavic tradition connected water with the substance of the soul (*O pogrebal'nykh obychaiakh*, p. 206).

5. PVL 1:117-19.

6. Gal'kovskii, *Bor'ba*, 2:58, 65, 93, 99.

7. Ibid., pp. 60, 121, 125-27, 139-40, 305-308; RIB 6:4.7.

8. Gal'kovskii, *Bor'ba*, 2:164-75, 179-83.

9. RIB 6:37.53, 54.

10. Short ZSL, 29; Expanded ZSL, 86; PRP 1:238.7, 241.3, 245.6; Shchapov, *Drevnerusskie*, pp. 23, 31, 38, 43, 47, 56, 60, 63, 67, 71, 74, 77, 83.

11. According to Ia. N. Shchapov, grave robbery was no more than simple theft, a reflection of "class society," (*Kniazheskie*, p. 78). Also see PRP 1:250-51.

12. Evel Gasparini, "Studies," pp. 114-15, 125-26, 129, 131, 133.

13. RIB 6:58.5, 60.14 ("If [wives] do not love their husbands and wash their bodies with water, and give that water to [their] husbands..."). Also see Iaroslav's Statute ("If a wife plots against her husband with poison . . ." [PRP 1:271.52; Shchapov, *Drevnerusskie*, pp. 90, 98-99, 102, 106, 132]).

14. PRP 2:41.6. Shchapov interprets this particular jurisdiction as an example of the collision between the growing claims of church and secular courts ("K istorii sootnosheniia," pp. 178-79).

15. PRP 1:269.37; Shchapov, *Drevnerusskie*, pp. 89, 97, 102, 105.

16. RIB 6:274, 283.

NOTES TO CHAPTER 6

17. PVL 1:14-15; PSRL 2:10; PSRL 25:339-40. For a brief discussion of the function of the marriage festivals, see Shchapov, *Kniazheskie*, p. 283.

18. RIB 6:18.30.

19. See James A. Brundage, "Concubinage and Marriage," p. 8.

20. Several terms are used in medieval texts to indicate marriage by abduction: *uvolochiti* (PRP 2:41.6); *umykan'e* (PRP 1:238.7); and *umytsi* (PRP 3:427.7). The terms *smil'noe* and *poshiban'e* are both associated with forced sexual intercourse. See PRP 1:249, 277; PRP 2:129; Pavlov, "Istoriia," pp. 491-92.

21. RIB 6:13-14.24. According to one cleric, traditional dances (*pliasaniia*) had considerable patronage even in the sixteenth century: the participants "began to commit fornication with other men's wives and with daughters-in-law, sisters-in-law and with godmothers and then they approached idols and began to offer sacrifices to the idols" (Gal'kovskii, *Bor'ba*, 2:188-89).

22. RIB 6:99-100.7-8. These articles were appended to the Council's canons beginning, evidently, only with the fifteenth century.

23. PRP 1:269.33; Shchapov, *Drevnerusskie*, pp. 89, 97, 101, 131, 135; RIB 6:31.33. This is mentioned briefly by Shchapov, who claims that the use of cheese was secularized for later Muscovite marriages (*Kniazheskie*, p. 244; "Brak i sem'ia," pp. 217).

24. RIB 6:272, 279.

25. GBLOR, f. 173.III, no. 108, fol. 27.

26. RIB 6:847, 851.

27. GPBOR, f. 588, no. 1572, fols. 9v.-10.

28. See PRP 1:238.7, 241.3, 245.6, 259.1-2, 260.5-6, 260.16, 261.21; PRP 3:426.4, 427.7, 428.33-34.

29. PRP 2:41.6; Shchapov, *Drevnerusskie*, pp. 15, 18, 20, 21, 23, 31, 38, 43, 46, 55-56, 60, 63, 67, 71, 74, 77, 83; PRP 3:426.4; Short ZSL, 33; Expanded ZSL, 37-39.

30. PVL 1:85.

31. Shchapov, *Kniazheskie*, pp. 131-33; PRP 1:237.3. Some form of the tithe was omitted only in the Varsonof'ev redaction, so that Shchapov is inclined to admit the tithe to the archetype of Vladimir's Statute (Shchapov, *Kniazheskie*, pp. 37, 116, 127, 318; "Tserkov' v sisteme," pp. 297-326). At approximately the same time the new Smolensk episcopacy also received a tithe guarantee from Prince Rostislav (PRP 2:39.3). The origins of the tithe in Russia were the subject, in part, of a classic dispute late in the nineteenth century. See Suvorov, *Sledy*, pp. 189-95; Pavlov, *Mnimye*, pp. 136-45; Suvorov, *K voprosu*, pp. 336-50. For a recent conservative view on church income, see I. Ia. Froianov, "Tserkovno-monastyrskoe zemlevladenie," pp. 87-95.

32. I. U. Budovnits, *Monastyri na Rusi*, pp. 46-47, 74-75.

33. PRP 1:242.6, 245-46.11; Shchapov, *Drevnerusskie*, pp. 24, 32,

40, 44, 47, 57-58, 63, 67, 71, 78-79. The entire history of this section of the Statute and the role of Biblical and South Slavic components is surveyed by Shchapov (*Kniazheskie*, pp. 81-86). Also see Shchapov, "Iz istorii," pp. 99-104.

34. PRP 1:237, 241, 244-45; Shchapov, *Drevnerusskie*, pp. 15, 18, 20, 23, 31, 38, 43, 46, 55, 61, 62, 67, 71, 74.

35. For example, PRP 1:265. See Shchapov, *Kniazheskie*, pp. 243, 257, 281. However, Shchapov attributes the formation of the Statute's archetype to the late eleventh or early twelfth century, a judgment which, as noted above, is not too persuasive (ibid., p. 293).

36. RIB 6:229-34; PRP 2:212.1, 300.109. Article 1 of the Novgorod Judicial Charter generally is dated to 1385 (PRP 2:229; Cherepnin, *Russkie feodal'nye arkhivy*, 1:381). Rozhkova's view, to the effect that the last section of the Pskov Judicial Charter is actually the oldest, dating from the early fourteenth century, seems to have carried the day (*K voprosu*, pp. 32-36). Cherepnin tried to date the Pskov Charter's last articles to a somewhat later time (*Russkie feodal'nye arkhivy*, 1:440-42; Cherepnin and Iakovlev, "Pskovskaia sudnaia gramota," pp. 258, 295). Other views are summarized in PRP 2:283-85.

37. A handful of immunity grants survives from the fourteenth century (ASEI 1, no. 1 [a forgery]; ASEI 2, nos. 9, 24, 42, 340; ASEI 3, nos. 53, 116, 178, 190, 322, 324, 325). I am indebted to Marc Zlotnik for these references. The history of the early expansion of clerical jurisdiction, based upon a particular history of the church statutes, is presented by Shchapov ("K istorii sootnosheniia," pp. 172-89).

38. PVL 1:86-87.

39. Short ZSL, 2b; Expanded ZSL, 9.

40. PSRL 25:75.

41. Sergeevich, *Lektsii*, p. 436.

42. PRP 1:238.7, 241.3, 245.6; Shchapov, *Drevnerusskie*, pp. 15, 19, 21, 23, 31, 38, 43, 47, 56, 63, 67, 71, 77, 83; Expanded ZSL, 80-84. Church-state claims over inheritance are discussed by Shchapov ("K istorii sootnosheniia," pp. 175-77).

43. Expanded RP, 90-95, 98-106; PRP 2:293.53, 297.88-89; 1497 Sudebnik, 60.

44. See, for example, the testament of Ivan Kalita, one of the oldest surviving wills. In an appropriate mix of Christian theology and legal capacity, Ivan affirmed the Holy Trinity and his own sinful nature while averring his sound mind. He noted that the document was witnessed by "my spiritual father Efrem, my spiritual father Fedosii, my spiritual father Priest Davyd" (DDG, no. 1).

45. Roman law came to regard written evidence highly, without abandoning witnesses. See H. F. Jolowicz and Barry Nicholas, *Historical Introduction*, p. 443; *Corpus Juris Civilis, The Civil Law*, 5:225 (III.10), 231-32 (IV.4).

NOTES TO CHAPTER 6

46. Although the usual explanation now is to tie the appearance of written evidence to secular and clerical courts alike, there can be little argument with the fact that the bulk of the medieval secular chanceries were nonetheless made up of churchmen. See Ralph V. Turner, "Clerical Judges," p. 75. On the appearance of written evidence see R. Van Caenegem, "The Law of Evidence," pp. 299-303; John H. Langbein, *Prosecuting Crime*, pp. 135-36.

47. Despite the fact that legislation affecting church courts was the first to ban ordeals, recent scholarship suggests that in this as in other respects church law anticipated a process also underway in secular courts in various parts of the Continent. See John W. Baldwin, "Intellectual Preparation," p. 614.

48. If the church was not the primary force behind reform, the church's move toward rationalizing judicial process was at least more noticeable than secular judicial reforms. See Langbein, *Prosecuting Crime*, pp. 133-38; Van Caenegem, "The Law of Evidence," pp. 297-305; Walter Ullmann, "Some Medieval Principles," p. 12.

49. See Szeftel, "Le Jugement," pp. 267, 288-90.

50. Baldwin, "Intellectual Preparation," p. 615. One notices that private libraries of seventeenth-century Muscovite activists included several treatises on law, but what effect this reading had is hard to establish. See S. P. Luppov, *Kniga v Rossii v XVII veke*, pp. 106, 109, 124.

51. See George Ostrogorsky, *History of the Byzantine State*, trans. Joan Hussey, rev. ed. (New Brunswick, N.J.: Rutgers University Press, 1969), pp. 159-60; Lipshits, *Ekloga*, pp. 13, 163-64; Lipshits, *Pravo i sud*, pp. 198-200.

52. The Macedonian Emperors themselves saw fit to condemn their predecessors' effort, the Ecloga, as a "perversion of good laws, harmful to the State and fit only to perpetuate foolishness" (E. H. Freshfield, *A Manual*, p. 51).

53. For more specific criticisms leveled by Peter the Chanter against the arbitrariness and ineffectiveness of ordeals, see Baldwin, "Intellectual Preparation," pp. 620-36. To my knowledge no record of any similar analysis survives from any medieval Russian source, or even from as late as the seventeenth century.

54. Solov'ev, *Istoriia*, 2:656.

55. Ibid., 1:343-47.

56. Ibid., 1:56, 96; PSRL 2:7.

57. A few examples must suffice. The second volume of PRP, which includes documents from the twelfth to fifteenth centuries, is subtitled "Monuments of Law of Feudally Fragmented Rus'" (PRP 2:3). The second section of the appropriate volume of the series *Ocherki istorii SSSR*, detailing events of the twelfth and thirteenth centuries, is carried under the heading "Feudal Fragmentation" (*Ocheki istorii SSSR*, 1:265).

58. B. D. Grekov, *Kievskaia Rus'*, pp. 450-51.

59. See *Ocherki istorii SSSR*, 1:61, 67-69; cf. B. D. Grekov, "Rabstvo i feodalizm," pp. 5-66.

60. Since rural sites inevitably are less rich in material to excavate, the towns constitute a better source for archeologists. Furthermore, because urban settlements represent a higher stage of exploitation, it has proved convenient to use the towns as a kind of model for the entire process of feudalization which, it is assumed, took place throughout the Russian lands. See *Ocherki istorii SSSR*, 1:124-28.

61. For example, see Tikhomirov, *Krestianskie i gorodskie vosstaniia*, pp. 107-13, 130-48; Cherepnin, "Obshchestvenno-politicheskie," pp. 131-39, 154-63, 175-95, 229-78.

62. To illustrate the variety of views on particular social categories, see PR 2:166-82, 198-205, 439-81.

63. To sample the speculation, see PR 2:256-59, 261-70.

64. Expanded RP, 3, 19; Also see Short RP, 13, 20; Expanded RP, 4-6, 70.

65. Expanded RP, 5-6, 19. One may note that the English hundred was responsible for the *murdrum*, a penalty similar to the *vira*, and also the hundred acted as a pool of frankpledges for its members (Cam, *Hundred*, pp. 2, 124).

66. Expanded RP, 77; Pollock and Maitland, *History*, 2:578.

67. See, for example, *Istoriia russkoi literatury*, 10 vols. (Moscow-Leningrad: AN SSSR, 1941-56), 2.1:352.

68. See the examples cited in *Slovar' russkogo iazyka*, 2:83. The *verevka* (in the sense of a rope) was known to the Englishman, Richard James, who was in Muscovy early in the seventeenth century (B. A. Larin, *Russko-Angliiskii slovar'-dnevnik*, pp. 75, 358).

69. O. Miller, *Opyt*, pp. 136-37.

70. See F. I. Leontovich, "O znachenii vervi," p. 9; Leontovich, "Zadruzhno-obshchinnyi kharakter," pp. 131, 138-39; Leontovich, "K voprosu," p. 27.

71. B. D. Grekov, *Politsa*, pp. 73, 247.59a. Other allusions in the Poljica Statute reinforce the kinship connections with the *verv'* (ibid., pp. 231.36c, 253.62). See Kosven, *Semeinaia*, pp. 138, 153, 157, 159.

72. Expanded RP, 36.

73. Expanded RP, 39.

74. See A. N. Nasonov, *Russkaia zemlia*, p. 28; Charles J. Halperin, "Concept," pp. 29-33.

75. See Kochin, *Materialy*, pp. 126-28.

76. PVL 1:27, 116, 160.

77. PVL 1:12 (*Slovenskaia zemlia*), 40.

78. Halperin, "Concept," p. 34. For more detailed elaboration of this point, see Halperin, "The Russian Land," pp. 7-103.

79. Nasonov, *Russkaia zemlia*, p. 25.

NOTES TO CHAPTER 6

80. See G. P. Fedotov, "Mat'-zemlia," pp. 3-18; Halperin, "Concept," p. 32; Halperin, "Russian Land," p. 21.

81. Paul Bushkovitch, "*Rus'*," p. 300.

82. V. L. Komarovich, "Kul't roda," pp. 88-90.

83. See PSRL 1:413; PSRL 10:29-30.

84. Short RP, 28-32, 35-37, 39-40; Expanded RP, 42-45, 69, 71, 75-76, 79-84.

85. Short RP, 34; Expanded RP, 72, 73.

86. Short RP, 19-26; Expanded RP, 11-14.

87. See, for example, GVNP, no. 81; *Paterik Kievskogo Pecherskogo monastyria*, p. 13; Shchapov, "Tserkov' v sisteme," pp. 326-27; Grekov, *Kievskaia Rus'*, pp. 139-42; O. M. Rapov, *Kniazheskie vladeniia*, pp. 232-38.

88. Short RP, 13.

89. S. V. Iushkov, *Ocherki*, pp. 9-11; Iushkov, *Obshchestvenno-politicheskii stroi*, p. 86; V. V. Mavrodin, *Obrazovanie*, pp. 122-24; Kosven, *Semeinaia*, pp. 153-85.

90. PVL 1:43. Compilation of the PVL took place late in the eleventh and early in the twelfth centuries, although some individual sources certainly were older (Likhachev, *Russkie letopisi*, pp. 147-72).

91. PRP 2:39.3, 117, 140.22.

92. See note 39 above.

93. S. B. Veselovskii, *Selo*, pp. 13-14; N. P. Pavlov-Sil'vanskii, *Sochineniia*, 3:42; Vasmer, *Etimologicheskii slovar'*, 3:295.

94. L. V. Alekseev has been especially interested in plotting the location of settlements by means of archeological data. In one interesting study he demonstrated that the Smolensk tribute points identified in Rostislav's Statutory Charter were, in the main, located along greater or lesser waterways ("Ustav," pp. 104-105 and map after p. 106). More general and less complete information may be found in N. N. Voronin, *K istorii*, p. 32.

95. Voronin, *K istorii*, pp. 19-20.

96. Veselovskii, *Selo*, pp. 13-16; Voronin, *K istorii*, p. 27.

97. V. V. Sedov, *Sel'skie poseleniia*, pp. 30, 33-34.

98. Dal', *Tolkovyi slovar'*, 3:400; *Slovar' sovremennogo russkogo literaturnogo iazyka*, 10:191.

99. Veselovskii, *Selo*, p. 16.

100. Expanded RP, 47-55.

101. The most notable works on pre-Muscovite towns are M. N. Tikhomirov, *Drevnerusskie goroda* (Moscow: Politizdat, 1956); A. M. Sakharov, *Goroda severo-vostochnoi Rusi XIV-XV vekov* (Moscow: MGU, 1959). For a somewhat haphazard survey of the historiography, see A. L. Khoreshkevich, "Osnovnye itogi," pp. 34-50.

102. See M. N. Tikhomirov, "Spisok russkikh gorodov," pp. 223-25; M. G. Rabinovich, "Poseleniia," p. 241. As Rabinovich and A. M.

Sakharov both point out, there is some question over what exactly constituted a city in the late fourteenth century (Sakharov, *Goroda*, p. 17).

103. P. P. Tolochko, *Istorychna topohrafiia*, p. 174; M. N. Tikhomirov, *Srednevekovaia Moskva*, pp. 67-68; Tikhomirov, *Drevnerusskie goroda*, pp. 138-41.

104. Christopher Dawson, ed., *The Mongol Mission*, pp. 29-30.

105. The Mongol raids in northeast Russia seem to have been every bit as destructive as those later against Kiev. The Tale of the Destruction of Riazan' summarizes the results of the Mongol attack on Riazan': "And not one man remained alive in the city. All were dead. All had drunk the same bitter cup to the dregs. And there was not even anyone to mourn the dead" (Serge A. Zenkovsky, ed., *Medieval Russia's Epics*, p. 202).

106. See V. T. Pashuto, *Aleksandr Nevskii*, pp. 127-32.

107. See P. I. Zasurtsev, "Postroiki," pp. 163-64.

108. The archeological evidence is summarized in M. W. Thompson, *Novgorod the Great*, pp. 64, 68-87, 92-94, 98-101.

109. See Podvigina, *Ocherki*, pp. 95-100; V. V. Mavrodin and S. N. Orlov, "K voprosu," pp. 89-99; B. A. Rybakov, *Remeslo*, pp. 716-23.

110. Direct allusion to master-apprentice relations appears only in the Pskov Judicial Charter (PRP 2:299.102), but as Rybakov notes, in the context of then current crafts, similar relations probably existed elsewhere (*Remeslo*, pp. 700-705).

111. Rybakov, *Remeslo*, pp. 706-12; PRP 2:291.39, 41.

112. Although archeological evidence of a money economy exists for the earliest and later periods, Novgorod seems to have operated without a money economy in the twelfth, thirteenth, and fourteenth centuries (Podvigina, *Ocherki*, pp. 70-72; I. G. Spasskii, *Russkaia monetnaia sistema*, pp. 53-67).

113. See M. V. Sedova who plots the frequency of unearthed pagan and Christian medallions ("Iuvelirnye izdeliia," pp. 259-60).

114. See, for example, Short RP, 21, 26, 28, 31, 34, 38-40; Expanded RP, 40-43, 45, 82-84.

115. For an approximate placing of the various tribes on the East European plain, see P. N. Tret'iakov, *Vostochnoslavianskie plemena*, p. 119. More details on the Slavs' relations with the non-Slavic tribes appear in Tret'iakov's *Finno-Ugry, balty, i slaviane na Dnepre i Volge* (Moscow-Leningrad: Nauka, 1966).

116. PVL 1:80-81.

117. Tikhomirov, *Drevnerusskie goroda*, pp. 174-75.

GLOSSARY

birich Known primarily from Novgorod where he evidently executed certain police duties. According to the Novgorod Judicial Charter he summoned witnesses and litigants as did several other Novgorodian bailiffs.

boiarskii sud Highest level of Muscovite judicial authority; literally, "boyar court."

detskii "Youth." One of the prince's junior servitors similar to the *otrok*. Assisted in administering the iron ordeal as prescribed by the Expanded Pravda. Also separated litigants in inheritance disputes, and in thirteenth-century Smolensk escorted litigants to trial and helped execute judicial decisions.

d'iak Judicial secretary, first in Novgorod and later in Muscovy. Compiled record of court proceedings and decisions and probably also wrote up various documents arranging trial dates. In Muscovy he deputed much of this work to the scribes (*pod'iachie*), but he signed all the documents.

dobrye liudi "Good men" or locally respected citizens. See *luchshie liudi*.

doklad Referral by which Muscovite judges of lower echelons sent court transcript to Moscow for final decision.

dokladnyi spisok Record of litigation used in referral procedure in Muscovite courts.

dovodchik Known exclusively from documents of northeast Russia where he acted as bailiff for the judicial staff of a *namestnik*.

druzhina Princely retinue.

dvorianin Princely servitor who may have occasionally performed police functions.

dvorskii Muscovite court official charged by the 1497 Sudebnik with carrying out judicial decisions.

golova Literally, "head." Used in medieval legal texts to express homicide composition (*za golovu*).

golovnichestvo "Head fee," that is, homicide composition.

grivna Monetary unit whose value was based upon weight of a given commodity, principally silver and furs. By the thirteenth century four grivny of the latter equaled one silver grivna. See *kuna*.

iabednik Calumniator who attempted to profit from false accusations and slanderous suits.

iabetnik Mentioned among the protected princely officials in the Short Russkaia Pravda, and occasionally in other documents of a later time. His association with other Novgorodian bailiffs suggests that he may have fulfilled some police duties, but no specific indication of such work survives. Perhaps a variation of *iabednik*.

izornik Pskov tenant-farmer.

izvetnik Mentioned only rarely and exclusively in Novgorod sources where he was charged with the delivery of court summonses.

Knigi zakonnye Collection of Byzantine statutes on marriage, criminal law, and procedural aspects of testimony, along with a revision of the so-called Farmers' Law.

Kormchaia Kniga "Pilot's Book," a compendium of church canons, epistles, sermons, Byzantine secular legislation, and certain forms of Russian law. Known in three basic redactions: Efrem, Serbian, and Russian.

kuna Descriptive of one form of medieval monetary calculation derived from weight of furs (*kuny*). Sometimes generalized to refer to money in any form.

liudi Freemen.

luchshie liudi "Better men," the local citizens who commanded respect, and therefore often served as witnesses in land litigation.

mechnik Literally, a "sword bearer" whose life and limb were protected by special regulation in the Short Pravda. Took part in administering the iron ordeal.

Merilo Pravednoe "Just Measure," a compendium of regulations devoted to the law. Consists of two parts: episcopal lessons, sermons, and other expositions on the theme of justice; and a selection of legal texts, Byzantine and Russian.

metel'nik Known only from the Russkaia Pravda, which assigned him a portion of the bloodwite collector's fees. Perhaps another name for *otrok*.

mir Community organization mentioned in the Short Russkaia Pravda.

namestnik Adjutant of the prince or other ranking official. Sometime in the fourteenth century assigned judicial duties, the exercise of which he accomplished with the help of his deputies (*tiuny*). In Muscovy he was part of the judicial hierarchy constructed from the prince's courts.

nedel'shchik "Week man," a bailiff attached to the grand prince's courts. He was the dominant bailiff in sixteenth-century Muscovy, where he summoned witnesses and litigants to trial, arranged trial postponements, and placed litigants on bond.

obida Offense or slander. Gradually converted into a sense of economic loss. Consequently, composition for certain non-lethal affronts was expressed as payment "for the offense" (*za obidu*).

ognishchanin Steward on prince's private estates.

otrok Literally, "youth." A member of the prince's retinue who accompanied the bloodwite collector on his excursions in search of princely revenue.

pechatnik Sealkeeper who affixed authenticating mark to all legally binding documents in Muscovy.

pisets Scribe mentioned only once in the Russkaia Pravda. Perhaps he accompanied the bloodwite collector on his rounds in early medieval

GLOSSARY   271

times. Later in Muscovy he was usually associated with population inventories and revenue collection exercises, but in Pskov the scribe was the official judicial clerk, and was charged with writing up the results of land litigation, court summonses, and default charters.

pod'iachii   Scribe in Muscovite court apparatus.

podvernik   Pskov court officer who was identified with other bailiffs.

podvoiskii   Perhaps originally a military servitor of high rank. As a judicial officer he was first recalled in Novgorod in the early thirteenth century. The Novgorod Judicial Charter charged him with summoning witnesses to court, while other texts show him presenting litigants to the judge as well. Both Muscovite and Pskov law continued using him as a court bailiff.

pogost   Tribute collection point and administrative center which originated from primitive settlement patterns around a communal burial ground where pagan rites connected with ancestor veneration took place.

poklep   False, unproven accusation known first from the Russkaia Pravda.

polichnoe   Muscovite physical evidence of theft: "materials recovered from [defendant's] safekeeping." Also occasionally referred to as a separate jurisdiction or judicial fee.

posadnik   Originated as prince's representative in various medieval centers. Sometime in the early twelfth century separated from princely administration, and became locally selected mayor. In Novgorod he was one of the chief judges who heard litigation together with the prince's judge (*namestnik*).

poslukh   (pl. *poslusi*)   Witness with two different functions: character referent; and attestor present at conclusion of contracts.

potok   An ambiguous reference to some form of judicial sanction, possibly confinement or exile. In the Russkaia Pravda paired with *razgrablenie*.

pozovnik   Constable who, as the name indicates, summoned litigants and witnesses to trial in Novgorod and Pskov.

pravaia gramota   Judgment charter which appended judicial decision to litigation record.

pravedchik   Known exclusively from northeast Russia as one of Muscovy's bailiffs, regularly recalled in fifteenth-century documents.

pristav   A bailiff, known first from a Novgorodian thirteenth-century text where he was identified simply as a princely servitor. But in Pskov and Novgorod he was clearly the predominant court bailiff, a position he also held in late fourteenth- and fifteenth-century Muscovite courts. Charged with summoning litigants and witnesses, arresting thieves and debtors, and guarding defendants.

prodazha   Ultimately a pecuniary judicial sanction, although originally it must have indicated a more general form of princely income.

put' Literally, "path" or "route" associated with tribute collection in early Russia. Also applied to an administrative unit in Muscovy.

razboi Recidivist serious criminal activity, especially homicide and assault.

razboinik Recidivist robber or murderer.

razgrablenie Property confiscation as a form of judicial sanction.

riad Contractual agreement or testament.

riadovnik Contract laborer.

smerd Peasant agriculturalist.

sof'ianin Bailiff of the Novgorod Archbishop's court.

starozhilets Muscovite "long-time resident" who, like a *znakhar'*, was expected to know the status and history of land under litigation. Occasionally he was called upon to pace off land boundaries.

sudnye muzhi "Men of court" prescribed to be in attendance at Muscovite court proceedings so as to allow them later to verify, if necessary, the court record.

svidetel' Muscovite eyewitness.

svod Confrontation procedure used in theft cases.

tatebnoe Physical evidence of theft as described in the Russkaia Pravda. An early variant of *polichnoe*.

tiun From an early time identified as a judge representing the prince's interests in Smolensk, Novgorod, and Muscovy. As recalled in the Russkaia Pravda he also held various jobs in the prince's household and estates. A slave, unless he obtained an exemption agreement before entering on his duties.

tysiatskii The "thousand-man," a member of the prince's military retinue as identified in the Russkaia Pravda. Later in Novgorod he was known as a judge with his own staff of subordinate judges.

verv' (v'rvnaia) Local community, perhaps sharing kinship bonds, which bore legal responsibility for its members in homicide complaints.

vidok The Russkaia Pravda's term for eyewitness.

vina A Novgorod corruption of the term for bloodwite (*vira*). Also used elsewhere to indicate fault and financial sanction.

vira Bloodwite. The *dikaia vira* was a general bloodwite, payment of which was incumbent upon a local community (*verv'*) that did not identify and yield the killer. The *vira* thereby protected the homicide.

virnik Bloodwite collector who received twenty percent of the 80-grivna bloodwite payable for the murder of certain princely personnel. Probably formalized only late in the eleventh or early twelfth century. Accompanied by an assistant (*otrok*) in executing his duties.

volkhvy "Seers," the priests / priestesses of pagan religion in medieval Russia.

volostel' Rural equivalent to the Muscovite *namestnik*. Known as a judge from early documents, and also recalled in that capacity in Novgorod, Pskov, and Smolensk.

GLOSSARY 273

Zakon Sudnyi liudem "Court Law for the People," a Slavic revision of the Byzantine Ecloga. Survives in three basic redactions: Short, believed to have been compiled somewhere among the West Slavs in the ninth century; Expanded, a revision undertaken probably in Novgorod late in the thirteenth or early fourteenth century; Concordance, a fifteenth-century combination of the Short and Expanded redactions.

zemlia "Land," a territorial designation used by the Russkaia Pravda in defining confrontation procedure. Also bore pagan religious meaning connected with ancestor veneration.

znakhar' "One who knows," witness as to custom in Muscovite land litigation.

SOURCES CITED

Unpublished Sources

Leningrad. Arkhiv Akademii nauk SSSR. fond 192. Personal archive of V. N. Beneshevich.

Leningrad. Gosudarstvennaia ordena trudovogo krasnogo znameni publichnaia biblioteka imeni M. E. Saltykova-Shchedrina. Otdel rukopisei.
    fond 351. Collection of Kirill-Beloozero Monastery.
    fond 560. Basic Collection.
    fond 588. Collection of M. P. Pogodin.
    fond 717. Collection of Solovetskii Monastery.
    fond 728. Collection of Sophia Library.

Moscow. Gosudarstvennaia ordena Lenina biblioteka SSSR imeni V. I. Lenina. Otdel rukopisei.
    fond 98. Collection of E. E. Egorov.
    fond 173. Collection of Moscow Ecclesiastical Academy.
    fond 209. Collection of P. A. Ovchinnikov.
    fond 247. Collection of Rogozh Cemetery.
    fond 256. Collection of N. P. Rumiantsev.
    fond 304. Collection of Troitse-Sergiev Lavra.

Moscow. Gosudarstvennyi istoricheskii muzei. Otdel rukopisei.
    Chudov Collection.
    Synod Collection.
    Uvarov Collection.

Moscow. Tsentral'nyi gosudarstvennyi arkhiv drevnikh aktov.
    fond 135. State repository of ancient charters and manuscripts.

Published Sources

Akty feodal'nogo zemlevladeniia i khoziaistva XIV-XVI vekov. 3 vols. Moscow: AN SSSR, 1951-61.

Akty istoricheskie, sobrannye i izdannye Arkheograficheskoiu komissieiu. 5 vols. + index. St. Petersburg, 1841-43.

Akty iuridicheskie, ili Sobranie form starinnogo deloproizvodstva, izd. Arkheograficheskoi kommissii. 1 vol. + index. St. Petersburg, 1838-40.

Akty, otnosiashchiesia do grazhdanskoi raspravy drevnei Rossii. Edited by A. Fedotov-Chekhovskii. 2 vols. Kiev, 1860-63.

Akty russkogo gosudarstva: 1505-1526 gg. Moscow: Nauka, 1975.

Akty, sobrannye v bibliotekakh i arkhivakh Rossiiskoi imperii Arkheograficheskoiu ekspeditseiu imp. Akademii nauk. 4 vols. + index. St. Petersburg, 1836-58.

Akty sotsial'no-ekonomicheskoi istorii Severo-Vostochnoi Rusi kontsa XIV-nachala XVI v. 3 vols. Moscow: AN SSSR, 1952-64.

Alekseev, Iu. G. "Chastnyi zemel'nyi akt srednevekovoi Rusi (ot Russkoi Pravdy do Pskovskoi Sudnoi Gramoty)." *Vspomogatel'nye istoricheskie distsipliny* 6 (1974):125-41.

———. "Naimit i gosudar' Pskovskoi sudnoi gramoty." In *Obshchestvo i gosudarstvo feodal'noi Rossii. Sbornik statei posviashchennyi 70-letiiu akademika L'va Vladimirovicha Cherepnina.* Moscow: Nauka, 1975, pp. 22-29.

———. "Paleograficheskie nabliudeniia nad spiskami Pskovskoi Sudnoi gramoty." *Vspomogatel'nye istoricheskie distsipliny* 10 (1978):70-103.

Alekseev, L. V. "Gramota Rostislava Mstislavicha Smolenskogo 1136 g. v svete dannykh arkheologii." In *Belaruskiia starazhytnastsi. Materialy konferentsyi pa arkheolohii BSSR i sumezhnykh terytoryi.* Minsk: Vydevetski savet, 1972, pp. 185-89.

———. "Ustav Rostislava Smolenskogo 1136 g. i protsess feodalizatsii Smolenskoi zemli." In *Słowiane w dziejach Europy. Studia historyczne ku uczczeniu 75 rocznicny urodzin i 50-lecia pracy naukowej profesora Henryka Łowmianskiego.* Poznan: Uniwersytet im. Adama Mickiewicza, 1974, pp. 85-113.

Allott, A. N.; Epstein, A. L.; and Gluckman, Max. "Introduction." In *Ideas and Procedures in African Customary Law.* Edited by Max Gluckman. Oxford: Oxford University Press for the International African Institute, 1969, pp. 1-81.

Andenaes, Johannes. "The General Preventive Effects of Punishment." *University of Pennsylvania Law Review* 114 (1966):949-83.

———. "General Prevention—Illusion or Reality?" *Journal of Criminal Law, Criminology and Police Science* 43 (1952):176-98.

Andreev, Mikhail. "Iavliaetsia li *Zakon Sudnyi Liud'm* drevnebolgarskim iuridicheskim pamiatnikom?" In *Slavianskii Arkhiv. Sbornik statei i materialov.* Moscow: AN SSSR, 1959, pp. 1-22.

———. "K"m v"prosa za proiskhoda i s"shchnostta na Zakon" soudnyi liud"m"." *Godishnik" na Sofiiskiia universitet". Iuridicheski fakultet"* 49 (1957):1-60.

———. "Sur l'origine du *Zakon sudyni ljudem* (Loi pour juger les gens)." *Revue des études sud-est européenes* 1 (1963):331-44.

Andreevskii, Ivan. *O namestnikakh, voevodakh i gubernatorakh.* St. Petersburg, 1864.

Anichkov, E. V. *Iazychestvo i Drevniaia Rus'.* St. Petersburg, 1914.

Armstrong, C.A.J. "Some Examples of the Distribution and Speed of News in England at the Time of the Wars of the Roses." In *Studies in Medieval History Presented to Frederick Maurice Powicke.* Edited by R. W. Hunt, W. A. Pantin, and R. W. Southern. Oxford: Clarendon Press, 1948, pp. 444-53.

Artsikhovskii, A. V. *Novgorodskie gramoty na bereste (Iz raskopok 1952 goda).* Moscow: AN SSSR, 1954.

———. *Novgorodskie gramoty na bereste (Iz raskopok 1958-1961 gg.)*. Moscow: AN SSSR, 1963.
Artsikhovskii, A. V., and Borkovskii, V. I. *Novgorodskie gramoty na bereste (Iz raskopok 1953-1954 gg)*. Moscow: AN SSSR, 1958.
———. *Novgorodskie gramoty na bereste (Iz raskopok 1955 goda)*. Moscow: AN SSSR, 1958.
———. *Novgorodskie gramoty na bereste (Iz raskopok 1956-1957 gg.)*. Moscow: AN SSSR, 1963.
Artsikhovskii, A. V., and Ianin, V. L. *Novgorodskie gramoty na bereste (Iz raskopok 1962-1976 gg.)*. Moscow: Nauka, 1978.
Aubert, Vilhelm. "Competition and Consensus: Two Types of Conflict Resolution." *Journal of Conflict Resolution* 7(1963):26-42.
Austin, John. *Lectures on Jurisprudence*. 4th ed. 2 vols. London: John Murray, 1878.
Backus, Oswald P. III. "Legal Analysis and the History of Early Russian Law." *Slavic Review* 31 (1972):283-90.
Baldwin, John W. "The Intellectual Preparation For the Canon of 1215 Against Ordeals." *Speculum* 36(1961):613-36.
Ball, John C. "The Deterrence Concept in Criminology and Law." *Journal of Criminal Law, Criminology and Police Science* 46 (1955):347-54.
Barats, G. M. "Kritiko-sravnitel'nyi razbor ustava velik. kn. Vsevoloda o tserkovnykh sudakh." *Vestnik prava* 35, no. 11 (November 1905):165-211; 35, no. 12 (December 1905):127-63.
Barkun, Michael. "Conflict Resolution Through Implicit Mediation." *Journal of Conflict Resolution* 8 (1964):121-30.
———. *Law Without Sanctions: Order in Primitive Societies and the World Community*. New Haven: Yale University Press, 1968.
———, ed. *Law and the Social System*. New York: Lieber-Atherton, 1973.
Barton, Roy Franklin. *Ifugao Law*. University of California Publications in American Archeology and Ethnology. vol. 15, no. 1. Berkeley, 1919.
Begunov, Iu. K. "Kormchaia Ivana Volka Kuritsyna." *Trudy otdela drevnerusskoi literatury* 12 (1956):141-59.
Beliaev, I. D. "O sude namestnich'em na Rusi, v starinu." *Iuridicheskii zhurnal* 2, no. 7 (July 1861):289-304.
———. "O vyvoze v sud po drevnim russkim zakonam do Ulozheniia 1649 goda." *Zhurnal Ministerstva Iustitsii* 3(1860):97-143.
———. "Pole. Izsledovanie o drevnikh sudebnykh poedinakh." *Moskvitianin* 4, nos. 13-14 (July 1855):33-62.
Beliaev, P. I. "Pervichnye formy zaveshchatel'nogo rasporiazheniia." *Zhurnal Ministerstva Iustitsii* 5, no. 6 (June 1901):138-58; 5, no. 7 (September 1901): 137-72.
———. "Spetsial'noe naznachenie sudei i sudebnaia gramota v drevnem russkom protsesse." *Sbornik pravovedeniia i obshchestvennykh znanii* 8 (1898):1-16.

Benemanskii, Mikhail. *Zakon gradskii. Znachenie ego v russkom prave.* Moscow, 1917.
Beneshevich, V. N. "Avtoreferat izdaniia ustava kn. Vladimira." *Russkii istoricheskii zhurnal* 7(1921):181-84.
―――, ed. *Drevneslavianskaia kormchaia XIV titulov bez tolkovanii.* St. Petersburg, 1906-1907.
―――, ed. *Sbornik pamiatnikov po istorii tserkovnogo prava, preimushchestvenno russkoi tserkvi do epokhi Petra Velikogo.* 2 vols. Petrograd, 1914-15.
Bernadskii, V. N. *Novgorod i Novgorodskaia zemlia v XV veke.* Moscow-Leningrad: AN SSSR, 1961.
Berry, Lloyd E., and Crummey, Robert O., eds. *Rude and Barbarous Kingdom: Russia in the Accounts of Sixteenth-Century English Voyagers.* Madison: University of Wisconsin Press, 1968.
Birnbaum, Henrik. "On Old Russian and Old Scandinavian Legal Language." *Scando-Slavica* 8 (1962):115-40.
―――. "On Old Russian and Old Scandinavian Legal Language: The *Russkaja Pravda* and Medieval Swedish Law." In Henrik Birnbaum. *On Medieval and Renaissance Slavic Writing: Selected Essays.* The Hague: Mouton, 1974, pp. 234-59.
Bloch, Marc. *Feudal Society.* Translated by L. A. Manyon. 2 vols. Chicago: University of Chicago Press, Phoenix Books, 1964.
Bobchev, S. S. "Edin" pametnik" na starota b"lgarsko pravo." *Periodichesko spisanie na B"lgarskoto knizhnovno druzhestvo v" Sofiia* 62 (1901):613-45.
Bogdanovskii, A. *Razvitie poniatii o prestuplenii i nakazanii v russkom prave do Petra Velikogo.* Moscow, 1857.
Bohannan, Paul J. "The Differing Realms of Law." In *Ethnography of Law*, Supplement to *American Anthropologist* 67 (1965), pp. 33-42.
―――. "Ethnography and Comparison in Legal Anthropology." In *Law in Culture and Society.* Edited by Laura Nader. Chicago: Aldine Publishing Co., 1969, pp. 401-18.
―――. *Justice and Judgment Among the Tiv.* London: Oxford University Press for the International African Institute, 1957.
―――. "Patterns of Murder and Suicide." In *African Homicide and Suicide.* Edited by Paul Bohannan. Princeton: Princeton University Press, 1960, pp. 230-57.
―――. "Theories of Homicide and Suicide." In *African Homicide and Suicide.* Edited by Paul Bohannan. Princeton: Princeton University Press, 1960, pp. 3-29.
Bolkhovitinov, Evgenii. *Istoriia kniazhestva Pskovskogo.* 4 vols. Kiev, 1831.
Britsyn, M. A. *Iz istorii vostochno-slavianskoi leksiki.* Kiev: Naukova dumka, 1965.

SOURCES CITED

Brundage, James A. "Concubinage and Marriage in Medieval Canon Law." *Journal of Medieval History* 1 (1975):1-17.

Budovnits, I. U. *Monastyri na Rusi i bor'ba s nimi krest'ian v XIV-XVI vekakh*. Moscow: Nauka, 1966.

———. "O stat'e 12 kratkoi Pravdy Russkoi." In *Voprosy sotsial'no-ekonomicheskoi istorii i istochnikovedeniia perioda feodalizma v Rossii. Sbornik statei k 70-letiiu A. A. Novosel'skogo*. Moscow: AN SSSR, 1961, pp. 197-201.

Bullough, D. A. "Early Medieval Social Groupings: The Terminology of Kinship." *Past and Present*, no. 45(1969):3-18.

Bushkovitch, Paul. "*Rus'* in the Ethnic Nomenclature of the *Povest' Vremennykh Let*." *Cahiers du monde russe et sovietique* 12, no. 3 (July-September 1971):296-306.

Cam, Helen M. *The Hundred and the Hundred Rolls*. London: Methuen and Co., 1930.

———. *Liberties and Communities in Medieval England*. Cambridge: Cambridge University Press, 1941.

Chambliss, William J. "Types of Deviance and the Effectiveness of Legal Sanctions." *Wisconsin Law Review* (1967):703-19.

Cherepnin, L. V. "K voprosu o proiskhozhdenii i sostave Pskovskoi Sudnoi Gramoty." *Istoricheskie zapiski* 16 (1945):203-31.

———. *Novgorodskie berestianye gramoty kak istoricheskii istochnik*. Moscow: Nauka, 1969.

———. "Obshchestvenno-politicheskie otnosheniia v drevnei Rusi i Russkaia Pravda." In L. V. Cherepnin, A. P. Novosel'tsev, V. T. Pashuto, and Ia. N. Shchapov. *Drevnerusskoe gosudarstvo i ego mezhdunarodnoe znachenie*. Moscow: Nauka, 1965, pp. 128-278.

———. "Russkaia Pravda (v kratkoi redaktsii) i letopis' kak istochnik po istorii klassovoi bor'by." In *Akademiku Borisu Dmitrievichu Grekovu ko dniu semidesiatiletiia. Sbornik statei*. Moscow: AN SSSR, 1952, pp. 89-99.

———. *Russkie feodal'nye arkhivy XIV-XV vekov*. 2 vols. Moscow-Leningrad: AN SSSR, 1948-51.

———. "Sostav i proiskhozhdenie Novgorodskoi Sudnoi Gramoty." *Istoricheskie zapiski* 21 (1947):222-53.

———, ed. *Gosudarstvennoe drevlekhranilishche khartii i rukopisei. Opis' dokumental'nykh materialov fonda no. 135*. Moscow: Glavnoe arkhivnoe upravlenie pri Sovete Ministrov SSSR, Tsentral'nyi gosudarstvennyi arkhiv drevnikh aktov, 1971.

Cherepnin, L. V., and Iakovlev, A. I. "Pskovskaia sudnaia gramota. Novyi perevod i kommentarii." *Istoricheskie zapiski* 6 (1940):235-99.

Chernousov, E. "K voprosu o vliianii vizantiiskogo prava na drevneishee russkoe." *Vizantiiskoe obozrenie* 2 (1916):303-22.

Chernov, V. M. "K voprosu o bolgarskom vliianii na ustav Iaroslava." In

Iuvileinyi zbirnyk na poshanu akademika M. Hrushevs'koho. 2 vols. Kiev, 1928, 2:426-34.

Chichagov, V. K. *Iz istorii russkikh imen, otchestv i familii.* Moscow: Uchpedgiz, 1959.

Chiricos, Theodore G., and Waldo, Gordon P. "Punishment and Crime: An Examination of Some Emprical Evidence." *Social Problems* 18, no. 2 (Fall 1970):200-217.

Colson, Elizabeth. "Social Control and Vengeance in Plateau Tonga Society." *Africa* 23(1953):199-212.

Corpus Juris Civilis, The Civil Law. Translated by S. P. Scott. 17 vols. Cincinnati, 1932.

Dal', V. I. *Tolkovyi slovar' zhivogo velikorusskogo iazyka.* 3d ed. 4 vols., Moscow, 1903-1909.

Danailov, Georgi T. "Edin" pametnik" na starota b"lgarsko pravo." *Sbornik" za narodni umotvoreniia, nauka i knizhnina* 18(1901): 3-59.

Dawson, Christopher, ed. *The Mongol Mission.* New York: Sheed and Ward, 1955.

Dawson, John P. *A History of Lay Judges.* Cambridge, Mass.: Harvard University Press, 1960.

De Administrando imperio. Greek Text by Gyula Moravczik. English translation by R.J.H. Jenkins. Budapest, 1949.

Demchenko, G. V. "K voprosu ob uchastii zemskikh dobrykh liudei v drevnerusskikh sudakh." In *Sbornik statei po istorii prava posviashchennyi M. F. Vladimirskomu-Budanovu.* Kiev, 1904, pp. 153-75.

Demchenko, V. G. *Istoricheskoe izsledovanie o pokazaniiakh svidetelei.* Kiev, 1859.

Depp, F. *O nakazaniiakh, sushchestvovavshikh v Rossii do tsaria Alekseia Mikhailovicha.* St. Petersburg, 1849.

Dewey, Horace W. "Defamation and False Accusation (*Iabednichestvo*) in Old Muscovite Society," *Études Slaves et Est-Euorpéenes* 11, nos. 3-4 (Fall-Winter 1966-67):109-20.

―――. "The 1497 Sudebnik—Muscovite Russia's First National Law Code." *American Slavic and East European Review* 15 (1956):325-38.

―――. "Judges and the Evidence in Muscovite Law." *Slavonic and East European Review* 26, no. 86 (December 1957):189-94.

―――. "Muscovite *Guba* Charters and the Concept of Brigandage (*Razboj*)." *Papers of the Michigan Academy of Sciences, Arts and Letters* 51 (1966):277-88.

―――. "The Sudebnik of 1497." Ph.D. dissertation, University of Michigan, 1955.

―――. "Trial by Combat in Muscovite Russia." *Oxford Slavonic Papers* 9 (1960):21-32.

———, ed. and trans. *Muscovite Judicial Texts 1488-1556*. Michigan Slavic Materials, no. 7. Ann Arbor, 1966.
Dewey, Horace W., and Kleimola, Ann M. "Coercion by Righter (*Pravezh*) in Old Russian Administration." *Canadian-American Slavic Studies* 9 (1975):156-67.
———. "Promise and Perfidy in Old Russian Cross-Kissing." *Canadian Slavic Studies* 2 (1968):327-41.
———, eds. and trans. *Russian Private Law XIV-XVII Centuries*. Michigan Slavic Materials, no. 9. Ann Arbor, 1973.
———, eds. and trans. *Zakon Sudnyj Ljudem (Court Law for the People)*. Michigan Slavic Materials, no. 14. Ann Arbor, 1977.
D'iakonov, M. A. "Prof. Dr. Goetz, L. K. *Das russische Recht* (Russkaia Pravda). 1-er Band. Die alteste Redaktion des russischen Rechtes. Sttugt. 1910." *Izvestiia otdeleniia russkogo iazyka i slovesnosti Imperatorskoi akademii nauk* 16, no. 1 (1911):232-52.
Diamond, A. S. *The Comparative Study of Primitive Law*. London: The Athlone Press, 1965.
———. *The Evolution of Law and Order*. London: Watts and Co., 1951.
———. *Primitive Law, Past and Present*. London: Methuen, 1971.
Diev, I. "O virakh u rossiian X i XI st." *Russkii istoricheskii sbornik*. Edited by N. Pogodin. 1, bk. 2 (1837):30-66.
Diuvernua, N. *Istochniki prava i sud v drevnei Rossii*. Moscow, 1869.
Dopolneniia k aktam istoricheskim, sobrannye i izdannye Arkheograficheskoiu komisseiu. 12 vols. + index. St. Petersburg, 1846-72.
Drew, Katherine Fischer. *The Burgundian Code*. Philadelphia: University of Pennsylvania Press, 1972.
———. *The Lombard Laws*. Philadelphia: University of Pennsylvania Press, 1973.
Dukhovnye i dogovornye gramoty velikikh i udel'nykh kniazei XIV-XVI vv. Edited by S. V. Bakhrushin and L. V. Cherepnin. Moscow-Leningrad: AN SSSR, 1950.
Eaton, Henry L. "Cadasters and Censuses of Muscovy." *Slavic Review* 26 (1967):54-69.
Engel'man, I. E. *Sistematicheskoe izlozhenie grazhdanskikh zakonov, soderzhashchikhsia v Pskovskoi Sudnoi Gramote*. St. Petersburg, 1855.
English Historical Documents. Edited by David C. Douglas. 9 vols. to date. London: Eyre and Spottiswoode, 1955- .
Epifanov, P. P. "K voprosu o proiskhozhdenii Russkoi Pravdy." *Voprosy istorii*, 1951, no. 3, pp. 93-104.
Epstein, A. L. *Juridical Techniques and the Judicial Process: A Study in African Customary Law*. Manchester: Manchester University Press for Rhodes-Livingston Institute, 1954.
Evan, William. "Public and Private Legal Systems." In *Law and Sociology*.

Edited by William M. Evan. New York: The Free Press of Glencoe, 1962, pp. 165-84.

Ewers, G. F. *Drevneishee russkoe pravo v istoricheskom ego raskrytii.* Translated by I. Platonov. St. Petersburg, 1835.

Falk, Richard A. "International Jurisdiction: Horizontal and Vertical Conceptions of Legal Order." *Temple Law Quarterly* 32 (1958-59):295-320.

Fallers, Lloyd A. "Changing Customary Law in Busoga District of Uganda." *Journal of African Administration* 8 (1956):139-44.

———. "Customary Law in the New African States." *Law and Contemporary Problems* 27 (1962):605-16.

———. *Law Without Precedent.* Chicago: University of Chicago Press, 1969.

Fallers, Lloyd A., and Fallers, Margaret C. "Homicide and Suicide in Busoga." In *African Homicide and Suicide.* Edited by Paul Bohannan. Princeton: Princeton University Press, 1960, pp. 65-93.

Fedotov, George P. "Mat'-zemlia: K religioznoi kosmologii russkogo naroda." *Put'* 46 (January-March 1935):3-18.

———. *The Russian Religious Mind.* 2 vols. Cambridge, Mass.: Harvard University Press, 1946-66.

Filippov, A. N. "Iz inostrannykh otzyvov o Russkoi Pravde i ee kommentatorakh." *Uchenye zapiski instituta istorii Rossiiskoi assotsiatsii Nauchno-issledovatel'skikh institutov obshchestvennykh nauk* 2 (1927):311-37.

———. "Russkaia Pravda v izsledovaniiakh nemetskogo uchenogo." *Iuridicheskii vestnik* 6, no. 2 (1914):164-216.

———. *Uchebnik istorii russkogo prava (Posobie k lektsiiam).* 5th ed. Iur'ev, 1914.

Fletcher, Giles. *Of the Russe Commonwealth.* Edited by John V. A. Fine, Jr. and Richard Pipes. Cambridge, Mass.: Harvard University Press, 1966.

Florinskii, T. D. "Drevneishii pamiatnik bolgarskogo prava." In *Sbornik statei po istorii prava posviashchennyi M. F. Vladimirskomu-Budanovu.* Kiev, 1904, pp. 404-29.

Fogel', G. "O poklepnoi vire. Opyt vosstanovleniia i ob"iasneniia teksta Russkoi Pravdy." *Uchenye zapiski imperatorskogo Kazanskogo universiteta*, 1848, bk. 2, pp. 126-77.

Freshfield, E. H. *A Manual of Eastern Roman Law: The Procheiros Nomos.* Cambridge: Cambridge University Press, 1928.

Fried, Morton. *The Evolution of Political Society.* New York: Random House, 1967.

Friedman, Lawrence M. *The Legal System: A Social Science Perspective.* New York: Russell Sage Foundation, 1975.

Froianov, I. Ia. "Danniki na Rusi X-XII vv." *Ezhegodnik po agrarnoi*

istorii vostochnoi Evropy. 1965 g. Moscow: MGU, 1970, pp. 33-41.
———. *Kievskaia Rus'. Ocherki sotsial'no-ekonomicheskoi istorii.* Leningrad: LGU, 1974.
———. "Kniazheskoe zemlevladenie i khoziaistvo na Rusi X-XII vekov." In *Problemy istorii feodal'noi Rossii. Sbornik statei k 60-letiiu V. V. Mavrodina.* Leningrad: LGU, 1971, pp. 43-52.
———. "Tserkovno-monastyrskoe zemlevladenie i khoziaistvo na Rusi XI-XII vv." In *Problemy otechestvennoi i vseobshchei istorii. Sbornik statei*, no. 2. Leningrad: LGU, 1973, pp. 87-95.
Gal'kovskii, N. M. *Bor'ba khristianstva s ostatkami iazychestva v drevnei Rusi.* 2 vols. Moscow-Khar'kov, 1913-16.
Ganev, Venelin. *Zakon" Soudnyi liud'm: Pravno-istoricheski i pravno-analitichni prouchvaniia.* Sofia: B"lgarskata akademiia na naukite, 1959.
Gasparini, Evel. "Studies in Old Slavic Religion: *Ubrus.*" *History of Religions* 2 (Summer 1962):112-39.
Geiermans, G. L. "Tatishchevskie spiski Russkoi Pravdy." *Problemy istochnikovedeniia* 3 (1940):163-74.
Gibbs, Jack P. "Definitions of Law and Empirical Questions." *Law and Society Review* 2 (1967-68):429-46.
Gluckman, Max. "African Jurisprudence." *The Advancement of Science* 18, no. 75 (1962):439-54.
———. *African Traditional Law in Historical Perspective.* London: Oxford University Press for the British Academy, 1974.
———. "Concepts in the Comparative Study of Tribal Law." In *Law in Culture and Society.* Edited by Laura Nader. Chicago: Aldine Publishing Co., 1969, pp. 349-73.
———. *The Ideas in Barotse Jurisprudence.* New Haven: Yale University Press, 1965.
———. *The Judicial Process Among the Barotse of Northern Rhodesia (Zambia).* 2d ed. rev. Manchester: Manchester University Press for the Institute for African Studies, 1973.
———. *Order and Rebellion in Tribal Africa.* London: Cohen and West, 1962.
———. *Politics, Law and Ritual in Tribal Society.* Oxford: Basil Blackwell, 1965.
———. "The Reasonable Man in Barotse Law." *Journal of African Administration* 7 (1955):51-55, 127-31; 8 (1956):101-105, 151-56.
———, ed. *Ideas and Procedures in African Customary Law.* Oxford: Oxford University Press for the International African Institute, 1969.
Goebel, Julius, Jr. *Felony and Misdemeanor: A Study in the History of English Criminal Procedure.* New York: The Commonwealth Fund, Oxford University Press, 1937.
Golenishchev-Kutuzov, D. *Russkaia Pravda i Vizantiia.* Irkutsk, 1913.

Got'e, Iu. V. *Zamoskovnyi krai v XVII veke*. Moscow: Sotsekgiz, 1937.
Gramoty Velikogo Novgoroda i Pskova. Edited by S. N. Valk. Moscow-Leningrad: AN SSSR, 1949.
Green, Thomas A. "Societal Concepts of Criminal Liability for Homicide in Medieval England." *Speculum* 47 (1972):669-94.
Grekov, B. D. *Kievskaia Rus'*. Leningrad: Gospolitizdat, 1953.
———. *Politsa*. Moscow: AN SSSR, 1951.
———. "Rabstvo i feodalizm v drevnei Rusi." *Izvestiia Gosudarstvennoi Akademii istorii material'noi kul'tury* 86 (1934):5-66.
———, ed. *Russkaia Pravda po spiskam Akademicheskomu, Karamzinskomu i Troitskomu*. Moscow-Leningrad: AN SSSR, 1934.
———, ed. *Russkaia Pravda. Uchebnoe posobie*. Moscow-Leningrad: AN SSSR, 1940.
Gross, Charles. "The Medieval Law of Intestacy." *Harvard Law Review* 18, no. 2 (15 February 1904):120-31.
Gsovskii, V. V. "Medieval Russian Laws." *American Slavic and East European Review* 6 (1947):152-58.
———. "Roman Private Law in Russia." *Bullettino dell' Istituto di Diritto Romano* 46 (1939):363-75.
Gubidelnikov, Georgi G. "Zakon" soudnyi liud'm"." *Iuridicheski pregled"* 16, no. 2 (15 February 1908):100-105; 16, no. 3 (15 March 1908):149-56.
Halperin, Charles J. "The Concept of the Russian Land from the Ninth to the Fourteenth Centuries." *Russian History* 2 (1975):29-38.
———. "The Russian Land and the Russian Tsar: The Emergence of Muscovite Ideology, 1380-1408." *Forschungen zur osteuropäischen Geschichte* 23 (1976):7-103.
Hammer, Darrell P. "The Character of the Russkaia Pravda." *Slavic Review* 31 (1972):291-95.
———. "Russia and the Roman Law." *American Slavic and East European Review* 16 (1957):1-13.
Hart, H.L.A. *The Concept of Law*. 2d ed. Oxford: Clarendon Press, 1972.
Hellie, Richard. *Enserfment and Military Change in Muscovy*. Chicago: University of Chicago Press, 1971.
Henderson, Dan Fenno. "Promulgation of Tokugawa Statutes." *Journal of Asian and African Studies* 2 (1967):9-25.
Herberstein, Sigismund von. *Notes Upon Russia: Being a Translation of the Earliest Account of That Country, Entitled Rerum Moscoviticarum Commentarii*. Translated and Edited by R. H. Major. 2 vols. New York: Burt Franklin, 1968.
Heyd, Uriel. *Studies in Old Ottoman Law*. Oxford: Clarendon Press, 1973.
Hoebel, E. Adamson. "Law and Anthropology." *Virginia Law Review* 32 (1945-46):835-54.

―――. *The Law of Primitive Man.* Cambridge, Mass.: Harvard University Press, 1954.
―――. "Three Studies in African Law." *Stanford Law Review* 13 (1960-61):418-42.
Howell, P. P. *A Manual of Nuer Law.* London: Oxford University Press for the International African Institute, 1954.
Huber, Hugo. "Ritual Oaths as Instruments of Coercion and Self-Defense Among the Adaŋme of Ghana." *Africa* 29 (1959):41-49.
Iakovlev, A. I., ed. *Namestnich'i, gubnye i zemskie ustavnye gramoty Moskovskogo gosudarstva.* Moscow, 1909.
―――, ed. *Russkaia Pravda.* Moscow, 1914.
Iakovlev, A. I., and Cherepnin, L. V., eds. *Russkaia Pravda po spiskam Akademicheskomu, Troitskomu i Karamzinskomu.* Moscow, 1928.
Ianin, V. L. *Aktovye pechati Drevnei Rusi X-XV vv.* 2 vols. Moscow: Nauka, 1970.
―――. "Den'gi i denezhnye sistemy." In *Ocherki russkoi kul'tury XIII-XV vekov.* 2 vols. Moscow: MGU, 1969, 1:317-47.
―――. "K khronologii torgovogo ustava kniazia Vsevoloda." *Arkheograficheskii ezhegodnik za 1976 god.* Moscow: Nauka, 1977, pp. 60-68.
―――. *Novgorodskie posadniki.* Moscow: MGU, 1962.
―――. "O date Novgorodskoi Sinodal'noi kormchei." In *Drevniaia Rus' i slaviane.* Moscow: Nauka, 1978, pp. 287-92.
Isaev, M. M. "Ugolovnoe pravo Kievskoi Rusi." *Uchenye trudy vsesoiuznogo instituta iuridicheskikh nauk Ministerstva iustitsii SSSR* 8 (1946):153-76.
―――. "Ugolovnoe pravo Novgoroda i Pskova XIII-XV vv." *Uchenye trudy nauchnoi sessii vsesoiuznogo instituta iuridicheskikh nauk 1-6 Iiulia 1946 g.* Moscow, 1948, pp. 126-42.
Iushkov, S. V. *Izsledovaniia po istorii russkogo prava.* Vyp. 1. *Ustav kn. Vladimira.* Novouzensk, [1926].
―――. *K istorii drevnerusskikh iuridicheskikh sbornikov (XIII v.).* Saratov: Gosudarstvennoe izdatel'stvo, 1921.
―――. *Obshchestvenno-politicheskii stroi i pravo Kievskogo gosudarstva.* Moscow: Gosiurizdat, 1949.
―――. *Ocherki po istorii feodalizma v Kievskoi Rusi.* Moscow-Leningrad: AN SSSR, 1939.
―――. "Pravosudie mitropolich'e." *Letopis' zaniatii Arkheograficheskoi komissii za 1927-1928 gody* 35 (1929):115-20.
―――. "Russkaia Pravda kak kodeks russkogo feodal'nogo prava." *Problemy sotsialisticheskogo prava,* 1939, no. 4-5, pp. 72-89.
―――. *Russkaia Pravda. Proiskhozhdenie, istochniki, ee znachenie.* Moscow: Gosiurizdat, 1950.
―――. "Sudebnik 1497 g. (K vneshnei istorii pamiatnika)." *Uchenye*

zapiski Saratovskogo gosudarstvennogo universiteta imeni N. G. Chernyshevskogo 5, no. 3 (1926):1-46.

———. "Ustav kn. Vsevoloda (ko zovnishn'oi istorii pam"iatky)." *Iuvileinyi zbirnyk na poshanu Akademika Dmitriia Ivanovicha Bahaleia. Zapysky istorychno-filolohychnoho viddilu AN URSR* 51 (1927):405-24.

Jewel, Helen M. *English Local Administration in the Middle Ages.* New York: Barnes and Noble Books, 1972.

Jolowicz, H. F., and Nicholas, Barry. *A Historical Introduction to the Study of Roman Law.* 3d ed. Cambridge: Cambridge University Press, 1972.

Kafengauz, B. B. *Drevnii Pskov. Ocherki po istorii feodal'noi respubliki.* Moscow: Nauka, 1969.

———. "O proiskhozhdenii i sostave Pskovskoi sudnoi gramoty." *Istoricheskie zapiski* 18 (1946):295-326.

———. "O pskovskikh krest'ianakh XV-XVI vv." In *Akademiku Borisu Dmitrievichu Grekovu ko dniu semidesiatiletiiu. Sbornik statei.* Moscow: AN SSSR, 1952, pp. 132-39.

———. "Pskovskie izorniki." *Uchenye zapiski Moskovskogo gosudarstvennogo pedagogicheskogo instituta imeni K. Libknekhta* (seriia istoricheskaia) 2 (1939):28-48.

Kaiser, Daniel H. "Reconsidering Crime and Punishment in Kievan Rus'." *Russian History* 7 (1980):283-93.

Kalachov, N. V. "Merilo Pravednoe." In *Arkhiv istoriko-iuridicheskikh svedenii otnosiashchikhsia do Rossii.* Edited by N. Kalachov. 3 vols. Moscow, 1850-61, 1:28-40.

———. "O znachenii kormchei v sisteme russkogo prava." *Chteniia v imperatorskom obshchestve istorii i drevnostei rossiiskikh pri Moskovskom universitete*, 1847, no. 3, pp. 1-128.

———. "Ob ugolovnom prave po Sudebniku tsaria Ioanna Vasil'evicha." *Iuridicheskie zapiski Redkina* 2 (1842):306-408.

———. *Predvaritel'nye iuridicheskie svedeniia dlia polnogo ob"iasneniia Russkoi Pravdy.* 2d ed. Moscow, 1880.

———. "Pskovskaia Sudnaia Gramota." *Moskvitianin* 2, no. 2 (1848):165-78.

———, ed. *Tekst Russkoi Pravdy na osnovanii chetyrekh spiskov raznykh redaktsii.* Moscow, 1846.

Kalaidovich, K. F. "O poedinakh v Rossii voobshche, i v osobennosti o sudebnykh." *Russkii istoricheskii sbornik.* Edited by N. Pogodin. 1, bk. 4 (1838):3-38.

Kamentseva, E. I., and Ustiugov, N. V. *Russkaia sfragistika i geral'dika.* 2d ed. Moscow: Vysshaia shkola, 1974.

Kantorowicz, Hermann. *The Definition of Law.* Edited by A. H. Campbell with Introduction by A. L. Goodhart. New York: Cambridge University Press, 1958.

Karamzin, N. M. *Istoriia gosudarstva Rossiiskogo*. 7th ed. 12 vols. St. Petersburg, 1892. Reprint, The Hague-Paris: Mouton, 1969.

Karskii, E. F., ed. *Russkaia Pravda po drevneishemu spisku*. Leningrad: AN SSSR, 1930.

Kartashev, A. V. *Ocherki po istorii russkoi tserkvi*. 2 vols. Paris: YMCA Press, 1959.

Kaye, J. M. "The Early History of Murder and Manslaughter." *Law Quarterly Review* 83 (1967):365-95, 569-601.

Kazakova, N. A. "K izucheniiu Kormchei Vassiana Patrikeeva." *Trudy otdela drevnerusskoi literatury* 28 (1974):345-49.

Kelsen, Hans. *The Pure Theory of Law*. Translated by Max Knight. Berkeley: University of California Press, 1970.

Khoroshkevich, A. L. "K istorii vozniknoveniia *Zapisi o Dushegubstve*." In *Vostochnaia Evropa v drevnosti i srednevekov'e*. Moscow: Nauka, 1978, pp. 193-203.

―――. "Osnovnye itogi izucheniia gorodov XI-pervoi polovine XVII v." In *Goroda feodal'noi Rossii. Sbornik statei pamiati N. V. Ustiugova*. Moscow: Nauka, 1966, pp. 34-50.

King, P. D. *Law and Society in the Visigothic Kingdom*. Cambridge: Cambridge University Press, 1972.

Kleimola, Ann M. "Formulae and Formalism in Muscovite Judgment Charters." *Canadian-American Slavic Studies* 6 (1972):355-73.

―――. *Justice in Medieval Russia: Muscovite Judgment Charters (Pravye Gramoty) of the Fifteenth and Sixteenth Centuries*. Transactions of the American Philosophical Society. vol. 65, pt. 6. Philadelphia, 1975.

―――. "Law and Social Change in Medieval Russia: The Zakon Sudnyi Lyudem as a Case Study." *Oxford Slavonic Papers* n.s. 9 (1976):17-27.

―――. "Muscovite Judgment Charters (*Pravye Gramoty*) of the Fifteenth Century." Ph.D. dissertation, University of Michigan, 1970.

Kliuchevskii, V. O. *Sochineniia*. 8 vols. Moscow: Politizdat-Sotsekgiz, 1956-59.

Klochkov, M. *Ukazatel' slov i vyrazhenii vstrechaiushchikhsia v Sudebnikakh 1497, 1550, 1598 gg*. Iur'ev, 1902.

Kochakov, B. M. "Novgorodskaia Sudnaia Gramota." *Uchenye zapiski Leningradskogo pedagogicheskogo instituta* 5, no. 1 (1940):9-22.

Kochin, G. E. *Materialy dlia terminologicheskogo slovaria drevnei Rusi*. Moscow: AN SSSR, 1947.

―――. *Sel'skoe khoziaistvo na Rusi, kontsa XIII-nachala XVI v*. Moscow-Leningrad: Nauka, 1965.

Kolycheva, E. I. *Kholopstvo i krepostnichestvo (Konets XV-XVI v.)*. Moscow: Nauka, 1971.

Komarovich, V. L. "Kul't roda i zemli v kniazheskoi srede XI-XIII vv." *Trudy otdela drevnerussko literatury* 16 (1960):84-104.

Kopechnyi, F. F. "K etimologii slav. otrok"." *Etimologiia 1966.* Moscow: Nauka, 1968, pp. 54-61.
Kosven, Mark O. *Prestuplenie i nakazanie v dogosudarstvennom obshchestve.* Moscow-Leningrad: Gosudarstvennoe izdatel'stvo, 1925.
———. *Semeinaia obshchina i patronimiia.* Moscow: AN SSSR, 1963.
Kotliarevskii, A. *O pogrebal'nykh obychaiakh iazycheskikh slavian.* Moscow, 1868.
Kucherov, Samuel. "Indigenous and Foreign Influences on the Early Russian Legal Heritage." *Slavic Review* 31 (1972):257-82.
Kuper, Hilda and Kuper, Leo, eds. *African Law: Adaptation and Development.* Berkeley: University of California Press, 1965.
Kuz'min, A. G. "Ob etnicheskoi prirode Variagov (k postanovke problemy)." *Voprosy istorii,* 1974, no. 11, pp. 54-83.
la Fontaine, Jean. "Homicide and Suicide Among the Gisu." In *African Homicide and Suicide.* Edited by Paul Bohannan. Princeton: Princeton University Press, 1960, pp. 94-129.
Lancaster, Lorraine. "Kinship in Anglo-Saxon Society." *British Journal of Sociology* 9 (1958):230-50, 359-77.
Langbein, John H. *Prosecuting Crime in the Renaissance.* Cambridge, Mass.: Harvard University Press, 1974.
Lange, Nikolai. *Drevnee russkoe ugolovnoe sudoproizvodstvo (XIV, XV, XVI i poloviny XVII vekov).* St. Petersburg, 1884.
———. *Izsledovanie ob ugolovnom prave Russkoi Pravdy.* St. Petersburg, 1860.
Laran, Michel and Saussay, Jean, eds. *La Russie ancienne (IXe-XVIIe siècles).* Paris: Masson et Cie, 1975.
Larin, B. A. *Russko-Angliiskii slovar'-dnevnik Richarda Dzhemsa (1618-1619 gg.).* Leningrad: LGU, 1959.
Latkin, V. N. *Lektsii po vneshnei istorii russkogo prava: Moskovskoe gosudarstvo–Rossiiskaia imperiia.* St. Petersburg, 1888.
Laws of the Alamans and Bavarians. Translated by Theodore John Rivers. Philadelphia: University of Pennsylvania Press, 1977.
Laws of the Kings of England From Edmund to Henry I. Edited and translated by A. J. Robertson. Cambridge: Cambridge University Press, 1925.
Leont'ev, A. K. *Obrazovanie prikaznoi sistemy upravleniia v Russkom gosudarstve.* Moscow: MGU, 1961.
Leontovich, F. I. "K voprosu o proiskhozhdenii sem'i voobshche i o ee organizatsii po drevnemu russkomu pravu." *Zhurnal Ministerstva Iustitsii* 4, no. 6 (June 1900):1-45; 4, no. 7 (July 1900):1-47; 4, no. 8 (August 1900):78-117.
———. "O znachenii vervi po Russkoi Pravde i Politskomu statutu sravitel'no s zadrugoiu iugo-zapadnykh slavian." *Zhurnal ministerstva narodnogo prosveshcheniia* 134 (April 1867):1-19.
———. "Zadruzhno-obshchinnyi kharakter byta Drevnei Rossii." *Zhurnal ministerstva narodnogo prosveshcheniia* 174 (July 1874):120-51.

Likhachev, D. S. *Russkie letopisi i ikh kul'turno-istoricheskoe znachenie.* Moscow-Leningrad: AN SSSR, 1947.

———. *Tekstologiia.* Moscow-Leningrad: AN SSSR, 1962.

Lipshits, E. E. *Ekloga.* Moscow: Nauka, 1965.

———. *Pravo i sud v Vizantii v IV-VIII vv.* Leningrad: Nauka, 1976.

The Lithuanian Statute of 1529. Translated and edited with an Introduction by Karl von Loewe. Leiden: W. J. Brill, 1976.

Liubimov, V. P. "Novye spiski Pravdy Russkoi." In *Pravda Russkaia.* Edited by B. D. Grekov. 3 vols. Moscow-Leningrad: AN SSSR, 1940-63, 2:840-62.

———. "Ob izdanii *Russkoi Pravdy.*" *Problemy istochnikovedeniia* 2 (1936):299-314.

———. "Paleograficheskie nabliudeniia nad Akademicheskim spiskom Russkoi Pravdy." *Istorik-Marksist,* 1938, no. 5, pp. 156-61.

———. "Paleograficheskie nabliudeniia nad Troitskim spiskom Russkoi Pravdy." *Doklady Akademii nauk SSSR,* 1929, series B, no. 6, pp. 109-14.

———. "Spiski Pravdy Russkoi." In *Pravda Russkaia.* Edited by B. D. Grekov. 3 vols. Moscow-Leningrad: AN SSSR, 1940-63, 1:11-54.

Llewellyn, K. N., and Hoebel, E. Adamson. *The Cheyenne Way.* Norman: University of Oklahoma Press, 1941.

Logan, Charles H. "General Deterrent Effects of Imprisonment." *Social Forces* 51 (1972):64-73.

Lotots'kyi, Oleksandr. "Tserkovnyi ustav kniazia Volodymyra Velikoho." *Zapysky naukovoho tovarystva imeni Shevchenka* 138-40 (1925):7-44.

———. *Ukrains'ki dzherela tserkovnoho prava. Pratsi Ukrains'koho naukovoho instytutu,* vol. 5. Warsaw, 1931.

Luppov, S. V. *Kniga v Rossii v XVII veke.* Leningrad: Nauka, 1970.

Maine, Henry Sumner. *Ancient Law.* London: John Murray, 1861.

Maksimeiko, N. A. "Moskovskaia redaktsiia Russkoi Pravdy." *Problemy istochnikovedeniia* 3 (1940):127-62.

———. *Opyt kriticheskogo izsledovaniia Russkoi Pravdy.* Khar'kov, 1914.

———. "Russkaia Pravda i litovsko-russkoe pravo." In *Sbornik statei po istorii prava, posviashchennyi M. F. Vladimirskomu-Budanovu.* Kiev, 1904, pp. 382-95.

Markov, V. "Vopros o podlinnosti tserkovnykh gramot vkhodiashchikh v sostav novgorodskikh letopisei." *Bogoslovskii vestnik,* 1911, no. 6, pp. 361-67; 1911, no. 9, pp. 136-47; 1911, no. 10, pp. 331-44.

Marks, N. A., ed. *Russkaia Pravda po Sinodal'nomu spisku.* Moscow, 1910.

Martysevich, I. D. *Pskovskaia sudnaia gramota. Istoriko-iuridicheskoe issledovanie.* Moscow: MGU, 1951.

Matejka, Ladislav. "Diglossia in the Oldest Preserved Legal Codex of Novgorod." *Papers in Slavic Philology* 1 (1977):186-97.

Mavrodin, V. V. *Obrazovanie drevnerusskogo gosudarstva.* Leningrad: LGU, 1945.
Mavrodin, V. V., and Froianov, I. Ia. "Startsy gradskie." In *Kul'tura srednevekovoi Rusi.* Leningrad: Nauka, 1974, pp. 29-33.
Mavrodin, V. V., and Orlov, S. N. "K voprosu ob Ustave kniazia Iaroslava O mostekh." *Sovetskaia arkheologiia,* 1975, no. 2, pp. 89-99.
"Medieval Legal Procedure." In *Translations and Reprints From the Original Sources of European History.* vol. 14, no. 4. Philadelphia: Dept. of History, University of Pennsylvania, n.d.
Meichik, D. M. *Gramoty XIV i XV vv. Moskovskogo Arkhiva ministerstva iustitsii. Ikh forma, soderzhanie i znachenie v istorii russkogo prava.* Moscow, 1883.
———. "Russkaia Pravda XI v." *Iuridicheskii vestnik* 12 (1915):78-100.
Merilo Pravednoe po rukopisi XIV veka. Edited by M. N. Tikhomirov. Moscow: AN SSSR, 1961.
Mikhailov, P. E. *Iuridicheskaia priroda zemlepol'zovaniia po Pskovskoi sudnoi gramote.* St. Petersburg, 1914.
———. "Novye dannye dlia kommentariia Pskovskoi sudnoi gramoty." *Izvestiia otdeleniia russkogo iazyka i slovesnosti Akademii nauk* 18, bk. 2 (1913):132-42.
Miller, O. *Opyt istoricheskogo obozreniia russkoi slovesnosti.* 2d ed. St. Petersburg, 1865.
Milov, L. V. "K istorii drevnerusskogo prava XIII-XIV vv." *Arkheograficheskii ezhegodnik za 1962 god.* Moscow: AN SSSR, 1963, pp. 55-59.
———. "K istorii teksta Zakona Sudnogo liudem kratkoi redaktsii." *Sovetskoe slavianovedenie,* 1978, no. 6, pp. 97-101.
———. "K istorii teksta Zakona Sudnogo liudem prostrannoi redaktsii." In *Novoe o proshlom nashei strany. Pamiati akademika M. N. Tikhomirova.* Moscow: Nauka, Vostochnaia literatura, 1967, pp. 65-78.
———. "Novoe issledovanie o Zakone Sudnom liudem." In *Slavianskii arkhiv.* Moscow: AN SSSR, 1961, pp. 51-63.
———. "O drevnerusskom perevode vizantiiskogo kodeksa zakonov VIII veka (Eklogi)." *Istoriia SSSR,* 1976, no. 1, pp. 142-63.
Moore, Sally F. "Legal Liability and Evolutionary Interpretation: Some Aspects of Strict Liability, Self-Help and Collective Responsibility." In *The Allocation of Responsibility.* Edited by Max Gluckman. Manchester: Manchester University Press, 1972, pp. 51-107.
Morris, William Alfred. *The Medieval English Sheriff to 1300.* Manchester: Manchester University Press, 1927.
Mrochek-Drozdovskii, P. N. "Glavneishie pamiatniki russkogo prava epokhi mestnykh zakonov." *Iuridicheskii vestnik* 16, no. 5-6 (May-June 1884):74-131.
———. *Izsledovaniia o Russkoi Pravde. Uchenye zapiski Moskovskogo*

universiteta, otdeleniia iuridicheskogo, nos. 2, 4. Moscow, 1881, 1885.

———. "Izsledovaniia o Russkoi Pravde. Prilozheniia ko 2-mu vypusku." *Chteniia v Obshchestve istorii i drevnostei rossiiskikh pri Moskovskom universitete,* 1886, no. 1, pp. 1-245.

———. "Materialy dlia slovaria pravovykh i bytovykh drevnostei po Russkoi Pravdy." *Chteniia v Obshchestve istorii i drevnostei rossiiskikh pri Moskovskom universitete,* 1917, no. 3, pp. 1-128.

———. "Novoe izdanie Russkoi Pravdy." *Uchenye zapiski imperatorskogo Moskovskogo universiteta iuridicheskogo fakul'teta* 26 (1907):1-32.

———. "O drevnerusskikh iabetnikakh." *Chteniia v Obshchestve istorii i drevnostei rossiiskikh pri Moskovskom universitete,* 1884, no. 1, pp. 1-19.

———. "Pamiatniki russkogo prava vremeni mestnykh zakonov." *Uchenye zapiski imperatorskogo Moskovskogo universiteta iuridicheskogo fakul'teta* 20 (1902):1-78.

Mstislavskii, V. V. "O poklepnoi vire ili poniatie ob obvinitel'nom protsesse po Russkoi Pravde." *Iuridicheskii zhurnal,* 1861, no. 5, pp. 1-14.

Mysovskii, Kirill. "Drevnee russkoe tserkovnoe pravo v sviazi s pravom vizantiiskim." *Pravoslavnyi sobesednik,* 1862, no. 3, pp. 177-212; 1862, no. 6, pp. 139-72, 260-301; 1862, no. 7, pp. 3-31, 125-47.

Nader, Laura; Koch, K.; and Cox, B. "The Ethnography of Law: A Bibliographic Survey." *Current Anthropology* 7 (1966):267-94.

Nasonov, A. N. *Russkaia zemlia i obrazovanie territorii drevnerusskogo gosudarstva.* Moscow: AN SSSR, 1951.

Nazarov, V. D. "*Dvor* i *dvoriane* po dannym novgorodskogo i severovostochnogo letopisaniia (XII-XIV vv.)." In *Vostochnaia Evropa v drevnosti i srednevekov'e.* Moscow: Nauka, 1978, pp. 104-23.

Neilson, George. *Trial by Combat.* Glasgow: William Hodge and Co., 1890.

Nikitin, A. L. "Boltinskoe izdanie Pravdy Russkoi." *Voprosy istorii,* 1973, no. 11, pp. 53-65.

Nikitskii, A. I. *Ocherk vnutrennei istorii Pskova.* St. Petersburg, 1873.

Nikol'skii, N. K. "K istorii slavianorusskoi pis'mennosti." *Bibliograficheskaia letopis'* 3 (1917):110-24.

Nosov, N. E. *Ocherki po istorii mestnogo upravleniia russkogo gosudarstva pervoi poloviny XVI veka.* Moscow-Leningrad: AN SSSR, 1957.

Novgorodskaia pervaia letopis' starshego i mladshego izvodov. Edited by A. N. Nasonov. Moscow-Leningrad: AN SSSR, 1950.

Novgorodskie pistsovye knigi. Edited by P. I. Savvaitov, A. Timofeev, and S. K. Bogoiavlenskii. 6 vols. St. Petersburg, 1859-1910.

Obnorskii, S. P. *O iazyke Efremovskoi kormchei XII veka.* St. Petersburg, 1912.

———. "Russkaia Pravda kak pamiatnik russkogo literaturnogo iazyka." *Izvestiia Akademii nauk*, 7th series (Otdelenie obshchestvennykh nauk), 1934, no. 10, pp. 749-76.

"Ob osnovaniiakh russkogo tserkovnogo prava." *Khristianskoe chtenie* 24, pt. 4 (1846):302-44, 416-40.

"O pervonachal'nom sostave slavianskoi Kormchei knigi." *Khristianskoe chtenie* 29, pt. 1 (1851):535-60.

Ocherki istorii SSSR. Period feodalizma IX-XV vv. 2 vols. Moscow: AN SSSR, 1953-55.

Olearius, Adam. *The Travels of Olearius in Seventeenth-Century Russia.* Translated and edited by Samuel H. Baron. Stanford: Stanford University Press, 1967.

Opis' sobraniia rukopisnykh knig P. A. Ovchinnikova. f. 209. XIV v.-XIX v. Moscow: GBLOR, 1963.

Opisanie rukopisnogo otdela biblioteki akademii nauk SSSR. vol. 3, pt. 1: *Khronografy, letopisi, stepennye knigi, rodoslovnye, razriadnye knigi.* 2d ed. Compiled by V. F. Pokrovskaia. Moscow-Leningrad: AN SSSR, 1959.

Opisanie sobraniia V. M. Undol'skogo s No. 580-1422. Moscow, 1936-37.

Oraschakoff, Haralampi. "Ein Denkmal des bulgarischen Rechtes." *Zeitschrift für Vergleichende Rechtswissenschaft* 33 (1916):141-282.

Oreshnikov, A. S. "K istorii teksta Russkoi Pravdy." In *Vostochnaia Evropa v drevnosti i srednevekov'e.* Moscow: Nauka, 1978, pp. 151-55.

———. "K voprosu o sostave Kratkoi Pravdy." In *Lingvisticheskoe istochnikovedenie.* Edited by S. I. Kotkov. Moscow: AN SSSR, 1963, pp. 121-30.

Otchet imperatorskoi publichnoi biblioteki za 1886 g. St. Petersburg, 1889.

Otchet imperatorskoi publichnoi biblioteki za 1905 g. St. Petersburg, 1912.

Pakhman, S. V. *Istoriia kodifikatsii grazhdanskogo prava v dvukh tomakh.* 2 vols. St. Petersburg, 1876.

Pamiatniki istorii Kievskogo gosudarstva IX-XII vv. Edited by G. E. Kochin. Leningrad: Sotsekgiz, 1936.

Pamiatniki istorii Velikogo Novgoroda i Pskova. Edited by G. E. Kochin. Leningrad-Moscow: Sotsekgiz, 1935.

Pamiatniki russkogo prava. 8 vols. Moscow: Gosiurizdat, 1952-63.

Panov, Fedor. "Izsledovanie o novgorodskoi sudnoi gramote 1471 g. v otnoshenii k sudoproizvodstvu, preimushchestvenno grazhdanskomu." *Sbornik izdavaemyi studentami imperatorskogo Peterburgskogo universiteta.* 3 vols. St. Petersburg, 1857-66, 1:255-320.

Pashuto, V. T. *Aleksandr Nevskii*. Moscow: Molodaia gvardiia, 1974.
―――. "Cherty politicheskogo stroia drevnei Rusi." In L. V. Cherepnin, A. P. Novosel'tsev, V. T. Pashuto, and Ia. N. Shchapov. *Drevnerusskoe gosudarstvo i ego mezhdunarodnoe znachenie*. Moscow: Nauka, 1965, pp. 11-76.
Paterik Kievskogo Pecherskogo monastyria. St. Petersburg, 1911.
Pavlov, A. S. "Istoriia istochnikov tserkovnogo prava." *Bogoslovskii vestnik*, 1900, no. 2, pp. 207-30; 1900, no. 3, pp. 486-520.
―――. *Kanonicheskoe pravo*. Moscow, n.d.
―――. "Knigi zakonnye soderzhashchiia v sebe v drevnerusskom perevode vizantiiskie zakony zemledel'cheskie, ugolovnye, brachnye i sudebnye." *Sbornik otdeleniia russkogo iazyka i slovesnosti imperatorskoi akademii nauk* 38, no. 3 (1885):1-92.
―――. "K voprosu o podlinnosti tserkovnogo ustava sv. Vladimira." *Trudy VIII arkheologicheskogo s"ezda v Moskve*. 4 vols. Moscow, 1890, 4:72-73.
―――. *Mnimye sledy katolicheskogo vliianiia v drevneishikh pamiatnikakh iugoslavianskogo i russkogo tserkovnogo prava*. Moscow, 1892.
―――. *Pervonachal'nyi slaviano-russkii nomokanon*. Kazan', 1869.
Peshtich, S. L. *Russkaia istoriografiia XVIII veka*. 3 vols. Leningrad: LGU, 1961-71.
Picheta, V. I. "Litovskii statut 1529 g. i ego istochniki." In K. I. Jablonskis, ed. *Statut velikogo kniazhestva litovskogo 1529 goda*. Minsk: AN BSSR, 1960.
Pikhoia, R. G. "K voprosu o vremeni perevoda vizantiiskoi sintagmy XIV titulov bez tolkovanii v Drevnei Rusi." In *Antichnaia drevnost' i srednie veka. Sbornik 10 (K 80-letiiu M. Ia. Siuziumova)*. Sverdlovsk: Ural'skii universitet, 1973, pp. 308-11.
Pistsovye knigi Obonezhskoi piatiny 1496 i 1563 gg. Materialy po istorii narodov SSSR, no. 1. Leningrad: AN SSSR, 1930.
Podvigina, N. L. *Ocherki sotsial'no-ekonomicheskoi i politicheskoi istorii Novgoroda Velikogo v XII-XIII vv*. Moscow: Vysshaia shkola, 1976.
Pollock, Frederick, and Maitland, Frederic William. *The History of English Law Before the Time of Edward I*. 2d ed. 2 vols. Cambridge: Cambridge University Press, 1968.
Polnoe sobranie russkikh letopisei. 34 vols. to date. St. Petersburg-Moscow, 1846- .
Polnoe sobranie zakonov Rossiiskoi imperii. 45 vols. St. Petersburg, 1830.
Polosin, I. N. *Pskovskaia sudnaia gramota. Uchenye zapiski Moskovskogo gosudarstvennogo pedagogicheskogo instituta imeni V. I. Lenina*, kafedra istorii SSSR, vol. 65, no. 3. Moscow, 1952.
Porfiridov, N. G. *Drevnii Novgorod*. Moscow-Leningrad: AN SSSR, 1947.
Pospisil, Leopold J. *Anthropology of Law: A Comparative Theory*. New York: Harper and Row, 1971.

Pospisil, Leopold J. *Kapauku Papuans and Their Law.* Yale University Publications in Anthropology, no. 54. New Haven, 1958.

———. "Legal Levels and Multiplicity of Systems." *Journal of Conflict Resolution* 11 (1967):2-26.

———. "Multiplicity of Legal Systems in Primitive Societies." *Bulletin of the Philadelphia Anthropological Society* 12, no. 3 (1959):1-4.

———. "The Nature of Law." *Transactions of the New York Academy of Science* 18 (1956):746-55.

———. "Social Change and Primitive Law: Consequences of a Papuan Legal Case." *American Anthropologist* 60 (1959):832-37.

Pound, Roscoe. *An Introduction to the Philosophy of Law.* New Haven: Yale University Press, 1954.

———. *Social Control Through Law.* New Haven: Yale University Press, 1942.

———. *The Spirit of the Common Law.* Boston: Marshall Jones, Co., 1921. Reprint, Boston: Beacon Press, 1963.

Povest' vremennykh let. Edited by V. P. Adrianova-Peretts. 2 vols. Moscow-Leningrad: AN SSSR, 1950.

Pravda Russkaia. Edited by B. D. Grekov. 3 vols. Moscow-Leningrad: AN SSSR, 1940-63.

Presniakov, A. E. "[Review of] I. A. Stratonov, *K voprosu o sostave i proiskhozhdenii kratkoi redaktsii Russkoi Pravdy.* Kazan', 1920; S. Iushkov, *K istorii drevnerusskikh iuridicheskikh sbornikov (XIII v.).* Saratov, 1921." *Kniga i revoliutsiia* 2, no. 1 (1921):45-47.

———. *Kniazhoe pravo v Drevnei Rusi.* St. Petersburg, 1909.

———. *Lektsii po russkoi istorii.* 2 vols. Moscow: Sotsekgiz, 1938-39.

———. "Leopold Karl Goetz. *Das Russische Recht* (Russkaia Pravda). I-II tt. Sttugt., 1910-11." *Zhurnal ministerstva narodnogo prosveshcheniia* 42 (1912):153-67.

———. *Obrazovanie velikorusskogo gosudarstva.* Petrograd, 1918.

Priselkov, M. D. *Istoriia russkogo letopisaniia XI-XV vv.* Leningrad: LGU, 1940.

———. "Zadachi i puti dal'neishego izucheniia Russkoi Pravdy: po povodu vykhoda akademicheskoi 'Pravdy Russkoi' pod redaktsii Akad. B. D. Grekova." *Istoricheskie zapiski* 16 (1945):238-50.

Prochazka, Vladimir. "Le *Zakon" Sudnyj ljud'm"* et la Grande Moravie." *Byzantinoslavica* 28 (1967):359-75; 29 (1968):112-50.

———. "*Posluch"* et *vidok"* dans le droit slave." *Byzantinoslavica* 20 (1959):231-51.

Protas'eva, T. N., ed. *Opisanie rukopisei Sinodal'nogo sobraniia.* 2 vols. Moscow: Glavnoe arkhivnoe upravlenie, Arkheograficheskaia komissiia, Gosudarstvennyi istoricheskii muzei, 1970-73.

Pskovskaia Sudnaia Gramota, sostavlennaia na veche v 1467 godu. Edited by M. S. Vorontsov. Odessa, 1847.

Pskovskaia Sudnaia Gramota. Edited by N. D. Chechulin. St. Petersburg: Imperatorskaia arkheograficheskaia kommissiia, 1914.
Rabinovich, M. G. "Poseleniia." In *Ocherki russkoi kul'tury XIII-XV vv.* 2 vols. Moscow: MGU, 1969, 1:231-53.
Rapov, O. M. *Kniazheskie vladeniia na Rusi v X-pervoi polovine XIII v.* Moscow: MGU, 1977.
———. "O nekotorykh aspektakh kniazheskogo zemlevladeniia v Kievskoi Rusi." In *Stanovlenie rannefeodal'nykh slavianskikh gosudarstv (Materialy nauchnoi sessii pol'skikh i sovetskikh istorikov. Kiev, 1969 g.).* Kiev: Naukova dumka, 1972, pp. 90-115.
Redfield, Robert. *Primitive Law.* Chicago: Distributed by the University of Chicago Bookstore, n.d.
Rettig, Salomon. "Ethical Risk Sensitivity in Male Prisoners." *British Journal of Criminology* 4 (1964):582-90.
Riasanovsky, V. A. *Customary Law of the Mongol Tribes (Mongols, Buriats, Kalmucks).* Harbin: Artistic Printinghouse, 1929.
Roberts, John M. "Oaths, Autonomic Ordeals and Power." In *Ethnography of Law,* Supplement to *American Anthropologist* 67 (1965), pp. 186-212.
Romanov, B. A. *Liudi i nravy Drevnei Rusi.* Leningrad: LGU, 1947. 2d ed. Moscow-Leningrad: Nauka, 1966.
Rosenkampf, G. A. *Obozrenie kormchei knigi v istoricheskom vide.* Moscow, 1829.
Rozhkova, M. K. *K voprosu o proiskhozhdenii i sostave Pskovskoi Sudnoi Gramoty.* Moscow-Leningrad: Kniga, 1927.
Rubinshtein, N. L. "Drevneishaia Pravda i voprosy dofeodal'nogo stroia Kievskoi Rusi." *Arkheograficheskii ezhegodnik za 1964 god.* Moscow: Nauka, 1965, pp. 3-10.
Russkaia istoricheskaia biblioteka. 39 vols. St. Petersburg-Leningrad, 1872-1927.
Russkie dostopamiatnosti. 3 vols. Moscow, 1815-44.
Rybakov, B. A. *Remeslo Drevnei Rusi.* Moscow: AN SSSR, 1948.
Sakharov, A. M. *Goroda severo-vostochnoi Rusi XIV-XV vekov.* Moscow: MGU, 1959.
Salem, Richard G., and Bowers, William J. "Severity of Formal Sanctions as a Deterrent to Deviant Behavior." *Law and Society Review* 5 (1970-71):21-40.
Samokvasov, D. Ia. *Drevnee russkoe pravo.* Moscow, 1903.
Saturnik, Theodor. *Příspěvky k šířeni Byzantského prava u slovanů.* Prague, 1922.
Schapera, Isaac. *A Handbook of Tswana Law and Custom.* 2d ed. London: Oxford University Press for the International African Institute, 1955.
Schmid, Heinrich Felix. "La legislazione Bizantina e la practica giudiziaria

occidentale ne piu antico codice slavo." *Atti del Congresso internazionale di diritto Romano e di storia del diritto*, Verona, 1948. 4 vols. Milan, 1953, 1:395-403.

Schwartz, Richard D. "Social Factors in the Development of Legal Control." *Yale Law Journal* 63 (1953-54):471-91.

Schwartz, Richard D., and Miller, James C. "Legal Evolution and Societal Complexity." *American Journal of Sociology* 70 (1964-65):159-69.

Schwartz, Richard D., and Orleans, Sonja. "On Legal Sanctions." In *Law and the Social System*. Edited by Michael Barkun. New York: Lieber-Atherton, 1973, pp. 64-87.

Sedov, V. V. *Sel'skie poseleniia tsentral'nykh raionov smolenskoi zemli (VIII-XV vv.)*. Materialy i issledovaniia po arkheologii SSSR, vol. 92. Moscow: AN SSSR, 1960.

Sedova, M. V. "Iuvilirnye izdeliia drevnego Novgoroda." In *Materialy i issledovaniia po arkheologii SSSR*, vol. 65. Moscow: AN SSSR, 1959, pp. 223-61.

Select Historical Documents of the Middle Ages. Translated and edited by Ernest F. Henderson. London: G. Ball and Sons, 1925.

Selishchev, A. M. "O iazyke Russkoi Pravdy v sviazi s voprosom o drevneishem tipe russkogo literaturnogo iazyka." *Voprosy iazykoznaniia* 6, no. 4 (1957):57-63.

Semenchenko, G. V. "O datirovke Moskovskoi gubnoi gramoty." *Sovetskie arkhivy*, 1978, no. 1, pp. 53-58.

Seregny, Scott J. "The *Nedel'shchik:* Law and Order in Muscovite Russia." *Canadian-American Slavic Studies* 9 (1975):168-78.

Sergeevich, V. I. *Drevnosti russkogo prava*. 3d ed. 3 vols. St. Petersburg, 1903-1909.

———. *Lektsii i izsledovaniia po drevnei istorii russkogo prava*. 2d ed. St. Petersburg, 1899.

———. "Russkaia Pravda i eia spiski." *Zhurnal ministerstva narodnogo prosveshcheniia* 321 (January 1889):1-41.

———. *Russkaia Pravda v chetyrekh redaktsiiakh*. St. Petersburg, 1904.

Shakhmatov, A. A. *Obozrenie russkikh letopisnykh svodov XIV-XVI vv.* Moscow-Leningrad: AN SSSR, 1938.

———. *Povest' vremennykh let*. Vol. 1: *Vvodnaia chast'. Tekst. Primechaniia*. Petrograd, 1916.

———. *Razyskaniia o drevneishikh russkikh letopisnykh svodakh*. St. Petersburg, 1908.

Shakhmatov, M. V. *Ispolnitel'naia vlast' v Moskovskoi Rusi*. 3 vols. Prague: Russkii svobodnyi universitet, 1935-37.

Shchapov, Ia. N. "Brak i sem'ia v Drevnei Rusi." *Voprosy istorii*, 1970, no. 10, pp. 216-19.

———. "Iuzhnoslavianskii politicheskii opyt na sluzhbe u russkikh ideologov XV v." *Byzantinobulgarica* 2 (1966):199-214.

———. "Iz istorii gorodskogo upravleniia v Drevnei Rusi (Sluzhba mer i vesov).″ In *Goroda feodal'noi Rossii. Sbornik statei pamiati N. V. Ustiugova*. Moscow: Nauka, 1966, pp. 99-104.

———. "K istorii sootnosheniia svetskoi i tserkovnoi iurisdiktsii na Rusi v XII-XIV vv." In *Pol'sha i Rus'. Cherty obshchnosti i svoeobraziia v istoricheskom razvitii Rusi i Pol'shi XII-XIV vv*. Moscow: Nauka, 1974, pp. 172-89.

———. "K istorii teksta Novgorodskoi Sinodal'noi Kormchei." *Istoriko-arkheologicheskii sbornik*. Moscow: n.p., 1962, pp. 295-301.

———. "K kharakteristike nekotorykh letopisnykh trudov XV." In *Letopisi i khroniki. Sbornik statei 1973 g. posviashchen pamiati Arseniia Nikolaevicha Nasonova*. Moscow: Nauka, 1974, pp. 173-86.

———. *Kniazheskie ustavy i tserkov' v drevnei Rusi XI-XIV vv*. Moscow: Nauka, 1972.

———. "Nekotorye iuridicheskie i kanonicheskie pamiatniki v slavianskoi pis'mennosti XII-XV vekov." In *Metodicheskoe posobie po opisaniiu slaviano-russkikh rukopisei dlia svodnogo kataloga rukopisei khraniashchikhsia v SSSR*. Moscow: Arkheograficheskaia komissiia pri otdelenii istorii SSSR, 1973, pp. 261-73.

———. "Novoe o spiskakh Russkoi Pravdy." *Istoricheskii arkhiv*, 1959, no. 4, pp. 209-11.

———. "Novye spiski kormchikh knig, soderzhashchie Russkuiu Pravdu." *Istoriia SSSR*, 1964, no. 2, pp. 100-103.

———. "Novyi spisok kormchei Efremovskoi redaktsii." In *Istochniki i istoriografiia slavianskogo srednevekov'ia*. Moscow: Nauka, 1967, pp. 258-76.

———. "Novyi spisok Novgorodskogo ustava Sviatoslava Ol'govicha (Iz sobraniia E. E. Egorova)." *Zapiski otdela rukopisei GBL* 26 (1963):395-98.

———. "O sostave drevneslavianskoi Kormchei Efremovskoi redaktsii." In *Istochniki i istoriografiia slavianskogo srednevekov'ia*. Moscow: Nauka, 1967, pp. 207-15.

———. "Pervonachal'nyi sostav Rashskoi kormchei knigi 1305 g." *Zapiski otdela rukopisei GBL* 33 (1972):140-47.

———. "Pravilo o tserkovnykh liudiakh." *Arkheograficheskii ezhegodnik za 1965 god*. Moscow: Nauka, 1966, pp. 72-81.

———. "Prokhiron v vostochnoslavianskoi pis'mennosti." *Vizantiiskii vremennik* 38 (1977):48-58.

———. "Redaktsiia ustava kniazia Iaroslava Vladimirovicha." *Problemy istochnikovedeniia* 11 (1963):481-513.

———. "Retseptsiia sbornikov vizantiiskogo prava v srednevekovykh balkanskikh gosudarstvakh." *Vizantiiskii vremennik* 37 (1976):123-29.

———. "Russkaia Pravda v novykh spiskakh kormchikh knig XVI-XVII vv." *Arkheograficheskii ezhegodnik za 1969 god*. Moscow: Nauka, 1971, pp. 70-72.

———. "Smolenskii ustav kniazia Rostislava Mstislavicha." *Arkheo-

graficheskii ezhegodnik za 1962 god. Moscow: AN SSSR, 1963, pp. 37-47.

———. "Sobranie rukopisnykh knig I. Ia. Lukashevicha i N. A. Markevicha." *Zapiski otdela rukopisei GBL* 19 (1957):3-35.

———. "Tserkov' i stanovlenie drevnerusskoi gosudarstvennosti." *Voprosy istorii*, 1969, no. 11, pp. 55-64.

———. "Tserkov' kak feodal'naia organizatsiia v drevnei Rusi v X-XII vv." Candidate's dissertation, Moscow, 1964.

———. "Tserkov' v sisteme gosudarstvennoi vlasti drevnei Rusi." In L. V. Cherepnin, A. P. Novosel'tsev, V. T. Pashuto, and Ia. N. Shchapov. *Drevnerusskoe gosudarstvo i ego mezhdunarodnoe znachenie.* Moscow: Nauka, 1965, pp. 279-352.

———. "Ustav kniazia Iaroslava i vopros ob otnoshenii k vizantiiskomu naslediiu na Rusi v seredine XI v." *Vizantiiskii vremennik* 31 (1971):71-78.

———. "Varsonof'evskaia kormchaia." *Arkheograficheskii ezhegodnik za 1968 god.* Moscow: Nauka, 1970, pp. 93-101.

———. *Vizantiiskoe i iuzhnoslavianskoe pravovoe nasledie na Rusi v XI-XIII vv.* Moscow: Nauka, 1978.

———, ed. *Drevnerusskie kniazheskie ustavy XI-XV vv.* Moscow: Nauka, 1976.

Shchepkina, M. V.; Protas'eva, T. N.; Kostiukhina, L. M.; and Golyshenko, V. S. "Opisanie pergamentnykh rukopisei Gosudarstvennogo istoricheskogo muzeia." *Arkheograficheskii ezhegodnik za 1964 god.* Moscow: Nauka, 1965, pp. 135-234.

Shtamm, S. I., ed. *Sudebnik 1497 goda.* Moscow: Gosiurizdat, 1955.

Slovar' russkogo iazyka XI-XVII vv. Edited by S. G. Barkhudarov, V. I. Borkovskii et al. 6 vols. to date. Moscow: Nauka, 1975- .

Slovar' sovremennogo russkogo literaturnogo iazyka. 17 vols. Moscow-Leningrad: AN SSSR, 1948-65.

Smirnov, I. I. *Ocherki sotsial'no-ekonomicheskikh otnoshenii Rusi XII-XIII vekov.* Moscow-Leningrad: AN SSSR, 1963.

———. "Sudebnik 1550 goda." *Istoricheskie zapiski* 24 (1947):267-352.

———. "Ustavlen'e tat'by." In *Issledovaniia po otechestvennomu istochnikovedeniiu (Sbornik statei posviashchennykh 75-letiiu S. N. Valka).* Leningrad: Nauka, 1964, pp. 488-99.

Smith, M. G. "The Sociological Framework of Law." In *African Law: Adaptation and Development.* Edited by Hilda Kuper and Leo Kuper. Berkeley: University of California Press, 1965, pp. 24-48.

Smolenskie gramoty XIII-XIV vv. Edited by T. A. Sumnikova and V. V. Lopatev. Moscow: AN SSSR, 1963.

Sobolevskii, A. I. "Dve redaktsii Russkoi Pravdy." In *Sbornik statei v chest' Praskov'i Sergeevny Uvarovoi.* Moscow, 1916, pp. 17-23.

———. "Knigi zakonnye." *Zhurnal ministerstva narodnogo prosveshcheniia* 243 (February 1886):312-18.

Sochineniia Ivana Peresvetova. Edited by A. A. Zimin. Moscow-Leningrad: AN SSSR, 1956.

Sofiiskii vremiannik ili Russkaia letopis' s 882 po 1534 god. Edited by Pavel Stroev. 2 vols. Moscow, 1820-21.

Solov'ev, S. M. *Istoriia Rossii s drevneishikh vremen*. 15 vols. Moscow: Sotsekgiz-Mysl', 1962-66.

Spasskii, I. G. *Russkaia monetnaia sistema*. 3d ed. Leningrad: Gosudarstvennyi ermitazh, 1962.

Sreznevskii, I. I. *Materialy dlia slovaria drevnerusskogo iazyka po pis'mennym pamiatnikam*. 3 vols. St. Petersburg, 1893-1903. Reprint, Moscow, 1958.

———. "Obozrenie drevnikh russkikh spiskov kormchei knigi." *Sbornik otdeleniia russkogo iazyka i slovesnosti imperatorskoi akademii nauk* 65, no. 2 (1899):1-54, 1-207.

———. *Paleograficheskii snimok Russkoi Pravdy po Novgorodskoi kormchei knige XIII veka*. St. Petersburg, 1888.

Staden, Heinrich von. *Land and Government in Muscovy*. Translated and edited by Thomas Esper. Stanford: Stanford University Press, 1967.

Starostina, I. P. "K tolkovaniiu berestianoi gramoty no. 25." *Istoriia SSSR*, 1976, no. 1, pp. 171-74.

Stenton, Doris M. *English Justice Between the Norman Conquest and the Great Charter, 1066-1215*. London: George Allen and Unwin for the American Philosophic Society, 1964.

Stoglav. 2d ed. Kazan', 1887.

Stratonov, I. A. "K voprosu o sostave i proiskhozhdenii kratkoi redaktsii Russkoi Pravdy." *Izvestiia obshchestva arkheologii, istorii i etnografii pri Kazanskom universitete* 30, no. 4 (1920):385-424.

Stupin, M. N. *Istoriia telesnykh nakazanii v Rossii*. Vladikavkaz, 1887.

Sudebniki Ioanna III i Ioanna IV 1497 g. i 1550 g. Edited by M. Klochkov. Khar'kov: Istoriko-filologicheskii fakul'tet Khar'kovskogo universiteta, 1915.

Sudebniki XV- XVI vekov. Edited by B. D. Grekov. Moscow-Leningrad: AN SSSR, 1952.

Sudebniki Russkogo gosudarstva. Edited by N. Dobrotvor. Gor'kii: Gor'kovskii gosudarstvennyi pedagogicheskii institut imeni M. Gor'kogo, kafedra istorii SSSR, 1939.

Sukhov, A. A. "Obychno-narodnye i kniazheskie nakazaniia po drevnerusskomu ugolovnomu pravu." *Iuridicheskii vestnik* 5, nos. 7-8 (July-August 1873):44-116; 5, no. 9 (September 1873):35-44.

Suvorov, N. S. *K voprosu o zapadnom vliianii na drevnerusskoe pravo*. Iaroslavl', 1893.

———. *Konspekt tserkovnogo prava*. Moscow, 1909.

———. "O sledakh rimsko-katolicheskogo tserkovnogo prava v drevneishem russkom prave." *Izvestiia o zaniatiiakh sed'mogo ar-

kheologicheskogo s"ezda v Iaroslavle, no. 14. Iaroslavl', 1885, pp. 5-6.

———. *O tserkovnykh nakazaniiakh*. St. Petersburg, 1876.

———. *Sledy zapadnokatolicheskogo tserkovnogo prava v pamiatnikakh drevnego russkogo prava*. Iaroslavl', 1888.

———. *Uchebnik tserkovnogo prava*. Moscow, 1902.

Sverdlov, M. B. "Dvoriane v Drevnei Rusi." In *Iz istorii feodal'noi Rossii. Stat'i i ocherki k 70-letiiu so dnia rozhdeniia prof. V. V. Mavrodina*. Leningrad: LGU, 1978, pp. 54-59.

———. "K istorii teksta kratkoi redaktsii Russkoi Pravdy." *Vspomogatel'nye istoricheskie distsipliny* 10 (1978):135-59.

Szeftel, Marc. "La condition legale des étrangers dans la Russie Novgorodo-Kievienne." *Recueils de la Société Jean Bodin* 10 (1958):375-430.

———. "Le Jugement de Dieu dans le droit russe ancien." *Archives d'histoire du droit oriental* 4 (1949):267-93.

———. "Le Statut juridique de l'enfant en Russie avant Pierre le Grand." *Recueils de la Société Jean Bodin* 36 (1976):635-56.

———. "The Sudebnik of 1497: Paleographic Analysis, Composition and Sources." In *For Roman Jakobson*. Edited by Morris Halle. The Hague: Mouton and Co., 1956, pp. 547-52.

———, ed. and trans. *Documents de droit public relatifs à la Russie médiévale*. Brussels: Libraire encyclopedique, 1963.

Tatishchev, V. N. *Istoriia Rossiiskaia*. 7 vols. Moscow-Leningrad: AN SSSR-Nauka, 1962-68.

Thayer, James B. "The Older Modes of Trial." *Harvard Law Review* 5, no. 2 (15 May 1891):45-70.

Thompson, M. W. *Novgorod the Great*. London: Evelyn, Adams and Mackay, 1967.

Tikhomirov, M. N. *Drevnerusskie goroda*. Moscow: Politizdat, 1956.

———. *Issledovanie o Russkoi Pravde*. Moscow: AN SSSR, 1941.

———. *Krest'ianskie i gorodskie vosstaniia na Rusi XI-XIII vv*. Moscow: Politizdat, 1955.

———. "Krestininskii spisok Russkoi Pravdy." *Problemy istochnikovedeniia* 3 (1940):398-400.

———. *Posobie dlia izucheniia Russkoi Pravdy*. Moscow: MGU, 1953.

———. "Pravosud'e mitropolich'e." *Arkheograficheskii ezhegodnik za 1963 god*. Moscow: Nauka, 1964, pp. 32-55.

———. "Russkaia Pravda (k 200-letiiu otkrytiia pamiatnika)." *Istorik-Marksist*, 1939, no. 5, pp. 138-55.

———. "Spisok russkikh gorodov dal'nikh i blizhnikh." *Istoricheskie zapiski* 40 (1952):214-59.

———. *Srednevekovaia Moskva v XIV-XV vekakh*. Moscow: MGU, 1957.

———. "Vossozdanie russkoi pis'mennoi traditsii v pervye desiatiletiia tatarskogo iga." In M. N. Tikhomirov. *Russkaia kul'tura X-XVIII vv.* Moscow: Nauka, 1968, pp. 173-84.

———. "Zakon Sudnyi liudem kratkoi redaktsii v russkikh rukopisiakh." In M. N. Tikhomirov. *Istoricheskie sviazi Rossii so slavianskimi stranami i Vizantiei.* Moscow: Nauka, 1965, pp. 196-217.

Tikhomirov, M. N., and Shchepkina, M. V. *Dva pamiatnika Novgorodskoi pis'mennosti. Trudy gosudarstvennogo istoricheskogo muzeia*, vol. 8. Moscow, 1952.

Timofeev, A. G. *Istoriia telesnykh nakazanii v russkom prave.* 2d ed. St. Petersburg, 1904.

Tittle, Charles. "Crime Rates and Legal Sanctions." *Social Problems* 16 (1969):409-23.

Tittle, Charles, and Logan, Charles H. "Sanctions and Deviance: Evidence and Remaining Questions." *Law and Society Review* 7 (1973):371-92.

Tittle, Charles, and Rowe, Alan R. "Moral Appeal, Sanction Threat and Deviance: An Experimental Test." *Social Problems* 20 (1973):488-98.

Tolochko, P. P. *Istorychna topohrafiia starodavn'oho Kyeva.* Kiev: Naukova dumka, 1970.

Tret'iakov, P. N. *Finno-Ugry, balty i slaviane na Dnepre i Volge.* Moscow-Leningrad: Nauka, 1966.

———. *Vostochnoslavianskie plemena.* Moscow-Leningrad: AN SSSR, 1948.

Troitski, S. V. "Apostol slavianstva sv. Mefodii kak kanonist." *Zhurnal moskovskoi patriarkhii*, 1958, no. 3, pp. 38-51.

———. "Sv. Mefodii kak slavianskii zakonodatel'." *Bogoslovskie trudy* 2 (1961):83-141.

———. "Sviatoi Mefodii ili Bolgarskii kniaz' Boris sostavil Zakon Sudnyi liudem?" *Bogoslovskie trudy* 4 (1968):117-26.

Turner, Ralph V. "Clerical Judges in English Secular Courts." *Medievalia et Humanistica*, n.s. 3 (1972):75-98.

Ullmann, Walter. "Some Medieval Principles of Criminal Procedure." *Juridical Review* 59 (1947):1-28.

Unbegaun, B. O. "Le 'crime' et le 'criminel' dans la terminologie juridique russe." In B. O. Unbegaun. *Selected Papers on Russian and Slavonic Philology.* Oxford: Clarendon Press, 1969, pp. 203-17.

———. "La Fausse Évidence étymologique: Polonais *podvojski*, russe *podvojskij*." In *Symbolae Linguisticae in Honorem Georgii Kuryłowicz.* Wroclaw-Warsaw-Cracow: Polska Akademia Nauk, 1965, pp. 335-39.

———. "Russe et slavon dans la terminologie juridique." In B. O. Unbegaun. *Selected Papers on Russian and Slavonic Philology.* Oxford: Clarendon Press, 1969, pp. 129-35.

Unger, Roberto Mangabeira. *Law in Modern Society: Toward A Criticism of Social Theory.* New York: The Free Press, 1976.

Usachev, N. N. "Gramoty Smolenskoi stariny." In *Smolenskii krai v istorii russkoi kul'tury*. Edited by Ia. R. Koshelev. Smolensk: Smolenskii gosudarstvennyi pedagogicheskii institut imeni K. Marksa, 1973, pp. 15-22.
Ushakov, V. E. "Ustiuzhskaia Kormchaia." *Slavia* 30 (1961):20-40.
Uspenskii, F. I. "Drevneishii pamiatnik slavianskogo prava." *Iuridicheskii vestnik* 18, no. 4 (April 1886):700-713.
Ustav sviatogo velikogo kniazia Vladimira o tserkovnykh sudakh i o desiatinakh. Edited by V. N. Beneshevich. Petrograd, 1915.
"Ustavy v. k. Vladimira i Iaroslava o tserkovnom sude." *Khristianskoe chtenie*, 1851, pt. 2, pp. 422-52.
Ustiuzhskii letopisnyi svod. Edited by K. N. Serbina. Moscow-Leningrad: AN SSSR, 1950.
Ustrialov, F. N. *Izsledovanie Pskovskoi Sudnoi Gramoty 1467 goda*. St. Petersburg, 1855.
Valk, S. N. "I. N. Boltin i ego rabota nad Russkoi Pravdoi." *Trudy otdela drevnerusskoi literatury* 14 (1958):650-56.
———. "Russkaia Pravda v izdaniiakh i izucheniiakh 20-40 godov XIX v." *Arkheograficheskii ezhegodnik za 1959 god*. Moscow: AN SSSR, 1960, pp. 194-255.
———. "Russkaia Pravda v izdaniiakh i izucheniiakh XVIII-nachala XIX veka." *Arkheograficheskii ezhegodnik za 1958 god*. Moscow: AN SSSR, 1960, pp. 124-60.
———. "Tatishchevskie spiski Russkoi Pravdy." *Materialy po istorii SSSR*. 7 vols. Moscow-Leningrad: AN SSSR, 1955-59, 5:607-57.
Van Caenegem, R. "The Law of Evidence in the Twelfth Century." In *Proceedings of the Second International Congress of Medieval Canon Law*. Edited by Stephen Kuttner and J. Joseph Ryan. Vatican City, 1965, pp. 297-310.
Vansina, Jan. "A Traditional Legal System: The Kuba." In *African Law: Adaptation and Development*. Edited by Hilda Kuper and Leo Kuper. Berkeley: University of California Press, 1965, pp. 97-119.
Vašica, Josef. "Jazyková povaha Zákona sudného ljudem." *Slavia* 27 (1958):521-37.
———. "Kirillo-Mefodievskie iuridicheskie pamiatniki." *Voprosy slavianskogo iazykoznaniia* 7 (1965):12-33.
———. "K lexiku Zákona sudného ljudem." In *Slavistična revija* 10 (1957):61-66.
———. "K otázce puvodu Zákona sudného ljudem." *Slavia* 30 (1961):1-19.
———. "Origine Cyrillo-Methodienne du plus ancien code slave di *Zakon sudnyj ljudem*." *Byzantinoslavica* 12 (1951):154-74.
Vasil'evskii, V. G. "Knigi zakonnye." *Zhurnal ministerstva narodnogo prosveshcheniia* 243 (February 1886):317-51.

SOURCES CITED

Vasmer, Max. *Etimologicheskii slovar' russkogo iazyka*. Translated by O. N. Trubachev. 4 vols. Moscow: Progress, 1964-73.

Vernadsky, George. *Kievan Russia*. New Haven: Yale University Press, 1948.

———, ed. and trans. *Medieval Russian Laws*. New York: Columbia University Press, 1947.

Veselovskii, S. B. *D'iaki i podiachie XV-XVII vv*. Moscow: Nauka, 1975.

———. *Feodal'noe zemlevladenie v severo-vostochnoi Rusi*. Moscow-Leningrad: AN SSSR, 1947.

———. *Selo i derevnia v severo-vostochnoi Rusi XIV-XVI vv*. Moscow-Leningrad: AN SSSR, 1947.

Vinogradoff, Paul. *Roman Law in Medieval Europe*. Cambridge: Speculum Historiale, 1968.

The Visigothic Code (Forum Judicum). Translated and edited by S. P. Scott. Boston: Boston Book Co., 1910.

Vladimirskii-Budanov, M. F. "Das russische Recht (Russkaia Pravda)." [*Kievskie*] *universitetskie izvestiia* 51, no. 3 (March 1911):1-24.

———. *Khristomatiia po istorii russkogo prava*. 5th ed. 3 vols. St. Petersburg-Kiev, 1899.

———. *Obzor istorii russkogo prava*. 2d ed. St. Petersburg, 1888.

Voronin, N. N. *K istorii sel'skogo poseleniia feodal'noi Rusi*. Leningrad: Ogiz, 1935.

Wallace, Ernest, and Hoebel, E. Adamson. *The Comanches*. Norman: University of Oklahoma Press, 1952.

Wallace-Hadrill, J. M. "The Bloodfeud of the Franks." *John Rylands Library Bulletin* 41 (1958-59):459-87.

Weber, Max. *Max Weber on Law in Economy and Society*. Edited by Max Rheinstein. Translated by Edward Shils and Max Rheinstein. New York: Simon and Schuster, Clarion Books, 1967.

Westermarck, Edward. "The Blood-feud among some Berbers in Morocco." In *Essays Presented to C. G. Seligman*. Edited by E. E. Evans-Pritchard. London: Kegan Paul, Trench, Trubner, 1934, pp. 361-68.

Whitelock Dorothy, ed. and trans. *Anglo-Saxon Wills*. Cambridge: Cambridge University Press, 1930.

Wimberley, Howard. "Legal Evolution: One Further Step." *American Journal of Sociology* 79 (1973):78-83.

Zakon Sudnyi liudem kratkoi redaktsii. Edited by M. N. Tikhomirov and L. V. Milov. Moscow: AN SSSR, 1961.

Zakon Sudnyi liudem prostrannoi i svodnoi redaktsii. Edited by M. N. Tikhomirov and L. V. Milov. Moscow: AN SSSR, 1961.

Zakony velikogo kniazia Ioanna Vasil'evicha i Sudebnik tsaria i velikogo kniazia Ioanna Vasil'evicha, s dopolnitel'nymi ukazami. Edited by K. Kalaidovich and P. Stroev. Moscow, 1819.

Zasurtsev, P. I. "Postroiki drevnego Novgoroda." In *Materialy i issledovaniia po arkheologii SSSR,* vol. 65. Moscow: AN SSSR, 1959, pp. 262-98.

Zavadskaia, S. V. "O znachenii termina 'kniazh tiun' v XI-XIII vv." In *Drevneishie gosudarstva na territorii SSSR. Materialy i issledovaniia 1975 g.* Moscow: Nauka, 1975, pp. 157-64.

Zenkovsky, Serge A. *Medieval Russia's Epics, Chronicles and Tales.* Rev. ed. New York: E. P. Dutton and Co., 1974.

Zguta, Russell. "The Ordeal by Water (Swimming of Witches) in the East Slavic World." *Slavic Review* 36 (1977):220-30.

Zimin, A. A. "D'iacheskii apparat v Rossii vtoroi poloviny XV-pervoi treti XVI v." *Istoricheskie zapiski* 87 (1971):219-86.

———. "Feodal'naia gosudarstvennost' i Russkaia Pravda." *Istoricheskie zapiski* 76 (1965):230-75.

———. "Iz istoriografii sovetskogo istochnikovedeniia (Russkaia Pravda v trudakh S. V. Iushkova)." In *Problemy istorii obshchestvennoi mysli i istoriografii. K 75-letiiu akademika M. V. Nechkinoi.* Moscow: Nauka, 1976, pp. 275-82.

———. "K istorii teksta kratkoi redaktsii Russkoi Pravdy." *Trudy Moskovskogo gosudarstvennogo istoriko-arkhivnogo instituta* 7 (1954):155-208.

———. "Namestnicheskoe upravlenie v Russkom gosudarstve vtoroi poloviny XV-pervoi treti XVI v." *Istoricheskie zapiski* 94 (1974):271-301.

———. "Novye spiski Russkoi Pravdy." *Arkheograficheskii ezhegodnik za 1958 god.* Moscow: AN SSSR, 1960, pp. 323-30.

———. "O sostave dvortsovykh uchrezhdenii Russkogo gosudarstva kontsa XV i XVI v." *Istoricheskie zapiski* 63 (1958):180-205.

———. "Ustavnaia gramota kniazia Vsevoloda Mstislavicha." In *Akademiku Borisu Dmitrievichu Grekovu ko dniu semidesiatiletiia. Sbornik statei.* Moscow: AN SSSR, 1952, pp. 123-31.

Zimin, A. A., and Poliak, A. G. "Znachenie Russkoi Pravdy dlia razvitiia russkogo, ukrainskogo i belorusskogo feodal'nogo prava." *Sovetskoe gosudarstvo i pravo,* 1954, no. 4, pp. 116-22.

Zimring, Franklin E., and Hawkins, Gordon. *Deterrence.* Chicago: University of Chicago Press, 1973.

———. "Deterrence and Marginal Groups." *Journal of Research in Crime and Delinquency* 5 (1968):100-114.

Žužek, P. Ivan. *Kormčaja Kniga: Studies on the Chief Code of Russian Canon Law. Orientalia Christiana Analecta,* vol. 168. Rome, 1964.

INDEX

ancestor veneration, 180, 182-83
Archeographic Miscellany, 25, 28
arson, 66, 89, 121
Aubert, Vilhelm, 8
Austin, John, 4

bailiffs, 104-105, 107, 120-21, 125. See also *birich, detskii, dvorianin, dvorskii, iabetnik, izvetnik, mechnik, nedel'shchik, podvernik, podvoiskii, pozovnik, pravedchik, pristav,* and *sof'ianin*
Bal'zerov Miscellany, 28
Barkun, Michael, 105
Beneshevich, V. N., 25, 54, 199n
birich, 101-102, 109, 236n
Bloch, Marc, 131
bloodwite, 68, 71-78, 97, 116, 193n. See also *vina, vira*
Bohannan, Paul, 10
boiarskii sud, 119, 157
Boltin, I. N., 30, 201n
bribery, 115, 119-20, 125, 135, 242n
Byzantine law, 72-73, 89, 141, 144, 147, 154-55, 171-72, 174, 210n. See also Encloga and Procheiros Nomos

capital punishment, 29, 73, 77, 85, 87, 91-92, 121-22, 125, 139, 229n, 245n
Cherepnin, L. V., 59
church courts, 52, 170-71
church income, 170. See also tithe
Collection of Princely Statutes, 26
Collection of Russian Articles, 26-27
Collection of Thirty Chapters, 27
commune, see *verv'*
composition, 15, 64, 69, 76-77, 80, 88, 192n, 193n, 195n. See also wergeld
confirmation charters of Grand Prince Vasilii Dmitrievich, 26, 28, 55, 118
confrontment, 82-85, 116, 129-30, 152, 179

dan', 79, 181, 241n
default charter, 113, 121, 156, 258n
detskii, 101, 108
Dewey, Horace W., 41
d'iak, 112-13, 151, 161, 259n. See also scribe
Diamond, A. S., 10, 15
doklad, 106, 136, 138, 157, 160
dovodchik, 122-24, 246n
druzhina, 96, 232n
duels, 122, 133-35, 150-51, 245n, 249n, 254n, 255n, 256n
Dvina Administration Charter, 39-40, 116
dvoretskii, 246n
dvorianin, 84, 109, 239n
dvorskii, 125

Ecloga, 23, 47-48, 87, 144, 173, 265n
Evan, William, 8
evidence, 153, 155-56, 158-59, 161, 173. See also *polichnoe* and stolen property
eyewitness, 128, 149. See also *svidetel'* and *vidok*

flogging, 87, 91
Fotii, Metropolitan, 26, 55, 167, 169

Gluckman, Max, 9, 10, 15, 94
Goetz, L. K., 202n
golovnich'stvo, 65, 69
"good men," 92, 135-36, 138
Grekov, B. D., 33-34, 176

Hart, H.L.A., 6
Herberstein, Sigismund von, 124, 236n
Hoebel, E. Adamson, 10, 95, 232n
homicide, 64-65, 70-73, 193
horizontal legal systems, 7, 11, 15
horse theft, 65-67, 85-86

iabednik/iabetnik, 102-103, 140, 236n, 251n. See also *poklep* and slander
Iakovlev, A. I., 32

Iaroslav, Grand Prince (1015-1054), 43, 50, 54, 63, 100, 254n
Iaroslav's Statute, 25-26, 28, 50, 54-57, 213n
Iaroslav's Statute on Bridges, 25, 27-28
inheritance law, 155-56, 172, 235n
Ioann II, Metropolitan, 168
Iushkov, S. V., 24-27, 33, 35, 41, 49, 59, 200n, 203n, 211n
izvetnik, 102, 109, 236n

judgment charters, 121, 157-58

Kalachov, N. V., 31-33, 49, 71, 198n, 201n
Kalaidovich, K. F., 30, 40
Kantorowicz, Hermann, 5
Karamzin, N. M., 30, 201n
Karskii, E. F., 33
Kelsen, Hans, 6
kinship, 7-8, 11, 16, 43, 62-63, 71, 175, 179, 183, 195n
Kiprian, Metropolitan, 26, 28, 55
Kirill, Metropolitan, 20-21
kissing the cross, 134-35, 150-51, 254n. *See also* ordeals
Kliuchevskii, V. O., 124, 161
Knigi zakonnye, 60, 144-45, 216n, 252n
"known evil men" (*vedomye likhie liudi*), 92, 139-40
Kormchaia Kniga, 19, 21-22, 198n; Chudov Kormchaia, 23, 27-28, 47, 198n; Concordance Kormchaia, 23; Efrem Kormchaia, 19-21, 196n; Ferapontov Kormchaia, 46; Miasnikov Kormchaia, 21, 45; "Russian" Kormchaia, 19, 21; Serbian Kormchaia, 19-21, 46, 197n; Sophia Kormchaia, 21, 45, 47, 209n; Synod Kormchaia, 21, 44, 47, 50-51; Ukrainian Kormchaia, 21; Varsonof'ev Kormchaia, 47; Vladimir-Volynia Kormchaia, 21, 52-53
Kosven, M. O., 36
Krestinin, V. V., 29

law and social structure, 5-6, 8-10, 14-15
legal change, 3-4, 14-15, 164-65, 171, 174, 177, 187-88
likhie liudi. *See* "known evil men"
Liubimov, V. P., 35
lots, 150, 254n. *See also* ordeals

Maine, Henry Sumner, 8
Maitland, Frederic William, 64, 153
Maksimeiko, N. A., 34
marriage, 168-69, 263n
mayor, 106-108, 112. *See also posadnik*
mechnik, 100-101, 108, 235n
mediators, 7, 11-12, 14-15, 94-95, 105, 193n
Merilo Pravednoe, 23, 25, 27-28, 44-45, 47, 142, 209n
metel'nik, 99, 234n
Mikhailov, P. E., 39
Milov, L. V., 50
mir, 177
Moore, Sally Falk, 9
Mrochek-Drozdovskii, P. N., 201n
murdrum, 78, 266n
Musin-Pushkin Miscellany, 25, 30, 44
mytnik, 129

namestnik, 84, 90, 106-108, 116-18, 124, 147, 243n
nedel'shchik, 122, 124, 234n
nomocanons, 20, 196n
Novgorod Judicial Charter, 38, 205n
Novgorod Treaty with Gotland and German Towns (1189-1199), 37

oaths, 135, 144, 149-52, 253n, 255n. *See also* ordeals
obida, 70, 80-81, 85, 97
ognishchanin, 68, 70, 97, 109, 233n
okol'nichii, 119, 151
On Church People (*O tserkovnykh liudiakh*), 23, 28
On the Procedure for Theft (*O ustavlen'e tatby*), 87
On Witnesses (*O poslusekh*), 144-46, 172

INDEX

ordeals, 13, 101, 141, 148-50, 152, 173, 194n, 253-54n, 265n. *See also* duels, kissing the cross, lots, and oaths
otrok, 99, 117, 234n

paganism, 16, 46, 165, 167-69, 180, 186, 262n, 268n
Pavlov, A. S., 20, 49, 60, 145, 196, 212-13n
perjury, 135, 144, 147-48
pisets, 99-100, 112-13, 235n
poaching, 89-90
podvernik, 111, 240n
podvoiskii, 103-104, 108-109, 112, 122, 236n, 237n
pogost, 181-84
poisoning, 167, 262n
poklep, 140-41
polichnoe, 152-53. *See also* stolen property
poliud'e, 99, 234n, 241n
Poljica, 179
Pollack, Frederick, 153
posadnik, 106, 108, 238n. *See also* mayor
poslukh, 128, 130-32, 134-36, 142-44, 247n. *See also* testimony
postponement documents, 121
potok, 65-66, 86
Pound, Roscoe, 5
pozovnik, 85, 109, 113, 239n
pravedchik, 122-23
Pravilo zakonno, 26-27
Pravosudie Mitropolich'e, 34, 44, 59, 73, 77, 88, 141, 215-16n, 216n
Presniakov, A. E., 96
pristav, 104, 109-13, 122-23, 240n, 241n, 245n
Procheiros Nomos, 23, 48, 144, 173-74, 222n
prodazha, 72, 75, 78-79, 81-82, 88, 222n, 226n, 229n
Pskov Judicial Charter, 38-39, 205n, 206n, 264n
put', 114-15, 117, 242n

Questionary of Kirik, 21, 166

razboi, 71, 75, 97
razboinik, 65-66, 68, 71-72, 75, 78, 86, 221n
recidivism, 85, 91-92, 122, 139, 250-51n. *See also razboinik*
revenge, 14-15, 62-64, 76-77, 80, 188, 217n, 218n
riad, 98, 241n, 257n
Roman law, 173, 204n, 264n
Rosenkampf, G. A., 30, 49
Rostislav's Statute, 58, 215n
Rozhkova, M. K., 39
Rubinshtein, N. L., 36
Rukopisanie of Vsevolod, 27, 238n
Rumovskii, S. Ia., 29
Russkaia Pravda, 19, 26-27, 29, 36, 41-42, 208n, 209n; Abbreviated Pravda, 31, 34-35, 46, 67; Expanded Pravda, 18, 21, 23, 25, 28, 30, 43-45, 208-209nn; Short Pravda, 18, 29, 41, 43

sanctions, 6-8, 12-15, 62, 73, 113, 121, 226-27n, 237n, 245n
Schlözer, A. L., 29
scribe, 100, 161
seals, sealkeepers, 161-62
secretary, see *d'iak*
Selections from Mosaic Law, 23, 25
Sergeevich, V. I., 31-32, 37, 161
Shchapov, Ia. N., 22, 28, 42, 50, 53, 55, 57, 200n
slander, 122, 141, 148. *See also iabednik* and *poklep*
slaves, 83, 157
Smolensk Treaty of 1229, 37, 66
sof'ianin, 103, 109, 236n
Solov'ev, S. M., 175-76
Speranskii, M. M., 30
starosty, 232n
starozhil'tsy, 137-38
Statutory Regulation on Murder. See *Zapis' o dushegubstve*
stolen property, 140, 152, 256n
Stroev, P. M., 30, 40
Sudebnik of 1497, 40-41
Sudebnik of 1550, 40
sudnye muzhi, 136

sud proezdnoi, 99, 118, 234n, 258n
Suvorov, N. S., 196-97n, 212n, 213n
Sviatoslav O'lgovich, Prince, 74, 79
Sviatoslav's Statute, 58-59
svidetel', 135, 143, 147
Syntagma in Fourteen Titles, 20, 197n
Szeftel, Marc, 36

testament, 133, 153-55, 172
testimony, 131, 134-39, 141, 145-47. See also eyewitness, *poslukh*, *starozhil'tsy*, *svidetel'*, *vidok*, and *znakhar'*
Tikhomirov, M. N., 25, 34, 49, 59, 74
tithe, 51, 74-75, 170, 263n
tiun, 90, 97-98, 106-109, 124-25, 233n, 233-34n, 246n, 248n
Tobien, E. S., 31
torture, 82, 121, 140, 146-47, 229n
trial-date charters, 156
trial records, 113, 121, 157-58
tribute, see *dan'*
tysiatskii, 106-108, 238n

Ustiug Miscellany, 20, 47, 196n

Vernadsky, George, 36, 204n, 221n, 228n, 231n, 234n, 240n, 247n, 248n, 255n
vertical legal systems, 7, 11, 13, 15
verv', 65, 84, 141, 177-79, 266n
vidok, 129-30. See also eyewitness

vina, 140, 153, 229-30n, 251n. See also *vira*
vira, 65, 72-74, 76-77, 218n, 220n; *dikaia vira*, 65, 68-69, 71, 73-74, 78, 223n. See also bloodwite and *vina*
virnik, 74, 76, 78, 98-99, 223n, 224n, 232-33n, 234n
Vladimir Sviatoslavich, Grand Prince (980-1015), 50-51, 75-77, 165, 170-71, 175, 224n
Vladimir Council of 1273, 20-21, 144, 168, 197n
Vladimir Statute, 21, 25-26, 28, 50-53, 211-12n
volostel', 118
Vsevolod's Statute, 25, 58, 97, 215n

Weber, Max, 4-5, 16, 94-95, 105, 232n
wergeld, 68, 70, 72, 220n. See also composition
witnesses, 132-33, 142-43, 159. See also eyewitness, *poslukh*, *starozhil'tsy*, *svidetel'*, testimony, *vidok*, and *znakhar'*

Zakon Sudnyi liudem, 25, 28, 34, 46-49, 89, 141, 210n
Zapis' o dushegubstve, 118, 244n
zemlia, 177, 179-80
Zimin, A. A., 36, 59, 203-204n
znakhar', 136-37

Library of Congress Cataloging in Publication Data

Kaiser, Daniel H   1945-
  The growth of the law in medieval Russia.

  Bibliography: p.
  Includes index.
  1. Law—Russia—History and criticism.   I. Title.
Law   349.47'09   80-7535
ISBN 0-691-05311-1

Daniel H. Kaiser is Assistant Professor of History at Grinnell College.